PUSHKIN
A WRITER'S BIOGRAPHY

PUSHKIN
A WRITER'S BIOGRAPHY

YURI LOTMAN

Translated by
Ilya Nemirovsky with
David M. Bethea

Edited with a Preface
by David M. Bethea

ACADEMIC STUDIES PRESS
BOSTON
2026

Library of Congress Cataloging-in-Publication Data

Names: Lotman, I͡U. M. (I͡Uriĭ Mikhaĭlovich), 1922-1993, author. | Nemirovsky, Ilya, 2002- translator.

Title: Pushkin : a writer's biography / Yuri Lotman ; translated by Ilya Nemirovsky with David M. Bethea. Edited with preface by David M. Bethea.

Description: Boston : Academic Studies Press, 2025. | The biography makes up one section of a volume of Lotman's writings on Pushkin (pp. 21-184): Lotman, Yuri. Pushkin. St. Petersburg: Iskusstvo—SPB, 1995. | Includes bibliographical references.

Identifiers: LCCN 2024033501 (print) | LCCN 2024033502 (ebook) | ISBN 9798887196435 (hardback) | ISBN 9798887196442 (paperback) | ISBN 9798887196459 (adobe pdf) | ISBN 9798887196466 (epub)

Subjects: LCSH: Pushkin, Aleksandr Sergeevich, 1799-1837. | Poets, Russian—19th century—Biography. | LCGFT: Biographies.

Classification: LCC PG3350 .L69 2024 (print) | LCC PG3350 (ebook) | DDC 891.71/3 [B]—dc23/eng/20240724

LC record available at https://lccn.loc.gov/2024033501

LC ebook record available at https://lccn.loc.gov/2024033502

Copyright © Tallinn University, all rights reserved, 2025
Published by arrangement with ELKOST International Literary Agency

ISBN 9798887196435 (hardback)
ISBN 9798887196442 (paperback)
ISBN 9798887196459 (adobe pdf)
ISBN 9798887196466 (epub)

Book design by Tatiana Vernikov
Cover design by Ivan Grave

Published by Academic Studies Press
1007 Chestnut St.
Newton, MA 02464, USA
press@academicstudiespress.com
www.academicstudiespress.com

Contents

Preface. *David M. Bethea*	VII
Introduction	1
Chapter One. The Years of His Youth	9
Chapter Two. St. Petersburg, 1817–1820	32
Chapter Three. Pushkin's Southern Period, 1820–1824	56
Chapter Four. Mikhailovskoe, 1824–1826	118
Chapter Five. After the Exile, 1826–1829	143
Chapter Six. The Year Eighteen Thirty	167
Chapter Seven. The Boldino Autumn	188
Chapter Eight. A New Life	199
Chapter Nine. The Final Years	230
Endnotes	259
Index of Pushkin's Works Cited in the Book	317
Index	322

Preface

David M. Bethea

Pushkin has a famous line about the onset of inspiration in the fall, his favorite time of year: "And my fingers ask for the pen, the pen for the paper/ A minute [passes], and the verses freely flow."[1] Full disclosure: the writer of these lines admits without coyness that his fingers feel fidgety and less than obedient, the computer keys under those fingers rife with dead ends, and the words attempting to make sense less apt to flow when the topic is one genius writing about another genius's writing. How then to begin?

Enough of the twenty-first century has showed its face to declare confidently that Yuri Mikhailovich Lotman (1922–1993) was the greatest Russian literary scholar and cultural theorist of the second half of the twentieth century. His conceptualizing ardor was, as they say, a one-off. In terms of workload, sheer productivity, and elegance of thought he was modern Russian culture's elite Clydesdale, the horse who could pull the biggest informational load and whatever the context stand out with his special bearing—erudite, yet straightforward and matter of fact. Perhaps he was not as famous worldwide as Mikhail Bakhtin, whose key concept of dialogism accorded his philosophy of language longer legs, but within the domain of Russian scholars and thinkers there was no one held in higher esteem. To simplify, Bakhtin's focus was always on the interlocutor, the *sobesednik*, the other end of the idea that has been invited into the world, while Lotman's focus was more on the world, the context, the conditions for the idea to appear in the first place. And to continue the

---

[1] A. S. Pushkin, *Polnoe sobranie sochinenii v desiati tomakh* (Leningrad: Nauka, 1977), III:248. Hereafter cited as "*PSS*."

simplification, Bakhtin's native element was prose in its messiness, its middle, its loose ends and loopholes, while Lotman's native element was poetic/semiotic structure broadly applied, including terms and concepts like sign system, text and code, asymmetry and boundary, semiosphere, consciousness as translation, and *vzryv* (explosion) as cultural punctuation.

But more to the point, central to Lotman's scholarly output over the years were his many path-finding articles and books on Russia's ultimate poet, Aleksandr Sergeyevich Pushkin (1799–1837), the universally acknowledged "gold reserve" of the culture, the figure whose life and work, whose lyrics, epics, plays, fairy tales, stories, novel, letters, and history writing, all created against a backdrop of personal challenge and state oppression, most epitomizes what Russians tend to think of as their spiritual core. In this sense Pushkin's quickness of mind and the very elusiveness of that core make him the culture's greatest racehorse, its Secretariat. For who can explain where the horse found those reserves of strength to keep pulling away from the field in his legendary Belmont Stakes victory of 1973, and who can elucidate convincingly the seemingly miraculous internal growth of Pushkin in his Mikhailovskoye seclusion (1824–26), when, exiled and alone, he separates himself from his Byronic apprenticeship, burrows himself deep into Russian history and folklore, and writes a completely new, genre-defining drama (*Boris Godunov*), "with the gaze of Shakespeare" (*vzgliadom Shekspira*)? Thus, the mysterious shape to Pushkin's life in and through his creative work is what gave the myth of the poet its start and what caused, for example, a fellow poet like Apollon Grigoryev to write, in 1859, two decades after Pushkin's death,

> Pushkin is our everything. Pushkin is the representative of all that is *spiritual, special* in us, what remains our *spiritual,* our *special* after all encounters with the other, with different worlds. *Pushkin* is the only full esquisse of the Russian personality up to now, its purest form (*samorodok*), accepting into itself, during all possible encounters with

other special qualities and organisms, all that should be accepted, and rejecting everything that should be rejected.²

And so, this is perhaps a good place to start our brief discussion of Lotman's biography of Pushkin: Pushkin is "our everything" and Lotman is the finest interpreter we have of that "everything."

Let us jump in by taking a look at how Lotman conceptualizes the excavational process involved in restoring the life of a creative person, in this case Nikolai Karamzin (1766–1826), the great historian and belletrist whom Pushkin deeply admired and who served as the subject of Lotman's study *The Creation of Karamzin* (*Sotvorenie Karamzina*, 1987). What is noteworthy for us is how Lotman blends the pedagogical/"enlightening" with the scholarly/conceptual. This is a work he completed in the last few years of his life, but he did something similar (the pedagogical angle) when he wrote his Pushkin biography specifically for "Prosveshchenie" (Enlightenment), the Leningrad branch of the state publishing house whose large, accessible print runs were designed for teachers at secondary schools. Just as Pushkin takes on the role of unvarnished (but always entertaining) teller of the life of the people in his mature work of the 1830s (his so-called turn to "realism"), so too does Lotman, a thinker of surpassing sophistication across a broad range of disciplines, adopt the voice zone of a teacher of young people.

> On a green island amid the dark-blue sea there appeared a man. Here he decided to erect a temple. He broke up and carted blocks of marble, hewed them, cut capitals and friezes, erected columns and walls. But before doing that he constructed a temple in his imagination, and all that he erected in stone was simply the recreation of his already created ideal. This ideal was not something dead and immobile: in the head of the builder there swarmed designs, with the variants pressing in on each other, and the view from a hill or the form of a block of marble introduced corrections into the construction plans or into the figure of

---

2   http://dugward.ru/library/zolot/grigorjev_vzgljad.html.

a god. The builder was both bound and free: this was not the first temple he had built, and in his wanderings over the years he had made the rounds of hundreds of structures created by other geniuses. He knew what was necessary to build a temple and to escape that knowledge was not in his power. But he also knew that another's experience not only helps, it binds. And what he wanted to create was a *free* temple, one that had never existed before. The building grew, but so too grew, and changed, the ideal, which was, inexplicably, ahead of the [original] conception.

What was the builder thinking about, what brought him to this island, what was he trying to say with his work, and whom was he addressing? The only way of understanding is to be one of those who tread with the builder along the difficult and dusty roads of his life, who think over his thoughts on long nights, who experience his losses and hopes, his grievous humiliations and high soaring[s] of the soul...

Centuries pass. The temple has fallen, become overgrown, its scattered parts covered with earth. And in its place has arisen a green hill.

On the green hill amid the dark-blue sea there appeared a man. He had with him books, maps, and a shovel. He decided to restore the temple. He dug, extracted and cleaned off pieces of wall and statuary, he laid out on the green sward shining fragments of marble. He was a scientist and he knew the value of prosaic labor. Prior to this he had surveyed the proportions of many different temples. He understood the language of drafts, so dry to the uninitiated, to those who demand results and don't want to know at what cost such results are obtained. And now, after everything the earth could disgorge had been retrieved, it was time to put the scattered pieces back together.

But in the man's hands are only pathetic shards: much is missing, for along the shore there had grown up an entire village, built out of the stones of the former temple, and dozens of columns had been crushed into gravel as a new highway was being laid. The man's work gets a name—"reconstruction." In order for the fragments to assume a unified form once again it is necessary to see the temple in the mind's eye in its integral wholeness. And here what is required is a marriage of the most precise calculation, the multitudinous "boring" skills of the professional, [on the one hand,] and imagination, sometimes even fantasy [, on the other]. As it happens reconstruction is never irrefutable, definitive: after all, what needs to be restored is not some run-of-the-mill barracks but the creation of an individual genius, and what needs to be divined is not simply what was done by the builder but also what was rejected by him, what he didn't want to do, or what he wanted to do but couldn't. That which was built is only part of that which wasn't, the realized only part of the unrealized. The work of the reconstructor is co-creation [*sotvorchestvo*]. In order for him to restore the temple he has to recreate the entire spiritual world of the builder. He has to *resurrect him* [*voskresit' ego*].[3]

What emerges first and foremost from this astonishing passage is its unspoken self-referentiality. It is an allegory of scholarship to be sure, but it is also about Lotman himself. This speaker's voice is not that of a verbally "cloaked" artist/theorist in the manner of a stylish Derrida; as friend and coauthor Boris Egorov writes of Lotman's language in the Pushkin biography, it "is pure, transparent, aphoristic."[4] Here Lotman explains his concept (*sotvorenie*) by demonstrating how it progresses from the original creation to the secondary act of co-creation. The logic of the allegory states that the original genius of a builder had an *ideal* in his mind which he then made concrete in a specific idea or conception [*zamysel*]. The ideal as it were pulls the conception/*zamysel* forward and forces it to change under the power of circumstance (the hill that is different from a neutral flat space, the block of marble that already asks to be chiseled in a certain way). Lotman, always straightforward, always deliberate, says that the writer "constructs" his inner life in the same way: beginning as "a person born with great capabilities" he decides "to create himself as a good writer."[5] That is the writer's *intention*. Moreover, Lotman, who knew his Bakhtin and whose semiotic thinking was always recoding one text's rules into another's, goes on to say that the original builder was both "bound and free [*sviazan i svoboden*]." Nevertheless, this genius builder, who knew very well how other temples were constructed, wanted to build something Lotman calls a *"free* temple," in other words, one that departed from all previous

---

3   Iu. M. Lotman, *Sotvorenie Karamzina* (Moscow: Kniga, 1987), 11–12. My translation.
4   B. F. Egorov, "Lichnost' i tvorchestvo Iu. M. Lotmana," *Iu. M. Lotman. Pushkin* (St. Petersburg: "Iskusstvo-SPB," 1995), 17.
5   Ibid., 12.

temples, but was still recognizable as a temple. This is also, by analogy, the writer's *intention.*

Lotman does not downplay the gaps and indeterminacies in the restoration project. He says, "in the man's hands are only pathetic shards: much is missing, for along the shore there had grown up an entire village, built out of the stones of the former temple, and dozens of columns had been crushed into gravel as a new highway was being laid." Translation: there are certain questions that will never be fully answered by the restorer, some information that may be lost irretrievably. Who was Pushkin's secret love [*utaennaia liubov'*]? Did she ever exist? Also: the scholarly industry itself has its own momentum and can bury the shards of the original building in its own overgrowth of mythologizing. But this doesn't stop the restorer. Lotman goes on to say in the following paragraphs that the author of a "novel of reconstruction [*roman-rekonstruktsiia*]" does not have the right, as Tynyanov did in his novels about Pushkin, Küchelbecker, and Griboyedov, to place imagined speeches in the mouths of his heroes.

> He cannot fill in the absent fragments of columns with stones of his own making, no matter how certain he is that he has correctly guessed what is lost. His creative work [*tvorchestvo*] has a different nature and is carried out in a different sphere: his activity is directed toward the recreation of the integral ideal of personality [*vossozdanie togo tselostnogo ideala lichnosti*] which the hero of the biography created in his soul. This was the design according to which he constructed himself. We must discover, expose the design, to guess it out amongst others, from those that are possible and those that are impossible [...] and in so doing enliven the remaining fragments, confer meaning on them, force them to speak.[6]

Therefore, the scholar, à la Lotman, does not contrive [*izmyshliaet*], he searches and he compares [*ishchet, sopostavliaet*]. What inspires him, launches him so to speak, is what is already there. There is no place is his *roman-*

---

6   Ibid., 13.

rekonstruktsiia for conjecture, *domysel*, for the idea that does not already, because of the existing jagged edges of the fragment, connect up to the overarching design. And if imagination or invention [*vymysel*] does play a role (it does), it is a carefully pinioned one: based on the evidence, sensitively and plausibly parsed, of an existing document. Presented allegorically, Lotman's scholar-archaeologist is at best a kind of secondary or co-creator—hence the play on words in the title, "The Creation [<u>*Sotvorenie*</u>] of Karamzin"—a faithful accomplice who can, through sacrificing himself and giving himself over to his subject's original construction plans, get inside the head and heart of the departed *lichnost'*. Thanks to Lotman's meticulous sleuthing, the Karamzin of his inner biography comes alive as someone quite different from his sentimental heroes (the writer was anything but naïve) and as someone who created a cult of friendship (*iskusstvo nezhnoi druzhby*, lit. "art of tender friendship"), but who himself was "extraordinarily chary of soulful outpourings"[7]—all hard lacquered surface that only those closest to him got behind. Inside the young man who bounced around Europe registering with wide-eyed wonder the great personages and events surrounding the era of the French Revolution in *Letters of a Russian Traveler, 1789–90* (1797) was a shrewd and masterful teacher, someone in fact quite like his biographer. Indeed, it is the *difference* between one set of texts, the aestheticized structure of *Letters,* and another set of texts, the actual letters and documents detailing Karamzin's trip abroad, that lays bare the design [*plan*] by which Karamzin constructs himself, which in turn is a reflection of the implicit ideal (the "free temple"), of which Lotman spoke in his allegory.

* * *

Now, using this later Lotman text as entry point into the Pushkin biography, what can we say about the scholar's "recreation" (*vossozdanie*) of the poet's

---

[7] Ibid., 17.

attempt to find and live up to his "ideal self" (*tselostnyi ideal lichnosti*) in his life and his work and in the artistically shaped interaction of the two. First, the general vector or "through-line" in Lotman's thinking:

> As with other stages in his development as a person, here too Pushkin also reflected on what it meant to be a poet. Pushkin always constructed his personal life as that of a poet. And if Romanticism considered a poet to be a "strange person" (Lermontov's favorite expression), that is, a person fundamentally unlike those around him, then the central conviction for the Pushkin of the Mikhailovskoe period was the belief that a poet is "simply a person." (125)

Thus no matter the situation Pushkin "always construct(s) his personal life as that of a poet." The operative word here is "constructs." What does Lotman mean by this word, as he returns to the phrasing often? Moreover, the principal questions hanging over the entire telling of the biography require their own parsing: where did the sense of purpose come from, when did it first manifest itself, and what were the guard rails that kept it on track as the poet's life progressed through difficulties and disappointments? Lotman brings all his erudition to bear in order to isolate and retrieve these psychic *dominanta* from the poet's and others' written traces.

Pushkin, as we know, was not a favorite child in his family; when he was little he was pudgy, recalcitrant in his behavior, and in terms of his complexion and facial features reminiscent of Abram Petrovich Gannibal, his African great-grandfather on his mother's side.[8] These were traits that did not endear him to his parents, especially Nadezhda Osipovna.[9] Here we also need to bear in mind that the young Pushkin's male family role models, beginning with his

---

[8] The famous writer and statesman Ivan Dmitriev on seeing the boy Pushkin remarked, "What a little blackamoor!" Vikentii Veresaev, *Pushkin v zhizni* (Moscow: Sovetskii pisatel', 1936), I: 54–55.

[9] Nadezhda Osipovna was especially perplexed by the behavior of her oldest son, the chubby layabout Sasha, whose inactivity was for her a constant irritation. She also didn't like his obvious Negroid facial features, as that may have reminded her of a set of traits she was, in her Moscow social incarnation, trying to get beyond (cf. she was known in society

father Sergey Lvovich and his uncle Vasily Lvovich, were, while steeped in literary culture and in the case of Vasily Lvovich not without talent, not more than entertaining lightweights. They socialized with the literati of the day and they were quick with bons mots and impressively conversant in French and Russian literature,[10] but that was it. Perhaps more formative was the fact that from "Sasha's" first steps as a social creature he learned to read such leading Russian literary lights as Karamzin, Konstantin Batyushkov, and Ivan Dmitriev not as works or books but as living personalities—voices, gestures, body languages. A typical evening at the Pushkins' might have Sergey Lvovich acting out charades or declaiming Molière, Vasily Lvovich regaling the audience with anecdotes about Parisian fashions (all the while splashing those close by with the "sea-mist" of his uncontrollable spittle—a speech defect), and a famous guest such as Xavier de Maistre (Joseph's brother) holding forth in his myriad roles of general, author (*Voyage autour de ma chambre* [1794]), portraitist, and urbane interlocutor. It's true that Vasily Lvovich achieved a certain comic notoriety as the author of *The Dangerous Neighbor*, an unpublishable bawdy tale in verse, but when compared to his nephew, once the latter graduated the Lyceum and published his stunning mock epic *Ruslan and Liudmila* (1820), there was only one Pushkin. Likewise with Pushkin's younger brother Lev ("Lyovushka"), his surviving male sibling, whose role it was to do Aleksandr's bidding as a kind of agent in negotiations with editors and publishers. In short, and with only slight exaggeration, these other Pushkin family males

---

 as "the beautiful Creole"). In any event, it was clear to all that she preferred the other children to Aleksandr.

10 To give only one example of his sparkling wit, when asked at a social gathering by a plump Polish lady, "Est-ce vrai, M-r Pouchkine, que vous autres Russes, vous êtes des antropophages: vous mangez de l'ours [Is it true, Mr. Pushkin, that you Russians, who are cannibals, eat bear?]" he answered, tongue firmly in cheek, "Non, M-me: nous mangeons de la vache, comme vous [No, madame, we eat cow like you.]." (P. V. Annenkov, *Materialy dlia biografii. A. S. Pushkina* [Sankt Peterburg: Izd. P. V. Annenkova, 1855; rpt. Moscow: "Sovremennik," 1984], 9.)

are worth pausing on in these preliminaries not because they are significant but the opposite: the "weight" of the poet's genius, so to speak, does not originate with them—the verbal cleverness, the love of literature, the hours spent in the father's and uncle's libraries browsing risqué French tomes—yes. But that does not get one closer to the starting point of Aleksandr Pushkin's depth and universal appeal.[11]

On the other hand, as Lotman astutely demonstrates, the seriousness of purpose (still in inchoate form) that the temperamentally fidgety Pushkin needed to become Russia's greatest poet and most iconic creative personality was added first at the Lyceum through different channels. To begin with, there was the lifelong friendship with classmates like Anton Delvig and Ivan Pushchin and the special meaning of the Lyceum to the children that gave the teenage Pushkin a different, more lasting sense of validation and symbolic "family." The 19th of October 1811, the day the new school, which was inspired by tsarist advisor Nikolay Speransky's liberal ideas, was officially opened with all due pomp in the presence the tsar and the royal family, would remain in the Lyceans' minds a sacred moment for the rest of their lives. When in later years they would reconvene on this date, they would drink toasts to those who had departed into space (far-flung assignments or exile) or time (death) and commemorate them in anecdote and verse. In one of his numerous such anniversary pieces, "19 October [1825]," Pushkin will write, for example:

> Друзья мои, прекрасен наш союз!
> Он как душа неразделим и вечен—
> Неколебим, свободен и беспечен
> Срастался он под сенью дружных муз.

---

11 Typical of Pushkin's time was the fact that the women in his family, such as his grandmother Marya Alekseyevna and his nanny Arina Rodionovna, could be significant as nurturers and sources of linguistic authenticity, but not as models of civil authority and literary authorship. Still, that Pushkin was inspired by these women and that their images were reshuffled in his mind with the image of his favorite female goddess, the Muse, can be seen in his early poem "Sleep/Dream" (Son, 1816): *PSS*, I:164–69.

Куда бы нас ни бросила судьбина,
И счастье куда б ни повело,
Все те же мы: нам целый мир чужбина;
Отечество нам Царское Село.¹²

My friends, our union is a thing of beauty!
Like the soul it is inseparable and eternal—
Unshakable, free, without care
It grew up in the shadow of well-wishing muses.
No matter where fate might cast us,
No matter where fortune might lead us,
We remain the same: the entire world is a foreign place to us;
Our fatherland is Tsarskoe Selo.¹³

Delvig, probably Pushkin's closest friend of all, was legendary for his laziness and atrocious study habits. Yet Tosia or "the Sultan" was also endowed with a superb wit and fancy (his imagination and ability to weave tall tales were probably quicker than Pushkin's) and he was as dedicated to poetry and poetic values as his more famous classmate. In time he would become a comrade in arms in literary battles in the periodic press. Equally significant, he was the one who first "discovered" Pushkin and described mythopoetically the passing of the baton from the grizzled swan Derzhavin to this new Apollo. Pushchin, nicknamed "Big Jeannot," occupied the small *dortoir* room next door to Pushkin's at the Lyceum. His role was that of confidant, particularly in the evenings when the two boys spoke through the thin wall separating them about the day's happenings. It was Pushchin's job to soothe the hurt feelings of his temperamental classmate when the latter inevitably got into a confrontation with one of the other boys. It was also he who visited Pushkin during the latter's loneliest time in exile, when the poet was holed up in remote Mikhailovskoye under house arrest. The brotherly gesture occasioned one of Pushkin's most heartfelt lyrics, "To I. I. Pushchin" (1826), which begins with the line "My first friend, my priceless friend" (Moi pervyi drug, moi drug

---

12   *PSS*, II:245.
13   My translation.

bestsennyi).[14] Likewise when Pushchin, now himself in Siberian exile as a result of his participation in the 1825 Decembrist uprising, learned of Pushkin's death, he responded—and the words ring true to his character—that he would have offered his own breast to the duelist's bullet to save his former mate and the pride of Russian letters.

Next, in addition to friendship there was the love affair with the muses that was initiated against the natural beauty of the parks and gardens surrounding the Catherine Palace, home to the Lyceum at Tsarskoe Selo. This nexus of grand architecture and cultivated countryside lent itself almost magically to poetical musing; its meandering paths and viewing sites became the perfect hideouts for a budding versifier. As Pushkin tells us in the famous opening to chapter 8 of *Eugene Onegin*:

> В те дни, когда в садах Лицея
> Я безмятежно расцветал,
> Читал охотно Апулея,
> А Цицерона не читал,
> В те дни в таинственных долинах,
> Весной, при кликах лебединых,
> Близ вод, сиявших в тишине,
> Являться муза стала мне.
>   Моя студенческая келья
>   Вдруг озарилась; муза в ней
>   Открыла пир младых затей,
>   Воспела детские веселья,
>   И славу нашей старины,
>   И сердца трепетные сны.[15]

> In days when I still bloomed serenely
> Inside our Lycée garden wall
> And read my Apuleius keenly,
> But read no Cicero at all—
> Those springtime days in secret valleys,

---

14 *PSS*, II:306.
15 *PSS*, V:142.

> Where swans call and beauty dallies,
> Near waters sparkling in the still,
> The Muse first came to make me thrill.
>> My student cell turned incandescent;
>> And there the Muse spread out for me
>> A feast of youthful fancies free,
>> And sang of childhood effervescent,
>> The glory of our days of old,
>> The trembling dreams the heart can hold.[16]

The valleys are "secret, mysterious" (*tainstvennye*) because they first gave birth to private reverie; the water provides a setting for the swans, which become a Derzhavinian metaphor for poetry to Pushkin and his Lyceum mates; Apuleius with his adventure stories and sexual license are the more attractive forbidden fruit for these teenagers than stern Cicero; and the notion of withdrawal into the gardens ("v sadakh") and into the student cell (*kel'ia*) that somehow miraculously opens out into an illumination called the Muse—all this is integral to the "blooming" ("ia bezmiatezhno rastsvetal") of the future poet.

And last but not least, there was the boys' exposure to the most enlightened perspectives of the time, first from brilliant "older brother"-type mentors like Pyotr Chaadayev, and second from the best among the school's teaching staff. Chaadayev was the elegant hussar officer who had participated in the historic Battle of Borodino and who was quartered for a time at Tsarskoe Selo while Pushkin was a student at the Lyceum. Pushkin first met the young philosopher, whose sophisticated self-possession and command of the history of ideas were striking, at the Karamzins' in 1816 and immediately fell under his spell. "Pushkin's primary weapon against the degrading nature of his existence," explains Lotman about the poet's subsequent wanderings in the South, "was a deep belief in his own self-worth—instilled in him by Chaadayev—that prompted him to be decisive in every situation, no matter how insignificant,

---

16 James Falen's translation in the Oxford World's Classics.

and also to defend his proud independence (93)." Another influential interlocutor was Pushkin's favorite "professor"[17] at the Lyceum Aleksandr Kunitsyn, who, "intelligent, eloquent, and highly educated," exuded *amour-propre* and never tried "to ingratiate himself with the authorities."[18] In a sketch done by one of Pushkin's classmates, Aleksey Illichevsky, in which several of the professors are scampering up a plank (a kind of career ladder) to pay homage to then minister of education Count Aleksey Razumovsky, Kunitsyn is standing at the bottom and has his back turned to the grandee. In other words, in Kunitsyn the boys recognized someone who was his own person and they respected him for it. "Kunitsyn taught . . . those disciplines on the basis of which the pupils at the Lyceum learned about 'functions' (responsibilities) of the man and the citizen."[19] Nowhere else in Russia were educators talking about subjects like logic and morality in this way.[20] The schoolboy Pushkin saw the connection between Kunitsyn's independence and integrity as a person and his message of the "natural rights" (*estestvennye prava*) allotted to every human being, including the illiterate and downtrodden Russian serfs. It's perhaps then not too much of an exaggeration to say that the moral philosophy Pushkin gleaned from Kunitsyn, once it had sunk in, played a major role in helping to rid him of his frequent displays of shallowness and his eagerness to, as the Russian says, reach into his pocket for the *krasnoe slovtso*, the sparkling witticism, something that consistently got him into trouble in his youth, since his puns and epigrams were often aimed recklessly at those in authority. Kunitsyn's example inculcated

---

17 The teachers were called professors and, in several cases, possessed professor-like qualifications.
18 M. V. Basina, *V sadakh litseia. Na bregakh Nevy* (Moscow: Detskaia literatura, 1988), 33.
19 Ibid.
20 In Kunitsyn's words, spoken at the Lyceum's grand opening, "Preparing yourselves to be the protectors of laws, learn first of all to respect them yourselves, since the law, once broken by its guardians, has no sacred status in the eyes of the people." B. S. Meilakh, *A. S. Pushkin: Ocherk zhizni i tvorchestva* (Moscow: Izd. Akademii nauk, 1949), 9.

in the poet the humanistic gravitas and political and social broad horizons that were so obviously lacking in Sergey Lvovich, Vasily Lvovich, and Lev.[21]

These then were the guard rails (friendship-poetry-dignity) that were erected at the Lyceum and that, once attached to Pushkin's extraordinary memory, inexhaustible curiosity, and nonpareil verbal gift, kept him on track as he proceeded to adulthood.

Now let us move further into the poet's life and look at how Lotman presents the crucial, agonistic transition from the Romantic role-playing in the South to the understanding of the poet as "simply a person" in Mikhailovskoye. We will quote the passage at length and then see how it is projected forward in anticipation of "the life of the poet" in maturity.

> The idea that a poet's life, personality, and fate merge with his art, constituting for the reading public a kind of unitary whole, belongs to the Romantic era. In previous ages, works of literature existed largely independently of their authors. They were valued not for their connection to an author's individuality, but rather for their closeness to Truth—singular, eternal, "bright like the sun," as Descartes put it. The author's biography was viewed as largely extraneous to the work—it was never reflected in high genres (such as odes), nor even in middle genres, such as elegiac poetry; it was tolerated in lower genres, primarily comic ones, and even then, in the form of hints. Readers did not search the author's biography for keys to understanding his works.
>
> If an author's biography came to readers' attention (this was possible only if the author had achieved great renown and subsequently passed away), what would stand out in the biography were certain generalized iconic traits, which would liken the subject to a single idealized image. Everything that was idiosyncratic to the author was largely ignored: in effect, the biography vacillated between a saint's *vita* and a service record. First, pre-Romanticism, and then Romanticism proper, saw in a poet his genius—his unique and singular spirit expressing itself in the originality of a given work of art. The poet's creative work began

---

21 As Pushkin wrote in a draft of one of his Lyceum anniversary poems: "To Kunitsyn goes a tribute of the heart and of wine! / He created us, he nurtured our flame, / It was by him that the foundation stone was laid, / By him was our pure icon lamp lit" ("19 October 1825"). *PSS*, II:351.

to be looked at as one huge autobiographical novel, in which poems and epics formed chapters, and the biography itself functioned as plot. The two geniuses of Romantic Europe—Lord Byron and Napoleon—fixed in place these ideas: the former, having played out his personal life before all of Europe, by turning his poetry into a chain of fiery confessions; the latter, by showing that his very life could resemble an epic poem. [...]

The Romantic worldview was salvational to Pushkin because it gave him a way—so necessary to him then—of unifying his personality. Pushkin's time in St. Petersburg had greatly enriched him: he had interacted with a wide circle of progressive contemporaries, he had participated in discussions crucial to his age, and his intense love life had expanded his emotional world. His interactions with women and participation in the refined culture of feelings and matters of the heart developed his delicacy of mind, his ability to sense, notice and express emotional nuances, and not merely their primitive spectrum. Finally, his ability to enter into these different looks and modes enriched him with a sense of behavioral style. This resulted in Pushkin's extraordinarily developed talent of changing and adapting his personality in different situations, for being different. Later Pushkin singled out this attribute in Onegin: "How he was able to appear new" (6:9). (58–59)

From the broader context to the individual instance: we learn about the rules for writing in the age and then we learn about Pushkin's personality and how it takes in experience and responds to those rules. Anthologists often describe Pushkin as a "romantic poet." How inadequate the epithet if left unglossed! What Lotman does is show how Pushkin's *work on himself*, in and through his art, perfectly matches up with the emergence of Romanticism on the scene in Russia. This is, again, the notion of the poet "constructing himself" that we recall from the opening passage from the Karamzin book. The ideal of "the life of the poet," however "life" and however "poet" are defined in context, is the gravitational pull that dictates the decisions that need to be made. And as Lotman writes further on, "No matter what Pushkin did after having reached his creative maturity, he always remained, first and foremost, 'The Poet.' It was precisely this that he considered the core and defining element of his personality, and it was as a poet that he was perceived by his contemporaries. (69)"; and "It would be wrong to conceive of the process of "personality construction" as a strictly rational process: much like in art, the conscious plan of action coexisted with intuitive discoveries and moments of inspiration that informed the artist's decisions. Together they formed that blend of conscious and unconscious energies that are characteristic of any creative activity. " (93). And so, while Lotman's unequalled erudition supplies the dense sinewy contexts to each stage Pushkin passes through, the ideal of how Russia's consummate modern poet discovers himself and continues to grow is always in view. To finish up with a few examples chosen at random: Pushkin's so-called "secret love" whose referents in real-life scholars have disputed for decades and that Lotman argues is a mystification on the poet's part (75–80); the rejection of admittance to a Secret Society to which he desperately wanted to belong either because the members (i.e. future Decembrists) didn't want to subject Pushkin's gift to danger or because he was already under surveillance and as a personality could be flighty (98); money problems dogging him in the South and how they pushed him toward poetic flights in Kishinev/Chişinău and toward prosaic worries about unpaid bills in Odessa (101–2); his "frenemy" Aleksandr Rayevsky and the controversial poem "The Demon," which is perhaps less autobiographical than previously thought and which has more to do with the treachery and betrayal that are everywhere present in the atmosphere of the South (Karolina Sobanska, de Witt) (107–11); "simplicity" as a new poetic medium and the return to childhood (Pushkin sleeps in the nursery) and Arina Rodionovna's language and stories at Mikhailovskoye (125–27); solitary "Thought" (*Mysl'*) thrusting the poet into uncharted territory in Mikhailovskoye as opposed to social interactions holding him back in the South, coupled with the necessity of answering the riddle of the "people" (*narod*), which process eventuates in the "Shakespearean" realism of *Boris Godunov* (130–33); the turning to history/"historism" and historical writing and how to become a living link in history's chain through family (203–5); the construction of a "Home" (*Dom*) through

Krylov-inflected, juicily "Russian" letter writing to normally French-speaking wife Natalya Nikolayevna (208–12)—his attempt at "enlightenment" on a personal level—which when those letters were unceremoniously opened and read by the censorship was terribly offensive, an assault on his dignity (his family, his private space), to Pushkin. Virtually every page of the text has additional bricks fitting together into the "free temple" (the Karamzin allusion) of Pushkin's "life of the poet."

Perhaps the single most salient trait of Pushkin, which goes along with other traits like verbal virtuosity, curiosity, resilience, intelligence, but in the end may be more pronounced than any of them, is "flexibility and richness of Pushkin's inner self" (*gibkost' i bogatstvo dushi*) (59). One of the greatest lyric poets in the English tradition was John Keats, who defined the echt-Shakespearean attribute as "Negative Capability":

> Several things dove-tailed in my mind, and at once it struck me what quality went to form a Man of Achievement, especially in Literature, and which Shakespeare possessed so enormously—I mean Negative Capability, that is, when a man is capable of being in uncertainties, mysteries, doubts, without any irritable reaching after fact and reason—Coleridge, for instance, would let go by a fine isolated verisimilitude caught from the Penetralium of mystery, from being incapable of remaining content with half-knowledge. This pursued through volumes would perhaps take us no further than this, that with a great poet the sense of Beauty overcomes every other consideration, or rather obliterates all consideration.[22]

Obviously the negativity here is not an absence, but an all-encompassing presence, which brings us back to why Pushkin is Russia's "everything." Pushkin is "Russia's Shakespeare" not only because his reputation as a cultural gold standard is equivalent, but also because his "flexibility and richness of inner self" is precisely that quality that can accommodate "uncertainties, mysteries,

---

22 John Keats, *The Complete Poetical Works and* Letters [Cambridge Edition] (New York: Houghton, Mifflin and Company, 1899), 277.

doubts, without any irritable reaching after fact and reason." It is a Protean spirit that enters unseen and is everywhere and nowhere. And that is why Pushkin is Russia's ultimate artist and Yuri Lotman's densely packed, yet succinct biography, now in English translation, is the first place to look to make his acquaintance.

PUSHKIN

A Writer's Biography

Introduction

Seldom has one's personal fate been so closely intertwined with that of entire nations and peoples as was Pushkin's during his lifetime. In an 1831 poem, dedicated to the 14th anniversary of his graduation from the Lyceum, Pushkin wrote:

> How long, my friends, it's been, and twenty years
> Have passed, and what is there to see now?
> The tsar of old has passed away,
> We burned down Moscow; Paris was our capture.
> Napoleon's flame died out in prison;
> The ancient glory of the Greeks is resurrected;
> Another Bourbon's lost his throne.* (3:879–880)
>
> So have the winds of earthly storms
> By chance thus touched our lives as well. (3:277)

Neither Pushkin nor his classmates at the Lyceum had actually participated in any of these events, and yet the annals of the times were so integral a part of their personal biographies that Pushkin had every reason for declaring "We burned down Moscow." The "we" of the people, the "we" of the Lyceum ("We became men" in the same poem), and Pushkin's "I" all coalesce to form the image of a participant and contemporary of a great historical process.

---

* Pushkin's works are quoted here and throughout the book from the sixteen-volume *Polnoe sobranie sochinenii* [Complete collected works] (Moscow–Leningrad: Izdatel'stvo Akademii nauk SSSR, 1937–1949). Numbers before the colon will refer to the volume number; numbers after the colon will refer to page numbers. Square brackets within the text contain parts of the text crossed out by Pushkin; angled brackets indicate reconstructed portions based on textual conjectures.

Half a year after Pushkin's birth, on November 9, 1799 (on the 18th of Brumaire in the 8th Year of the Republic), General Bonaparte organized a coup d'état. Initially a consul, then a life-long consul, and finally the emperor, Napoleon[1] remained in power until his defeat and subsequent removal from power in 1814; after which he restored his power for a hundred-day-long period which ended with his decisive defeat at Waterloo, in 1815. He was thereupon exiled to the island of St. Helena. These years had been a time of endless turmoil for Europe and, starting from 1805, for Russia as well.

During the night between March 11 and 12, 1801, a coup d'état also took place, but in the opposite end of Europe, in St. Petersburg: a group of palace conspirators and Officers of the Guard barged into Paul I's[2] bedroom and viciously strangled him. The throne was then assumed by twenty-four-year-old Alexander I,[3] Paul's eldest son.

Early nineteenth-century youths had become accustomed to a life of unrest, campaigns, and battles. Death had become commonplace and was associated not with senility and disease, but rather with youth and valor. Battle-wounds were the objects of envy, not pity. Later, when Pushkin relayed the news of the emerging Greek revolts of 1821, he wrote of the movement's leader Alexander Ypsilantis: "Henceforth whether a dead man or a victor he shall belong to history—28 years old, an amputated arm, a noble aim—envy such a fate" (13:24). Not only is the fight for freedom viewed as a "noble aim," but so is the "amputated arm" (Ypsilantis,[4] a general of the Russian Imperial Army, lost his arm to a cannonball during the Battle of Leipzig, in 1813). An amputated arm could become an object of envy, as it signified that one had participated in the historical process. With hardly enough time to visit their homes in Petersburg, Moscow, or their familial estates, young men, during the small breaks afforded them between military campaigns, were in no rush to get married or to immerse themselves in social frivolities or familial squabbles: they locked themselves in their studies, read political tractates, and mused on the futures of Europe and Russia. Passionate disputes in friendly circles attracted them more than balls or the company of women. As Pushkin noted, the "storm of 1812" had struck. During the War of 1812, Russian society matured by decades. On August 15, 1812 (Moscow had yet to be surrendered!), the smart, educated, but, frankly, otherwise unexceptional socialite Maria Volkova[5] wrote to her friend, Varvara Lanskaia,[6] "Judge for yourself just how painful it is to see villains like Balashov [the minister of police, and general-aide-de-camp of Alexander I—Lotman][7] and Arakcheev[8] selling out such a lovely people! But I assure you that if they are as hated in St. Petersburg as they are in Moscow, then no good shall await them."*

The war ended with Russia's victory. Young cornets, ensigns, and lieutenants—

> Who, setting off on their own at age fifteen,
> In three wars grew accustomed to but camp
> and battlefield (7:246, 367)

—returned home as wounded battle officers imbued with a sense of having personally participated in History. They were categorically opposed to the idea that Europe's future should be decided by a group of monarchs gathered in Vienna and that Russia's future should be delivered into the hands of the harsh martinet Arakcheev.

The impossibility of returning to the status quo following the War of 1812 was widely understood in Russian society, which had undergone a national political ascent. Sharp-eyed observer and Livonian nobleman Timofei von Bock[9] wrote in a memorandum submitted to Alexander I: "The nation, illuminated by the glow of [burning] Moscow, is not the same nation whose strings were pulled by that Curlandian groom, Biron,[10] for 10 years."**

---

* Vladimir Kallash, *Dvenadtsatyi god v vospominaniiakh sovremennikov* [1812 in Contemporaries' Memoirs and Correspondences] (Moscow: Tovarishchestvo I. D. Sytina, 1912), 253–254.

** Anatolii Predtechenskii, "Zapiska T. E. Boka" [A Note by T. E. Bock], in *Dekabristy i ikh vremia* [The Decembrists and Their Time] (Moscow–Leningrad: Pushkinskii Dom,

Indicative in this regard is a plan for a tragedy that Griboedov[11] compiled called "1812": the main character was to be a certain peasant "M." (Griboedov had not come up with a name), a hero of the guerilla war effort who named, following victory, was to "reassume his place under his master's rod." Griboedov concluded his fragments with a telling postscriptum: "The former abominations." M. was to commit suicide. The idea that society could not revert to the "former abominations" of "ages past" (Chatsky's expression), was a given for many young officers returning from war. Risking their futures and rejecting the joys of youth and a brilliant career, these young officers took up the path of political struggle. The connection between 1812 and the later liberation movement was gauged by many Decembrists. Mikhail Bestuzhev-Ryumin[12] in a speech given at a conspiratorial meeting said, "The age of military glory ended with Napoleon. Now the time has come to free nations from the slavery which subjugates them. Could it be that Russians, who distinguished themselves with brilliant achievements in a war that was truly for the Fatherland, Russians that freed Europe from the yoke of Napoleon, will they not shake off their own yoke?"*

In 1815, the first secret revolutionary societies arose. On February 9, 1816, several officers of the guard, aged 20–25, all participants in the War for the Fatherland, established the Union of Salvation,[13] thereby turning a new page in Russian history. Freedom seemed natural to them, and struggle and death for its sake seemed an enviable celebration of life. Even the severe Pestel,[14] when located in a prison of the fortress and addressing not his confederates, but judges and henchmen, experienced once again the rapture of freedom as he thought back on those minutes: "I have become a republican in

---

    1951), 193. The note was originally written in French and translated for the publication. Bock would pay for his note with many years of imprisonment, and later he committed suicide in Viljandi.

*   *Vosstanie dekabristov* [The Decembrist Uprising], vol. 9 (Moscow–Leningrad: Izdatel'stvo Akademii nauk SSSR, 1950), 117.

my soul and can see no greater prosperity or good for Russia than a republican government. When I considered this subject with other members [of the organization] who shared my beliefs, we became so enthralled and excited with the mere image of the happiness Russia would share in, according to our understanding, that I and others were not only prepared to agree to, but to offer anything that could have assisted in the introduction and complete consolidation and establishment of such an order."*

The number of members in the secret society quickly rose, and in 1818 it was reorganized into the Union of Welfare[15]—a conspiratorial organization that strove to prepare Russia for top-to-bottom societal reorganization in the coming 10–15 years. They sought to achieve this through their influence on public opinion, pressure on the government, the infiltration of government offices, and the education of the younger generations in line with patriotism, a love of freedom, self-independence, and a hatred of despotism. The Union of Welfare's sphere of influence was wide-reaching and fruitful: in a country where all matters were under the purview of the government, and everything under the purview of the government was conducted secretly, the members of the Union of Welfare strove to engage in political matters transparently. During balls and other public gatherings, they discussed governmental deeds in an open manner, bringing to light cases of abuse of power, thereby forcing despotism and bureaucracy to relinquish their prime weapon: secrecy. The Decembrists produced a phenomenon which had previously not existed in Russia: public opinion. It was precisely public opinion that set the condition—new in Russia—about which Griboedov, through the mouth of Chatsky, said: "nowadays laughter frightens and reins in shame."**

---

*   *Vosstanie dekabristov* [The Decembrist Uprising], vol. 4 (Moscow–Leningrad: Izdatel'stvo Akademii nauk SSSR, 1927), 91.

**   Aleksandr Griboedov, *Sochineniia* [Works] (Moscow: Gosudarstvennoe izdatel'stvo khudozhestvennoi literatury, 1956), 24.

However, the wide-ranging scope of the Decembrists' activity, as well as their emphasis on transparency, came at a cost: the Union of Welfare eventually became bloated, due to the large number of casual joinees, which caused the conspiracy to almost fall through. By 1821, the government possessed a multitude of denunciations that contained extensive information on the secret society. This information was all the more alarming for the emperor, because the reactionary Holy Alliance, formed after Napoleon's downfall, was breaking up and failing: there was unrest in German universities, revolution in Naples, the Greek War of Independence, unrest in the Semenovsky Royal Guard regiment in St. Petersburg, rebellion in the military settlements in Chuguev, near Kharkiv—all this led the government to panic. A period of repression took root: unrest at the universities in Kazan and Petersburg was stifled (following strict investigations, the best professors were fired and instruction in a range of sciences was forbidden; the universities came to resemble a cross between a military barrack and a monastery), censorship and persecution increased; Pushkin and, somewhat later, poet and Decembrist Colonel Pavel Katenin,[16] were both exiled from St. Petersburg.

After illegally convening in these conditions in 1821 in Moscow, the Union of Welfare, having also found out that the government possessed complete lists of all the conspirators, declared the secret society liquidated. This was, however, a tactical move: in reality, after this initial decision, there followed another which restored the Union, making it smaller and yet more conspiratorial. This restoration, nevertheless, proceeded not without its troubles: the secret society became geographically split—into Northern[17] and Southern[18] factions—as well as politically: into moderates, who fled its ranks, and more decisive, mainly younger members, who replaced the leaders of the first wave of Decembrism. In the unfolding situation where the organization was collapsing, the society's members were forced to combat a resultant nearly ubiquitous pessimism and develop new tactics. The government, as many thought, was confidently celebrating its triumph. However, as often is the case, this reactionary victory proved to be illusory: public dissatisfaction, having been forced inwards, only began to foment, and by 1824, both the Northern and Southern societies of Decembrists embarked on a new period of political activity and began to directly prepare for a military revolution in Russia.

On November 19, 1825, in Taganrog, Alexander I unexpectedly died. The Decembrists had clearly intended the start of their "campaign" to coincide with the tsar's passing. On December 14, 1825, in St. Petersburg, on Senate Square, the first attempt at a revolution in Russia took place. Buckshot, fired at point-blank, dispersing the rebellious crowd, marked the failure of the revolt and the beginning of a new tsarist rule and a new era of life in Russia.

Nicholas I[19] commenced his rule as a cunning investigator and ruthless executioner: the five leaders of the Decembrist movement were hanged and 120 of their followers were sent to Siberia to do hard labor. The new reign set off under the banner of political terror: Russia was given over to the political secret police—the commissioned machine whose aim was search and repression. The Third Section of the Imperial Chancellery and the Gendarmes became a sort of peephole through which the tsar was able to observe a Russia behind bars. The crude and poorly educated Arakcheev was replaced by the well-educated and enlightened Benckendorf[20] and his assistant, Dubelt.[21] Arakcheev relied on the rod and controlled by shouting and poking; Benckendorf created an army of spies, making the denunciation of one's fellow a facet of ordinary life. If the Decembrists strove to elevate the level of public ethics, Benckendorf and Nicholas I, conversely, purposefully depraved society, persecuting personal freedom and independent opinion as political crimes.

However, the natural flow of life could not be totally arrested. Nicholas I saw his divine purpose in "freezing" Russia and slowing the development of a spirit of freedom in all of Europe. He sought to replace real life with bureaucratic mementos, and people in government—with faceless careerists, who were to help him, while fooling themselves, by creating a decorative imitation of a powerful and blossoming Russia. The historical reality, however, was depressing.

In such conditions, society began to give rise to new forces. All the power of Russia's national life became concentrated in literature during this time.

Such was Pushkin's era.

Chapter One

The Years of His Youth

Pushkin was born on May 26, 1799,* in Moscow, in the Skvortsov Dom on Nemetskaya Street to former Major and Moscow Commission bureaucrat Sergei Lvovich Pushkin[1] and his wife, Nadezhda Osipovna (née Hannibal)[2]. Besides them, the family consisted of an older sister named Olga and three younger brothers. The Pushkins were of noble blood. In his autobiographical sketches, Pushkin writes, "We trace our lineage to a Prussian émigré named *Radshi* or *Rachi* (a *noble man*,[3] as the chronicler writes, that is aristocratic, nobleborn). He came to Russia during the rule of St. Alexander Yaroslavich Nevsky.[4] He was the forefather of the Musins, the Bobrishchevs, the Miatlevs, the Povodovs, the Kamenskys, the Buturlins, the Kologrivovs, the Sherefedinovs and the Tovarkovs" (12:311). A shared kinship with a range of old boyar families had established a steady link between the Pushkins and "pre-fire Moscow" (that is, Moscow before the fire of 1812). Common sayings regarding this aristocratic kinship network included: "Be aware of your kinfolk and pay them respect," and "Whoever doesn't respect his ancestry brings shame upon himself; whoever is ashamed of his family has also brought shame on himself."

"My mother's lineage is even more curious," Pushkin continued, "Her grandfather[5] was a negro, the son of a powerful prince. The Russian envoy in Constantinople somehow managed to retrieve him from the seraglio, where he lived as an *amanat* [a hostage—Lotman], and sent him to Peter the First"[6] (12:311–312).[7] By the end of the eighteenth century, the Hannibals had intermarried with Russian aristocratic families and become the relatives of the

---

* All dates are given in the old style (that is, according to the Julian calendar—Transl.).

Rzhevskys,[8] Buturlins, Cherkasskys,[9] and Pushkins. Pushkin's parents were cousins thrice removed.

The Pushkins were far from wealthy. Thriftless and poorly organized, they spent their whole lives on the brink of bankruptcy, eventually steadily decreasing their financial support of Pushkin, and in the final years of his life, burdening the poet with their own debts. Sergei Pushkin's aristocratic frivolity was paired with an incessant stinginess. Pushkin's friend Prince Vyazemsky[10] described the following scene in his notes, "In point of fact, he was very miserly not really with regard to himself, but rather with regard to everyone at home. His son Lev[11] once dropped a shot-glass at dinnertime. His father flared up and, throughout the entire meal, growled, 'How could one (said Lev) lament a shot-glass, which costs 20 kopeks, for so long.' 'I beg your pardon, sir,' (his father retorted with feeling), 'not twenty, but thirty-five kopeks.'"*

The Pushkin family belonged to the educated portion of Moscow society. Pushkin's uncle, Vasily Lvovich Pushkin,[12] was a famous poet, and their house often hosted a range of famous writers. Even as a child, Pushkin had seen Karamzin,[13] who was then at the forefront of the burgeoning Russian literary field. Pushkin would have overheard many literary discussions.

The upbringing of the children, which the parents paid little heed to, proceeded on its own. From his studies at home the only thing Pushkin received was an excellent knowledge of French, while in his father's library he developed a passion for reading (also in French).

Nevertheless, the most distinguishing feature of Pushkin's childhood was how little and seldom he would recall it in the future. For an aristocratic child, one's Home is a complete world unto itself, replete with intimacy, loyalty, and personal memories, remaining relevant throughout one's life. In his memoirs,

---

* *A. S. Pushkin v vospominaniiakh sovremennikov* [A. S. Pushkin in Contemporaries' Recollections], 2 vols. (Moscow: Khudozhestvennaia literatura, 1974), 1:154 (henceforth *Contemporaries*, with specified volume and page—Transl.).

Sergei Aksakov[14] describes how his separation from his parents and the house where he had grown up became a childhood tragedy (he was sent from his parents' house to a gymnasium in Kazan); life outside his home had seemed to him utterly impossible. Leo Tolstoy's[15] childhood was far from idyllic (there was strife between his parents, his father was flighty and constantly in debt, before dying in bizarre fashion), but nevertheless, Tolstoy dedicated a deeply passionate tale to the topic of his childhood (appropriately named *Childhood*), where he detailed his first memories, his parents' house, and his mother. Lermontov's[16] childhood had been ruined by a severe family tragedy; he grew up not knowing who his real family was, with turmoil brewing between his closest relatives. And nonetheless, he carried a poeticized memory of his childhood and Home throughout his whole life.

> Outwardly immersed in their brilliance and vanity,
> In my soul I caress an older dream
> Of sacred sounds I heard in years now gone
> [...]
> And I see myself a child, and around me
> Are all my dearest places: that tall, old manor
> And the garden with the ruined greenhouse.*

Lermontov's father,[17] as he appears in Lermontov's poetry, is significantly poeticized and idealized, contrary to the biographical facts.

Pushkin abandoned his childhood home with ease and never reminisced about his mother or father in his poetry. References to his uncle, Vasily, quickly became unambiguously ironic. Despite this, he was not devoid of familial sentiment; his whole life he selflessly loved his brother and sister, devotedly assisted them monetarily, even when he was having financial troubles himself, without fail paying off his brother Lyovushka's debts, which had amounted to significant sums. Even with his parents he was more caring than they had ever

---

* Mikhail Lermontov, *Sobranie sochinenii* [Collected Works], 6 vols. (Moscow–Leningrad: Izdatel'stvo Akademii nauk SSSR, 1954), 2:136.

been with him. It is all the more telling that whenever Pushkin would seek to reminisce about his early days, without exception he would remember the Lyceum; he blotted out his childhood years from his life.* He was a man without a childhood.

But when his internal development led Pushkin to the idea of Home, to the poetry of his place, it turned out that it was not at all that home (or those homes) where he had spent his childhood days. His Mikhailovskoe estate became his quintessential Home; it was his ancestral estate with which his own biography had become intertwined—with his youthful memories of 1817 as well as his years of exile, but not with his childhood. The woman that gazed out of the estate's windows was not Pushkin's mother, but rather his peasant "mother," Arina Rodionovna.[18]

Childhood, however, is too vital a point in one's self-development to be crossed-out entirely without some sort of replacement. For Pushkin, the Lyceum replaced childhood as the point where he learned to differentiate between good and evil and which he would turn to for valuable recollections. Pushkin's ideas of the Lyceum as home, of the Lyceum instructors as older relatives, and of his classmates as brothers, mates formed towards the mid-1820s, when these memories already belonged to the relatively distant past, and the persecution, exiles, and slander haunting the poet forced him to seek support in idyllic memories.

---

* This is especially palpable in those rare cases when the demands of literary tradition forced him to treat the theme of childhood in his poetry. Thus, in the Lyceum-era "Epistle to Iudin," Pushkin incorporated aspects of the real Zakharovo village with which his childhood recollections were tied. However, the accompanying poetic image of the author musing on Horace and La Fontaine, beautifying his garden with shovel in hand, and welcoming guests to an idyllic countryside banquet with a wineglass in his hand is, of course, entirely abstract and contains nothing personal: Pushkin frequented Zakharovo from 1806 to 1810, that is, between the ages of seven and eleven—his behavior, of course, had nothing in common with this literary pose. A rare case of real echoes of his childhood impressions can be found in "A Dream" (1816). It is typical, however, that there it is not his mother that is mentioned, but his nanny ("Ah! Will I fail to mention my little mother...").

> My friends, our union is beautiful!
> Like the soul it is indivisible and eternal —
> Unshakeable, free, and without care,
> It grew under the protection of friendly muses.
> Wherever fate may cast us
> And wherever fortune may lead,
> We are the same: to us the entire world is a foreign land,
> Our home is Tsarskoe Selo. (2:425)

But the idealized memories from the Lyceum that became rooted in Pushkin's consciousness were a stark departure from reality. The Lyceum was an educational institution whose fate was something of a microcosm of the other reforms planned during the "beautiful beginning of Alexander's days." Like other institutions, it would suffer from a fatal combination of brilliant promises, broad designs in the complete absence of common goals and planning. The housing and external regimen of the Lyceum were initially allotted much attention: the students' uniforms were even discussed by the emperor himself. However, the syllabus was not thought through, and the staffing of professors was haphazard: in terms of preparation and pedagogical experience the majority of them could not have fulfilled the demands of a good gymnasium. Initially it was thought that Alexander I's younger brothers, Nicholas and Michael,[19] would receive their educations and be brought up at the Lyceum. This idea was likely Speransky's;[20] like many other forward-thinking men at court, he was concerned with how the grand dukes' personalities would develop, since in the future the fate of millions could depend on them. The teenaged Nicholas and Michael were accustomed to believing in the limitlessness and divine origin of their power and were deeply attached to the idea that the art of ruling consists of "Feldwebel science."* In 1816, General Peter Konovnitsin,[21] a distinctly conservative, yet honest military man and patriot, to whom Alexander I had entrusted the care of his brothers while

---

* I.e. in the study of military science and discipline. (Translator's note)

they were at war, clearly and deliberately wrote of the necessity of giving the grand dukes written instructions: "If the time comes that you will have to command the armed forces [...] try to improve the position of each and every soldier; do not demand the impossible from people. Firstly, ensure their necessary comfort and only then demand the exact and strict performance of faithful service. Shouting and threats only serve to frustrate and bring you no benefit."

At the Lyceum, the grand dukes were supposed to have been brought up among their peers, separated from the court. They would have been taught ideas more appropriate for their future positions, as opposed to "shouting and threats" and demanding "the impossible from people," both of which they had been inclined to from an early age. Had this plan been realized, Pushkin and Nicholas I would have been schoolmates (Nicholas was only three years older than Pushkin). Additionally, according to this plan, the other students at the Lyceum were intended for high-ranking government careers.

It would appear, however, that these plans were thwarted by the Empress Maria Feodorovna.[22] The reactionary forces that had set in after the War of 1812 which, among other things, resulted in Speransky's fall from grace, eventually led to the initial plans being thrown out, leaving Nicholas I terribly unprepared when he assumed the throne in 1825. As informed memoirist Vladimir Mukhanov wrote, "as far as the political sciences are concerned, there was no mention of them during the emperor's upbringing. [...] When it was decided that he would rule, the emperor himself was horrified as to his own incompetence."*

There was a positive side to all these changes for the Lyceum, however: although the fact that the court became uninterested in the Lyceum led to it losing a certain prestige, and the future of its alumni ceased appearing in its

---

* Vladimir Mukhanov, "Esche iz drevnikh zapisok" [More from Antique Notes], *Russkii arkhiv*, no. 5 (1897): 89–90.

original alluring light, it also happened that the interference of court circles in the life of the Lyceum became less noticeable.

The Lyceum was located in Tsarskoe Selo as was the emperor's summer residence. With the Lyceum occupying a wing of the Yekaterininsky Palace, its very location served to mark it as something of a royal educational institution. Nevertheless, Vasily Malinovsky,[23] the first director of the Lyceum, attempted to guard the school from the influence of the nearby court by strictly isolating the students. It would seem that Speransky also had had a hand in this, for he notoriously despised courtly circles and frequently sought to obstruct their political role in the government and their influence on the emperor. The Lyceum was thus separated from the surrounding courtly life; the students were let off the campus with great reluctance and only on special situations—even relatives' access to visits was limited.

In Pushkin's poetry, these practices of isolation became associated with images of monasteries, monastic life, and devilish temptations. This, in turn, was connected to Pushkin's constant desire to be rid of his chains and roam freely. As was stated above, Pushkin's poetic affection for his time at the Lyceum would come significantly later; when he actually attended the Lyceum, his primary mood was that of expectation to finish.

In Pushkin's verse, the Lyceum transforms into a monastery where a young monk tells himself:

> I gaze in tears through the bars on the window,
> Fingering my rosary beads,—

Yet the end of his time is associated with being freed from prison:

> But time will pass,
> And the locks will fall away
> From the stony gates,
> And the proud steeds will gallop
> Through valleys and mountains
> To sumptuous Petrograd;

> Rushing to my new home,
> I will abandon my cell
> And my fields and gardens;
> I'll leave my hood and chain under the table
> Defrocked and shaved as I am
> I'll run into your arms. (1:43)

Needless to say, lectures given by the teachers at the Lyceum left their mark on Pushkin. Many of Pushkin's teachers were progressive and erudite (for example, Alexander Kunitsyn[24] and Alexander Galich[25]). Pushkin, however, was far from an exemplary student.

The educational program at the Lyceum was extensive. The first three years were dedicated to the study of languages, "Russian, Latin, French, German," mathematics (at the same level as a technical gymnasium), literature and rhetoric, history, geography, dance, fencing, horseback riding, and swimming. In the upper classes, there was no strict program; the only thing specified by the charter were the disciplines that were to be studied: ethics, physics, mathematics, history, literature, and foreign languages. Not unexpectedly, the pairing of the ambitious nature of plan with the general ambiguity of the programs and requirements, as well as the general inexperience of the instructors, led to the students achieving only superficial levels of knowledge. Pushkin was justified in complaining to his brother in 1824 about the "inadequacy of his damned education" (13:121). Despite this, studies at the Lyceum also had their definite positive side: the so-called "Lyceum spirit" that the students of the first graduating class—Pushkin's class—would remember their entire lives and that soon would become the topic of numerous denunciations. It was this very "spirit" that Nicholas I later diligently drove out of the Lyceum.

Many different factors contributed to the unique atmosphere the Lyceum enjoyed: the small number of enrolled students; the youth of some of the professors; the humane character of pedagogical ideas, which, at their best, were geared towards displaying attention and respect to the students; the fact that, unlike other schools, there was no corporal punishment and a general sense of aristocratic honor and camaraderie was upheld among the students; and finally, Pushkin's class's position as the first alumni of the Lyceum—an object of love and attention. A number of professors held liberal views and some, such as Kunitsyn and Galich, later became victims of political persecution themselves. Their lectures were beneficial for their listeners. Thus, even though Pushkin did not achieve high marks in Kunistyn's classes, the fact that one of the chapters of Pushkin's lost novel *Fatam, or Human Reason* was titled "Natural Law" speaks for itself: Kunitsyn taught a course on natural law at the Lyceum. The course was dedicated to the study of naturally endowed human rights. The very fact that such a subject could be taught was a tribute to the liberal spirit of the Lyceum; later on, the subject was excluded from the curricula of Russian universities. However, teachers like Kunitsyn or Malinovsky, who was the director, instructed the students mainly not through lectures (Kunitsyn was never a gifted public speaker), but rather through teaching by example. They displayed proud independence and a "Spartan strictness" in their personal conduct. A spirit of independence and self-respect was cultivated among the students as well. Aside from leading ideas, the students also absorbed a certain behavioral model, which consisted in distaste towards slavishness and mindlessly obeying one's superiors and the will to independently think and act. The notorious journalist Faddei Bulgarin,[26] in a denunciatory note titled "On the Tsarskoselsky* Lyceum and Its Spirit" presented to Nicholas I in 1826, wrote: "In society, it is called the Lyceum spirit when a young man is disrespectful to his elders, is overly familiar with his superiors, haughty with his peers, and contemptuous towards those beneath

---

*   I.e. pertaining to Tsarskoe Selo (Translator's note).

him, except in those cases out of show where he needs to act as a supporter of equality."*

If we disregard the aggressive and denunciatory tone of the note, on one hand, and on the other, acknowledge that Bulgarin had no personal knowledge of the "Lyceum spirit" of the 1810s, but rather reconstructed it based on his impressions from later interactions with Delvig,[27] Pushkin, and other Lyceum graduates, and also that Bulgarin likely enriched this caricature by adding traits he associated with members of Arzamas and with the "liberalist" Turgenev brothers, then we arrive at a notable illustration of the behavior of a young "progressive," as he would have shown himself in society, from the end of the 1810s to the early 1820s. As concerns Bulgarin's accusation that they were contemptuous towards those beneath them, what he is likely referring to is a characteristic disdain of a free thinker toward someone servile, of a Chatsky toward a Molchalin.** It was for this attitude "from above," based on a heightened sense of self-respect, that the Molchalins and Poprishchins (Poprishchin is the hero in Gogol's[28] *Notes of a Madman*) did not forgive the Chatskys and Pechorins, just as Bulgarin could not forgive Pushkin and Delvig. Bulgarin, armed with the intuition of a denunciator, correctly gauged the connection between the "noble behavior" that the Lyceum students were taught to uphold and the behavior of young liberals often deemed offensive to "those who freely choose servility," as Pushkin put it.

For Pushkin, the Lyceum was most crucially the place where he first felt himself to be a poet. In 1830, Pushkin wrote, "I started to write when I was 13, and it was around that time that I was first published" (11:157).

> In those days, under the dark of oaken vaults,
> By waters flowing quiet

---

* Boris Modzalevskii, *Pushkin pod tainym nadzorom* [Pushkin under Secret Surveillance] (Leningrad: Atenei, 1925), 36.

** Characters from Aleksandr Griboedov's *Woe from Wit* (Translator's note).

> Along the corners of the Lyceum alleys,
> My Muse first thought to visit me.
> My student cell, which
> Thitherto had known no solace,
> All at once lit up—the Muse arrived,
> And set a feast of her endeavors.
> Forgive me, ye cold sciences!
> Forgive me, childish games!
> I am changed, I am a poet. (6:620)

The Romantic ideal of friendship was in vogue during this time at the Lyceum. Despite this, in reality the students naturally split into different groups, which often found themselves at odds. Pushkin belonged to several such groups but was never fully accepted in any given one. At the Lyceum there was a strong push toward literary activities, which was encouraged by the entire style of the teaching. Handwritten journals circulated with titles like "The Lyceum Sage," "The Inexperienced Quill," "For Pleasure and Purpose," and others. The poetical leader of the Lyceum, at least in the early years, was Illichevsky.[29] It is generally thought that Pushkin ardently sought to occupy the poetical forefront among his peers. Boris Tomashevsky has shown conversely, however, that certain key features of Pushkin's early verse (such as its connection to the epic tradition and other major genres) were not accepted by his peers, with the result that there was no consensus between the young Pushkin and the "literary opinions" of his peers at the Lyceum.**

Pushkin's closest friends included Delvig, Pushchin,[30] Malinovsky, and Küchelbecker.[31] Their friendship would last through Pushkin's entire life, leaving a deep mark on him. But there was more than meets the eye to their friendship. The students' political opinions were maturing, and each began holding their own free-thinking views. Many of the alumni became caught up in the Decembrist movement: Pushchin, Delvig, Küchelbecker, and Volkhovsky[32]

---

*   Boris Tomashevskii, *Pushkin*, 2 vols. (Moscow–Leningrad: Izdatel'stvo Akademii nauk SSSR, 1956), 1:40–41.

all belonged to the Sacred Artel of Alexander Muravyov[33] and Ivan Burtsev.[34] Pushkin did not receive an invitation to participate. Moreover, his friends hid their own participation from him.

In the future, when Pushkin would recall the Lyceum from the height of years passed since, all differences were resolved. His need for friendship "corrected" his memories. It was namely after their graduation, after the Lyceum was left far in the past, that these memories served as the cement that bound together the "Lyceum circle," which only became stronger as the years went by. Their brotherhood waxed rather than waned. One example makes this clear: on June 9, 1817, Delvig's farewell hymn was performed at their graduation ceremony:

> Farewell, my brothers! Hand in hand!
> We embrace for the final time.
> Fate has united us, perhaps,
> Only to forever separate us!
> Pause your gaze on each of us
> With a parting tear.
> Guard, O friends, guard
> This friendship with the same soul,
> With the same great striving for glory,
> For truth, not falsehood,
> In misfortune, proud patience,
> In good fortune, regards to all.*

The Lyceum students of the first graduating class obviously remembered this poem by heart and every line served as a code for them. In the future Pushkin more than once would use Delvig's poem as a code that allowed him in a few words to resurrect in the consciousness of his Lyceum friends the atmosphere of their youth. In a poem titled "19 October" (1825), dedicated to the anniversary of their graduation, Pushkin, addressing his classmate Fedor Matiushkin,[35] who was then completing a circumnavigation of the globe, wrote:

---

* Anton Delvig, *Polnoe sobranie stikhotvorenii* [Complete Collected Poems] (Leningrad: Khudozhestvennaia literatura, 1934), 286–287.

> You extended your hand over the seas,
> You carried us alone in your young soul
> And repeated to yourself: "Only to long be apart,
> Has mysterious fate, perhaps, sentenced us!" (2:425)

Delvig's lines—

> Fate has united us, perhaps,
> Only to forever separate us!

—are slightly changed in Pushkin's version, but his classmates would have definitely recognized them. Even more noteworthy is another example: the famous lines from the "Epistle to Siberia"—

> In the depths of Siberian mines,
> Preserve your proud patience (3:49)

—which are an unambiguous reference to Delvig's hymn:

> In misfortune, proud patience.

For Delvig these lines were an elegiac topos, whereas Pushkin filled them with real-life meaning. The move by most of the Lyceum students from Tsarskoe Selo to St. Petersburg, where they were to start their careers—whether civilian or military—is an elegiac "eternal parting"; the circumnavigation of the globe is a real-life "long-term parting"; the "In misfortune, proud patience" is a poetic topos. The "proud patience" "in the depths of Siberian mines" had an entirely different meaning. These poetic quotes had an additional hidden connotation. Readers who purchased the Northern Flowers almanac for 1827 had no way of knowing whose words Pushkin used here for his sailor-friend—only Pushkin's classmates could have known. Though never published in the poet's lifetime "To Siberia" made the rounds of all those doing hard labor in Siberia as well as to those much farther away, but the full meaning of "proud patience" could have been gauged only by

Pushkin's classmates, in particular, Pushchin and then, considerably later, Küchelbecker.

In Pushkin's mind, the Lyceum was transformed into an ideal community of friends, and his friends, in turn, became an ideal audience for his poetry.

Pushkin's relationships with his friends, as stated, could be strained. Even those who were very well-inclined toward him could not help but recall, later on, how easily he took offense and how he would often behave in a brash and defiant manner. Ivan Pushchin wrote in his memoirs:

> Pushkin, from the very beginning, was more irascible than most and thus was not particularly well-liked: such is the fate of the eccentric among his peers. It's not that he tried to act out any particular role among us or shocked us with his eccentricities, as is often the case with others; but sometimes he found himself in inopportune situations, which arose due to his inappropriate jokes and awkward barbs. He would then find it hard to extricate himself from the situation. This led to new blunders, which never escape the attention of one's classmates. As his roommate (on the other side of his room was a blank wall), we would, in lowered voices, after everyone had fallen asleep, talk through the partition about the blunder of the day; it was during these conversations that I clearly saw how sensitive he was to all this nonsense and how worried he was by it. Together, to the best of our ability, we tried to smooth out any rough spots that arose, but this was not always possible. He possessed a strange blend of excessive courage and shyness, and both these aspects constantly manifested themselves at the wrong time, as a result of which he would suffer himself. It sometimes happened that both of us would make a blunder, I would smooth it over, but he could not find it in himself to make it right. Most importantly, he lacked what is called *tact*.

"All of this was the reason," Pushchin concludes, "that his own attachment to his peers at the Lyceum was far from immediately well-received." Pushchin was a sharp-eyed observer. His continuous interactions with Pushkin over the course of six years allowed him to make an exceptionally astute observation regarding his friend's personality: "To really love him, you had to look at him with the sort of complete benevolence that knows and sees all the rough edges of his character and his flaws, accepts them, and ends by coming to love them in your friend and comrade."*

Pushkin, the unloved child in his family, whose personal development came unevenly and awkwardly, was always deeply insecure. This resulted in bravado, showing off, an urge to come first. At home he was considered a laggard, so at school he constantly sought to demonstrate his physical ability, strength, and self-reliance. The same Pushchin, even fifty years later, still expressed great puzzlement in his memoiristic sketches, writing that Pushkin, who was significantly better-read than his classmates, had never been vain about his erudition and learning and did not seem to even value them: "Anything that was scholarly was worthless to him, and it was as if he only wanted to prove that he was a master at running, jumping over chairs, throwing a ball etc. Even in these things it was a question of his pride—there were many awkward conflicts as a result."**

Pushkin himself testified to the fact that before "the Muse appeared" in his "student cell" there was a time

> when I would oft prefer
> A well-thrown ball to a rare poem.
> I held scholasticism for rubbish
> And would jump into the garden o'er the gate.***
> It would happen I was sometimes diligent,
> Sometimes lazy, sometimes stubborn,
> Sometimes cunning, sometimes direct,
> Sometimes meek, sometimes rebellious,
> Sometimes sad, sometimes silent,
> And sometimes heartily loquacious. (6:619)

---

*   *Contemporaries*, 1:82–83.
** *Contemporaries*, 1:74.
*** Pushkin was writing about youthful pranks. The tsar would complain to Engelhardt, the director of the Lyceum: "Your pupils [...] have been removing my ripe apples through the fence and beating the guards" (*Contemporaries*, 1:91).

All memoirists are united in their descriptions and evaluations of the great impression that the War of 1812 left on the students of the Lyceum. Let us cite Pushchin once more: "Our life at the Lyceum was merging with the lives of the whole Russian people: the storm of 1812 was approaching. Its events had a great impact on our childhood. It started when we accompanied the Guard regiments as they were passing by the Lyceum."** The impressions from these years, needless to say, set the tone of the civic pathos and early-set freethinking of many of the Lyceum students' views, including Pushkin's. The events of the war were also influential for the students in another regard: history appeared right from the pages of textbooks at the gates of the Lyceum. To immortalize one's name and pass it on to descendants it was no longer necessary to have been born in earlier mythological times or to a royal family. Not only "the man of fate," Napoleon Bonaparte, the son of minor Corsican aristocrats, who became the emperor of France and who re-carved the European landscape, but also any of the young Guard officers who had passed by the Lyceum on the way to their deaths at Borodino, Leipzig, or Montmartre were now "men of history." In one of his final poems (on October 19, 1836) Pushkin wrote:

> Do you remember? Brigade after brigade flowed by
> With our elder brothers we then parted
> And, dejected, returned to the cover of our studies,
> Envious of him, who to his death,
> Was filing past us… (3:432)

The reserved style of Pushkin's later poetry is generally devoid of poetical embellishment. "Envious of him, who to his death, / Was filing past us" is not a rhetorical figure, but rather a precise psychological description of the Lyceum students' feelings. A heroic death that allowed one to achieve immortality did not seem frightening—on the contrary, it was glorious. This only

---

*   *Contemporaries*, 1:81.

intensified the pain of having been born too late. Leo Tolstoy astutely captured these feelings in Petya Rostov's words in *War and Peace*: "'anyway, I cannot study anything now when…'—Petya paused and deeply blushed, but finished his thought—'when the Fatherland is in danger.'"*

Poetry was the answer to everything. It became a form of self-justification and a promise of immortality. It was precisely immortality that became the sole measure of poetry worthy the name in Pushkin's circle. Pushkin was 16 years old when Derzhavin[36] "consecrated" him as a poet, and Delvig, in 1815, in the September edition of the *Russian Museum* [Rossiiskiy Muzeum] journal, greeted him (Pushkin had only published a select few poems at this point) with the following verses:

> Pushkin! He can't seek cover in the woods;
> His lyre will give him away with its loud singing,
> And he'll be raised immortally above the crowd of mortal men
> By Apollo as he celebrates triumphant on Olympus.**

Pushkin had never been strongly attached to his parents. However, it would appear that a need for attachment was exceptionally strong. This affected the majority of relationships Pushkin had with his older contemporaries. On the one hand, he was always ready to rebel against any authority; condescension and patronage from his older peers were unbearable to him. On the other hand, he was drawn towards them, was starved for their attention, and their recognition of him was a necessity. He wanted their friendship. The cult of friendship was inseparable from pre-Romantic literature: Schiller[37] and Karamzin, Rousseau[38] and Batyushkov[39] all contributed to a dense "mythology" of friendship. Literary tradition, nonetheless, only supplied the

---

* Lev Tolstoi, *Sobranie sochinenii* [Collected Works], 22 vols. (Moscow: Pravda, 1980), 6:92.

** Delvig, *Polnoe sobranie stikhotvorenii*, 192.

rhetorical forms and words; in Pushkin's life and poetry, these were complemented by a very real lack of friendship and intimacy that greatly affected Pushkin, who always reluctantly thought back to his family and early childhood.

Pushkin's friendships with the Lyceum students, as we have seen, did not always go smoothly. This, in part, explains his longing for friendship with his older peers who included Chaadaev,[40] Kaverin,[41] members of Arzamas, Karamzin, the Turgenevs, and Fedor Glinka.

If we were to divide Pushkin's social life into three distinct periods, we would see the following. From the Lyceum on to his life in Odesa, during his exile, Pushkin's friends were predominantly older than him, more experienced, and higher up in official rank. Pushkin actively sought to ignore these distinctions. He once told Karamzin: "'So, you prefer slavery to freedom.' (Kara[mzin] flared up and called me a slanderer.)" (12:306). To Mikhail Orlov,[42] hero of the War of 1812, recipient of the keys to Paris, favorite of the emperor and idol of the regular soldiers, head of the Chișinău Decembrist society, Pushkin, "getting worked up, accidentally let out," "You think, general, like an old woman." "Pushkin, you are speaking impertinently, be careful," Orlov replied.*

And nevertheless, Pushkin's friendships with these older men certainly did not pass on equal terms. Pushkin's friends were almost always also his teachers. Some taught him to be firm and stoical in civil society (like Chaadaev or Fedor Glinka). Others, such as Nikolai Turgenev,[43] taught him political economy. Others still, like Kaverin and Molostvov,[44] admitted him to the secret revelries of the hussars; finally, some like Krivtsov[45] "corrupted" him with materialism. To even consider the possibility of any reciprocal influence by Pushkin on these people is pointless. In 1824, Pushkin wrote the following bitter quatrain on friendship:

---

* *Contemporaries*, 1:351.

> What's friendship? Hangover's faint ardor,
> Insult's free speech,
> The exchange of vanity, idleness
> Or patronage's dishonor. (2:460)

During the Mikhailovskoe period Pushkin began to be drawn more to people closer to his own age. His relationships with his Lyceum classmates attained a new and special value during this time. His epistolary friendship with Vyazemsky flourished—even though the latter was somewhat older than Pushkin, he by no means fit the role of a mentor, nor did he aspire to that role. In the role of publisher-friend (due to his wanderings in exile Pushkin very much needed help in this area, inasmuch as he was deprived of the ability to carry on business transactions on his own) the venerable Gnedich[46] was replaced by Pletnev.[47] From among the political conspirators it was the "young ones"—Ryleev[48] and Bestuzhev[49]—who attracted Pushkin; from among the poets, it was his coevals—Delvig, Baratynsky,[50] and Yazykov[51]—who did.

In the 1830s Pushkin's circle of friends is joined by younger writers who were only just beginning literary careers—Ivan Kireevsky,[52] Pogodin,[53] Gogol (who becomes a close working colleague of Pushkin), Koltsov,[54] and even Belinsky[55] (despite all the differences in their literary views and their cultural and everyday habits). Pushkin's younger brother's friends (Nashchokin,[56] Sobolevsky[57]) became his friends as well. The constant renewal of his circle of friends would become for Pushkin one of the traits signifying his brave acceptance of the eternal movement of life.

Zhukovsky[58] occupied a unique place among Pushkin's friends. A deep and subtle lyric poet who unlocked the mysteries of poetry's plangent sounds, Zhukovsky was also gifted in another way: he was undoubtedly the kindest person in Russian literary history. Kindness, gentleness, receptiveness—these also require talent, and Zhukovsky possessed this talent in the highest degree. When Pushkin was still a student at the Lyceum, Zhukovsky was already a famous poet. In 1816, Pushkin dedicated an epistle to Zhukovsky that began with the line, "Bless me, O Poet..." In these words was an acknowledgement of the distance between Zhukovsky, the author of the renowned patriotic poem on the War of 1812, and Pushkin, who was then a poetic novice. However, in Zhukovsky's relation to the beginning poet there was neither an attitude of patronage, so unbearable to Pushkin, nor one, also annoying, of moralizing. Zhukovsky was able to find the correct tone, one of a loving older brother whose seniority does not get in the way of equal relations. This made Pushkin and Zhukovsky's friendship particularly long-lasting. Even here, however, matters were not always smooth: occasionally, Zhukovsky would try to moralize with Pushkin, and in Pushkin's final months, he completely lost his ability to understand the poet's inner life. Pushkin, in turn, never disguised his creative differences from his older friend, sometimes even accentuating the fact with epigrammatic sharpness. Nevertheless, among Pushkin's longest friendships that with Zhukovsky belongs next to those with Delvig and Pushchin.

Pushkin's circle of friends during the Lyceum period—the hussars in Tsarskoe Selo, the writers of the Arzamas group (those young men of letters who rallied around Karamzin's "new literary style" and Zhukovsky's Romanticism), and Karamzin's family—all of these were incredibly beneficial in the development of the poet's mind and views as well as his public and literary positions. They also had an effect on his character. Among the hussars, Pushkin could feel like a grownup; with Karamzin, he could enjoy a sort of familial and domestic comfort, something he had lacked as a child. His unexpected and touching love for Ekaterina Karamzina,[59] Karamzin's wife, was likely largely defined by his need for some kind of motherly love (she was more than twice his age—nineteen years older than him!). There is no reason to view this as deep, hidden passion. Yury Tynianov,[60] who wrote a detailed work on Pushkin's "unnamed love," highlights the fact that it was precisely Karamzina whom Pushkin wanted to see before his death.* However, this can only be understood if we examine the other names that Pushkin remembered during his final minutes.

Anyone who has seen another person dying and suffering from gaps in their consciousness knows of the unexpected ability these people display in recalling their long-past and seemingly long-forgotten childhood. On his deathbed, Pushkin neither recalled his mother, who had recently passed away, nor asked after his father, brother, or sister. Yet he remembered the Lyceum: "It's a pity that neither Pushchin nor Malinovsky are here; I'd have found it easier to die." "Karamzina? Is Karamzina here?" Pushkin asked.** He was returning to the world of his Lyceum life.

The Lyceum effectively replaced Pushkin's childhood. The departure from childhood and the entry into "adult" life was perceived by Pushkin, eager to leave the Lyceum behind, as something solemn. He conceived of his adulthood as the time when he would be consecrated as a figure in Russian literature, like a knight taking a vow to protect his lady. For the youth who knew the culture of chivalry through the ironic poems of Voltaire,[61] Ariosto,[62] and Tasso[63] such a "consecration" had a double meaning: solemn and tinged with pathos, on the one hand, and burlesquely parodic, on the other—the pathos and the irony didn't cancel each other out, but went hand-in-hand. During his time at the Lyceum, Pushkin had already been twice consecrated as a poet. The first consecration took place on January 8, 1815, during the exam signaling the students' graduation from the lower to the upper form. Pushkin's meeting with Derzhavin did not in reality have that conventionally symbolic (and certainly not theatrical) character that we ascribe to it, looking back and knowing as we do that on that day in the lyceum hall there came together the greatest Russian

---

*   Iurii Tynianov, "Bezymennaia liubov" [The Unnamed Love], in *Pushkin i ego sovremenniki* [Pushkin and His Contemporaries] (Moscow: Nauka, 1969), 217.

**   *Contemporaries*, 2:332, 349.

poet of the eighteenth century, who had only a year to live, and the greatest Russian poet of all time. In all actuality, Derzhavin had already several times before this passed on his lyre to younger poets:

> To you, as inheritance, Zhukovsky,
> I bequeath this ancient lyre
> And I above the slippery abyss of my grave
> Can now bend my brow.*

Pushkin himself later described the meeting with a characteristic blend of humor and lyricism: "Derzhavin arrived. He came into the entryway and Delvig heard him asking the porter, 'Hey, brother, where's the privy?' This prosaic request disappointed Delvig." "Derzhavin was very old. [...] He sat supporting his head with his hand. His face was inexpressive; his eyes were vacant, his lips were drooping" (12:158). This passage was written around the same time as Pushkin's description of the old countess in *The Queen of Spades*: "The countess sat there, all sallow, her drooping lips twitching. [...] Her opaque eyes revealed the complete absence of thought" (8:240). This is no coincidence: in both cases, Pushkin is representing images of the outlived and departed eighteenth century, distilled as it were in a single, withered face.

This meeting of the departing poet and the beginning poet during Pushkin's final exams is unlikely to have shocked Pushkin's contemporaries, who were otherwise occupied by their routine bureaucratic, political, and court concerns. Only a limited circle of close friends, who had begun to value Pushkin's gifts, could have grasped its meaning. But for Pushkin himself, it was one of the most important events of his life. He felt like a page being knighted: "I was finally summoned. I read my 'Recollections at Ts[arskoe] S[elo]' while standing two paces away from Derzhavin. It's impossible for me to describe what I felt then: when I reached the line where Derzhavin's name is mentioned,

---

*   Gavrila Derzhavin, *Stikhotvoreniia* [Poems] (Leningrad: Sovetskii pisatel', 1933), 386.

my adolescent voice rang out, and my heart started beating from ecstasy and excitement… I don't remember how I finished reading, I don't remember where I ran off to. Derzhavin was delighted; he asked for me, wanted to embrace me… They looked for me, but I was nowhere to be found…" (12:158).

Pushkin's second consecration occurred when he joined Arzamas—an unofficial literary society which brought together young and provocative writers who enjoyed sending up the literary "old believers" at their playful meetings. Members of Arzamas were followers of Karamzin; they regarded Derzhavin's house with a comic condescension, as it was the place where the literary "archaists" solemnly convened. Pushkin was accepted into Arzamas during the autumn of 1817, a time when inner strife had beset the literary society. For Pushkin, this acceptance carried another deeper meaning: he had been accepted into the literary world. His recruitment into a fighting band of young writers—Romantics, mockers, pursuers of "the Bygone Age"—drew a line beneath the period of his childhood and years of study. He felt he had entered the company of known poets.

Chapter Two

St. Petersburg, 1817–1820

The Lyceum had become Pushkin's home. Home, as a poetic symbol, would with the passage of years come to represent what were Pushkin's most cherished thoughts as well as Culture's highest values. In time the idea of life's journey would be imagined as a *return home*. At the time of the fourth anniversary of the events on Senate Square, on December 14, 1829, Pushkin suffered a bout of home-sickness, leading him to travel to Tsarskoe Selo. This idea of return is central to a poem that was started on that very day but ultimately left unfinished. It is no coincidence that even the poem's title ("Recollections at Tsarskoe Selo"*) harkens back to the poet's famous final exam at the Lyceum:

> Troubled by recollections,
> Filled with sweet longing,
> Your beautiful gardens, on the sacred twilight,
> I enter with lowered head,
> So did that Biblical youth, the [mad] spendthrift,
> Who having drained his vial of repentance to the last drop,
> Saw, at last, his native abode,
> And bent his head and wept. (3:189)

During Pushkin's youth, Home (viz. the Lyceum, St. Petersburg) signified a cell of captivity. Living there meant being kept by force, while fleeing meant achieving one's desires. Beyond the walls of Home, space and freedom envisioned. When Pushkin was at the Lyceum, St. Petersburg became that

---

* The word "recollections" is used here and in the Lyceum poem to mean slightly different things: in 1814, the poet spoke of historical recollections prompted by the monuments at Tsarskoe Selo and the defeat of Napoleon as a result of the latter's failed Russia campaign of 1812; in 1829, he referred to both personal and historical recollections.

space, and when he was in St. Petersburg, it was the countryside. This thought process would leave its imprint on Pushkin's perception of his own exile to the south of Russia in a surprising manner: rather than viewing it as a forced expulsion, he preferred to consider it as a voluntary escape from captivity to freedom.

Before the reader and before himself Pushkin takes on the image of the Fugitive, the voluntary Exile. Sometimes this image, borrowed from European Romanticism's arsenal of images, contains actual biographical content, as in the lines—

> Scorning both the voice of reproach,
> And the calls of sweeter hopes,
> I shall travel to foreign lands,
> Shaking the ashes of the fatherland off my travel clothes (2:349)

—are reflected in Pushkin's actual plans to "quietly take his hat and cane in hand and travel to see Constantinople." However, more often it is Pushkin's poetic thinking that transforms reality. In the prose of Pushkin's life it was a forced exile to the south, while in his verse he is

> A seeker of new impressions,
> I fled you, fatherly lands... (2:147)

In his verse the Lyceum is an abandoned monastery, St. Petersburg—a brilliant and alluring place of escape. But in reality everything was otherwise: Pushkin's parents moved to St. Petersburg and Pushkin simply came home from the Lyceum. What is interesting is what is not there in Pushkin's creative work of this period (1817–1820) that then shows up in *The Little House in Kolomna* and *The Bronze Horseman*: e.g. the house in Kolomna, "right by [the Church of the Holy Virgin's] Intercession," Klokachev's[1] house on the Fontanka Embankment, and other impressions from these St. Petersburg outskirts where, as Gogol wrote, "everything is quiet and retired." While at the Lyceum Pushkin constantly wrote epistles to his sister,[2] but during his St. Petersburg period there are neither mentions of his sister nor any "domestic" themes whatsoever.

Pushkin lived in St. Petersburg from the beginning of June 1817 (on June 9 the graduation ceremony took place at the Lyceum and on June 11 Pushkin was already in the city) until May 6, 1820, when he departed for his southern exile along the road to Tsarskoe Selo. Pushkin's plans for a military career, which he had been entertaining, had to be abandoned: his father, fearing the expenses (service in the Guards required large outlays), insisted on the civil service. Pushkin was enrolled in the Collegium of Foreign Affairs and on June 13, together with Küchelbecker and Griboedov, took his oath.

St. Petersburg caught Pushkin in its swirl. In a hurry to reward himself for six years of enforced isolation he donned a wide, black tailcoat with uncut tails (such a tailcoat was called *à l'américaine*—its showy crudeness the peak of fashion and refinement) and a wide-brimmed hat *à la bolivar* (the brims were "so wide that it was impossible to pass through narrow doorways without taking it off").*

There were times in Pushkin's life when he would find his best company in a book and his best occupation in solitude and contemplation. His time in St. Petersburg from 1817 to 1820 could not have been more different. The reason for this lay not solely in the fact that the young poet's unspent forces passionately sought an outlet. In unison with these forces there also boiled and seethed Young Russia. In Russian history these years possess a unique, nonpareil countenance. The successful conclusion of the war with Napoleon awakened in Russian society a feeling of its own strength.

The right to engage in political activity seemed something that had been achieved irrevocably. Young people were filled with a thirst for action and faith in Russia's potential. A conflict with the state and its "old men" was already

---

*   Mikhail Pyliaev, *Staroe zhit'e: ocherki i rasskazy* [Old Living: Sketches and Tales] (St. Petersburg: Tipografiia A. S. Suvorina, 1892), 104.

Chapter Two. St. Petersburg, 1817–1820 | 35

clearly looming on the horizon, but no one yet believed in its tragic character. A characteristic trait of the time was a striving to unite forces. Even the reading of a book, an activity traditionally linked in cultural history with solitude, was carried out jointly. As Kantemir[3] wrote about reading at the beginning of the eighteenth century,

> I'll lock myself
> In the pantry, and for the sake of dead friends,
>   deprive myself of the living.*

In the late 1810s–early 1820s, reading in Russia took the form of friendly interaction; people read together just as they thought together, disputed together, drank together, and discussed state decrees or theatrical news together. Pushkin, addressing Yakov Saburov,[4] a hussar, placed in one series the following activities:

> [...] I strolled with Kaverin,
> Cursed Russia [with] Molostvov,
> Read together with my Chaadaev. (2:350)

Pyotr Kaverin, who had been a student at the University of Göttingen,** was a hussar, a duelist and reveller, and member of the Union of Welfare. He not only "strolled" (i.e. caroused) with Pushkin, but also "popped a cork into the ceiling" with Onegin in the fashionable restaurant *Talon* on Nevsky Prospekt. Pamfamir Molostvov, a liberal and great eccentric, was in the Life Guards. Like merry-making or conversing, reading also requires a companion. The character of such reading is wonderfully illustrated in a story told by the Decembrist Ivan Yakushkin.[5] In 1818 he became acquainted with Colonel

---

*   Antiokh Kantemir, *Sobranie stikhotvorenii* [Collected Poems] (Leningrad: Sovetskii pisatel', 1956), 59.
**   A center of German Idealist philosophy (Translator's note).

Pavel Grabbe.[6] During their conversation Grabbe's orderly brought him his hussar's uniform—the dolman and mentik—as the colonel was preparing to present himself to Arakcheev. "The conversation hit on the ancient historians. At the time we were all passionately in love with the ancients: Plutarch,[7] Livy,[8] Cicero,[9] Tacitus,[10] and others were for each of us almost our favorite books. Grabbe also loved the ancients. On my table there lay a book from which I read to Grabbe several letters of Brutus[11] to Cicero, in which the former, having decided to act against Octavius,[12] chides the latter for his cowardice. During the reading Grabbe apparently (i.e., noticeably—Lotman) became impassioned and told his man that he wasn't leaving, and we proceeded to dine together. After that he never appeared before Arakcheev."*

The pursuit of friendship, common society, and brotherhood became the defining feature of Pushkin's behavior during these years. The energy with which he aligned himself with different literary and friendly circles can appear surprising. One factor is worthy of note: each circle that attracted Pushkin's attention during these years had a distinct literary-political profile; each counted among its members people who had undergone fire in literary battles and were covered in actual battle scars; their tastes and opinions were already formed, their judgements and goals categorical.

As a rule, membership in one circle excluded participation in another. Pushkin stood out among such members as someone searching among those who had found what they were looking for. Here the issue was not only his age, but Pushkin's life-long (though still inchoate), deeply characteristic avoidance of any one-sided thinking: when joining this or that circle, he would, with the same ease with which he adopted the styles of Russian poetry in his Lyceum verse, adopt the dominant style of the circle, its type of behavior, and the speech of its participants.

---

* Ivan Yakushkin, *Zapiski, stat'i, pis'ma* [Notes, Articles, Letters] (Moscow: Izdatel'stvo Akademii nauk SSSR, 1951), 20.

But just as the mastery of established stylistic and generic norms became more striking in a given poem of the Lyceum period, so too did it become more "Pushkinian." Something similar to this took place in 1817–1820 with regard to the construction of the poet's personality. Mastering with extraordinary ease the "conventions of the game" established in a given circle, and assuming the style of friendly interaction suggested by one of his instructor-interlocutors, Pushkin did not disappear into other characters and norms. He was searching for himself.

Pushkin's ability to change, moving from one circle to another and seeking out social exchanges with very different people, was not always greeted with approval by the Decembrists. Even his close friend, Decembrist Ivan Pushchin, wrote:

> Pushkin, a man of liberal views, had a lamentable habit of betraying his noble character; quite often he would anger me and the rest of us by, for example, loitering near the orchestra to converse with Orlov,[13] Chernyshov,[14] Kiselyov,[15] and others. [...] You'd say to him: 'What sport is there for you, dear friend, in bothering with these people: you shan't find sympathy in any one of them, etc.' He'd patiently listen and then begin tickling you, embracing you, which he would always do when he had nothing to reply. And then you'd look, and Pushkin would be in the company of the lions again!*

Brother of a Decembrist, barely thirty years old, son of a Catherine-era grandee, his military career begun at the Battle of Austerlitz (where he received a golden saber for bravery), wounded seven times at Borodino, a major general at thirty, commander of a Horse Guard regiment, favorite of the emperor—Alexei Orlov had many stories to tell. Alexander Chernyshov, a year younger than Orlov, had also experienced much in life: his numerous long conversations with Napoleon and his excellent personal knowledge of the entire staff surrounding the emperor made this adjutant-general an interesting

---

*   *Contemporaries*, 1:98.

conversationalist as well. Pavel Kiselyov, a smart and clever high-flyer, promoted at just thirty-one to major-general, someone capable of being at the same time both a close advisor to Alexander I and a best friend of Pestel, also quickly made a career for himself. All three individuals, in the activist spirit of the Alexandrine Age not standing aloof to "free-thinking" ideas, became in time highly successful state bureaucrats.

It is precisely the above-quoted observation by Pushchin that allows us to make the claim that Pushkin's position in this circle was not that of a rapturous youth, but rather that of a curious observer. Even the perceptive Pestel had failed to figure out Kiselyov, having believed in the sincerity of the latter's friendship and free-thinking and having paid for it with his life, while the twenty-year-old Pushkin wrote the following about him in an epistle to Alexei Orlov:

> I shan't rest my hopes
> On General Kiselyov
> He is very kind, there is no question,
> A foe of treachery* and fools ...
> But he serves at court: his promises
> Cost him nothing. (2:85)

While at the Lyceum, Pushkin, who had been elected in absentia to Arzamas and given the nickname of *Sverchok***, was keen to take part in the activities of the literary society. However, once his wish could become a reality, Arzamas's purely literary agenda seemed anachronistic with formation of the Union of Welfare. From February to April 1817 Arzamas welcomed Nikolai Turgenev and Mikhail Orlov; in the autumn Nikita Muravyov[16] became a member as well.

---

*   This phrase is registered more explicitly in manuscript form: "tyrants." (2:561).
** Russian for "cricket" (Translator's note).

Each of these individuals was an active member of a politically conspiratorial group. They looked at literature not as something of independent value, but only as a means of promoting political propaganda. By this point in time the political interests of the "old" Arzamas members (Prince Pyotr Vyazemsky, Denis Davydov[17]) had also been activated. Telling in this respect is the following diary entry made by Nikolai Turgenev on September 29, 1817: "The day before yesterday we had an Arzamas meeting. By chance we turned away from literature and began discussing domestic politics. All agreed on the necessity of abolishing slavery."* Pushkin, it would seem, was also present at this assembly.

Arzamas had not been ready to engage in political activity and eventually fell apart. Nevertheless, it was there apparently that Pushkin became close with Nikolai Turgenev and Mikhail Orlov, and it was these connections during this time that decisively supplanted old attachments and friendships. Karamzin, Zhukovsky, Batyushkov—heroes of the language's elegance and its "new style," heroes in the battles against the Beseda group (i.e. the "archaists" of "Colloquy")—all faded in Pushkin's mind before these preachers of freedom and civic virtues.

Nikolai Turgenev occupied a unique role among Pushkin's friends. To start with, he was ten years older than him. Having inherited stern ethical principles and a deep religiosity from his freemason father,[18] Turgenev combined a hard, dry wit—often inclined to doctrinairism—with an exalted, if somewhat bookish, love for Russia and its people. The struggle against slavery ("boorishness," as he expressed it on his own specific political vocabulary) was an idea that he carried throughout his life.

Contrary to his older brother Alexander,[19] who was known for his mild character and who expressed his liberalism mainly in his tolerance for others' viewpoints, Nikolai Turgenev was intolerant, demanded that others be

---

*   *Arzamas*, 2 vols. (Moscow: Khudozhestvennaia literatura, 1994), 1:436.

uncompromising, was harsh in his own decision-making, and in conversation was sarcastic and categorical. Pushkin was a regular guest at Turgenev's apartment. Turgenev's political views in these years mostly corresponded to those of the moderate wing of the Union of Welfare, which he joined in the latter half of 1818. It was Turgenev's hope to attain the emancipation of the serfs through the intercession of the state.

However, at this time no one believed in the tsar's good intentions. Nonetheless, the members of the Union of Welfare hoped to apply pressure on progressive elements in society, to which Alexander I would be forced, willy-nilly, to yield. It was with this goal in mind that the Union of Welfare considered it imperative that public opinion be established in Russia, which the political conspirators would then wield through literature and the press. In this way literature was assigned a subservient goal. Problems of a purely artistic nature were of little concern to Nikolai Turgenev, who wrote in 1819: "Where might a Russian glean those necessary rules of civic spirit? Our literature has hitherto been limited almost entirely to poetry. Prose compositions do not touch upon matters of politics." And later: "Poetry and fine literature in general cannot fill our soul."*

Graduate of the University of Göttingen, diplomat and government figure, author of books on political economy, Nikolai Turgenev regarded poetry rather dismissively, making an exception only for politically useful, agitational verse. It was with this perspective that he attempted to imbue Pushkin. His younger brother Sergei,[20] a diplomat beginning his career, fully concurred with him, ruminating in his diary: "Zhukovsky wrote to me saying that, to judge by [my] portrait, he could see that my eyes shone with liberal ideas. He's a poet, but I would tell him truthfully that his talent will be lost should he not

---

*   Vasilii Semennikov, "Materialy dlia istorii russkoi literatury i dlia slovaria pisatelei epokhi Ekateriny II" [Materials for the History of Russian Literature and for a Reference Book of Writers from the Period of Catherine II], *Russkii bibliofil*, no. 5 (1914): 17.

dedicate it to all that is liberal. It is only with such [liberal-minded] poems that one might hope to attain immortality… People write to me again about Pushkin, that he is a developing talent. Ah, would that they hasten him to properly inhale the breath of liberty and instead of crying over himself, his first song might be to Freedom."** "Crying over himself" refers to elegiac poetry, which the Turgenevs, as indeed most Decembrists, looked upon harshly.

Nikolai Turgenev had a clear influence on Pushkin's poem "The Village." Also characteristic in this regard is the beginning of the "Ode to Liberty," which features an outspoken rejection of love poetry in favor of a freedom-loving Muse. One should not, of course, take the influence here too literally; the idea of condemning love poetry and juxtaposing to it political poetry was a virtual commonplace in Decembrist and adjacent circles. Vyazemsky, who trod a different, completely original path, expressed the same idea in similar imagery of "Indignation" (1820):

> And from the forehead, wrinkled with thought,
> I tore away the wreath of soulless joys.
> […]
> My Apollo is indignation!
> By his flame, from my unbound lips
> Will fall disgraceful silence
> And bold verse will catch fire.

In Pushkin's poem:

> Come, tear the wreath from me,
> Smash my effete lyre…
> I long to sing Freedom to the world,
> And vanquish vice on the thrones. (2:45)

---

*   Nikolai Turgenev, *Pis'ma k bratu S. I. Turgenevu* [Letters to His Brother S. I. Turgenev] (Moscow–Leningrad: Izdatel'stvo Akademii nauk SSSR, 1936), 59.

The "Ode to Liberty" is linked to Nikolai Turgenev's ideas not only through its opposition of love poetry and political verse, but also through its entire cluster of thoughts, its relation to the French Revolution and to Russian autocracy. The ode expressed the political views of the Union of Welfare, and Nikolai Turgenev's thoughts were reflected in it directly.*

Nikolai Turgenev was a strict moralist—there was much in Pushkin's behavior and poetry that did not please him. Pushkin's edgy pranks directed at the state, his epigrams and his careless attitude towards service (Turgenev himself occupied high positions in the State Council and the Ministry of Finance and took service very seriously) caused him to "chastise and shame" Pushkin. According to Alexander Turgenev, he "more than once let [Pushkin] understand that one cannot accept one's salary for doing nothing and disparage the individual who gives it." Once Turgenev's condemnation of Pushkin "for his epigrams, etc., aimed at the government" reached such a pitch that Pushkin challenged Turgenev to a duel, albeit immediately he recanted it and apologized.**

Nikolai Turgenev was not the only link between Pushkin and the Union of Welfare. Pushkin apparently also became acquainted with Fedor Glinka in autumn 1817. Glinka was the descendant of a poor but ancient family of Smolensk noblemen. A man of small height, sickly from childhood, Glinka was renowned for his bravery during the war (his uniform was stubbed with medals both Russian and foreign) and for his keen love of humanity. Even Speransky, who compared to such political figures as Arakcheev seemed a model of sensitivity, chided Glinka for his "un-Russian" impressionability, saying: "You

---

*   There is an entirely plausible biographical hypothesis according to which Nikolai Turgenev directly instigated the beginning of the writing of the "Ode to Liberty" in his apartment through the windows of which the Mikhailovsky Castle—where Paul I had been killed—could be seen (for more see Tomashevskii, *Pushkin*, 1:147–148).

** *Pamiati dekabristov* [In Memory of the Decembrists], vol. 2 (Leningrad: Izdatel'stvo Akademii nauk SSSR, 1926), 122.

can't mourn everybody buried in the churchyard!" Glinka was a famous writer and an extremely active member of different secret Decembrist organizations during their early stages. Combining his role as one of the leaders of the Union of Welfare with that of adjutant to then Governor-General of St. Petersburg Mikhail Miloradovich,[21] Glinka was able to provide crucial services to the secret societies as well as to aid in mitigating the severity of Pushkin's fate in 1820.

In 1819, Glinka was chosen as chairman of the Free Society of Lovers of Russian Literature in St. Petersburg, an organization that would go on to play a key role in uniting different writers from the Decembrist movement. Pushkin experienced keenly the influence of Glinka in person—his great spiritual purity and firmness of character. To some extent Glinka drew Pushkin into legal activity that was being secretly controlled by the conspiratorial groups.

Other points of contact between Pushkin and the Union of Welfare can be noted. Even earlier, while still at the Lyceum, Pushkin met Nikita Muravyov. When their acquaintance was renewed upon Muravyov's joining Arzamas, Muravyov was one of the organizers of the first secret Decembrist society—the Union of Salvation. Apparently it was through Nikita Muravyov that Pushkin was drawn to participate in meetings of the Union of Welfare that were not strictly conspiratorial but rather intended to spread the influence of the society. Many years later, when he was working on the tenth chapter of *Eugene Onegin,* Pushkin described such a meeting:

> Famous for their sharp eloquence,
> This family's members would gather
> At agitated Nikita's,
> At careful Ilya's.
> [...]
> A friend of Mars, Bacchus, and Venus,
> Lun[in] would sharply offer up
> His decisive measures
> And mutter in inspired fashion.
> Pu[shkin] read his [satirical] Noëlles,

> And melan[choly] Yak[ushkin],
> It seemed, silently revealed,
> His regicidal dagger. (6:523–524)

These lines were long viewed as the fruit of poetic imagination: Pushkin's participation in such gatherings seemed impossible. However, in 1952, Militsa Nechkina[22] published the testimony of Decembrist Ivan Gorstkin,[23] who said at his investigation (here one should take into account the tactical urge, completely understandable on Gorstkin's part, to lessen the importance of said meetings): "At first we would meet eagerly, but later it was difficult to gather ten people; a couple times, I was at P[rince] Ilya Dolgoruky's.[24] He was, it seems, one of the leaders then. It was at his place that Pushkin read his poems; everyone was in raptures over their wit; people would tell all sorts of stories, read, whisper—everyone was there. There was never any general conversation. [...] I frequented evening meetings at Nikita Muravyov's, and it was there that I would often come in contact with people who had nothing to do with the secret society."*

If we add to the picture the fact that Lunin[25] and Yakushkin, both named in the poem and both important figures in the Decembrist movement, were acquaintances of Pushkin's in these years, then the poet's relations with the Decembrists becomes sufficiently clear. (Pushkin met Lunin on November 19, 1818 as they were seeing off Batyushkov who was on his way to Italy; they became so close that Pushkin snipped off a strand of Lunin's hair before Lunin departed St. Petersburg in 1820. Yakushkin was introduced to Pushkin by Chaadaev.) However, the picture is not complete unless we take into account one more aspect.

We have already mentioned how the ethical ideal of the Union of Welfare was colored in tones of heroic asceticism. The genuine citizen was thought of

---

* *Literaturnoe nasledstvo* [The Literary Heritage], vol. 58 (Moscow: Izdatel'stvo Akademii nauk SSSR, 1952), 158–159.

as a stern hero who, for the sake of the general good, rejects happiness, merry-making, and feasting. Filled with love for his homeland, he does not waste his spiritual powers on amorous interests. Not only does the poetry of elegant eroticism elicit condemnation from him, so too do the "unearthly" love elegies of Zhukovsky: the latter weaken the citizen's soul and are useless for the cause of Freedom. As Ryleev wrote,

> Love won't come to mind:
> Alas! My fatherland is suffering,
> My soul, upset by heavy thoughts,
> Thirsts for freedom alone.*

Later, in Chişinău, Vladimir Raevsky,[26] imprisoned in the Tiraspol Fortress, called on Pushkin to

> Leave love to other singers!
> Can one sing love where blood is spurting ...?**

The ethic of heroic self-sacrifice, which juxtaposes citizen and poet, hero and lover, Freedom and Happiness, was characteristic of a broad sampling of freedom lovers from Robespierre[27] to Schiller. There were, however, other ethical considerations: eighteenth-century Enlightenment in its battle with Christian asceticism created a different concept of Freedom. In this instance, Freedom was not opposed to Happiness, but rather coincided with it. A truly free person was one of seething passions, of unshackled inner powers, one who dared to desire and attain what he desired—a poet and a lover. Freedom meant a life that could not be contained by any bounds, that overflowed its limit, while self-restraint implied a kind of spiritual slavery. A free society cannot be constructed on the basis of asceticism and the self-sacrifice of the

---

* Kondraty Ryleev, *Polnoe sobranie stikhotvorenii* [Complete Collected Poems] (Leningrad: Academia, 1934), 104.

** Vladimir Raevskii, *Stikhotvoreniia* [Poems] (Leningrad: Sovetskii pisatel', 1952), 149.

individual person. On the contrary, it is [only] the [free] society that will guarantee the person an unheard-of richness and flowering.

Pushkin was, to an extraordinary degree, deeply and originally attached to the culture of the eighteenth-century Enlightenment. In this respect, of the Russian writers of his century, he can be compared only to Herzen.[28] As for Pushkin's love for the life, it is impossible to separate his temperamental traits from his theoretical positions. Telling here is the fact that, almost at the same time as he was writing "Ode to Liberty," with its clearly expressed concept of heroic asceticism, Pushkin penned his madrigal to Golitsyna[29] ("An inexperienced lover of foreign climes..."), in which two high human ideals of equal value are presented:

> A citizen with a noble soul,
> Lofty, fiery, and free

and

> A woman—not with a cold beauty,
> But with one fiery, captivating, and alive. (2:43)

Freedom leaves its mark on them both.

This attitude shaped the poet's personal, everyday behavior. To exist in a constant state of passionate tension was not a concession Pushkin made to his temperament, but rather a conscious decision on how to live. If Love was a sign of this endless burning flame, then Mischief and Laziness were conventions designating Pushkin's unwillingness to accept the lifeless discipline of the state bureaucracy. In opposing the proper order of workaday Petersburg, Mischief and Laziness acted as a protest against the conventions of decorum and as a refusal to take seriously the whole world of governmental values. However, they also simultaneously opposed the seriousness of the civic pathos of the Decembrist ethic.

The boundary between the Decembrists and the liberally minded younger circles adjacent to them divided in two the sphere of ethics and the area of everyday habits and behavior. Fedor Glinka, famously philanthropic despite not having a dime to himself, would cover himself with his overcoat instead of a blanket, but if he needed to buy the freedom of a serf actor, he would deny himself tea and switch to hot water to make it happen. His motto was severe poverty and labor.

Delvig and Baratynsky were also poor:

> Where, in a dismal little house, the fifth company of the Semenovsky Regiment was quartered,
> There lived the poet Baratynsky with Delvig, another poet.
> They lived quietly, not paying much for the flat;
> They owed the store and seldom ate at home.*

Their motto, however, was a merry poverty and laziness. For Delvig, Baratynsky and the other poets of their circle, merriment was a literary pose: Baratynsky, a melancholic in life, wrote an entire epic poem called *Feasts* which glorified carefree merriment. A self-denying dreamer in his poetry, Zhukovsky in his day-to-day life was much more equanimous and cheerful than Batyushkov, a hedonist in his verse and someone unfortunate and seriously ill in life. Pushkin made "poetic" behavior the norm for the real. Poetic mischief and everyday "rebelliousness" became the characteristic traits of his real-life behavior.

Pushkin's mentors and guides—from Karamzin to Nikolai Turgenev—failed to grasp that he was laying out a path that was new and *his own;* to them he had simply veered from the correct path. The brilliance of Pushkin's talent was blinding, and the older poets and cultural and political figures considered it their duty to ensure that his talent be preserved for Russia. They deemed it necessary to guide him on a familiar and well-understood path. The unfamiliar seemed dissolute to them. Pushkin was constantly surrounded by many who wished him well, but few who truly understood him. He would grow tired of

---

* Delvig, *Polnoe sobranie stikhotvorenii*, 429. The poem was written by Delvig together with Baratynsky (1819).

moral lessons and of the fact that he was still considered a boy; sometimes out of spite he would affect boyishly immature behavior.

Zhukovsky used to say at the Arzamas meetings, "The cricket, having dug himself / into the hole of prank, shouts from there, in verse, I'm lazy..." (telling here is the view that behavior that is permitted "in verse" is forbidden in real life).* Alexander Turgenev, as he said himself, used to chastise Pushkin on a daily basis for "laziness and [for his] neglect of his own education. Additionally, his taste for brazen womanizing and eighteenth-century freethinking, which was equally brazen."** Batyushkov wrote to Turgenev, saying, "It would do good to lock him up in Göttingen and spoon-feed him milk-soup and logic for three years or so."***

The meaning of "mischief" to the youth of Pushkin's circle is best shown by The Green Lamp. It was a friendly literary and theatrical society that arose in the spring of 1819. They would assemble in the house of Nikita Vsevolozhsky.[30] It used to be that a range of murky rumors surrounded the society, which greatly affected Pushkin's first biographers, who imaged the society as some kind of club for the debauched youth of those days, who organized orgies. Subsequent publications of the society's 'protocols' and other related documents have proved sufficient to dispel such notions. The fact that The Green Lamp[31] was led by such people as Fedor Glinka, Sergei Trubetskoy,[32] and Yakov Tolstoy[33]—all of whom were active members of the Decembrist movement—should be proof enough of the serious and socially significant nature of the society and its assemblies. Publications of works that were read at assemblies, as well as analyses of the group's historical and literary interests, demonstrate the group's firm connections to the Decembrist movement.

---

*   *Otchet Imperatorskoi Publichnoi biblioteki za 1884 god* [Report of the Imperial Public Library for 1884] (St. Petersburg: Tipografiia V. E. Balashova, 1887), 162.

**   Aleksandr Pushkin, *Pis'ma* [Letters], vol. 1 (Moscow-Leningrad: Pravda, 1926), 19.

*** Konstantin Batiushkov, *Sochineniia* [Works], vol. 1 (Moscow: Khudozhestvennaia literature, 1989), 517.

These materials impressed researchers to such a degree that many posited that The Green Lamp was nothing more than an affiliate organization of the Union of Welfare (indeed, the Union's constitution encouraged the proliferation of such organizations). This is, however, an oversimplification. Undoubtedly, The Green Lamp was somewhat under the auspices of the Union of Welfare, which sought to exert its influence on the former. Nonetheless, The Green Lamp, in its focus, was far removed from the atmosphere supported by the Union of Welfare; that is, one of ethical rigidity and civil service. Rather, it combined the freethinking and the genuine social interests of the Union with an atmosphere of play, exuberant merriment, and demonstrative challenges to any forms of self-purported "seriousness." Ideas of rebelliousness and freethinking flow through Pushkin's poems and letters connected to The Green Lamp. This, however, carried a mischievous tone fundamentally alien to the seriousness of the Union of Welfare.

On October 27, 1819, Pushkin wrote the following to Pavel Mansurov,[34] his friend from The Green Lamp, who had left to serve in Arakcheev-controlled Novgorod (i.e. around Novgorod there were military settlements):

> The Green Lamp has flamed out—seems it's extinguished—and that's a shame—there's still oil (that is, our friend's champagne). Write to me, my brother, will you write to me, my dearie. Tell me about yourself—about the military settlements. I need all this—because I love you—and I despise despotism. Goodbye, sweetie. Sver[chok] [cricket] A. Pushkin (13:2).

The combination of phrases like "I despise despotism" and "my dearie," "sweetie" (and other, significantly more unconstrained expressions) was typical for The Green Lamp and completely foreign to the spirit of the Decembrist underground.

Mention of the singular aspects of Pushkin's position gave rise in conspiratorial circles to the idea that the poet had "not sufficiently matured" and did not deserve trust. And if the people who knew Pushkin personally and loved him softened that judgement with comforting considerations about how, being positioned outside the secret society, Pushkin was aiding the cause of freedom with his verse (Pushchin), or with reference to the necessity of guarding the poet's talent from dangers associated with the actual revolutionary struggle (Ryleev after all didn't protect himself!), then to those people at the periphery of the Decembrist movement, those who were not acquainted with Pushkin and had been fed on third-hand rumors, came interpretations of the following type: "By his character and his cowardly nature, by his life of debauchery, he will make a denunciation immediately to the government about the existence of the Secret Society."* It was these words of flagrant unfairness that were said by Ivan Gorbachevsky,[35] a Decembrist of rare fortitude, an honorable and brave man. And while saying this he cited such sacred Decembrist authorities as the hanged Sergei Muravyov-Apostol[36] and Mikhail Bestuzhev-Ryumin. Mikhail Bestuzhev,[37] whose markings cover the manuscript, was in full agreement.

The Union of Welfare was not a "conspiratorial" organization in the sense given this word in the subsequent revolutionary tradition; the fact of the Union's existence was widely known. It is typical, in this regard, that when Mikhail Orlov asked General Nikolai Raevsky[38] for his daughter's hand, one of the terms of the marriage was Orlov's exit from the secret society. Thus, Raevsky not only knew of the society's existence, but even knew who its specific members were, and he discussed these matters as one settling the terms of his daughter's dowry.

Having constantly interacted with its members, Pushkin, obviously, knew of the society's existence and clearly sought to join it. The fact that he was not invited and was frequently met with polite but firm refusals from friends as close as Pushchin was incredibly hurtful for him. Pushkin was frequently

---

* Ivan Gorbachevskii, *Zapiski dekabrista* [Notes of a Decembrist] (Moscow: Zadruga, 1916), 300.

Chapter Two. St. Petersburg, 1817-1820 | 51

pained and offended, on the one side, by the patronizing advice of his elders, and on the other, by the distrust of his friends. This illuminates the tension and nervousness that Pushkin felt during these years. These circumstances help explain, for example, why Pushkin was always ready to be offended and in response to fight a duel. In the summer of 1817, Pushkin—for practically no reason—challenged his old uncle, Semen Hannibal*; Nikolai Turgenev; his classmate Modest Korf;[39] Major Denisevich, and apparently many others. Ekaterina Karamzina wrote to her brother, Prince Vyazemsky, that "Mr. Pushkin has duels every odd day; thank God, they're not fatal."** Not all duels could be smoothed over, however, and many had to be settled on "the field of honor": in the fall of 1819, Pushkin dueled Küchelbecker (who had issued the challenge); both shot in the air and the matter ended with their reconciliation. Later, Pushkin admitted to Fedor Luginin[40] that he had had a serious duel in St. Petersburg (there is a hypothesis that his opponent was in fact Ryleev).

During this period of spiritual trouble, Pushkin's budding friendship with Pyotr Chaadaev was a source of salvation.

Pyotr Chaadaev, whom Pushkin had met at the Karamzins' when he was still a Lycean, was one of the most remarkable people of his time. Having grown up in the house of historian Mikhail Shcherbatov[41] (his grandfather), where he received a brilliant education, Chaadaev joined, at sixteen, the Semenovsky Regiment of the Guard, which marched all the way from Borodino to Paris. During the period at hand, he served in the Hussar Regiment as the aide-de-camp to Illarion Vasilchikov,[42] the Commander of the Guard Corps,

---

* Lotman means Pavel Hannibal (Translator's note).
** Ekaterina Karamzina, "Pis'ma E. A. Karamzinoi P. A. Viazemskomu" [E. A. Karamzina's Letters to P. A. Vyazemsky], *Starina i novizna*, no. 1 (1897): 98, quoted in *Letopis' zhizni i tvorchestva A. S. Pushkina, 1799-1826* [A Chronicle of A. S. Pushkin's Life and Works], ed. Mstislav Tsiavlovskii (Leningrad: Slovo, 1991), 201.

and quartered at the Demutov Traktir* in St. Petersburg. "Chaadaev was handsome and distinguished himself not so much with hussar as with English or even Byronic manners; he enjoyed brilliant success in the St. Petersburg society of those days."**

Chaadaev was part of the Union of Welfare, but he was not an active member: its tactics of gradual spreading propaganda and freedom-loving ideas and philanthropy seemed not to have interested him. Chaadaev was taken with the desire for glory—great, unheard-of glory—which would forever imprint his name in the sacred texts of Russian and European history. Napoleon's example caused his head to spin, and the idea that he was specially chosen for something, that he had drawn a special lot, never left him during his lifetime. He wanted to be a Russian Brutus or Marquis de Posa,*** regardless of whether he would have to stab a tyrant in the name of freedom or sway him to his side with a fiery speech. What was important to Chaadaev was something else: the future must hold the fight for freedom, a heroic death, and immortal glory. When, in 1821, Pushkin wrote of Chaadaev's study—

> Where you're always a sage, sometimes a dreamer
> And the dispassionate observer of the flighty crowd (2:189)

—the poet's is overtaken by an atmosphere of greatness. Chaadaev taught Pushkin to prepare himself as a person whose great name would be inherited by his descendants. Chaadaev also gave lessons to Pushkin and demanded that

---

* An inn on the Moika river, close to Nevsky Prospekt.

** Dmitrii Sverbeev, *Zapiski* [Notes], vol. 2 (Moscow: Tipo-litografiia Tovarishchestva I. N. Kushnerev i Ko., 1899), 386.

*** Brutus was an ancient Roman political figure who participated in the organization of Caesar's assassination; in eighteenth- and early nineteenth-century literature, he features prominently as an image of a republican hero. Marquis de Posa is the main character in Schiller's *Don Carlos*—a republican who seeks to exert his influence on a tyrant.

he "stand on equal footing with the enlightenment of the age." These lessons did not lower, but raised Pushkin in his own eyes.

The great future which Chaadaev bid Pushkin prepare himself for was only partially connected to poetry: in Chaadaev's study at the Demutov Traktir discussion apparently touched upon how the heroic acts of Brutus and Cassius[43]—the repeal of tyranny with one blow of the sword—might be repeated in Russia. In his memoirs, the Decembrist Yakushkin recounted how in 1821, in Kamenka, in order to divert the suspicions of Alexander Raevsky[44] (the general's son), they *played* a scene in which they organized a secret society, only to turn it into a joke, whereupon Pushkin passionately cried: "I just saw my life ennobled and a high purpose before myself."* "A life ennobled by a high purpose" and "a high-minded purpose"—these phrases point to Pushkin's dream of a higher destiny. Even death is enviable if it leads a calling that "belongs to history." Pushkin's conversations with Chaadaev taught him to view his own life as "ennobled by a high purpose."

Only the context of conversations about regicide can explain Pushkin's proud words:

> And on the ruins of tyranny
> They shall inscribe our names! (2:72)

Why would the names of Chaadaev, a "twenty-odd-year-old young man who has never written anything or distinguished himself in any field," as one memoirist caustically characterized him, and Pushkin, who never actively participated in politics and was not even admitted to the ranks of Decembrists, be inscribed on the ruins of tyranny? We usually uncover the strangeness of these verses by imagining that they are being addressed to all the freedom-loving youth of the era, while the poet writing them is already conceived of in the light of his subsequent fame. At the time when this poem was actually written,

---

*   *Contemporaries*, 1:366.

however, it could only have been understood as an expression of ardent and heroic plans.

It was precisely in these plans that Pushkin found support in one of the bitterest moments in his life. There are numerous testimonies by contemporaries confirming Pushkin's personal charm, his giftedness as a friend, and his talent as a lover. Nonetheless, he could also engender hatred and he always had enemies. In St. Petersburg, in 1819–1820, there were goodly number of people willing to denounce Pushkin's poems, words, and actions to the government. Vasily Karazin,[45] a troubled and jealous man, prone to ambition himself, worked particularly hard to this end. Another's glory elicited his own genuine suffering. His denunciations, which were brought before Alexander I, were especially harmful to Pushkin, who was accused of personally offending the tsar: the vindictive and suspicious Alexander could forgive even the bravest political ideas, but he never forgave or forgot personal offenses against him.

On April 19, 1820, Nikolai Karamzin wrote to Ivan Dmitriev: "There gathers above [our] local poet Pushkin if not a dark cloud, at least a cloud, and one containing a thunderclap (this is between us): serving under the Liberals' banner, he has written and circulated poems on liberty, epigrams against the rulers, etc., etc. The Police have found out about this, etc. Investigations are feared."*

During this time, when Pushkin's fate was being decided, and the poet's friends were pleading his case before the emperor, a disgusting rumor made its way around St. Petersburg that Pushkin had been secretly flogged by the order of the government. It had been initially spread by renowned adventurer, duelist, and gambler Fedor Tolstoy[46] (often known by his nickname, "The American"). Pushkin did not know who had spread these rumors initially and was completely shaken, considering himself to be irrevocably humiliated and

---

* Nikolai Karamzin, *Pis'ma k I. I. Dmitrievu* [Letters to I. I. Dmitriev] (St. Petersburg: Tipografiia Imperatorskoi Akademii nauk, 1866), 286–287.

his life destroyed. Not knowing whether to commit suicide or kill the emperor whom he considered as partially to blame for the rumors, Pushkin ran to Chaadaev. Chaadaev consoled him: he proved that a man with a higher purpose must despise rumors and rise above his persecutors.

> At the time of my doom, suspended over a hidden abyss,
> You supported me with your vigilant hand;
> You filled your friend with hope and calm;
> Penetrating the depths of my soul with a stern gaze,
> You animated it with a word of advice or rebuke;
> Your flame flared up in love for the sublime;
> And bold patience was reborn in me anew,
> Now the voice of libel could not wound me,
> I learned to hate and to despise. (2:188)

The efforts of Karamzin, Chaadaev, Fedor Glinka somewhat mitigated Pushkin's fate: neither Siberia, nor Solovki became the places of his exile. On May 6, 1820, Pushkin left St. Petersburg for the south of Russia having been appointed to serve in the chambers of Lieutenant-General Ivan Inzov.[47]

Chapter Three

Pushkin's Southern Period, 1820–1824

Pushkin journeyed to Yekaterinoslav,* where the governor of international colonies in the Russian south, Ivan Inzov, resided, and to whose office Pushkin was assigned. Inzov, shortly thereafter, was appointed viceroy of Bessarabia and subsequently, of the Novorossiysk region; he wielded considerable administrative power. Strictly speaking, Pushkin was not exiled; his exit from the capital was presented as an administrative transfer.

Pushkin served in the Ministry of Foreign Affairs and his St. Petersburg supervisor, the liberal minister Count Ivan Kapodistrias,[1] at the emperor's insistence, detailed all of Pushkin's "faults" to his soon-to-be new supervisor, Ivan Inzov. This move, however, largely backfired. Inzov was a natural brother of Nikolai Trubetskoy,[2] a freemason and friend of Nikolai Novikov;[3] he had been brought up in the atmosphere that had permeating Novikov's circle. In his later life, he combined an inherent courage (Inzov participated in tens of battles under Suvorov,[4] Miloradovich, and Kutuzov,[5] and commanded regiments at Trebbia and Novi and a whole division at Leipzig) with an impulse towards philanthropy (he was made an honorary member of the French legion for his humane attitude towards French prisoners during the War of 1812). A Spartan in his everyday life and a childhood friend of Radishchev-loving[6] poet Ivan Pnin,[7] he secretly sympathized with the youth's liberal causes. Count

---

*   Now Dnipro, Ukraine (Translator's note).

Kapodistrias's letter thus only recommended Pushkin to him, and Inzov immediately took Pushkin under his wing.

Pushkin's itinerary ran to the side of the main Moscow highway: through Luga, Velikie Luki, Vitebsk, Mogilev, Chernigov, and Kyiv. Up to Tsarskoe Selo he was joined by his friends Delvig and Yakovlev.[8] From there he traveled on accompanied only by his servant Nikita Kozlov.[9] His St. Petersburg life lay behind him, and ahead lay only the road. Thus begun Pushkin's period of wanderings, his life without a permanent place, without domesticity. It lasted until August 9, 1824, when Pushkin set foot in his ancestral home at Mikhailovskoe.

This long road, having torn Pushkin away from his colorful life in St. Petersburg, afforded him the chance to look around himself and take stock.

The picture he had of himself was the following: on June 11, 1817, he came to St. Petersburg, a youth with great expectations; on May 6, 1820, he rode through the outpost at Tsarskoe Selo as a poet who had earned acclaim among a wide readership. On May 15, Timkovsky,[10] a censor, signaled his permission for the publication of Pushkin's narrative poem *Ruslan and Liudmila* (it was eventually published in full towards the end of July). However, fragments of the poem had already been published in the spring, while other portions, even before the poet's exile, had circulated by word of mouth in St. Petersburg literary circles. *Ruslan and Liudmila* provoked mixed reactions, many of which were far from positive (the critical debates reached their peak when Pushkin was already in the south). Nonetheless, one thing was beyond doubt, both in Pushkin's eyes and in the eyes of his readers: from now on his path in life was clear—he was not a mischief-maker who wrote verse, he was a Poet.

Pushkin's awareness of this fact filled him with a feeling of respect for his vocation and told him that his period of studying under others was over: now it fell to him—not to his wise teachers—to determine the character of his art and his behavior. The latter question acquired a new meaning: how should a Poet comport himself? Pushkin became aware that thenceforth his person, his behavior, even his appearance were mysteriously, but firmly tethered to his poetry.

The idea that a poet's life, personality, and fate merge with his art, constituting for the reading public a kind of unitary whole, belongs to the Romantic era. In previous ages, works of literature existed largely independently of their authors. They were valued not for their connection to an author's individuality, but rather for their closeness to Truth—singular, eternal, "bright like the sun," as Descartes[11] put it. The author's biography was viewed as largely extraneous to the work—it was never reflected in high genres (such as odes), nor even in middle genres, such as elegiac poetry; it was tolerated in lower genres, primarily comic ones, and even then, in the form of hints. Readers did not search the author's biography for keys to understanding his works.

If an author's biography came to readers' attention (this was possible only if the author had achieved great renown and subsequently passed away), what would stand out in the biography were certain generalized iconic traits, which would liken the subject to a single idealized image. Everything that was idiosyncratic to the author was largely ignored: in effect, the biography vacillated between a saint's *vita* and a service record. First, pre-Romanticism, and then Romanticism proper, saw in a poet his genius—his unique and singular spirit expressing itself in the originality of a given work of art. The poet's creative work began to be looked at as one huge autobiographical novel, in which poems and epics formed chapters, and the biography itself functioned as plot. The two geniuses of Romantic Europe—Lord Byron[12] and Napoleon—fixed in place these ideas: the former, having played out his personal life before all of Europe, by turning his poetry into a chain of fiery confessions; the latter, by showing that his very life could resemble an epic poem.

In Russia, Zhukovsky, Denis Davydov, and Ryleev all connected their lives, in different and complex ways, to their poetry. This Romantic worldview, which was not yet an established tradition, but rather a living literary (and, broader, cultural) sensibility that hovered in the air, provided a firm foundation for Pushkin during this stage of his artistic career. Drawing from it, Pushkin proceeded farther, creating not only a completely unique art of the world, but also a completely unique art of life.

The Romantic worldview was salvational to Pushkin because it gave him a way—so necessary to him then—of unifying his personality. Pushkin's time in St. Petersburg had greatly enriched him: he had interacted with a wide circle of progressive contemporaries, he had participated in discussions crucial to his age, and his intense love life had expanded his emotional world. His interactions with women and participation in the refined culture of feelings and matters of the heart developed his delicacy of mind, his ability to sense, notice and express emotional nuances, and not merely their primitive spectrum. Finally, his ability to enter into these different looks and modes enriched him with a sense of behavioral style. This resulted in Pushkin's extraordinarily developed talent of changing and adapting his personality in different situations, for being different. Later Pushkin singled out this attribute in Onegin: "How he was able to appear new" (6:9).

This capability testified to the flexibility and richness of Pushkin's inner self [lit. 'soul']. It also, however, showed the danger this held for that self's inner integrity. Excessive flexibility and variety threatened the post's sense of self. Here Romanticism arrived just in time. It not only helped Pushkin become the poetic mouthpiece of his generation, it aided him in building his own character.

One of the basic requirements that Romanticism put before the personality of the genius was immutability, dedication to a single passion, integrity. "*One man*—he was always cold, *unwavering*," Lermontov wrote of Napoleon (in a poem titled "The Last Housewarming," 1841), endowing him with the features of a Romantic hero.

Just as Pushkin in this period replaces the stylistic variety of previous years with a unified Romantic style, so too does the poet's personal behavior orient itself to a single model. The Romantic hero becomes this ideal, this norm.

The Romantic mode of behavior, when viewed by subsequent eras, was often criticized for its lack of sincerity; people saw it as nothing more than an attractive mask. Needless to say, the Romantic era produced its fair share of Grushnitskys*—superficial and petty lovers of the well-turned phrase, who donned the Romantic mantle to hide (from themselves in the first place) their own insignificance and lack of originality. But at the same time it would be a grave mistake to forget that this worldview and this type of relationship to one's milieu could also produce a Lermontov or a Byron. To equate Romanticism to the era's small change would be profoundly incorrect.

A characteristic feature of Romantic behavior was its conscious orientation on this or that literary type. The Romantically attuned young man defined himself using the name of one of the personages common to Romantic mythology: the Demon or Werther, Melmoth or the Wandering Jew, the Giaour or Don Juan.** He would also assign to people in his milieu roles of literary (or historical) heroes. Perceived in this way the artificial world and everyday reality became doubles. Moreover, for the Romantic this artificial world was more real than the "vulgar" reality around him. Thus did he see and understand the world and people.

The bookish nature of these physic constructions did not betoken an insincerity or mannered element in the best representatives of the generation.

---

* Refers to a vulgarly Romantic character from Mikhail Lermontov's *A Hero of Our Time* (Translator's note).

** Werther is the main character of Goethe's *The Sorrows of Young Werther*—a tragically in-love youth who commits suicide out of misery; Melmoth—from English writer Charles Maturin's *Melmoth the Wanderer*—is a mysterious villain and demonic seducer; Ahasuerus ("The Eternal Jew")—a perpetual wanderer rejected by God and men) is a character in a range of Romantic works; the Giaour and Don Juan are characters in the tradition of Romantic rebels and wanderers from Byron's poems.

Quite the opposite: it often went hand in hand with a genuine naïveté. An obvious example perhaps is Pushkin's Tatyana,* who:

> Imagining herself a heroine
> Of her beloved authors,
> A Clarissa, Julia, Delphine,
> [...] in the quiet of the woods
> She wandered with a dangerous book,
> In which she searches and finds
> Her secret fire and her dreams. (6:55)

"Having appropriated for herself / Another's ecstasy, another's sorrow," Tatyana also assigns Onegin a role played by one of the best known heroes of "the British muse." The bookishness of these feelings does not prevent them from being both sincere and profound.

The primary traits of the Romantic hero included loneliness, disenchantment, "indifference to life and its pleasures," and "the premature aging of the soul"—these became "the distinguishing features of young people in the 19th century" (13:52), as Pushkin wrote to Vladimir Gorchakov. The Romantic hero was always en route; his world was the road. Behind him lay his abandoned homeland, which had become a prison to him. All ties with his native region have been severed: in love he had met with betrayal, in friendship—the poison of slander.

> Deceit in friends, disbelief in love,
> And hell in everything the heart cherishes...**

But the wanderer also doesn't stop in a foreign land. Any halt for him is forced. Whether detained somewhere because he has been taken prisoner by the wild, but freedom-loving inhabitants of an exotic country, or whether tied to a place by an affair of the heart, prison or happiness is for him, in equal

---

*   From *Eugene Onegin* (Translator's note).
** Delvig, *Polnoe sobranie stikhotvorenii*, 163.

measure, captivity. He escapes from prison or breaks off his romance in order to continue his proud and solitary wanderings.

The phrase *"premature aging of the soul"* contains two different hidden motifs (which are often combined). The "aging" might be caused by the deadening effects of slavery reigning in the homeland of the fugitive. In that case, the plot takes on a political coloring, and the hero who has been taken prisoner by "savages" merely trades one form of slavery for another:

> And is the trade so horrible?
> At home, for chains! Abroad, captivity!*

However, another motif is also possible: on his faraway homeland the fugitive has left behind a secret, unrequited—something criminal—love. This love is bereft of hope. The fugitive has etched it from his heart, but with his heart now faded for love, he cannot respond to the youthfully fresh feeling of the "wild maiden." Thus does the myth of a secret, unrequited love arise.

This was, in general outline, the mythology of the Romantic personality. As we will see, Pushkin was far from blindly adhering to its schemas. Nevertheless, he was well aware that Romanticism was a fact of the general cultural consciousness of the epoch and that the reader viewed him, the man and the poet, precisely through this prism.

By playing a sui generis game with these still new cultural categories, Pushkin stylized in part his own behavior to fit them, but also in part, through the charm and authority of his human image, sought to shape how readers perceived them.

In the middle of May Pushkin passed through Kyiv. It was there that he met a score of his St. Petersburg acquaintances, including the family of famous general Nikolai Raevsky, hero of 1812. It seems likely that it was through

---

*   Aleksandr Griboedov, *Polnoe sobranie sochinenii* [Complete Collected Works], vol. 2 (St. Petersburg: Notabene, 1999), 230.

Zhukovsky that Pushkin made Raevsky's acquaintance. Pushkin also knew the general's son, Nikolai Raevsky "the younger,"[13] with whom he had been on friendly terms in St. Petersburg. On May 17, he arrived in Yekaterinoslav, where his new service was to take place.

In fact, there was no service to speak of. Inzov greeted Pushkin warmly and already by May 21 sent positive reports about him to St. Petersburg. Shortly thereafter, following a swim in the Dnipro River, Pushkin came down with a bad cold. While he was ailing, the Raevsky family, which happened to have been traveling through Yekaterinoslav, picked him up and brought him with them to the Caucasus. In a letter to his brother from September 24, 1820, Pushkin described this—for him—highly significant journey in the following way:

> Inzov gave me his blessing for my journey—I entered the carriage sick, but in a week's time had fully recovered. I lived in the Caucasus for two months. The waters were very necessary for me and helped a great deal, especially the hot sulfur ones. Incidentally, I took baths in the warm acidulous sulfur waters, the iron waters, and in the cold acidulous ones. These medicinal springs are located nor very far apart, in the last spurs of the Caucasian Mountains. I am sorry, my friend, that you could not see the magnificent range of mountains with me, with their icy summits, which from afar in the clear twilight look like strange, many-colored, and motionless clouds. I regret that you could not climb with me to the sharp peak of the five-ridged Beshtu, or Mashuk, and of Iron, Stone, and Serpent Mountains. [...] I have seen the banks of the Kuban and our guardian Cossack villages—I have looked with admiration at our Cossacks. Eternally on horseback, eternally ready to fight, eternally on guard! I traveled in sight of the hostile fields of the free mountain peoples. Sixty Cossacks were convoying us; behind us was being dragged a loaded cannon, with a lighted slow match. [...] From there we set off by sea, past the southern shores of Tavrida [Crimea], to *Gurzuf*, where Raevsky's family was. At night aboard the ship I wrote an elegy, which I am sending you; send it off to Grech[14] without a signature. The ship sailed in front of mountains covered with poplars, grapes, laurels, and cypresses; Tatar settlements were dotted everywhere. The ship stopped in sight of Gurzuf, I spent three weeks there. My friend, I spent the happiest moments of my life in the midst of the

family of the honorable Raevsky. I did not see in him the hero, the glory of Russian troops; I loved in him a man of lucid mind, of a simple and beautiful soul, an indulgent, solicitous friend, and a host who is always kind and affable. A witness of the Age of Catherine,[15] a memorial of '12; a man without prejudices, with a strong character, and yet a sensitive person who, without intending it, draws to himself everyone capable of understanding and appreciating his lofty qualities. His older son is going to be more than merely well known. All his daughters are a delight; the oldest is an extraordinary woman. Judge whether I was happy: a free and untroubled life in the circle of a dear family, a life which I so love and which I had never enjoyed; a happy, southern sky; a marvelous region; scenery which gratifies the imagination: mountains, orchards, the sea. My friend, my cherished hope is to see the southern shore and the Raevsky family again. (13:17–19)*

On the night of August 19, 1820, Pushkin, together with Raevsky, arrived in Gurzuf on the navy brig "Mingrelia." During his journey, while onboard the ship, he wrote an elegy entitled "Extinguished is the orb of day...," which heralded a new period in his poetry. He stayed in Gurzuf until the beginning of September, where he "swam in the sea and gorged on grapes" (13:251). He wrote his *Notes on the Don and Black Sea Cossacks*, which is no longer extant, as well as a few elegies. He also started working on *The Prisoner of the Caucasus*. It was here that he discovered for himself two new poets—André Chénier[16] and Lord Byron—and started studying the English language systematically.

In the beginning of September, Pushkin, together with Nikolai Raevsky père and fils, left Gurzuf on horseback. They rode past Alupka, Simeiz, Sevastopol and Bakhchisarai, where they visited the Khan's palace, after which they headed towards Simferopol. In mid-September, Pushkin left Crimea and via Odesa traveled to Chișinău (Kishinev), where by this time Inzov had relocated his official residence.

---

*   This long quote in translation from Pushkin's famous letter to his brother Lev about his trip through Crimea with the Raevsky family is adapted (i.e. slightly modified for precision) from J. Thomas Shaw, ed. and trans., The Letters of Alexander Pushkin (Madison: University of Wisconsin Press, 1967), 75–77.

The short holiday which fate had gifted Pushkin was now over. Chişinău was no quiet backwater: it lay at the crossroads of many crucial political and military conflicts of the age. Life in Chişinău raised difficult questions, questions which demanded answers. In various ways it returned Pushkin to the same problems that he had faced in St. Petersburg. But now the poet had changed.

Pushkin lived in Chişinău, with various comings and goings, from September 21, 1820 to July 2, 1823. Here he experienced hope in the Greek rebellion as well as disenchantment at its demise; here he imbibed the "before battle" atmosphere of Orlov's circle while also witnessing that circle's destruction, even before the latter could enter into open warfare against autocracy. Thus did Pushkin live through moments of upsurge and moments of bitter disappointment.

Pushkin's sojourn in Crimea, despite its short duration (only a few weeks), played a huge role in his subsequent life and poetry. It laid the foundation for many of the creative plans that were developed and transformed in the poet's consciousness. But the Crimea of this time was also connected to various real-life impressions of great significance. The image of Crimea entered into Pushkin's concept of happiness. On February 2, 1830, he wrote Karolina Sobańska,[17] "In my moments of deepest regret, I am drawn to, and revived by, the thought that one day I will have a piece of land in Crimea" (14:63, 399).

The Crimean and Caucasian landscapes dressed Pushkin's Romantic concepts in living flesh. That which in Europe had come into vogue as "orientalism" (the "east") quickly turned into a system of literary clichés, but now, before the eyes of the poet, came alive as everyday reality. Romanticism which in St. Petersburg seemed an exotic fairytale, in the Caucasus turned out to be life and truth. This led Pushkin to search for Romantic traits within himself. The Romantic worldview allowed him to merge his psychic [lit. "soulful"] world and the surrounding landscape into a unified picture with a single meaning.

Pushkin's moods during these two months were far from a replication of Romantic standards, however. The Romantic world is tragic and self-absorbed. Such, for instance, is the world of Lermontov's experiences during his time in the Caucasus. Pushkin's world was different: St. Petersburg, with its insults and passions, was simply blotted out for a time—it is no coincidence that throughout this entire period Pushkin did not write a single letter, which is in stark contrast to the many letters he wrote while in Chișinău and Odesa. His small world narrowed to the Raevsky family; his large world expanded to the vistas of the Caucasus and Crimea.

The Raevsky family was going through one of its happiest moments: the famed, battle-scarred General Raevsky was a happy father and a charming interlocutor; he was full of vigor and energy; and his sons, whose names from early childhood had resounded throughout Russia, were preparing for glorious futures.*

Raevsky's beautiful, well-educated, and intelligent daughters added an atmosphere of romantic femininity. What awaited the family in the future—the bitterness of failure felt by their eldest, Alexander; the heroic and tragic fate of [daughter] Maria Nikolaevna;[18] the death of General Raevsky himself who would not let go, up until the very last minute, of a portrait of his daughter who had followed her Decembrist husband to Siberia—all of this was as yet

---

* In 1813, Raevsky was asked the following by his adjutant, Konstantin Batyushkov: "Pardon me, Your Excellency! Was it not you who took his children and a banner, went to the bridge, and repeated 'Forward, young ones; my children and I will open the path to glory' or something like that?" Raevsky laughed and responded: "I would never speak so ornately, you know it yourself. It's true, I was in front. The soldiers were hesitating, and I tried to inspire them. There were adjutants and orderlies with me. On the left, many were shot and wounded, the buckshot stopped with me. But my children were not there at the time. My younger son was gathering berries in the woods (he was just a child than, and a bullet tore through his trousers; that is all, this anecdote was dreamed up in Petersburg. Your friend (Zhukovsky) sang it in verse. Illustrators, journalists, novelists made use of this convenience, and I was consecrated as a Roman. Et voilà comme on écrit l'histoire! (And that is how history is written!)." See Konstantin Batiushkov, *Opyty v stikhakh i proze* [Experiments in Verse and Prose] (Moscow: Nauka, 1977), 413–414.

unthinkable to the happy cavalcade. What stood out here at this moment was that atmosphere of family happiness and mutual love that Pushkin, by his own admission, "had never enjoyed," but eagerly desired. Pushkin was accepted into this circle without condition, as if he had been a member of their family, and, moreover, as an equal and not as a child: Raevsky's young daughters were younger than Pushkin and also strove to acquit themselves as grown women, while General Raevsky, conversely, was noted for his almost childlike simplicity (compare Batyushkov's description: "Raevsky is very intelligent and remarkably sincere, even to the point of childishness.")

The small world of the Raevsky family reproduced in miniature, as it were, a utopia in which all human connections rested on love and equality. Around them, however, spread out a different world: the bellicose, wild, and free world of mountain-dwellers and the equally free world of border-dwelling Cossacks. This world knew perpetual war, but did not know slavery (if looked at from the perspective of the political ideas that Pushkin received at the Lyceum and in St. Petersburg). The small world attracted Pushkin with its love and happiness, the large world with its energy and wild freedom. They both cast their spell on him.

In these conditions, the Romantic poetry of exile, of tragic egoism, and of the urge to curse one's surroundings and hide oneself in the soul's proud and gigantic images was not supported by Pushkin's own lived experience and personal emotions. This led to the fact that Romantic consciousness and Romantic individualism were expressed in Pushkin's worldview in rather muted form. For along this path of Romantic appropriation, braking its movement, there rose up a set of ideas that had long since entered firmly into Pushkin's mindset (primarily from Rousseau): the happy life in harmony with Nature; freedom that is proud and defiant and purchased by rejecting civilization; and the strength of feelings found in the simple man. "A prematurely aged soul," in this light, seemed no longer the fate of genius, but a disease of a son of civilization, a disease unknown to children of Nature.

The existing biographical literature employs two main approaches for explicating the relationship between 'Pushkin the Poet' and 'Pushkin the Man'. According to the first of these, the poet is completely sincere in his creative work and thus his poetry, revealing the depths of his personality, becomes the ideal biographical source. According to the second, the poet, in the moment he is creating, is transformed as it were into a different person. As a result, the poet has two biographies: one real-life, the other creative. "With Pushkin what strikes one is the lack of correspondence between his real-life experiences and their reflection in his poetry," claimed Vikenty Veresaev.*[19]

Contemporary psychology rejects both interpretations of the creative personality as simplifications. The poet's personality is, of course, unitary and doubtless connected to a wide range of impressions coming to him from the external world. However, being embedded in various social connections, this personality speaks to the world in many languages, and the world responds in many voices. Consequently, a single person, when entering into different collectives and shifting his orientation toward a goal, can change himself—sometimes within very significant limits.

This is especially true of an artist whose reactions to the external world are distinguished by their complexity and variety. Instead of the concepts "Poet—a passive camera fixing in place external impressions" and "Poet—a contradictory mix of the banal and the sublime" there arises the idea of the creative personality as a complex combination of socio-psychological mechanisms that yield reactions characterized not only by a dependency on external conditions, but also on a free, active transformation of the world in the poet's consciousness.

No matter what Pushkin did after having reached his creative maturity, he always remained, first and foremost, 'The Poet.' It was precisely this that

---

* Vikentii Veresaev, *V dvukh planakh: stat'i o Pushkine* [On Two Levels: Essays on Pushkin] (Moscow: Nedra, 1929), 135.

he considered the core and defining element of his personality, and it was as a poet that he was perceived by his contemporaries.

From this point forward Pushkin would have to think constantly about what a poet is, how he should be in his art and his life, how he should take into account (or struggle with) what his readers expect from him, and which ideas in the surrounding society are connected to that understanding. It would be difficult to find an artist who thought more about, and expressed himself more broadly on, the theme "What is the essence of a poet, what should be his relationship to the world."

Having recognized himself as a poet, Pushkin found himself in at least three specific situations: 1) Poet and literature; 2) Poet and political life (for Pushkin, the world of anti-governmental conspiratorial struggle); 3) Poet and everyday life (the world of daily routine). Of course, in all these situations he acted as a poet, and this poet, Alexander Pushkin, had a distinctly individual face. Nevertheless, in each of situations the individual and the poetic was realized in different, idiosyncratic ways. It is only in their totality that the true face of Pushkin in life arises.

In identifying himself as a poet, Pushkin inevitably had to become a littérateur as well; that is, he had to pursue concrete literary connections and earn his spot in the "feisty workshop" of writers, with their professional interests and concerns. Pushkin's letters provide ample material regarding his participation in literary life. The memoirs and diaries of close friends and random acquaintances show him engaged in political disputations at Mikhail Orlov's table or during dances in the houses of Chișinău "society." However, the epicenter of Pushkin's life, its most fully experienced and intense hours, are not reflected in these documents; they were connected to his creative work and took place behind closed doors.

Pushkin came to reside at one end of Inzov's house, in a room on the first floor, and he remained there even after the house had been partially destroyed by an earthquake and Inzov had left. Pushkin enjoyed living among the ruins. Along with the wasteland and vineyards that surrounded the house, the setting dovetailed with his idea of himself as a "fugitive" who lived in a "desert," as he called noisy Chișinău. (The city was significantly overpopulated during this time. Having been essentially a small settlement, it was stuffed to the brim with Russian bureaucrats, Moldovan landowners who had relocated to the new administrative center, soldiers and officers of Mikhail Orlov's division, and, after the beginning of the Greek Revolution, with refugees from Turkey and Turkish Moldova, as well as with the families of volunteers from Ypsilantis's army.) "I'm alone in Moldova, which is deserted for me" (13:19), wrote Pushkin: it was "deserted" alone "for him" in his poeticization.

Here Pushkin wrote *The Prisoner of the Caucasus*, *Gavriiliada*, *The Robber Brothers*, a large number of lyrics (among them "The Black Shawl," "The Dagger," "To V. L. Davydov," the epistle "To Chaadaev," "Napoleon," "To Ovid," "The Song of Prophetic Oleg"), a series of critical essays, and began *The Fountain of Bakhchisarai* and *Eugene Onegin*.

This large group of works did not present itself as a mechanical sum of separate texts, but rather as a unity. Its unifying center was the image of the author. This image, arising from the poet's works, intermingled in complex ways with the facts of his life, stylized in Romantic fashion: on the one hand, becoming the property of the readers, it influenced how new Pushkin texts were perceived, and on the other, it had a rebounding effect on the author's own behavior.

The main feature of this image was its aspect as "fugitive poet" vs. "exile poet." In a way the "fugitive," who has voluntarily abandoned his homeland, and the "exile," who has been forced to leave, look like synonyms in this system of ideas. It is typical that in the narrative poem *The Gypsies* even the bear, whom Aleko leads around on a chain, is called "the fugitive of his den" (4:188), although clearly in Romantic terminology it ought to be called a prisoner (*uznik*). However, between these two ideas-images there was also an obvious distinction, as they influenced the poet's actual biography and its public interpretation in different ways.

With the appearance of Byron's *Child Harold's Pilgrimage* the *fugitive poet* became one of the leading topoi of European Romanticism. It was convenient inasmuch as it encapsulated the opposition "the captivity of stuffy cities" (4:185), the closed world of slavery and civilization, on the one hand, and the free expanse of the wild steppe, the limitless "desert of the world," where the Romantic hero wanders, on the other. This interpretation of the hero as both exile and fugitive had the end result of fixing him to a specific place of incarceration, thus turning him from a "hero of movement" to a "hero of immobility," which contradicted Romantic poetics. As a result, whenever the prison theme enters a Romantic biography, it becomes invariably linked to notions of escape or a desire to escape.

The image of the fugitive is also tied to the theme of disenchantment. Having left behind in his homeland, his heart, and spiritual bloom, the hero flees his native home that has become a prison and yet won't cease to pine for it. Transposing directly this common Romantic stamp onto his biographical circumstances Pushkin in his elegy "Extinguished is the orb of day…" altered his exile into a voluntary flight:

> Fly, O ship, and carry me to distant lands
> Through the fearsome whims of treacherous seas,
> > But only not to the sad coasts
> > Of my misty homeland,
> > That country, where in passion's flame,
> My feelings first flared up,
> Where gentle muses secretly smiled on me,
> > Where, in the tempests, there faded
> > My lost youth,
> Where light-winged joy betrayed me
> And gave over my cold heart to suffering.
> A seeker of new impressions,
> > I fled you, fatherly lands;
> > I fled you, children of delight,
> Momentary friends of momentary youth. (2:146-147)

In the first chapter of *Eugene Onegin* this image is further complicated by a picture of double outcast status: the poet, lonely and longing in one homeland, is condemned in another, Africa, to yearn for a Russia he has left behind.

> Under the skies of my Africa,
> I sighed after dusky Russia,
> Where I suffered, where I loved,
> Where I buried my heart. (6:26)

This picture is in turn linked to Pushkin's insistent habit at the time of highlighting his "African heritage in his mother's side," as he reminded his readers in a footnote to the first publication of the chapter (it is telling that subsequently he would replace the footnote with a blank reference to the first edition). In a letter to Delvig Pushkin wrote of his brother Lev: "I feel that we will be friends and brothers not only because of our shared African blood" (13:26).

The image of the exiled outcast was aligned with different psychological qualities: here what was needed was not the "prematurely aged soul," but conversely, energy and a willingness to fight. As a result, the type of authorial personality shifted as well:

> A sullen Slav, I spent no tears (2:219);

> I am the same as I was before;
> I do not bow to the ignoramus,
> I argue with Orlov, drink little,
> And I do not sing flattering entreaties
> To Octavius in blind hope. (2:170)

A major role in Pushkin's self-reflection at the time was played by the Roman poet Ovid,[20] who was exiled by Emperor Augustus[21] to the mouth of the Dunai [the Danube River]. Pushkin's identification with Ovid, as well as his identification of Alexander I with the sly despot Augustus, who concealed vengefulness beneath a mask of grandeur, provided a real-life role for Pushkin to adopt as well as a scale by which to measure his own significance. The

Poet who is persecuted by Power is on the same level as that Power (this idea is what Pushkin had in mind in 1825, when he wrote that Napoleon *honored* Mme de Staël[22] by persecuting her; see 11:29 [italics—Lotman]). For Alexander I (and later, Vorontsov[23]) Pushkin was a middling bureaucrat subject to government sanction. Pushkin, however, offered himself and his readers a different storyline: he was Ovid, a poet exiled by a tyrant. Further on began a contrast, however. Ovid, the cowardly and pampered singer of the south, the author of elegies and erotic verse, pleaded for forgiveness from Augustus; [versus:] "A severe Slav, I shed no tears" (2:219); "I sing no flattering entreaties / To Octavius in blind hope" (2:170; Octavius—Emperor Augustus).

The images of the prisoner, the fugitive, and the exile are concentrated in Pushkin's artistic works. But they go beyond the individual poetic instances in which they appear, permeating the letters Pushkin sent north, and also, apparently, his conversations, covering the poet with a certain figurative cloak and thus stylizing his personality and fate in the eyes of his contemporaries. We will cite just one example from many that are possible. In a letter to his brother from August 25, 1823, Pushkin informs him of his transfer to Odesa (information which seemed good news at the time) and of the fact that in order to resolve certain practical issues related to the transfer he needed to travel to Chişinău once more:

> Vorontsov arrived, received me very graciously, and announced that I will now be under his supervision and that I am to remain in Odessa—which I think is good—but a new sorrow has constricted my chest—I am sorry for the chains I left behind. I came to Chişinău for a few days, spent them in an ineffably elegiac manner—and, [subsequently,] having abandoned the city for good, I sighed for Chişinău" (13:67).

Pushkin's description of his emotions is profoundly sincere and psychologically perfectly natural. But in order to fully understand those emotions one must account for the fact that the expression "I sighed for Chişinău" is a slightly adjusted rendering of the last line of Lord Byron's *The Prisoner of Chillon* as translated by Zhukovsky:

> When, beyond the gates of my prison,
> I took a step towards freedom—
> I sighed for my prison.

Pushkin had grown tired of Chișinău, a city that became especially burdensome for him after the rout of Orlov and Vladimir Raevsky's circle. Nonetheless, Chișinău was no prison, and Odesa was no liberation. But the need to see himself through the prism of the Romantic hero (in this case, the famous Geneva prisoner François Bonivard[24]) was so insistent that he described nearly all of his feelings in a letter by employing quotations that were completely transparent to his addressee:

> And new tears from my eyes
> Flow, and a new sadness
> Constricted my chest... I felt sorry
> For my abandoned chains...

The type of poetic personality that Pushkin was creating was in large part comprised of the motif of an eternal, secret, unrequited love. Later, Pushkin ironically referenced this motif in a list of de rigueur attributes of Romanticism, calling it "high-flown fantasies":

> At that time, I found necessary
> Wastelands, the pearly edges of the waves,
> The roar of the sea, the masses of cliffs,
> And the ideal of the proud maiden,
> And nameless torments... (6:200)

This same required Romantic motif, which by the 1840s had become vulgarized, is also cited by Lermontov:

> All poets cursed the crowd,
> And praised the family circle,
> Everyone's souls soared to the heavens,

> And all invoked, in silent prayers,
> N.N.* of unprecedented beauty,
> And it all became a terrible turn-off.**

But in 1821–1823 Pushkin was far removed from an ironic disposition towards this theme. Moreover, he worked with exceptional energy to create around his poetry and personality an aura of mystery and hints at his secret passion. In this case he was no stranger to ironic play with the reader and sometimes even explicit mystification.

The theme of secret love unites the cycle of lyric poems with a "Crimean" background or coloring and makes itself felt in the narrative poem *The Fountain of Bakhchisarai*. However, it presents itself more powerfully not in the poems themselves, but in the author's commentaries on them, which direct the literary circles of those years toward a specific type of reception.

In December 1823, in St. Petersburg, Alexander Bestuzhev and Kondraty Ryleev published an almanac entitled *The Polar Star* [Polyarnaya Zvezda].

---

*   A common way of referencing an anonymous (or mystified) addressee in Russian poetry (Translator's note).

** Mikhail Lermontov, *Sobranie sochinenii* [Collected Works], 6 vols. (Moscow–Leningrad: Izdatel'stvo Akademii nauk SSSR, 1954), 1:475. The necessity of employing this subsequently quickly vulgarized cliché was so great that even Pushkin's uncle, Vasily Pushkin, felt himself impelled to indulge in a mysterious, unrequited passion:

> I love… and no one knows it
> And conceal this tender truth within my soul.
> I alone know… though me heart wails,
> Though day and night I long for her;
> But beloved is my suffering to me,
> And I vowed to love her without respite.

The danger of constructing Romantically tinged biographies on the basis of such verses can be attested to by the following written by a contemporary of the author: "The objects of his singing were usually maidens who had just about graduated from their petty-skirts. A man of short stature, stout, toothless, with bad skin, who perpetually gelled up the scant remnants of his hair, he was incredibly tearful and had lost his mind very early. He would fall in love of jealousy. This was told to me by the objects of his affections himself who are now mostly middle-aged women" (Mikhail Semevskii, "K biografii Pushkina" [Towards Pushkin's Biography], *Russkii vestnik*, no. 84 (1869): 86).

Among a series of Pushkin's poems published in the almanac there appeared the elegy "Sparser grows the flying range of clouds..." The elegy was published in full, but as can be seen from an angry letter that Pushkin immediately sent to Bestuzhev, the poet had asked the editors to omit the final lines of the poem:

> When on the huts the shadow of the night descended—
> And a young maiden searched for you in the darkness
> And called your name to her friends. (2:157)

Pushkin was furious. In another letter to Bestuzhev he wrote:

> May God forgive you! But you have brought shame on me in the current *Star* by publishing the final three lines of my Elegy; it was also the devil, by the way, who made me write in *The Bakh.[chisarai] Fount. [ain]* some sensitive lines and immediately recall my elegiac beauty. Imagine my despair when I saw them published—the journal might fall in her hands. What will she think when she sees how eagerly I talk about her *with one of my S[t. Peters]B[urg] friends.** Does she have to know that I did not name her, that the letter was opened and published by Bulgarin, that the damned Elegy was delivered to you by the devil knows whom, and that no one is at fault. I must admit, I value a single thought of this woman's higher than all the opinions of every journal in the world and all our public. My head is spinning (13:100–101).

This quote shows, it would seem, that Pushkin dedicated the elegy to a woman whom he was in love with, that it was her that he referred to in his letter that Bulgarin accidentally got hold of and partially published, and that he wished to keep these intimate lines a secret. And because Pushkin carefully hid this woman's name, scholars have arrived at the conclusion that the elegy is an unwilling confession of the poet's, a testimony as to his secret love.

A close examination of the facts, however, raises a score of doubts. First and foremost, although the elegy was delivered to Ryleev and Bestuzhev by

---

* The words italicized by Pushkin are an imprecise quotation from Faddei Bulgarin's note titled "Literary News" published in the fourth number of *Literary Notes* in 1824.

"the devil knows whom," it is apparent that only its author could have spread the poem among his friends (which at that time meant spreading it among the era's leading readership). It was completely his decision whether or not to keep it secret. Then, knowing that Bestuzhev was intending to publish the elegy, Pushkin did not forbid the publication, but only vetoed the publication of the final three lines. Pushkin thus, if anything, draws attention to them by accentuating the fact that they include a secret important to the author (which is unclear from the text itself). If one considers that Pushkin's aim was to conceal a secret, as opposed to the creation of an air of mystery around the elegy, then why did he not request that the final *two* lines of the poem be omitted (seeing as the first of the three could easily be included and presented as a syntactically complete dependent clause)? If Bestuzhev had heeded Pushkin's requests and omitted the last *three* lines, then the poem would have appeared as an unfinished fragment in print, intriguingly playing on the final line's consequent lack of a corresponding second rhyme. Combined with an admission on the author's part that the final three lines could not be published due to their intimate nature (and this information would have become then available to a certain circle of readers), such a publication would have surrounded the elegy with mystery and closely tied it to Pushkin's biographical legend.

But even more questions arise: Pushkin's words that he valued a single thought of this woman's higher than all the opinions of his readership sound alluringly sincere. Her name has, needless to say, fascinated biographers, because this "young maiden," named the Evening Star, is the likeliest candidate for Pushkin's "secret love." In this regard, because in the Gurzuf elegy Pushkin could have been referring to either one of Raevsky's daughters or their friend, Maria Raevskaya (later Volkonskaya, one of the famous "Decembrists' wives," who followed her husband to Siberia) who was often considered an especially likely candidate. However, after scholar Boris Tomashevsky[25] proved through written materials that "the young maiden" refers to General Raevsky's eldest daughter, Ekaterina Raevskaya[26] (who soon after married Mikhail Orlov), the characterization of Pushkin's words in his letter to Bestuzhev must be altered: Pushkin valued Ekaterina's beauty and character, but there could not have been talk of any serious love towards her; her marriage to Mikhail Orlov only raised a few silly jokes (in 1825 in a letter to Prince Vyazemsky Pushkin called her "a glorious wench"—13:226). If we add to this that in the fragment of the letter published by Bulgarin it was not her at all that was referred to, we must conclude that Pushkin was engaging in a sort of mystification with Bestuzhev, and, through him, with the wider circle of readers he valued most, in order to surround his elegiac poetry with an air of Romantic legend, presenting the verses as his heart's lyrical diary.

This is even more evident with regard to *The Fountain of Bakhchisarai*. Pushkin consciously spread rumors among literary circles in Petersburg, before the appearance of *Fountain*, about a direct connection between the poem and its author. In a letter from August 25, 1823, sent from Odesa, Pushkin wrote to his brother:

> Tumansky[27] is here. He's a good man, but he lies sometimes—for inst., he is writing a letter to [someone in] St. Petersburg where, among other things, he mentions me: Pushkin opened his heart and porte-feuile* to me without hesitation—love, etc.—a phrase worthy of V. Kozlov;[28] the matter is that I read him fragments from *The Fountain of Bakhchisarai* (my new poem), having said that I would rather not publish it because many places in it refer to a woman with whom I was stupidly in love for a long time and because I don't think the role of Petrarch[29] suits me. Tumansky accepted all this as if I were trusting him with my heart and is anointing me as one of the Shalikovs—help me!** (13:67)

There is much that is strange in this letter: first of all, Pushkin could easily have refused to disclose anything about the connections between *The Fountain*

---

*   The French word for briefcase.
** Prince Pyotr Shalikov was a sentimentalist writer. He was widely regarded in literary circles as a comical figure.

of Bakhchisarai and his life to Tumansky, who was a famous gossip. Second of all, as the text of the letter shows, Tumansky actually showed Pushkin the letter that he had written, and Pushkin could easily have requested that Tumansky not send it: he could even have forced him (Pushkin, throughout his life, had challenged opponents to duels for much less than this apparently sensitive matter). Pushkin not only failed to do this, but he also sent a fragment from this letter to his brother Lev—who had not heard of the new poem—asking that he prevent this rumor. Considering, similarly, Lev's well-known capacity for gossip, this cannot be interpreted as anything but a conscious effort on Pushkin's part to enable the rumor to spread throughout the various literary circles.

In the same letter he adds a note: "So be it, I'll send Vyazemsky my *Fountain* in which I let loose a bunch of nonsense about love—but what a shame!" (13:68). Studies of the poem's manuscripts disappoint in this regard, however: there was no "nonsense about love" (about which Pushkin repeatedly wrote to his friends) included. The final variant of the poem was published without any significant departures from the manuscripts.

All of this indicates Pushkin's conscious and deliberate effort to create a "second biography" for himself in literature, which would serve as a context connecting his works in the eyes of his readers.*

But the poet's relationship to literature also included another side, one that was inherently at odds with the ideals and demands of Romanticism. Pushkin desperately lacked money: his salary at his middling position was negligible, his father practically refused to support him monetarily (even such a comic show of support as the delivery of his father's old suits to Chișinău

---

* There is a telling detail here: in 1822, *The Prisoner of the Caucasus* was published with a portrait of Pushkin as a child in an engraving made by Georg Heytman. Pushkin was depicted wearing a soft shirt with an unbuttoned collar. This detail would force readers to recall a similar portrait of Byron likewise wearing a soft shirt with a poetically unbuttoned collar.

was the subject of a prolonged correspondence). Throughout all this, Pushkin found that he could earn significant royalties as his poetry grew in popularity and demand.

There were many obstacles in the way, however: Russia's complete absence of copyright laws, which defended authors' rights and regulated the legal aspects of publishing, together with Pushkin's exile status which forced him to turn to intermediaries, who were often incompetent, uninterested, and sometimes even dishonest. But there was another, even more significant obstacle: in Russian literature during that time there was the idea that poetry was a gift of the gods, as opposed to a form of labor, and that receiving payment for poetry was degrading for a poet.

Pushkin's personal circumstances forced him into the position of a professional writer—a position at odds with Romantic notions of the poet as an "idle layabout." Pushkin's lucid mind allowed him to see that the Romantic legend which he tried so hard to cultivate is destroyed by this attitude. In a letter to Alexander Turgenev from May 7, 1821, he wrote: "[L]et the fleeting friends of my fleeting youth know that they should send me money and that, in so doing, the seeker of new sensations will be greatly in their debt" (13:29). "Fleeting friends of my fleeting youth" and "the seeker of new sensations" are quotes from Pushkin's famous elegy "Extinguished is the orb of day…." Combining these quotes with requests for money, Pushkin deliberately collides two worlds—that of poetry and that of prosaic life. Thus, the poet appears to belong to both. The fight ahead for author's rights was long and cruel, but Pushkin eventually emerged triumphant, creating the foundations for professional literature and copyright law in Russia.

Pushkin's first epic poem was published when he was already in the south. It was published to great material success. *The Moscow Telegraph* later wrote: "*Ruslan and Liudmila* appeared in 1820. Then, all the copies were bought out and for a long time there have not been any copies available for purchase. Especially avid hunters were forced to pay 25 rubles and even had to resort to copying it down by hand."* Despite the significant revenue it generated, Pushkin hardly earned anything. The lion's share belonged to Nikolai Gnedich, the poem's publisher. Certain scholars have been inclined to rebuke Gnedich for dishonesty.** But according to the standards of the time, Gnedich had not done anything disreputable. The concept of literary property did not exist then, and the publisher of any poetic anthology pocketed money for the work not only of dead, but also of living poets. Publishing was considered a "lowly" profession and, as such, was monetarily compensated, but poetry could only be degraded with a royalty. It is characteristic that in eighteenth-century journals, translators were paid royalties, but a poet would have been offended if offered money ("inspiration is not for sale"). The same Gnedich, when publishing the works of his friend Konstantin Batyushkov, out of the 15,000 rubles of revenue that the publication brought, paid the author only 2,000 rubles, leaving the rest for himself. Nobody would have thought to rebuke him. Pushkin, however, felt that he was a new type of writer, and he did not want to accept the amateurish and unprofessional nature of publishing then. In a letter to Grech from September 21, 1821, offering his second epic poem *The Prisoner of the Caucasus* (this time going around Gnedich, which severely offended the latter), he wrote, ironically highlighting the business end of the relations between the poet and his publisher: "I would like to send you a fragment from my *Prisoner of the Caucasus*, but I am much too lazy to send it; would you like to buy a whole piece of the poem? It is 800 lines long; the width of every line is 4 feet; it is cut into two songs. I'd pass it along for cheap, to negate its short shelf-life" (13:32–33). Gnedich was able to repel other publishers (it can be assumed that this was done not out of greed, but from his gallant

---

* Anonymous, "Sovremennaia russkaia bibliografiia" [Contemporary Russian Bibliography], *Moskovskii telegraf*, no. 5 (1828): 77–78.

** Sergei Gessen, *Knigoizdatel' Aleksandr Pushkin* [Alexander Pushkin as a Publisher] (Leningrad: Academia, 1930), 34–35.

desire to occupy the role of Pushkin's patron and publisher), and the second poem once again brought its author 500 rubles in the form of a royalty, while bringing its publisher around 5,000 rubles.* However, Pushkin eventually emerged victorious.

With the help of his friend Pyotr Vyazemsky, who published his third narrative poem, *The Fountain of Bakhchisarai,* Pushkin attained an exceptionally high royalty by the standards of the time. Russian journals, which were taken up with intense polemics regarding Romanticism that had been spurred by Pushkin's poem and Vyazemsky's foreword, simultaneously noted the royalty side of its publication as the beginning of a "European" attitude towards poetry in Russia.

These two sides of the poet in his stance toward literary affairs were as of yet opposed and not combined into one—they were to coalesce only in the subsequent, realist period of Pushkin's writing.

Pushkin's time in Chişinău was marked by a particularly sweeping range of connections between the poet and the Decembrist movement. The Second Army of General Pyotr Wittgenstein,[30] situated in the south, was a refuge for the most significant figures in the Union of Welfare. Europe, paralyzed after the fall of Napoleon, was experiencing a new revolutionary awakening. The liberation movement in Russia was quickly gaining strength. Pushkin dove into this atmosphere headfirst. However, unlike in St. Petersburg, he was no student knocking on the doors of the chosen ones—in his eyes, he was a Poet and sought to define his place—the place of a Poet among Citizens.

The atmosphere which Pushkin experienced in Chişinău was different from that of St. Petersburg primarily in that the former was an atmosphere of *action*. Echoes of the revolutions that shook Europe, in Spain, Greece, Naples, and Piedmont, reached Chişinău much more directly. In January 1821 there arose a rebellion in Turkish Moldova headed by Tudor Vladimirescu;[31]

---

*   Gessen, *Knigoizdatel' Aleksandr Pushkin,* 40.

subsequently, Alexander Ypsilantis, the son of the Moldovan ruler and a Greek, made his way over the Prut River—the border between Russia and Turkish Moldova—and, having arrived in Iași, called upon the Greeks of the Ottoman Empire to raise a general rebellion. Pushkin found himself in the heat of it all.

The Decembrists, like other broadly liberal circles in Russia, had hoped that Alexander I would keep his semi-official promises to support the Greeks (who were also Orthodox Christians) and engage in a war of liberation against tyranny that would reverberate throughout Russia's domestic policy as well. Pushkin awaited war and was prepared to participate in it. He began studying Turkish and begged his friends to quit their efforts at returning him to St. Petersburg. It is during this time that Pushkin interacted very closely with Chișinău-based circles of Greek insurgents. In the beginning of March 1821, he wrote (it would seem, to Decembrist Vasily Davydov):

> I am writing to inform you of developments that will have consequences significant not only for our parts, but for all of Europe. Greece has risen in rebellion and declared its freedom. [...] I saw a letter written by one insurgent: he describes with passion the ritual of consecrating the banners and sword of Prince Ypsilantis, the ecstasy of the clergy and the people, and the precious minutes of Hope and Liberty. [...] The rapture of their minds has reached the highest level, all of their thoughts are directed towards a single object—the independence of their ancient Fatherland. In Odesa I just missed a curious sight: in the shops, in the streets, in the inns—everywhere were gathered crowds of Greeks who were selling their property for pennies; purchasing instead sabers, rifles, pistols; everyone was speaking about Leonidas,[32] Themistocles;[33] everyone was heading to the fortunate Ypsilantis's regiment (13: 22–23).

The Greek Rebellion not only granted Pushkin feelings of political enthusiasm ("precious minutes of Hope and Liberty"), it also allowed him to closely observe one of the key political developments of his era and see it from all its sides. This was one of the lessons to which Pushkin is indebted for his superbly clear political mind, which would later shock foreign diplomats in St. Petersburg in the 1830s. Pushkin saw the tragic divide that occurred among the Greek rebels—the bloody conflict between the Vladimirescu's mostly peasant army and Ypsilantis's aristocratic command, which was complicated by nationalist oppositions between Moldovans and Romanians on the one hand, and Greeks on the other. He bore witness to the complicated relationships between the leadership of the rebellion, the commanders of the Second Russian Army, and figures from Russian secret societies. It was these events, apparently, that brought Pestel to Chişinău. During this time, Pushkin took part in a "conversation [with Pestel] of a metaphysical, political, ethical et al. nature." "He is one of the most original minds I've seen" (12:303), writes Pushkin in his Chişinău journal. Together with Pestel, he apparently took part in talks with the leaders of the Greek Rebellion. Many years later, in 1833, Pushkin recorded in his journal many extremely interesting details regarding Pestel's diplomatic activity that demonstrate the poet's insider knowledge. Further developments in the Rebellion caused Pushkin to become greatly disappointed in Ypsilantis. If the practical developments of the Rebellion brought Pushkin to reflect on the tragic problem faced by the Decembrists of the interrelation between a folk movement and the revolutionary activity of an educated aristocratic minority, then the personal flaws that Pushkin saw in Ypsilantis caused him to doubt the Romantic cult of the "great man." Later, in his manuscripts for *Ezersky*—a planned epic poem—in justifying his turn to a simple, "nongreat" man, Pushkin noted: "Why do I bother with paltry heroes? What am I to do . . . I have seen [Yps(ilantis), Paske(vich),[34] Ermolov[35]]" (5:410; this is crossed out by Pushkin).

Pushkin's greatest influence during this period, however, was that of Mikhail Orlov and the Chişinău Decembrists that gathered around him—especially Vladimir Raevsky.

Mikhail Orlov arrived in Chişinău in the summer of 1820, taking up the command post of the 16th division. He declined posts that were, potentially, greater opportunities—to the disappointment of Alexander I—in order to be able to independently command a large military unit. This was necessary for his subsequent revolutionary military plans. "16,000 under my command. [...] One can make quite a joke with such a number," Orlov wrote to Alexander Raevsky shortly after receiving his new command post.* From the context of the letter it is clear that Orlov meant military action against Turkey. Nevertheless, Semen Landa's**[36] recent research has shown that for Orlov, participation in the Greek Rebellion in 1820 was part of his plan for a subsequent Russian revolution. Orlov was a member of the Decembrist Order of Russian Knights—an organization that was oriented towards tactics of decisive action. Initially, he hoped to gain command of a division closer to Moscow, as opposed to one on the border. "What a difference it would have made had I received a division in Nizhny Novgorod or Yaroslavl. I would have felt like a fish in water." With a homebase in either of these cities, Orlov could have realistically conceived of an advance towards Moscow which, at the time, was hardly supported by any troops of its own. It is no coincidence that the like-minded Count Dmitriev-Mamonov[37] was building a genuine fortress on his massive estate near Moscow, supplied with artillery which could have served as a superior base of support in the event of such an operation. Similarly, the Count was gathering a banner passed from Minin[38] to Pozharsky[39] as well as the bloody shirt of Dmitry the Tsarevich.[40] Both of these relics were filled with meaning: one was supposed to sanctify the advance of Orlov and Mamonov with

---

*   Mikhail Orlov, *Kapituliatsiia Parizha. Politicheskie sochineniia. Pis'ma* [The Surrender of Paris. Political Works. Letters] (Moscow: Izdatel'stvo Akademii nauk SSSR, 1963), 225.

**   Semen Landa, *O nekotorykh osobennostiakh formirovaniia revoliutsionnoi ideologii v Rossii 1816–1821* [On Certain Peculiarities in the Formation of Revolutionary Ideology in Russia 1816–1821] in *Pushkin I ego vremia* [Pushkin and His Time] (Leningrad: Izdatel'stvo Gosudarstvennogo Ermitazha, 1962), 148–168. See also Semen Landa, *Dukh revoliutsionnykh preobrazovanii* [The Spirit of Revolutionary Changes] (Moscow: Mysl', 1975), 169–179.

a historical symbol; the latter was meant to signify the abrogation of the Rurik[41] line and a negation of the Romanovs'[42] claims to the Russian throne.

Orlov, however, was already distrusted at court: his requests to command a division were repeatedly declined, and he was ultimately given a division at the periphery of the empire. After initially being discouraged, he then quickly devised a bold plan to tie the Greek Rebellion to a potential Russian counterpart. Semen Landa introduced notes by Greek historian Philemon[43]—who was close to Ypsilantis—that had previously eluded scholars. These notes show that in talks between Ypsilantis and Orlov, the pair came to an agreement that if Orlov's participation in Greek affairs (unsanctioned by his higher-ups) were to infuriate Alexander I, causing him to declare Orlov *non grata* in St. Petersburg—that is, if Orlov's actions were to provoke a civil war in Russia—Orlov "with the Russians [that is, with his own division—Lotman] would join the princedoms as an independent commander," receiving in turn a base in Wallachia and Turkish Moldova from which to engage in revolutionary warfare against the St. Petersburg government. Aside from this, Orlov counted on support from other divisions who were in on the conspiracy, from Wittgenstein's army and, to some degree, from such military leaders as Kiselyov, Ermolov, and Raevsky Sr. Having arrived in Chișinău, Orlov immediately began preparing his division for military action. He gathered officers around himself who were members of the secret society and expelled followers of Arakcheev, all while also earning personal loyalty and love from his soldiers.*

Orlov was by no means a romancer or dreamer when, in 1821, at a meeting of the Union of Welfare, in response to news that the government had unraveled some elements of the conspiracy, he offered a plan of immediate revolutionary action.

---

* See Vasilii Bazanov, *Vladimir Fedoseevich Raevskii* (Moscow–Leningrad: Izdatel'stvo Akademii nauk SSSR, 1949), 27–88.

Such was the situation in Chișinău when Pushkin arrived there. Orlov's closest comrades—Major Vasily Raevsky,[44] his adjutant Konstantin Okhotnikov,[45] General-Major Pavel Pushchin[46]—were all members of the Union of Welfare. It was these people that had the greatest political influence on Pushkin in Chișinău. Pushkin was always welcome at Orlov's house. He was a regular guest at dinners given by Orlov and, similarly, a regular opponent of the latter in the political disputes that frequently broke out at the house. Pushkin, however, was treated as an equal despite their differences in age and rank. Orlov's wife, Ekaterina, wrote to her brother on November 23, 1821: "We see Pushkin very often; he argues with my husband about every matter imaginable. His latest preoccupation is Charles-Irénée Castel, abbé de Saint-Pierre's eternal peace. He's convinced that the governments of the world, perfecting themselves, will eventually create an eternal and global peace and that then no one's blood will be spilled, except for that of people with strong personalities and passions, with enterprising spirits, whom we now call great men—these people will then be deemed disruptors of the public peace."* During this time, Pushkin was rereading the project of eternal peace in Rousseau's retelling of Saint-Pierre (in general, he was greatly interested in the Genevan philosopher then). This reading was especially relevant at this point in time, as it touched on questions of natural human freedom, peoples' sovereignty (the supreme power of the people), and the rights of nations. Pushkin's disagreements with Orlov, however, were of a friendly nature (compare his epistle to Gnedich: "I argue with Orlov and seldom drink").**

---

*   Mikhail Gershenzon, *Istoriia molodoi Rossii* [The History of Young Russia] (Moscow–Petrograd: Gosudarstvennoe izdatel'stvo, 1923), 34. Compare Ekaterina Orlova's letters to the same addressee: "Our house is perpetually filled with noisy disputes on philosophical, political, literary, and other topics. I hear them all the way down the hall" (Ibid.).

** See Mikhail Alexeev, "Pushkin i problema vechnogo mira" [Pushkin and the Problem of "Eternal Peace"], in *Pushkin* (Leningrad: Nauka, 1972).

The political context of Pushkin's interest in issues of "eternal peace" is that the leadership of the reactionary union of countries that emerged victorious following the Napoleonic Wars was operating under the motto of establishing peace in Europe. Having deemed Napoleon the demon of war, the Vienna Congress pompously declared a period of eternal peace. This motto, which in 1815 still had something of a liberal color to it, would later be turned into a reactionary imperative against the emerging revolutionary activity; or in Pushkin words, the idea of pacification "brought the world quiet slavery as a gift" (2:310).

As a result, those that bore a revolutionary mentality during these years were inclined to view things in martial terms. The sympathies of western European liberals were increasingly often with Napoleon, and revolutionary ideas were often closely intertwined with notions of revolutionary warfare. In this case, warfare was viewed as a means of protecting the interests of one's country after liberty had been established. The idea that relations between nations lay beyond morality (because they were based on "natural law") gave rise to an aggressive conception of Russian foreign policy once a revolution has taken place (Pestel), an idea which, for instance, in the hands of Orlov's friend Dmitriev-Mamonov, took on an explicitly confrontational nature. Mamonov's conception of a revolutionary government in Russia, following the Napoleonic tradition, involved an emphasis on "great power" status, with Mamonov projecting sweeping territorial expansions in northern, central, and southern Europe ("the composition of a project regarding an advantageous war against the Persians and an incursion into India").* Orlov, a longtime comrade of Mamonov's through the Order of Russian Knights, seemingly supported his friend's ideas, at least in part.

---

* *Iz pisem i pokazanii dekabristov* [From Letters and Testimonies of Decembrists] (St. Petersburg: Izdatel'skii dom M. V. Pirozhkova, 1906), 147.

For Pushkin, who was engaged in disputes with Orlov and working on a manuscript dedicated to eternal peace during this time, a different approach was characteristic. He rejected the idea of a peace produced by a union of monarchs, opting rather for a peace resulting from a union of revolutionary governments (he derived this idea from his reading of Rousseau). In a fragment of his, quoting Rousseau's words that a path towards peace can be initiated only by "means violent and terrible for humanity," he concluded: "It is evident that these terrible means of which he spoke are revolutions. And so they have come" (12:189 and 480).*

It is telling that in those very days, when Pushkin was propounding the idea of eternal peace at Orlov's house, the poet wrote a poem titled "War" that ends with the following line: "Why has the first battle not yet flared up?" (2:167). Revolutionary warfare (in this case, the Greeks' war of liberation) was for him not a negation of peace, but rather the singular path towards the permanent eradication of war. For Orlov (and for many other Decembrists), Liberty, much as happened with the French Revolution in the eighteenth century, was meant to usher in a series of wars whose ultimate objective was to be the consolidation of Russia's greatness; for Pushkin, Liberty was to bring Peace.

The most important political questions discussed in Orlov's circle and at Raevsky's house, nevertheless, concerned domestic policy. Pushkin's political views during these months are well-illustrated by his colleague Pavel Dolgorukov's[47] unguarded journal notes: "Pushkin has been chastising the government, landowners, he speaks sharply and convincingly." Pushkin "suddenly

---

* Pushkin's fragment manages to preserve the live intonations of his disputes with Orlov. The concluding words: "I know that all of these arguments are very weak, seeing as the testimonies of such a silly little boy as Rousseau, who could not win one little battle, carry no weight" (12:189–190, 480). These are of course an ironic reformulation of Orlov's own words originally addressed to a different "silly little boy who could not win one little battle"—that is, to Pushkin himself. See Mikhail Alexeev, *Pushkin i problema vechnogo mira*.

produced the following syllogism for us: 'Earlier in history, nations rose up against each other, now the king of Naples[48] is waging war against the people, the Prussian king[49] wars against his people, as does the Spanish king;[50] it is not difficult to predict which side will emerge victorious.' There was a deep silence after his words."

> The viceroy was riding to the hunt with his rifle and dog. During his absence, the table was set for the domestic servants, where I dined together with Pushkin. The latter, feeling himself at liberty to express his thoughts, began espousing his favorite text regarding the government in Russia. Smirnov,[51] the translator, was apt to disagree with Pushkin, and the more he refuted his arguments, the more Pushkin got worked up, angry, and lost his patience. Finally, every level of society earned a rebuke: civil officials were blackguards and thieves, generals were brutes for the most part, only the classes that worked the land were found worthy of respect. Pushkin was especially harsh on the Russian aristocrats. He found that it was necessary to hang them all and that, if this were to happen, he would happily tighten the nooses around their necks."*

These attitudes were reflected in the poet's works. His constant interactions with Orlov, Raevsky, and other Chișinău Decembrists allowed him to accurately express the most radical political ideas coursing within the Decembrist movement in 1821–1822. He decidedly positioned himself as a supporter of tyrannicide—an idea that was gaining traction throughout the various circles of the conspiracy.

Pushkin did not enjoy remaining cooped up in Chișinău, and General Inzov, who treated Pushkin with truly touching solicitude, freely let him go out as he wished. The places that Pushkin frequented included Vasily Davydov's[52] estate Kamenka, not far from Kyiv, as well as Tulchyn and Vasylkiv.** These trips only strengthened his connections to the southern Decembrists.

---

* *Contemporaries*, 1:360–361; notes from April 30, May 27, and July 20, 1822

** Tulchyn and Vasylkiv were two centers with Decembrists organizations in the South.

The political verse that he wrote at this time defined his special role among the Decembrists. Such poems as "The Dagger," "Napoleon," "O loyal Greek wife, cry not, he died a hero…" demonstrated the close connection he had to the political conspirators. Even more telling were his epistles to Vasily Davydov ("While General Orlov…") or to General Pushchin ("Through smoke, blood, and clouds of arrows…"). If the first group of poems were of a political-agitational nature dedicated to a wider readership, the latter group were conspiratorial messages sent from one member of the conspiracy to another. Poems from the latter group are written in a language of hints, with political cryptography (in one case, based on certain little phrases from their friendly political circle; in another case, it was based on the conspiratorial language of the Freemasons, seeing as the poem was dedicated to Pushkin's 'brother' from *Ovid*—a Chișinău-based Freemason lodge, which was frequented by Decembrists).

The portrait of Pushkin in Chișinău presented here would not be complete without mentioning another side. Pushkin's domestic life was difficult: the reputation of an exile; constant financial troubles coupled with the need to repeatedly interact with people from different social classes; an insignificant rank; the ambivalence of a poet's place in society—all of this made him rather vulnerable to insult. In general, when we think of the popular Russian image of Pushkin, we imagine a complete absence of spiritual pressure or victimhood, a man full of strength and life—but this often leads one to forget how difficult and vulnerable his position really was. As an author, he was unable to protect his rights due to the fact that he was located far from the centers of literary life as well as the fact that legally the literary profession at this time was surrounded by ambiguity. As a participant in political life, he constantly had to take account of the idea that his deep conviction in the many-sidedness of the poetic personality was often perceived by others as an insufficient commitment to political struggle or even "spoiledness," "flippancy," or "levity." As a person—this became evident in Chișinău—he was fated to bear the brand of "poet," forever facing unceremonious curiosity and a persistent expectation that he acquits himself in a manner consistent with the behavioral clichés of a "poetic personality."

In these circumstances, it took truly a great deal of both poetic and personal genius to avoid being seduced by many of the vulgar masks of the societal masquerade and stay true to his personality, which he worked on constantly, as opposed to falsely portraying himself as a

> Melmoth,
> A cosmopolitan, a patriot,
> A [Childe] Harold, a quaker, a hypocrite. (6:168)

And so he could construct his personality firmly and confidently, creating it continually as he would an original and finished work of art.

It would be wrong to conceive of the process of "personality construction" as a strictly rational process: much like in art, the conscious plan of action coexisted with intuitive discoveries and moments of inspiration that informed the artist's decisions. Together they formed that blend of conscious and unconscious energies that are characteristic of any creative activity.

A collegial secretary and a poet in a world where everything was defined by rank; a man without means constantly facing financial troubles in a society of wealthier people who constantly and casually spent large sums of money; a civilian among military men; a twenty-year-old youth among military officers and proud Moldovan boyars: Pushkin was a person whose dignity was constantly being undercut. What others received from birth as their natural inheritance and what was passed on to them as their aristocratic sheen—"the chill of calm pride"—was taken from Pushkin. He had to acquire everything by himself, without titles, without patronage, without money, without even tact in everyday behavior and a "good" upbringing. His only support was his genius.

Pushkin's primary weapon against the degrading nature of his existence was a deep belief in his own self-worth—instilled in him by Chaadaev—that prompted him to be decisive in every situation, no matter how insignificant, and also to defend his proud independence. Even the malignant Vigel,[53] in describing Pushkin's character, noted his "strong judgment which endlessly stirs in him," as well as a "feeling of honor with which he was full."* This is the key to understanding Pushkin's numerous duels in Chişinău and his conflicts with different members of Chişinău "society."

In the autumn of 1822, Pushkin wrote a letter to Lev—a characteristic honor code written by one situated in a hostile environment:

> Your behavior will determine your reputation for long to come and, perhaps, your well-being.
>
> You will have to deal with people whom you do not know yet. From the very beginning, think as poorly of them as you can: in the end, you won't be too mistaken. Don't judge people based on your own heart which, I'm sure, is noble and kind and, most importantly, still young; despise them in the most polite way possible: this is a means of protecting yourself from minor prejudices and minor passions, which will inhibit you upon entering society.
>
> Be cold with everyone; familiarity is always harmful; be especially prudent in allowing it when engaging with your superiors, no matter how kind they are to you. They will be quick to cast you aside and happy to insult you when you least expect it.
>
> Don't display complaisance and keep in check a cordial disposition if it takes hold of you: people don't understand and will readily perceive it as obsequiousness because they are always happy to judge others by themselves.
>
> Never accept favors. Favors, more often than not, are treachery. Avoid patronage because it enslaves and humiliates.
>
> I would caution you against the allurements of friendship, but I lack the decisiveness to harden your soul in a time of the most delightful illusions. All I can tell you about women would be completely useless. I would only note that the less we love a woman the likelier it is that we might possess her. This entertainment, however, is worthy of an old monkey from the 18th century. As far as the woman that you will come

---

*   *Contemporaries*, 1:219.

to love is concerned, I hope from the bottom of my heart that you will have her.

Never forget a deliberate offense: be of few words or be completely silent and never respond to an insult with insult.

If your means or circumstances don't allow you to shine in public, don't try to hide that which you lack; choose the other extreme instead: cynicism, through its harshness, can often impress the vain opinions of society, whereas vainglory's minor gimmicks will make one seem worthy of being laughed at and despised.

Don't take loans; it's better to tolerate your needs; believe me, it's not as bad as it seems, and either way it's better than the inevitability of ending up without one's honor or seeming so.

The rules which I have laid out have been obtained at the cost of bitter experience. It would be good if you were able to absorb them without needing to undergo what I did. They might relieve you of days of rage and anguish. Sometime in the future you'll hear my confession; it will come at a high cost to my self-esteem, but this will not stop me, if telling so concerns your happiness. (13:49–50 and 524)

These bitter lines tell us not only about a great and difficult life experience, but also about Pushkin's skill at strict self-analysis and conscious molding of character, and the removal of everything from that character that did not conform to a well thought out norm of behavior.

Orlov lived like a lord in Chişinău:* in his house there reigned the kind of merriment that consumes the young and bold who have made the decision of doing battle. With his brave actions in defending soldiers, Orlov was able to obtain the affection of those below him—an affection that approached worship. "His kindly disposition, his magnificent appearance, his always merry face, his accessibility—all these earned the soldiers' trust and ecstatic attachment. When inspecting troops at the front, the soldiers—without awaiting his greeting of 'Hello, brothers!'—greeted him with a loud 'hurrah!'" wrote Vladimir

---

* Vigel recalled: "He rented out a row of three or four houses and began living not as a Russian general, but as a Russian boyar" (*Contemporaries*, 1:222).

Raevsky.* A secret agent of the government wrote in a denunciation: "The lower ranks say: the commander of the division (M. F. Orlov) is our father, he has enlightened us, the 16th division is called *Orlovshchina*... In public and even in the coffee-houses, Pushkin berates not only the military command, but even the government."** Everyone was filled with impatience—from the commander of a division to an exiled poet.

Colonel Nepenin,⁵⁴ a commander of a regiment and member of the Union of Welfare, expressed the general mood to Raevsky: "What's there to talk about. [...] My regiment is ready. I can vouch for my officers and soldiers—I'm sick of not doing anything."***

Throughout all this, news of the situation in Chişinău was reaching the government. Clouds were gathering over Orlov and his circle.

In 1820, Alexander I was in Opava for a congress dedicated to the suppression of revolutionary movements in Europe. On October 28, he was notified about a rebellion in the Semenovsky Regiment. Although this event was in no way tied to the Decembrist movement, the emperor was convinced that "there were other reasons at work there." "I ascribe this to the work of secret societies," he wrote to Arakcheev.**** The government started keeping tabs on the secret societies more closely. In 1821, a member of the Central Council of the Union of Welfare, Mikhail Gribovsky,⁵⁵ a provocateur, provided the government with a detailed denunciation elucidating of the character and aims of the Union of Welfare. Mikhail Orlov was named among the "zealous members." Surveillance was established over the Chişinău grouping.

---

*   *Literaturnoe nasledstvo* [The Literary Heritage], 104 vols. (Moscow: Izdatel'stvo Akademii nauk SSSR, 1931–), 60:1:89.

**   Anonymous, "K istorii ssylki poeta A. S. Pushkina v iuzhnuiu Rossiiu" [Towards a History of the Poet A. S. Pushkin's Exile to Southern Russia], *Russkaia starina*, no. 12 (1883): 654–670.

***   *Literaturnoe nasledstvo*, 60:1:85.

**** Nikolai Shil'der, *Imperator Aleksandr Pervyi* [Emperor Alexander the First], vol. 4 (St. Petersburg: Izdanie A. S. Suvorina, 1898), 185.

Two events testify to the degree to which Pushkin was involved in the events developing around him: firstly, his participation in discussions regarding the role of secret societies at the Davydovs' Kamenka estate, and secondly, the service he performed for the Decembrists by alerting Vladimir Raevsky to the latter's impending arrest.

In November 1820, Mikhail Orlov, together with fellow Decembrist Ivan Yakushkin, set off for Chișinău from Moscow for a meeting of the Union of Welfare. On their way there the pair stopped at Kamenka where many talented members of secret societies in the south were gathering. Pushkin was there too at the Davydov brothers' request. A striking picture of the meeting is preserved in Yakushkin's memoirs:

> We spent all our evenings in Vasily Lvovich's lodgings, and our evening conversations were greatly entertaining for everyone. Raevsky, who himself did not belong to the secret society, though he suspected its existence, looked at everything unfolding around him with tense curiosity. He didn't believe that I simply arrived at Kamenka by chance and wanted to know the real reason I came. During the last evening Orlov, Vasily Davydov, Okhotnikov, and I decided to act in such a way as to confound Raevsky with regard to our membership in the secret society. In order to keep stricter order during our discussions, we elected Raevsky as the president. [...] Orlov offered to discuss the question of whether the establishment of a secret society in Russia would be useful. He himself expressed every possible reason for and against a secret society. Vasily Davydov and Okhotnikov were in agreement with Orlov's opinion. Pushkin passionately sought to prove all the uses that a secret society could bring Russia.

At the end of the discussion, everything was turned into a joke. Pushkin "arose, blushing, and said with a tear in his eye: 'I have never been as miserable as I am now; I just saw my life ennobled and a high purpose before myself, and it turned out that this was all just a mean joke.' In this moment, he was certainly magnificent."*

---

*   *Contemporaries*, 1:365–366.

The other occurrence has to do with the arrest of Major Vladimir Raevsky. Pushkin, as Raevsky himself notes in his memoirs, had accidentally overheard a conversation between Generals Sabaneev[56] and Inzov in which the former demanded Raevsky's arrest. Pushkin was then able to warn the Decembrist about the danger the latter faced. Raevsky had time to burn "everything he found expendable."* Raevsky was bold and incautious and he failed to take Pushkin's warning seriously; after his arrest the government seized a pile of important documents. One can only assume that had it not been for Pushkin's warning, the results of the house search would have been even more catastrophic for the secret society.

These occurrences clearly demonstrate both Pushkin's proximity to the southern conspirators, his organic embeddedness both in their everyday and psychic lives, and his desire to tie his fate to a "high purpose," as well as certain reservations on the part of the conspirators.

Why did the Decembrists of the Second Army, despite their closeness to Pushkin and the latter's clear desire to participate, not offer him membership in the secret society? It seems that there was a double caution at play: on the one hand, they did not want to endanger the poet's talent,** and on the other hand, they recognized that the exiled Pushkin was the object of heightened attention on the government's part and that, being unrestrained both in character and temperament, he might attract additional attention. At the same time, the parochialism of the Decembrists regarding their attitude to art and artists must be noted.

---

*   *Literaturnoe nasledtsvo*, 60:1:76.
** There is some evidence originating with Mikhail Volkonsky, the son of the Decembrist, that "his father had been instructed to accept him (Pushkin) in the Society and that his father did not fulfill this," safeguarding the poet's talent (*Literaturnoe nasledstvo*, 58:163). If this is true, this evidence would most aptly be applied to the Odesa period, when Pushkin often met with Volkonsky.

The Union of Welfare's charter presented lofty ethical demands for potential members. However, the practice of accepting members was less strict: Vadkovsky[57] light-heartedly accepted Shervud[58] (whom he hardly knew himself); the latter turned out to be a traitor. Pestel covered the spending of official funds illegally spent by Mayboroda,[59] a captain of his regiment, and accepted the unreliable captain's membership in the Southern Society. Mayboroda repaid this with treachery, denouncing the society to the government. Even if we cast these telling occurrences aside, one could still point out that Pyotr Kaverin's reputation as a carouser, bretteur, and rogue did not prevent his being admitted to the society. One could cite other examples.

Pushkin's case was entirely different: what caused problems was precisely the richness and complexity of his personality. Pushkin's rigid political mentors felt that they were unable to control his behavior and that one could expect only the unexpected from him. They were in awe over Pushkin's poetry, but only partially, rejecting certain aspects of it. Similarly, from Pushkin's behavior they demanded more of that one-sidedness which they saw as foundational to civic heroism.

The rout of the Chişinău circle began in February 1822. An investigation was taken up against Orlov. Although he was formally suspended as the commander of the division only in April 1823, the "Orlov episode" was practically over by spring 1822. An atmosphere of surveillance, denunciations, and the destruction of the entire circle of friends and like-minded thinkers made Pushkin's stay in Chişinău exceptionally difficult, and he was obviously elated when he got the chance to transfer to service in Odesa.

In spring of 1823, the administrative structure of the Russian south was experiencing changes: the Novorossiysk general-governorship and Bessarabian viceregency were concentrated in one pair of hands. Mikhail Vorontsov was appointed the commander of the *krai* and his chancellery was moved to Odesa. Pushkin was assigned to Vorontsov's chancellery. On August 25, 1823, he wrote to his brother: "How I'd like, my soul, to write a whole novel for you about the last three months of my life. Here's the thing: my health has long demanded saltwater baths; with great effort I managed to convince Inzov to let me go to Odesa—I left my Moldova and appeared in Europe—the restaurants and Italian opera reminded me of the old days and, honest to God, refreshed my soul. Meanwhile, Vorontsov arrived and received me very nicely, and they informed me that I would be transferred to his administration, that I am to remain in Odesa" (13:66–67).

Pushkin stayed in Odesa until August 1, 1824. This short period of his life would turn out to be one of the most complex and contradictory.

To a superficial observer Pushkin was taken in by the pleasures of life in a big city with restaurants, a theater, Italian opera, a brilliant and diverse society that starkly contrasted with the provincial life in Chișinău. With its social connections and theater life, Odesa recalled Petersburg; with its unconstrained society of military liberals it recalled Kyiv, Chișinău, and Kamenka; and with the sea, the French and Italian spoken in the streets, the French newspapers circulating without censorship, and duty-free wine, it reminded one of Europe. The life took Pushkin in its embrace.

> As it happens, at dawn
> When the cannon sounds from a ship,
> I run down the steep bank
> And head to the sea.
> Then, with a hot pipe in hand,
> Enlivened by the salty waves,
> Like a Muslim in his paradise,
> I drink of my thick eastern coffee.
> I take a stroll. Already the benevolent
> Casino opens; the clinking of cups
> Is heard there; out on the balcony
> The billiard marker steps out, half asleep,
> With broom in hand, and by the porch,
> Two merchants have just met.
> And suddenly the square is bright with colors.
> All comes to life; and here and there
> Some rush with business, some without,

> But mainly with business.
> A child of calculation and courage,
> The merchant goes to watch the flags,
> To find out whether the heavens
> Have sent him familiar sails.
> What new goods
> Have entered during this quarantine?
> Have the barrels of expected wine arrived?
> And what of the plague? And where the fires?
> And is there famine or war
> Or some similar news?
> But we, lads, without sorrow,
> Amongst the solicitous merchants,
> Only await our oysters
> As they travel from banks of Tsargrad.*
> What of the oysters? They've come! Oh joy!
> Gluttonous youth flies
> To swallow from the sea-shells
> These fat and lively recluses
> Lightly drizzled in lemon juice.
> Noise, arguments—a light wine
> Brought up from the cellars
> To the table by hospitable Othon.**
> The hours fly by band our frightful tally
> In the meantime grows imperceptibly.
> But the evening darkens so blue,
> It's time for us to go to the Opera… (6:203–204)

The picture Pushkin paints of his life in Odesa is certainly accurate—such was the reality in which he dwelled. But this was not the only reality; it was, so to speak, a poetical-holiday reality. There was also a prosaic reality that could not have looked more different. First and foremost, Pushkin was tormented by the poverty which he felt much more acutely in Odesa than he did in Chișinău, where he could always dine with Inzov, Orlov, Krupensky,[60] Bologovsky,[61] where life was more patriarchal, where there were fewer

---

*   A somewhat archaic name for Istanbul (Constantinople) (Translator's note).
** A famous restauranteur in Odesa (Pushkin's commentary).

temptations, and where a softened semi-shared sense of poverty could don poetic garments with much greater ease. In Chișinău, poverty reminded him of poetry, in Odesa, unpaid debts.

Pushkin wrote to his brother:

> Let my father know that I can't live without his money. With the current censorship, it's impossible to live by the pen; I have never learned the carpenter's craft;* I can't become a teacher, although I know religious law and the first four rules, but I serve [...] not of my own volition—and resignation is impossible. Everything and everyone deceives me—whom can I depend on, it would seem, if not on my loved ones. I won't live on Vorontsov's bread—I don't want to and that's it—an extreme might lead to an extreme (13:67).

Several months later, also to his brother:

> If only I had money, but where can I get it? As far as fame is concerned, it's difficult in Russia to be satisfied with it. Russian fame is flattering some V. Kozlov** whom his Petersburg acquaintances flatter, but any half-decent person would despise both of them. *Mais pourquoi chantais-tu?* [but why do you sing? (Fr.)—Lotman] I respond to Lamartine's[62] questions: I sing like a baker bakes, like a tailor sews, like Kozlov writes, like an apothecary poisons—for money, for money, for money—such am I in the nakedness of my cynicism (13:86).

---

*   The noxious nature of the hint contained in Pushkin's claims of having not learned the carpenter's craft are revealed when one considers that Mikhail Vorontsov had learned the carpenter's craft in his childhood. His father, the Russian ambassador to England, wrote on September 2/13, 1792, from Richmond to his brother in Russia regarding the inevitability of a Russian revolution: "We won't see it, neither you nor I, but my son will. Therefore, I've decided to train him in some craft, either as a welder or a carpenter, so that when his vassals come to him and say that they don't want to know him anymore or that they want to divide his lands amongst themselves, he would be able to earn a living with his labor and have the honor of becoming a member of the future Penza or Dmitrov municipality." The fact that Vorontsov had learned the carpenter's trade was evidently discussed in his Odesan circles and was known to Pushkin, who regarded it ironically.

**   Vasily Kozlov was a minor writer (not to be confused with the famous blind Romantic poet, Ivan Kozlov!).

To Vyazemsky, with a request to swiftly send along his royalties:

> [S]end them here. There is no reason for them to earn interest. They won't stay long with me, though I'm truly no spendthrift. I'll pay off my old debts and start writing a new epic. Thankfully, I don't belong to our writers of the 18th century: I write for myself and publish for money, and not for the smiles of the fair sex (13:89).

The prosaic life of Odesa involved dust, dirt, a lack of water; and the poetic life—the sea, wine, opera, and women. Both were real, and it was possible to exist in both, depending on how linguistic and experiential styles were shifted.

There was also a world of care and disillusion more bitter and tormenting. It was this that gave Pushkin's time in Odesa its chief coloring.

The above-cited line from a description of Odesa dialogues—"And where's the plague? And where are the fires?"—initially read as follows in the manuscripts: "And where are the Cortes and the fires?" The Cortes are the Spanish parliament that was convened after the revolution led by Rafael del Riego.[63] Conversations on this topic were not happy for Pushkin. The revolution was quashed by a French military intervention conducted at the command of the Holy Alliance. Riego was hanged despite the oath given by the Spanish king. Dmitriev-Mamonov wrote Orlov: "Saving t[yrants] is like forging chains for yourself heavier than the ones you want to destroy. What about the Cortes! They've been exiled, tortured, condemned to death, and by whom? By the brute whose crown they saved!"*

His remarks on the Greek rebellion were also tinged with bitterness. "Greece disgusts me," Pushkin wrote to Vyazemsky (13:99). Among his friends there were even rumors that Pushkin had become an enemy of the Greek rebellion, and he was forced to explain his position: "The matter of Greece rouses my deepest sympathies which is precisely why I'm bitter seeing

---

* *Iz pisem i pokazanii dekabristov*, 153.

how these miserable people have been tasked with the sacred responsibility of defending liberty" (To Vasily Davydov [?], 13:105 and 529).

Nonetheless, the main source of Pushkin's disillusion and bitterness was elsewhere: it is difficult to overstate how shocked Pushkin was by the rout of the Chișinău circle, Raevsky's arrest, and Orlov's suspension, the spectacle of open violence and lawlessness on the part of the regime, cowardice and treachery from people that a day prior seemed like-minded comrades or, at the very least, decent people.

In order to properly convey the degree to which Pushkin was struck by the rebellion's rout, let us cite one particular occurrence. In the latter half of January 1824, Pushkin went on a tour of Bessarabia together with his friend Liprandi.[64] When they were in Tiraspol, where Vladimir Raevsky was languishing in the fortress' prison, Pushkin received an offer from General Sabaneev, Raevsky's main enemy and the person conducting the case against him, to visit his friend in prison. The offer was made during a friendly dinner (Liprandi's brother[65] was Sabaneev's adjutant and a trusted advisor; he introduced Pushkin to the general). Liprandi, recounting this occasion in his memoirs, confirms that the offer "was made by Sabaneev with the earnest desire to please him (Pushkin) and Raevsky."* The temptation was certainly very strong, but Pushkin categorically rejected the offer. Much must have been taking place in Pushkin's soul in order that he, a person inherently trusting, exhibited (here entirely well-founded) suspicion in this situation, correctly diving a provocation. Moreover, when Liprandi later asked him why he declined the general's offer, Pushkin answered ambiguously: he was likely also suspicious that Liprandi would betray him (he was perhaps justified in this as well).**

---

*   *Contemporaries*, 1:337.
** See Bazanov, *Raevskii*, 9–20.

Betrayal and treachery became a constant theme in Pushkin's thoughts. Later, reflecting on this period, Pushkin would write:

> I espied...
> A traitor in a comrade who shook
> My hand at a feast: any and all around me
> Seemed a traitor or an enemy. (3:996)

These moods were called forth not only by personal impressions: the rout of the Chișinău circle also coincided with a period of crisis in the development of the Decembrist movement. The disillusion with the strategy of longer-term propaganda (a position typical for the Union of Welfare) together with the Decembrists' pivot to tactics of military revolution created entirely new objectives, in light of which the separation of the leading men of the day from the people looked especially menacing. The solitary Romantic hero was chastised for his egoism and his inability to understand the people, whereas the people were rebuked for their slavish patience. The Enlightenment idea of the natural goodness and reason of humanity was subjected to a thoroughgoing doubt. All of this called forth a tragic mood amongst the Decembrists. Trubetskoy declared: "We cannot write a constitution in line with the spirit of the people, for we do not have sufficient knowledge of our Fatherland," and Pestel remarked to his confidante Baryatinsky,[66] "that he is quietly withdrawing from the society, because it is all child's play which could be fatal for us, and that they should do what they will." Bobrishchev-Pushkin "a year and a half or a bit earlier [...] began to seriously doubt" the tactics and success of the Decembrists' affairs.

A tragic mood seized the hearts of many leading public figures: on September 12, 1825, Griboedov wrote to his friend Stepan Begichev:[67] "It is time to die," hinting at the possibility of suicide.

In the context of these moods, the extreme pessimism of a number of Pushkin's own declarations becomes immediately clear:

Whoever has lived and thought cannot but
Despise people in his soul. (6:24)

[And I cast my gaze upon] the people,
I saw their haughty, base,
[Vicious], flippant judges,
Their fools, so near to wickedness.
Before their cowardly throng,
[Cruel], vain and cold
[The noble] [voice] of truth is [ridiculous]
And centuries-old experience in futile. (2:293)

These attitudes hold a prominent place in such Odesa-period poems as "Of freedom the solitary sower…," "The Demon," "The motionless sentinel slumbered at the royal threshold…," "Why where you sent here and who sent you?"*

---

* One of the chief issues for Pushkin, as for the Decembrist circles, was that of assessing Napoleon. In the Lyceum years, under the impression of other tendencies in society around the time of the War of 1812, Pushkin wrote "Napoleon on the Elba" (1815), filled with condemnations of Napoleon as a "ravager" who "shackled Europe in chains." However, during the reactionary years that followed the victory of the anti-Napoleonic allies, when the Holy Alliance was striving to restore the prerevolutionary order in Europe and establish it forever, Napoleon came to be reassessed as a "son of the revolution," who destroyed the feudal order in Europe. This notion was coupled with the Romantic image of the "man of fate," a demonic genius who had shocked the world with the sheer effort of his titanic will. As a result of these ideological shifts, critiques of Napoleon were no longer met with sympathy in leading circles, and Raevsky subjected Pushkin's "Napoleon on the Elba" to harsh and biting criticism.

However, the image of Napoleon upset the Decembrists for another reason as well. Amidst discussions of questions pertaining to tactics for the liberation movement, two tendencies could be discerned: the more moderate, which demanded that all revolutionary changes be conducted within strictly democratic procedures, and the more decisive, which insisted on the necessity of a revolutionary dictatorship. Proponents of the former pointed out that the French revolutionary dictatorship morphed into a military dictatorship, thus calling attention to the dangers of Bonapartism. Decembrists were especially troubled by the ambitiousness exemplified by Pestel and Mikhail Orlov. Certain moderate figures even instituted a secret system of surveillance over the former, fearing his attraction to power and dictatorial tendencies. Napoleon became the riddle posed to freedom lovers by history. The correct solution to the riddle, it seemed, would determine the fate of the Russian revolution. It tortured Pushkin as well: "Why were you sent here and who sent you?" (2:314). Pondering the lessons afforded by history vis-à-vis the fates of

Europe in the early nineteenth century, Pushkin had arrived at the following formula: the French Revolution of the eighteenth century, which was the natural result of the Enlightenment, had declared great truths:

> The *knizhniki* portended, [the tsars] grew alarmed,
> The crowds stirred before them
> The exposed altars stood desolate,
> [The tempest of freedom] loomed.
> And suddenly it came... the ancient tablets
> Fell in ashes and blood, and shattered. (2:314)

The *knizhniki* ('philosophes') were Enlightenment philosophers who undermined superstition and the moral power of the church ("the ... alters stood desolate"). "The ancient tablets" signify ancient laws destroyed by the revolution. However, the revolution did not bring about the triumph of virtue and the establishment of a Kingdom of Liberty. Freed from the "ancient tablets" of feudalism, the French had remained adherents to a slavish spirit, and when the "Man of Fate" arrived, they changed their old chains for new ones:

> The Man of Fate appeared, the slaves fell silent anew,
> The swords and chains sounded. (1:314)

> You quenched the thirst for power
> Amongst the slaves, 'til they were enraptured,
> Led their regiments into battle,
> Would wreathes around their chains. (1:214)

In Pushkin's mind, the historical results of Napoleon's rule were, on the one hand, the awakening of Russia which had fueled Decembrism ("He indicated the High Lot to the Russian people" (2:216)), and, on the other hand, the rise of a new type of European: the ambitious, calculating egoist:

> Proud and naked came Debauchery,
> And before [?] it [?] hearts froze,
> In exchange for power, the Fatherland was forgotten,
> In exchange for gold, brother sold brother.
> The madmen declared: there is no Liberty,
> And the people believed them.
> [And no different, in their words, were],
> Good and evil, everything turned to shadows—
> Everything was given over to disdain,
> As earthly dust is given over to the wind. (2:314)

The fifth and sixth lines are reformulations of scripture: "The madman denies God's existence in his heart" [Ps. 52:2–3—Transl.]. This is important context: Pushkin deifies Freedom in verses dedicated to the impossibility of establishing it in a world of egoism and self-interest. In later works (e.g. "To a Grandee"), the post-Napoleonic world of egotism would be directly defined as bourgeois in nature. This would become one of the keys to understanding Hermann in *The Queen of Spades*, itself coming to (parodic) fruition

In the memoiristic and scholarly literature there exists a widespread, narrowly biographical reading of the central poem of the cycle: "The Demon." Scholars have typically viewed it as a portrait of Alexander Raevsky, which Pushkin composed in the poem, according to Vigel. Such a reading is overly simplistic and does not account for how the creative process works in Pushkin's case, automatically subordination it to the vagaries of biography. If this had come from Pushkin's contemporaries, who were far from understanding the scale of Pushkin's creative accomplishment, it would be forgivable. They typically perceived him as a writer of poems "for friends and acquaintances." In Chişinău there was once a reader who, upon reading the following line from Pushkin's "The Black Shawl"—"The Armenian kissed the unfaithful maiden" (2:151)—took it to refer to himself and became angry with the poet.

The numerous remarks by Pushkin's contemporaries that he was describing in his verse some person well-known to him carries the same weight as the response of "The Black Shawl's" disgruntled reader. Among "the choir of contemporaries" there is one perspective which is typically left unaccounted for—that of Pushkin himself, who strongly disagreed with a simple biographical reading of this poem as a literary photograph of one of his acquaintances. Responding to a critic who hinted transparently in a journal that "Pushkin's Demon is not an imaginary creature,"* Pushkin wrote: "[I believe that the critic is mistaken.] Many are of the same opinion, with some even indicating the person whom Pushkin apparently wanted to depict in his strange poem.

---

with Gogol's Chichikov [in *Dead Souls*—Transl.] and tragic fruition with Dostoevsky's Raskolnikov [in *Crime and Punishment*—Transl.]. Chichikov's similarity to Napoleon is no coincidence. The image of Napoleon becomes one of the polysemantic symbols in Pushkin's consciousness that unifies the literary and scientific: historically it is tied to the birth of "the age of money"; psychologically, to endless ambition and hatred for people and morality; literarily, to Romantic demonism.

* See Boris Tomashevskii, "Commentary," in Aleksandr Pushkin, *Polnoe sobranie sochinenii*, vol. 7 (Moscow–Leningrad: Izdatel'stvo Akademii nauk SSSR, 1950), 662.

I think they are wrong; at the very least, I see a different objective in 'The Demon'—something more moral" (11:30). In general, a straightforward biographical reading of the poet's works is always risky: in the most dramatic moments of his time in Odesa, Pushkin created the idyllic stanzas of the second chapter of *Eugene Onegin*.

Pushkin's friendship with Alexander Raevsky left its mark on his life in Odesa, having defined his relationship to a wide range of Odesan society. Raevsky had arrived in Odesa a deeply unhappy and broken man. An excessive sense of ambition had been fostered in him from an early age: not yet seventeen years old he was hailed as a hero and a hero's son; at the age of twenty-two he was a colonel, becoming fully convinced that fate had allotted him a lofty career path. This idea was further nurtured by people surrounding him. In 1820, after having only just met Alexander Raevsky, Pushkin wrote that the latter "will be more than just famous" (13:19). Subsequently, there followed a deep sense of disillusionment: he lacked the necessary intelligence, strength of character, and courage to follow an unconventional path to success, and yet he despised official paths. Having found himself in the position of a mediocrity (though he was a clever person and not a mediocrity), he became bitter, secretly envying his father and probably Pushkin too for the latter's early success. He found some consolation in horrifying provincial ladies with his sharp tongue and Mephistophelean jests. In Odesa, he delighted in his scandalous fame as a violator of social convention and in the fear he caused among members of "polite" society.

Raevsky was tied to Pushkin through a sort of "play at friendship," which in Pushkin's mind was far removed from the friendships to which the poet had been accustomed to in Chişinău. Similarly, there existed between them a "play at literature," which was carried over into their daily lives. Each of the participants of this circle received a literary name, which would dictate his typical behavior, with their lives becoming transformed into an improvised drama. Raevsky was named "Melmoth." This name came from Charles Maturin's[68] novel, belonging to a wicked character who sold his soul to Satan, a destroyer of a pure female soul that could not resist his charms (the novel was a literary innovation during the time). This name forced Raevsky to adopt a "demonic" mode of behavior (another name given to Raevsky was "The Demon"). Other participants in this game also bore Romantic masks. Kyivan landlord Wacław Hański was deemed "Lara," Byron's demonic hero, and his wife Ewelina[69] was called "Atala" after the Romantic wild woman from Chateaubriand's[70] eponymous novel. Names from Pushkin's poetry were also widely adopted: one of the female participants of the game was called Tatyana (it is unclear who precisely). It seems that Pushkin also had such a name, though it remains unknown.

Playing out these Romantic roles in their lives, the participants of this game behaved boldly and provocatively in society, offending the petty feelings of decorum. All concepts were to be demonically inverted: love was to be rejected, but hatred was irresistible; friendship implied treachery. Thus, Pushkin wrote with pleasure in a letter to Raevsky about his "insidious" plans to "blacken" his "rival" in the eyes of their shared passion Karolina Sobańska:

> I won't show your epistle to Mme. Sobańska as I had initially intended to do, concealing only that which prompted your interest in the Melmoth character; so, here's what I plan to do. I will read her only fragments from your letter, with the necessary omissions. From my end, I have prepared a fulsome, beautiful response to your letter where I bash you just as much as you bashed me in your letter. I start by saying: "You shan't trick me, dearest Job Lovelace;* I see your vanity and weakness in your feigned cynicism [the 'treachery' here lies in revealing his friend's cynicism to have been contrived!—Lotman]," etc., with the rest in the same vein. Don't you think this will create an impression? (13:70–71 and 526).

---

* Job is a character from the Bible who bemoaned God's cruelty; Lovelace is the seducer character from Samuel Richardson's *Clarissa*—a typical instance of play with literary masks.

This game had different meanings for its different players. Raevsky treated it as an opportunity to occupy an extravagant position in society, which greatly soothed his offended pride. For Pushkin, this play at literary passions and treachery afforded him an escape from the world of real treachery which he glimpsed during his final months in Chișinău and which never left him in Odesa. This world of treachery was following everywhere on Pushkin's heels: behind the thin layer of "Byronism" and "Melmothism" was a true abyss of administrative and police demonism. Let us cite one example. In the just cited letter from Pushkin to Raevsky, Pushkin mentioned Karolina Sobańska, carelessly noting, "My passion has significantly weakened." This seems to have been highly unlikely. Later, after many years had passed, in 1830, on the eve of his wedding, he wrote to Sobańska: "Today marks nine years since the day I first saw you. That day was decisive in my life. The more I think about it, the more I become convinced that my existence is inextricably tied to yours; I was born to love you and follow you—any other care on my part is delusion or folly" (14: 62–63, 399). This was an earnest and passionate feeling on Pushkin's part. But who was this Karolina-Rosalia-Tekla Sobanskaya, née Rzewuska, Cerkovic by her second husband, and Lakura by her third? She was a Polish beauty from an educated and noble family, who received a brilliant education. Her praises had been sung by Mickiewicz,[71] who had been madly in love with her, and by Pushkin, whose debt to her involved "becoming drunk with a love most convulsive and torturous." She was also the lover and *political spy* of General Ivan Witt,[72] the governor of the southern military settlements. Witt, a personality dirty in all respects, entertained far-reaching ambitious designs. Having known of the existence of the secret society (Pestel had even hoped to bring him on as a co-conspirator and was prepared to marry his daughter, a pockmarked old-maid), he had been weighing to whom it would be most beneficial to sell out: the Decembrists to the government or, in the case of the former's triumph (which he didn't exclude), the government to the Decembrists. By his own initiative, he spied on Alexander and Nikolai Raevsky,

Mikhail Orlov, and Vasily Davydov, and then, at the decisive moment, sold them all out. A target of special surveillance for him was Pushkin, to whom he attached a spy (Boshnyak[73]) even at Mikhailovskoe, a place far removed from his administrative sphere. Sobańska, a society lady, the sister of Balzac's[74] lover, then wife, was also Witt's spy, gathering information on Mickiewicz and Pushkin.* How naive seem the salon "treacheries" of the Melmoths and Demons of Odesan society in 1824 compared to such real treachery!

The game, however, turned out to be an unreliable escape. The thirst for real life; a life free, bright, inaccessible to political calculations; a life elemental and thus true (its parallel was the image of the sea in poetry)—all this poured itself out into that profound need to love that consumed Pushkin in Odesa.

The structure of life in Pushkin's time was such that love occupied an exceptional position. Love was the main content of a maiden's life until she got married, filling the thoughts of a young society woman. It was a natural and central subject in discussions amongst women and it imbued poetry with itself. It required both the ritual process of falling in love and the carrying out of the rites of confessing one's love, writing love-letters, etc. All of this had well-developed forms of "the science of tender passion," and, as a rule, was far removed from actual passion. Pushkin had paid an early and abundant tribute to this life of the heart which, to a significant degree, was a ritualized game.

According to the authoritative testimony of Maria Volkonskaya, "as a poet, [Pushkin] considered it his obligation to fall in love with all pretty women and young girls whom he met. [...] In essence, he only loved his muse and poeticized everything he saw."** Such is the testimony given by this intelligent woman whom many scholars have nominated as Pushkin's "secret love." Here

---

*   Later she served as a spy for Benckendorf. Exiled from Russia after the Polish Revolt of 1830, once she had lost the trust of Benckendorf, who had suspected her of sympathy to the Polish cause, she bitterly complained of the Russian government's ungratefulness.

**   *Contemporaries*, 1:214–215.

is another observation from Liprandi who had been closely acquainted with the poet in Chișinău: "Pushkin loved all good-looking and liberal chatterboxes."* All of this makes Pushkin's truly profound Odesa passions all the more striking. His love for Sobańska, Amalia Riznich,[75] and Elizaveta Vorontsova[76] so passionately and tormentingly filled his short time in Odesa that it is psychologically impossible to suppose the absence of a connection between such extreme emotional tension and the intellectual and cultural crises that Pushkin faced during this time.

Pushkin met Amalia Riznich, the twenty-year-old wife of an Odesan commersant in July 1823 and experienced a strong if, apparently, short-lived love for her. Riznich was tall with wonderfully expressive eyes and a long black braid; she dressed extravagantly, donning exorbitantly long dresses and men's hats with gigantic brims. Scholars have struggled to determine which poems from this period are connected to these feelings of Pushkin's. Among these, the poem written on her death (she died in 1825, in poverty in Italy) "Under the blue sky of your native country..." must be included, as well as possibly "For the shores of a distant fatherland..."

Undoubtedly, the following humorous verses from *Fragments from Onegin's Travels* refer to her:

> And the lair, where dazzling with beauty,
> The young negress,
> Selfish and languid,
> Is surrounded by a throng of slaves?
> She heeds and does not heed
> The cavatina and the pleas,
> Or the joke that's part flattery...
> While in a corner her husband dozes. (6:205)

So too refer to her the following totally serious verses, which the poet deleted from *Onegin* due to their deeply intimate nature:

---

*   *Contemporaries*, 1:290.

> I should not like to trouble
> The peace of the grave with vain reproof;
> You are gone, O you, to whom
> I, in my tempestuous youth,
> Was indebted for bitter experience
> And a sensuous instant of paradise.
> As a sickly child is instructed,
> You, clouding my tender soul,
> Taught it deep bitterness.
> You roused my blood with bliss,
> Caused love to stir within it
> And brutal jealousy to seethe. (6:611)

In early May 1824, Riznich left Odesa. By this point, Pushkin's feelings towards her had been displaced in his soul by feelings for others no less tumultuous.

Elizaveta Vorontsova (née Countess Branicki) was the wife of Pushkin's superior, Mikhail Vorontsov. She was seven years older than the poet, which was certainly significant, as Pushkin was 25 at the time. She appeared younger, however, was pretty and had the graceful charm of a Polish woman of society. Pushkin met her in autumn 1823. The attention he was used to bestowing upon young, good-looking women quickly turned into a deep and serious attachment. However, among the various claims made by memoirists and biographers, it is difficult to tell truth from fable when it comes to Pushkin and Vorontsova. Perhaps the most reliable source is that of Vera Vyazemskaya,[77] the wife of Prince Vyazemsky, Pushkin's close friend. She wrote the following when informing her husband about Pushkin's departure from Odesa: "I was the only one he trusted with his disappointments and I bore witness to his weakness, because he was distraught by having to leave Odesa, in particular due to a certain feeling that grew within him during his last days, as can happen. Don't say anything about this; once we meet, we can discuss this less opaquely; there are reasons to end these conversation. Be quiet, although this is all very chaste and serious, but only on his end."*

Pushkin's love for Vorontsova became intertwined with struggles of an entirely different nature: his relationship with his superior was pulled into a tight, inextricable knot. Vorontsov's jealousy only colored this conflict slightly; its roots lay elsewhere.

Among the myriad events, conflicts, and clashes of Pushkin's life one unchanging feeling prevails: that of his personal dignity. For him, it lay at the heart of his social ideals, for if one did not believe in one's own value, there could be no talk of freedom, neither public nor private. It was this feeling of self-worth that defined Pushkin's behavior both amongst his friends and his foes. This feeling of self-worth determined his readiness to spill blood at any moment, defend his honor, and magnificently stand his ground with a dueling pistol aimed directly at him (the usual distance between opponents at duels in Russia was short—from six to twelve paces). His feeling of self-worth motivated him to struggle for his compensation as a writer, because he clearly understood that "poetic" poverty, as it was conceived of in literature, in reality simply meant being deprived of independence—for Pushkin a synonym of honor. Thus it was, on this basis, inevitable that Vorontsov and Pushkin would clash.

Mikhail Vorontsov was the son of the Russian ambassador to England, Semen Vorontsov,[78] an Anglophile and often critical voice. He was educated in England. He participated in the military campaigns of 1812–1814 and bravely fought at Borodino. In 1815–1818, he commanded a Russian division in France and made a name for himself as a liberal and even oppositional military commander, having been the first commander in the history of the Russian army to repeal corporal punishment throughout the ranks. Alexander I was

---

* Letter by Vera Viazemskaia to Petr Viazemskii, 1 August, 1824, Item 3275, Inventory 1, Collection 195, Tsentral'nyi Gosudarstvennyi Arkhiv Literatury i Iskusstva, St. Petersburg, Russia, quoted in Tatiana Tsiavlovskaia, *Khrani menia, moi talisman* ["Safeguard me, my talisman"], *Prometei*, vol. 10 (1974): 30.

suspicious of him, whereas liberals in the early 1820s were largely sympathetic. In his heart, however, Vorontsov was unprincipled and arrogant toward those he commanded. Decembrist Sergei Volkonsky[79] characterized him as a "person with insatiable vanity, incapable of working with others, ungrateful to those who helped him in any way, and careless with his means."*

1822–1823 became a turning point for Vorontsov: the time that was safe or even advantageous for liberal careerists was coming to an end. One was forced to choose between the road that led to the scaffold and the road that led to steps of the Winter Palace and Arakcheev's chambers. The Decembrists chose one path, whereas their kind acquaintances, associates, and even friends like Kiselyov and Vorontsov chose a different one. When the emperor traveled to the south in 1824, Vorontsov shocked all who were in attendance with his servility that crossed the limits of propriety. Vorontsov was arrogant, proud, and behaved more like an English lord than a Russian general, but he lacked a feeling of self-worth. Such was the man who became Pushkin's immediate superior.

Vorontsov had no intention of offending Pushkin: quite the opposite, he adopted his customary condescendingly benevolent tone which simultaneously affirmed the courtesy of a superior and the requisite distance between him and his subordinates. Pushkin called this the tone of "the offensive courtesy of a time server." To Vorontsov, poetry was nonsense. Vigel recorded the following conversation with Vorontsov in his papers: "He said to me once, 'It seems like you like Pushkin: would you mind inclining him towards some more productive activity under your supervision?' 'Please, such people are only capable of being great poets,' I responded. 'Then what are they good for?' he responded to me."** Pushkin sharply and scrupulously defended his dignity against the grandee's attacks. This brought on complications that were further

---

*   Sergei Volkonskii, *Zapiski* [Notes] (St. Petersburg: Sinodal'naia Tipografiia, 1902), 325.
**   *Contemporaries*, 1:227.

complicated by jealousy. Pushkin wrote to Alexander Turgenev: "Vorontsov is a vandal, a court cad, and a petty egoist. He sees a collegiate secretary in me, whereas I, I confess, see myself otherwise" (13:103).

Vorontsov, who felt himself no match for his opponent's wit and talent, but who also refused to view him as anything more than a lowly bureaucrat in his offices, eventually began to denounce Pushkin to his superiors. While preserving a liberal mask, he assured their acquaintances that he had the poet's best interests in mind: "Pushkin, instead of learning and working, will stray from the path even more. Seeing as I have nothing to rebuke him for except idleness, I will give a good review of him to Nesselrode[80] and ask the latter to be well-inclined towards him."* Vorontsov surrounded Pushkin with a network of spies, read his letters, and constantly set the St. Petersburg authorities against him. The conflict over the assignment to "inspect the locusts" had been prompted by Vorontsov. Pushkin tried to resign, but in his position as a disgraced bureaucrat this could only be interpreted as insolence and rebellion.

Such was the situation when the Moscow police read Pushkin's letter in which he confessed to being intrigued by "atheistic teachings." That was enough. On July 8, 1824, Pushkin was removed from his duties through an order from the high authority. On July 12, Nesselrode, the minister of foreign affairs, informed the Governor-general of Estland and Lifland[81] that by the emperor's decree, Pushkin was relieved of his official duties and would be exiled to the Pskov region. On August 1, 1824, Pushkin, accompanied by his peasant caretaker, Nikita Kozlov, left Odesa.

During the period of his southern exile, Pushkin's name became famous to the entire reading public of Russia. He found out what success and fame meant. The basis for his renown was formed by his long poems, which would later be called his "southern poems," due to their place of composition, as well

---

* *Literaturnoe nasledstvo*, 58:42.

as to their specifically "southern" Romantic atmosphere, which reminded readers of Byron's "eastern poems."

On February 20, 1821, Pushkin concluded *The Prisoner of the Caucasus* (published 1822); throughout 1821–1822, he worked on *The Robber Brothers*; during summer 1823, he finished working on *The Fountain of Bakhchisarai*. These long poems, all unified by a common Romantic spirit, prompted heated critical discussions and brought Pushkin the unequivocal recognition of his readers.

"These poems were being read by all literate Russia; they went about in notebooks, were rewritten by young women, by lovers of verse, by schoolboys at their desks, hiding from their teacher's gaze, by merchants sitting in their stalls."*

Pushkin became famous as "the singer of the Caucasus" and the idol of the Romantic youth. Pushkin was outrunning his fame, however: on May 9, 1823, breaking his ties with literary Romanticism, he began work on *Eugene Onegin* and, at the end of same year, on *The Gypsies*. His creative work sought out new paths. And this new creativity demanded a new sensibility. A long-developing biographical catastrophe sped up this process.

His months in Odesa were reminiscent of a plot-filled adventure novel: interactions with political conspirators, with a network of spies cast about; love and jealousy; a lofty persecutor; the help of women in love with him; plans to escape abroad (Vera Vyazemskaya even secured funds for Pushkin to put this plan into action); and in the background the faces of all social classes and nationalities, including "a retired corsair," Ali the Moor, in Cossack pantaloons and a pistol in his belt, whose society Pushkin liked to frequent. Now, the stage decorations have been changed: the road stretched out before Pushkin again. That road led home. Up ahead lay his quiet Mikhailovskoe estate.

---

*   Vissarion Belinskii, *Polnoe sobranie sochinenii* [Complete Collected Works], vol. 7 (Moscow: Izdatel'stvo Akademii nauk, 1955), 320.

Chapter Four

Mikhailovskoe, 1824–1826

Pushkin arrived at his Mikhailovskoe estate on August 9, 1824. In his manuscripts to *Onegin's Travels*, he wrote:

> I, from the lovely southern ladies
> From the [plump] Black Sea oysters,
> From the opera, from the dark boxes,
> And, thank God, from the grandees,
> Have left for the shadowy Trigorsky woods,
> For a far-off, northern district,
> And gloomy was my arrival. (6:505)

Pushkin's arrival was truly gloomy. He had grown tired from his wanderings and poverty. The "home" to which he had been sent was, strictly speaking, a place of exile. As if to underscore the unnaturalness of such a combination, the poet's father had the indecency to take upon himself the responsibility of maintaining surveillance over his exiled son. This led to exceptionally heated conflicts between father and son and, eventually, to the departures from Mikhailovskoe of the poet's father, mother, brother, and sister. Pushkin was left alone at Mikhailovskoe in the company of his childhood nanny, Arina Rodionovna.

The exile at Mikhailovskoe was a harsh ordeal: separation from his beloved, loneliness, financial troubles, the absence of stimulating conversation, friends, entertainment had the potential to turn Pushkin's life into a continuous moral torture. Vyazemsky wrote that in order to withstand such torment one had to be "an epic hero of the spirit" and he was seriously concerned that Pushkin would lose his mind or take to drink. Pushkin, however, possessed a dynamic genius capable of breathing life into his surroundings: instead of submitting to his surroundings, he transformed them.

Pushkin's stay in Mikhailovskoe was enforced and was, on occasion, unbearably sorrowful. By temperament, the poet adored merriment, crowds, friendly circles, and lively conversations. This enforced loneliness, daily monotony, and the dependence his rural life had on the whims of the weather—all of these things were unfamiliar and sometimes torturous for him. Nonetheless, it can rightly be said that Pushkin's time at Mikhailovskoe was not only productive for him as a poet, but also life-saving for him as a person.

Pushkin's life in Mikhailovskoe became the reverse of everything he had been used to up to that point. Instead of crowds of acquaintances and expended energy, loneliness and concentration. His everyday life was impoverished, but not nomadic, following a firmly established, longstanding routine. "Events" were rare and rare and measured on an entirely different domestic, even room-sized, scale: the receipt of letters or a trip to Trigorskoe would become adventures that colored moods for days, and sometimes weeks.

But the chief event, the main sphere of activity throughout this period, was Pushkin's creative work. The poet's activity now transferred itself deep into his psyche. In this state of concentration on self, the external and enforced circumstances of biography became integrated with the immanent, organic demands of art. All of this was colored in distinct tones thanks to the unexpected shift in impressions brought about by living in a different landscape (Pushkin left Odesa in the hottest part of the southern summer, whereas his first impression of northern nature after not having seen it for four years was that of autumn). Folk living and folk poetry, the atmosphere of the provincial gentry's quaint and quiet cultural nests—so far removed from the bureaucratic primness of the "milords Worontsovys'"* (sic!)—struck him upon his arrival

---

*   Lotman remarks here that in the Russian, Pushkin writes Vorontsov's surname in a contrived English manner (Translator's note).

and imparted a special tone to his Mikhailovskoe exile. In his development as a writer, much of this was tied to the impressions of daily life that surrounded him; the very landscapes and details of this life looked different to Pushkin because he now viewed them through the eyes of a realist. Here what were causes and what effects were constantly changing places.

The turnabout that took place in Pushkin's writing in Mikhailovskoe and that expressed itself in the penning of works with a definite realist quality, had been prepared for not only by the poet's earlier creative work, but also by his complex lived experience. The experiences of Pushkin the person exerted an exceptionally powerful influence on his creative work. This influence, however, was not as simplistic as that imagined by Pushkin scholar Mikhail Gershenzon,[1] who sincerely believed that if a poem was written about the winter, then Pushkin must have been looking at snow as he composed it; however, when confronted with the dating—*September 7. Boldino*—of the autograph of the poem "Demons," Gershenzon concluded that the landscape is not real, but allegorical. The logic is as follows: he saw snow, he wrote about snow, he felt the approach of love (despite Pushkin's own admission: "I, in loving, was deaf and dumb. Love passed, and [then] the Muse appeared"), he wrote that he recognized "these omens." All it takes is an elementary acquaintance with psychology to understand that even the process of baking pirozhki (meat pies) or cutting leather boots requires more complex cognitive mechanisms. Let alone the psychology of artistic creation.

The connection between personal impressions and artistic creations is significantly more complex. On the one hand, the sphere of a poet's personal life experience is more fluid and "random" than the domain of an era's collective experience, which determines the appearance of such phenomena as "Romanticism" or "Realism." This makes that personal sphere more dynamic, more fluid. On the other hand, such phenomena as "Romanticism" (or its artistic offshoots), belonging to the facts of an era, influence the personal behavior of the poet and, in turn, become facts of his own biography. It is here that a countervailing process enters the action. A crucial element of creative work is self-observation; in creating imaginary situations and imaginary characters, the poet sometimes lives their lives. Thus, when embodying the poet's actual behavior, this or that norm of cultural existence becomes simultaneously for him both the object of observation and of distanced analysis. This is a step in the direction of turning from the author's position to that of being a theme in his work. Embodiment in life becomes a step toward depiction in literature. In this regard, Pushkin's "southern period" was like a grand school for him.

Romantic behavior required that one conduct oneself in life in accordance with a certain literary model which became a mask or double of the given person. Everything that was quotidian, simple, extraliterary was studiously eliminated from real life; if eliminating it proved to be impossible, one sought to ignore it, for it was "improper" to speak of it.

Such a literary mask became a person's constant companion, a second personality. With its help, the Romantic was able to understand himself better and present a public face, suggesting that others interpret his character in accordance with this mask. It was not only Pushkin's Tatyana who "imagined herself the heroine / of her beloved creators," many young people of the 1820s behaved similarly. Let us cite an example: in 1828, Anna Olenina,[2] a young lady not yet twenty years old, freed herself of a childhood infatuation with Alexei Lobanov-Rostovsky[3] (he was a widower, twenty years her senior; the infatuation bore a bookish Romantic nature and was entirely Platonic). Analyzing her feelings, she wrote the following in her diary:

> *June 20. Priiutino.*
> How much have you, in so few days,
> Managed to feel and experience!
> In the rebellious fire of passions
> How terribly did you burn!
> The slave of a wearisome dream,
> In the anguish of the soul's void
> What could your soul still desire?

As penance, you wail
And, as madness, you laugh.

Such was the real state of my heart at the end of the last troubled winter.*

The verses that Olenina quotes, originally dedicated to the famous beauty Agrafena Zakrevskaya,[4] known for her explicit and scandalous love affairs, were penned by Baratynsky. Zakrevskaya, the object of Pushkin's, Baratynsky's, and Vyazemsky's romantic feelings, was a woman of nearly thirty who figured in poetry of the time as the epitome of the turbulent Romantic heroine. Pushkin, in his verse, called her "a lawless comet" and used her as a prototype for numerous female characters. Of course, Olenina with her dreamy, childlike

---

* Contemporaries, 1:266. In this regard, the manner in which the Decembrist Pyotr Kakhovsky confessed his love to Sofia Saltykova (Delvig's future wife) is characteristic: in order to express his feelings and find words appropriate for them, he found it necessary to place himself in the position of literary heroes from Romantic poems and to quote famous poetic texts. The confession went as follows: "On that day, he read a multitude of poems, and I [Saltykova] helped him when he would forget a line, declaiming:

> By an unfathomable, wondrous power
> My whole being is drawn to you—

I almost committed a great faux pas; if I had not remembered myself and said what I had thought at the moment, I would have perished. Here's what it was:

> I love you, dear Kakhovsky,
> My soul is intoxicated with you...

Thankfully, I responded with 'prisoner' [the word from the original poem—Transl.], to which he responded in kind with a glowing look and a joyous voice:

> Hope, you are my goddess,
> Hope, a ray of light in my soul!"

And here's the parting: "He would not release my hand which he held tightly. A poem which he had frequently quoted could have well applied to me at the moment:

> Pale, like a shadow, she trembled;
> In the hand of her lover lay
> Her cold hand..."

(Boris Modzalevskii, *Roman dekabrista Kakhovskogo, kaznennogo 13 iunia 1826 g.* [The Romance of Decembrist Kakhovsky, Executed on June 13, 1826] (Leningrad: Gosudarstvennoe izdatel'stvo, 1926), 61, 67.)

infatuations had nothing psychologically in common with either Zakrevskaya or the woman in Baratynsky's poem. This, however, in no way prevented Olenina from identifying herself with such a literary mask and seriously trying to play out the role of the *femme fatale*.

Romantic behavior required that one grow into one's literary mask, as opposed to changing it. A poet was to forever be a poet, a melancholic, a melancholic; an enthusiast, to endlessly demonstrate the fire in his soul; and a dreamer, to ever be submerged in despondent musings. In this regard, as we have observed, Pushkin's Romantic behavior in the south was already characterized by its originality: rather than involving a disposition towards a singular mode of behavior, it implied a whole set of potential "masks," which the poet varied, changing types of behavior. In Odesa, when the shift in styles of behavior and the, as it were, "change of face" in Raevsky's company turned into its own idiosyncratic game, the very nature of Romantic behavior became a tangible fact of culture. This resulted in two consequences. On the one hand, the poet was able to observe Romantic psychology externally, as a mask that had been removed, which laid the groundwork for viewing the Romantic character at a distance and for understanding it objectively. On the other hand, it was precisely in everyday behavior that a "play with styles"—a rejection of Romantic egocentrism and the psychological possibility of accounting for another point of view—was formed.

Both these principles became critical to Pushkin's 'realist' work in the latter half of the 1820s and, most principally, to *Eugene Onegin*. The basic causes informing these principles lay in the sprawling processes of cultural movement, in the logic governing the development of the poet's creative thought, but the experience of shaping his personality also played a large role. The development of a "play with styles" in life and a play with contrasts in poetry had common psychological root and common goal—the path to simplicity.

As with other stages in his development as a person, here too Pushkin also reflected on what it meant to be a poet. Pushkin always constructed his personal life as that of a poet. And if Romanticism considered a poet to be a "strange person" (Lermontov's favorite expression), that is, a person fundamentally unlike those around him, then the central conviction for the Pushkin of the Mikhailovskoe period was the belief that a poet is "simply a person."

Now the poetic becomes identified with the ordinary, the everyday, whereas the exceptional appears contrived and theatrical—deprived of *truth* and poetry. Pushkin learns to observe the world through the perspective of another person, changing his point of view and, thus, himself changing, entering myriad different situations in his life. This is the *real-life* perceptual equivalent to literary realism.

This approach allowed one to find poetry and the sources of beauty, truth, and wisdom in places which, to the Romantic, would seem routine, mediocre, prosaic, and vulgar. The details of exile largely reverted to the background for Pushkin, while to the foreground there emerged in the rural life and northern landscape surrounding him the image of Home. This world was tinged with a poetics of the intimate, and though the poet's real childhood had nothing to do with Mikhailovskoe, it came to replace the lost childhood and the absent childhood memories. Pushkin's life at Mikhailovskoe was modest, even scanty. He did not occupy the front rooms of the house (admittedly, the master's house at Mikhailovskoe was small and unseemly; these rooms along the façade were only nominally "front rooms")—these latter were left locked and unheated through the winter, following the family's departure. Ivan Pushchin recalled:

> Alexander's room was next to the porch with a window overlooking the courtyard, through which he saw me when he heard the bell. In this small room (in Nikolai Ge's[5] famous painting *Pushchin visits Pushkin at Mikhailovskoe*, the room is presented far bigger than it was in real life— Lotman) there was a bed with a canopy, a writing desk, a bookshelf, and so on. Everywhere was a poetic disorder, with scattered sheets of paper covered in writing, and chewed and burnt pieces of feathers

were strewn about (he had always written with quills, which were barely able to be held in his fingers). The entrance to his room was straight from the corridor; across the hall was the door to his nanny's room.*

The rooms located in this part of the manor house were usually intended for children and servants (here, in particular, the girls' room was located); the adult nobles occupied the main rooms facing the facade. Apparently, Pushkin was placed in this room when he arrived from the south, and the house was occupied by his parents. But the fact that even after their departure he did not move to the formal rooms and stayed in the children's room (he did not even use the room with the billiard table, according to Pushchin's testimony), is as significant as the noticeable revival of "Lyceum memories"** during this period. It is as though a psychological return to childhood takes place.

Pushkin was known for monitoring his spiritual development and marking its milestones.*** In this respect, he decisively differed from poets such as Byron or Lermontov, whose spiritual ideal was characterized by constancy and who constructed their internal image as unchanging. However, for Pushkin, progress was conceived as a return. In the well-known poem "To ***" ("I remember a wonderful moment..."), there is a concept of spiritual development: the initial "pure" state of the soul—spiritual darkness—is a rebirth as a return to a bright beginning. This bright, "childlike" ideal of moral strivings also colored life at Mikhailovskoe.

---

*   *Contemporaries*, 1:106.

** It is indicative that it was precisely during this period that Pushkin first executed a retrospective poetic treatment of the Lyceum—"19 October" (1825). The only work related to earlier Lyceum anniversaries is perhaps the draft of his poem "I do not regret you, the years of my spring…"

*** Between stages in his development, Pushkin was apt to reassess everything he had written up to that point, compiling summary poetic collections. Thus plans for publications arose in 1820 (which did not come to fruition), 1824 (completed in 1824), and 1828 (published in 1829).

The poet's daily life was notably simple, completely devoid of any "landlord" responsibilities of activities. Even common activities for a nobleman in the countryside, such as hunting, were excluded from his existence.

Pushkin's chief activity at Mikhailovskoe was literature. The question of the poet's attitude towards life, towards other people, about the nature of poetic behavior and the relationship between the poetic and the real occupies him in two aspects: how to write and how to live. And again, everyday behavior precedes creativity, showing him the way. In Odesa, Pushkin discovered in his life a conscious stylistic "polyphony"—in Mikhailovskoe it entered his work. In Mikhailovskoe, Pushkin demonstratively defended his right to the prose of everyday life; literary prose came later, in his works of the late 1820s, triumphantly establishing itself in the Boldino autumn of 1830. Poetic behavior is "strange," unusual behavior that only exceptional personalities can carry out on the exceptional moments (therefore, "non-exceptional," prosaic moments from their lives are completely discarded: the life of a poetic personality consists as if of segments in which they are on stage, and in moments of prosaic revelations—he, like other people, needs to eat or spit—he as if goes behind the scenes and "ceases to exist"). Prosaic behavior is ordinary, natural, and in line with the behavior of other people. At the same time, it is connected to the fact that a person is not ashamed of ordinariness, internally does not oppose it to "lofty" life. No, simplicity itself is perceived as poetry. This view determined Pushkin's attitude towards the poet's fate. Here a combination of business professionalism with the idea of truth as the highest value predominates.

Romanticism, from this perspective, appeared as a system that foregrounded poses. In contrast to this, the reverse ideal involved a behavioral mode fundamentally opposed to posing and any preconceived role. This is not to say that the Romantic mode of behavior was forgotten, however. It would be preserved in the cultural arsenal (for instance, Pushkin would re-adopt it when faced with lighter and more superficial love affairs), but as a game; it would thenceforth be employed with a tinge of irony and parody.

Chapter Four. Mikhailovskoe, 1824–1826

On September 26, 1824, Pushkin wrote the poem titled "Conversation of a Bookseller with a Poet," which he published as a preface to a separate edition of the first chapter of *Eugene Onegin*. It was a declaration of the poet's right to a truthful and prosaic attitude towards life. The poem is written as a dialogue between a man of poetry (the Poet) and a man of prose (the Bookseller), in which the intersection of different views on poetry ends with an affirmation of simplicity as truth, the boldness of a free, unpretentious view of life:

> The Bookseller:
> […]
> Listen to the useful truth:
> Our age is a merchant; in this iron age
> There is no freedom without money.
> […]
> Let me just say to you:
> Inspiration is not for sale,
> But a manuscript can be sold.
> […]
> The Poet:
> You're absolutely right. Here's my manuscript. Let's make a deal.
> (2:329–330)

The time spent in Mikhailovskoe coincided with Pushkin's intense struggle for the professionalization of literary work. The question of royalties was dictated not by greed, but by the fight for at least that relative freedom and human dignity that material independence gave in Russia, with a conscious refusal of the traditional sources of existence for a Russian nobleman: service and landlord income.

During this period, Pushkin enthusiastically engaged in his publishing affairs. The collection entitled *Poems by Alexander Pushkin*, to which the author attached great literary (as well as commercial) value, demanded much effort. Firstly, Pushkin had to obtain a manuscript notebook of poems which he lost to Nikita Vsevolozhsky after incurring a loss of 1000 rubles in a card game. Following discussions facilitated through Alexander Bestuzhev and his brother, Pushkin recovered the notebook. The process of adding new poems and editing old ones began. On December 30, 1825, the book was published with an epigraph from the Roman poet Propertius,[6] which in translation reads: "A youth sings of love, whereas a man sings of troubles."

But the Latin word *tumultus* means not only "noise," "alarm," but also "riot," "rebellion," "uprising." The censor's approval for the book was given on October 8, 1825, but the poet had the opportunity to remove the epigraph, which after December 14, 1825 acquired dangerously relevant meaning. Karamzin, looking at the epigraph, was horrified and wrote to Pletnev: "What have you done? Why is a young man destroying himself?"* The collection, which includes, among others, the poems "André Chénier," "Bacchic Song," "Napoleon," "To Licinius," and a brilliant selection of love poetry, was published two weeks after the suppression of the uprising on Senate Square as a voice of hope, breaking the silence of the frozen literature. The unprecedented success of the collection among readers of the day is best evidenced by the fact that on February 27, 1826 (two months after the release of the collection), Pletnev wrote to Pushkin: "I no longer have a single copy of Alexander Pushkin's poems, and I congratulate him on that. More importantly, a war has begun among booksellers when they found out that they could no longer get anything from me" (13:263).

Poems by Alexander Pushkin went on sale on December 30, 1825. Their unprecedented success in the history of Russian literature was a public fact. Pushkin's verses inspired hope, reminding people of life. The way readers eagerly grabbed the thin volume of poems felt like a sign of the arrival of a new era: the opposition of solitary Romantic heroes had been dispersed by bayonets and bullets; now it was time for a different, more dangerous opposition

---

* Petr Bartenev, "Eshche novye pis'ma Pushkina" [More New Letters by Pushkin], in *Russkii arkhiv*, no. 7 (1870): 1366; quoted in *Letopis' zhizni i tvorchestva A. S. Pushkina, 1799–1826*, 588.

to the government—the anonymous and indestructible opposition of societal forces. And the fact that the first glance of this new societal resistance turned to Pushkin's lyrics was filled with deep historical significance. After all, there could have been a different reaction: a reader, oppressed by the gloomy atmosphere of the December 1825 capital, could have easily overlooked a small book of poems of 200 pages. There were surely more serious concerns at hand! But something else happened: in a difficult and tragic moment, the eyes of the Russian public turned hopefully to Pushkin.

During his years in exile in Mikhailovskoe, Pushkin became recognized as the first poet of Russia. The obligatory epithets of "the Lyceum Pushkin," "the nephew Pushkin," "the younger Pushkin" (to be distinguished from his uncle, the poet Vasily Pushkin) disappear when his name is mentioned in the correspondence of contemporaries. Now he simply becomes "Pushkin," and when referring to Vasily Pushkin, the explanatory "uncle" is added. The publication in March 1824 of *The Fountain of Bakhchisarai*, with an introduction by Vyazemsky; in February 1825, the first chapter of *Eugene Onegin*; and at the end of the same year, *Poems by Alexander Pushkin*, the journal polemics around these publications, the dissemination (mainly through his brother Lev, against the will of the poet himself) of his unpublished works, place him in a position significantly higher than other Russian poets. Delvig, in a letter dated September 28, 1824, calls his friend "the great Pushkin," and writes: "No one among Russian writers has turned our hearts of stone as you have" (13:110); and Zhukovsky in November of the same year expressed himself even more definitively: "You were born to be a great poet [...] By the authority given to me, I offer you the first place on the Russian Parnassus" (13:120).

Pushkin realized that this situation imposed a special responsibility on him, and he began preparing for a new role as an organizer of a literary movement. The Decembrists had a strong influence on the development of Russian journalism, but according to Pushkin, none of the existing journals at the time had a leading position in literature. The state of literary criticism also did not satisfy him. Ryleev's and Bestuzhev's yearly almanac *The Polar Star* had a significantly higher level of participation and a higher degree of literary orientation than all other journals. It began to be published in 1823 and brought together the most significant literary forces of that time. However, in 1824–1825, signs of a rift began to appear between the group, led by Ryleev-Bestuzhev, that had gathered strength around the idea of Decembrist citizenship, on one hand, and the moderately progressive poets such as Delvig, Baratynsky, and others. Delvig's organization of the almanac *Northern Flowers*, which competed with *The Polar Star*, contributed to the escalation of tensions. Both almanacs sought to secure Pushkin's participation.

In this, as in several other instances, Pushkin behaved deliberately and cautiously, consciously not associating himself with any literary groups or parties. At the same time, he firmly pursued *his* program, which mainly boiled down to the following: almanacs, small annual booklets, could not by their very nature be operational and capable of guiding literary publications. For this, a journal was needed. And Pushkin, anticipating the development of literature, began to promote the idea of creating a thick literary journal. He clearly wanted to concentrate the leadership of the journal in his own hands, but understood that such a publication should unite all of Russia's honest and talented writers (precisely *unification* was an important point of his program). The journal should not speak on behalf of any one group, but be an authoritative legislator of literary opinions. A special place would be given to criticism, and Pushkin began cautious negotiations with two of his friends—leading critics of two warring literary camps, Vyazemsky and Katenin—preparing for their unified presence in one journal. The literary defeat that followed December 14, 1825 thwarted these plans.

Isolated in the Pskov backwoods, Pushkin was tied to literary life only via his letters, which were read by sharp-eyed police officials, lost in the mail, or sent through friends. However, his main literary work was done at home, at his writing desk. In Mikhailovskoe, Pushkin wrote and read a great deal, listened carefully to the language and poetry of the people. In his letters, he often mentioned his laziness, his frequent horseback rides, saying little about his work, but he continuously asked for new books. In reality, he lived in an atmosphere of almost constant creative tension, writing and learning. During this time, he completed *The Gypsies*, wrote *Boris Godunov,* finished the third and wrote the fourth to sixth chapters of *Eugene Onegin, Count Nulin,* and several dozen poems, including such significant ones as "To the Sea" (completed in Mikhailovskoe), "Imitations of the Koran," "The Bridegroom," "19 October," "André Chénier," and many others.

Pushkin worked on several important literary-critical articles dedicated to the question of the folk nature of the literary language. His work on his notes was a great effort, which he destroyed after December 14, 1825. In addition to this, he worked on preparing a collection of poems for 1826 and an unfinished manuscript of epigrams. It is clear how intense Pushkin's literary life was during this period and how intense his daily work routine must have been. He read a lot during this time: Pushkin received a superficial and unsystematic education at the Lyceum; in the 1830s, however, he impressed his contemporaries with his deep and exceptionally broad knowledge of world literature, history, politics, and journalism. A sizable part of this knowledge was gained by him in Mikhailovskoe. Finally, we must consider his (nearly academic, by the standards of the time) interest in folklore, which he satisfied both with printed materials and by recording oral sources. He would write to his brother: "In the evening I listen to stories—this is how I compensate for the flaws in my damned upbringing. What a delight these fairy tales are! Each one is like an epic poem!" (13:121). Arina Rodionovna was, it would seem, a talented storyteller with an expressive manner of performance and wide-ranging repertoire.

This intense labor, which Pushkin concealed under the guise of "light idling," was not born simply of Pushkin's desire for education; he had a clear objective in mind. In St. Petersburg and in the south, Pushkin felt as though he was the pupil of his Decembrist friends. His intellectual efforts were directed towards "becoming the era's equal in enlightenment" (2:187), reaching the level of his teachers and gaining their recognition. However, the heavy thoughts visited upon Pushkin in 1823 led to deep doubts regarding the notion of a revolution without the people. At the same time, the Russian people stood out as a great riddle: their innate strength combined with their slavish patience was baffling.

The main idea of Pushkin's intellectual efforts at this time is focused on understanding the force without which any political protest is doomed in advance: the people. His position as a thinker is changing: in the south he was among a crowd of friends, and the main task was not to fall behind; now he realizes that he has broken ahead, that he is all alone on his intellectual path. In this position, Thought became his greatest weapon. In the south, the relationship between the poet and the politician was depicted as follows: the politician-conspirator knows the ways and the goals, and the poet, his assistant, spreads these ideas among readers, inspires and ignites fighters before the battle. His task is honorable, but the main work is done by Orlov or Pestel, Nikolai Turgenev or Nikita Muravyov. Now the picture is painted in a different light: the ways are yet to be known, the methods, to be weighed; the main thing is to understand what the people are and to be understood by them. In these conditions, thought becomes the most important action, and it is the poet-thinker, armed with the strict truth of his art, who turns into a lead fighter. Ryleev calls on Pushkin to write a poem in the spirit of the Decembrists: "... you are near Pskov: there the last flashes of Russian freedom were extinguished. The actual territory of inspiration. And will Pushkin really leave this land without an epic poem?" (13:133). Pushkin did not end up writing a long poem on the Pskov Republic, but he did write *Boris Godunov*, not a Romantic confession employing history as a means, but a drama-investigation. History, like folklore, turns out for Pushkin to be a path to understanding the psychology of the Russian people, and the historical past, studied without romantic bias, becomes a means of understanding the present.

Chapter Four. Mikhailovskoe, 1824–1826

It wasn't only books, among them, first of all, Karamzin's *The History of the Russian State*, it was also the surrounding area that was conductive to historical studies: the places around Mikhailovskoe were filled with memories of the Livonian War and Stephen Báthory's[7] siege of Pskov, while the Hannibal estates reminded one of the era of Peter the Great and the eighteenth century. Historical works, folk songs, and surrounding landscapes were all interconnected. *Boris Godunov* is a testament to the triumph of realism in Pushkin's work. Orienting himself on the Shakespearean tradition, Pushkin consciously rejected the Romantic tendency of turning characters into mouthpieces of their author's ideas. Vyazemsky wrote to Alexander Turgenev: "The truth is arresting, the soberness, the calm. It's difficult to discern the author at all. It is not a theatre of dolls on a string being moved along by some puppeteer."*
Boris Godunov is a tragedy that is simultaneously permeated with the spirit of the politics of Pushkin's day, as well as a faithful representation of the era described. Revealing the doomed nature of a political power divorced from its people, Pushkin captured at the same time the contradictory position of the people [narod], who possess in complex mixture both strength and weakness. The fates of all political powers are thus determined by "the people's opinion." However, the people's consciousness does not rise above condemning "King Herod" and contrasting him to the "murdered child." In reality the new tsar would also turn out to be a murderer. The people recoil from him in horror. And so the circle closes.

Boris Godunov was a drama-investigation. Among Pushkin's ideals regarding the poetic personality a new aspect had come to the forefront: the poet-thinker, the poet-scholar, like Karamzin, but combined with the poet who does not "think wise thoughts slyly," who, possessing a simple feeling of

---

* Petr Viazemskii, "*Pis'mo Aleksandru Turgenevu*" [Letter to Alexander Turgenev], Russkii arkhiv, no. 11 (1885): 39, quoted in Pushkin, *Polnoe sobranie sochinenii*, 7:421.

truth and morality approaches the "people's opinion," like a chronicler. Pushkin called the combination of these positions "Shakespeare's gaze."

This general change in the tone of life also influenced Pushkin's style of leisure. Never before had solitude occupied such a prominent place in his life: solitary horseback rides, solitary "two-ball" games of billiards, reading. Pushkin's circle during this time was almost entirely comprised of the neighboring landowning family of Praskovya Osipova.[8] Osipova at this point was just over forty years old. She was an intelligent, brilliantly educated woman from a cultured noble family. Her father, Alexander Vyndomsky,[9] worked at the *The Conversant Citizen* [Beseduiushchii Grazhdanin] journal and had personally known Novikov and Radishchev; he had also been a Freemason, and his books and papers were stored at Osipova's Trigorskoe estate. Osipova, who spoke foreign languages, kept up with literature.

The Trigorskoe library housed not only Russian books, but also the latest European literary novelties. The house was full of young people: Osipova had three sons from her first marriage to Nikolai Vulf,[10] the eldest of whom, Alexei,[11] became a close friend of Pushkin, and two daughters, Anna[12] and Evpraksiya.[13] The elder, Anna, was only six months younger than Pushkin, while Evpraksiya was ten years younger than him: in the autumn of 1824, she turned fifteen. In addition, from her second marriage, Osipova had two daughters aged four and one year. Furthermore, her stepdaughter, Alexandra,[14] who was nineteen years old, was also being raised in the house. Alexei Vulf, a student at the University of Derpt (now Tartu), would come home with his friend, the young poet Nikolai Yazykov, also a student at Derpt. Pushkin formed close relationships with this noisy and young family: he had a warm friendship with Praskovya Osipova throughout life, dedicated poems to the young ladies, was even alternately infatuated with Anna and Alexandra, measured waistlines with Evpraksiya, whose waist was slimmer, and praised the moonshine she made for friendly feasts. It was here, to Trigorskoe, that Pushkin's St. Petersburg acquaintance, the twenty-four-year-old Anna Kern,[15] Osipova's niece, would also come to visit. The beauty Kern (née Poltoratskaya) was married off at sixteen to an elderly general. By the time she arrived in Trigorskoe, she had already separated from her husband and had experienced several romantic affairs. In Trigorskoe-Mikhailovskoe, she had a passionate, albeit short-lived, romance with Pushkin. The story of this romance is very telling in what it shows about Pushkin's overall personal development as mirrored in his love life.

Anna Kern was not only a beautiful, but also a kind, sweet woman with an unhappy fate. Her true calling should have been a quiet family life, which she eventually achieved, marrying again, already after forty, and very happily. However, at the time when she met with Pushkin at Trigorskoe she was a woman who had left her husband and who enjoyed a rather ambivalent reputation. Pushkin fell in love with her. Pushkin's romantic behavior, however, still firmly adhered to those forms of conventional posing that had already been discarded in other spheres of life for the sake of simple self-expression. Precisely because romantic relationships between people are an area demanding true responsibility, where the most insignificant nuances of expression can receive serious significance, here what are especially convenient and what last longer are the familiar, readymade, and ritualized formulas and stylistic clichés.

Pushkin's sincere feelings towards Anna Kern, when he needed to express them on paper, were transformed in accordance with the conventional formulas of poeticized love. As soon as they were expressed in verse, this love became subordinated to the literary rules of Romantic love poetry, transforming Anna Kern into a "genius of pure beauty."* Meanwhile in letters to Kern herself Pushkin complained:

> What's the reason you're not naive? (13:214, 256)
> You are incapable or (what is worse) you don't want to have mercy on people. A pretty woman is her own mistress [sebe khoziaika] of course

---

*   The fact that Pushkin utilized a quote from Zhukovsky's poems "I, my young muse, it happened…" and "Lalla Rukh"—"Ah! She does not dwell amongst us / That genius of pure beauty"—additionally reinforces the notion of this image as literary convention.

[there is a pun in the original French that is difficult to translate here; "her own mistress" can also mean mistress in the romantic sense—Lotman], free to be someone's lover. Good Lord, I do not intend to preach you sermons, but you should still respect your husband, or else no one will want to be a husband. Do not diminish the importance of this métier too much; it has to exist in the world (13:212, 545).

In a letter to Alexei Vulf (whom he pretended to be jealous of), Pushkin wrote in a completely different, artificially rude tone characteristic of correspondence between men during the time, where he calls Kern "the whore of Babylon" (13:275). In one of his letters to Kern he even offers for her choosing two variations of a possible meeting (and he greatly desires a meeting!): a romantic meeting and a prosaic one. He writes:

If you're sick of your husband then leave him, but do you know how you should do it? You should abandon the whole family there, take the post horses to Ostrov [Anna Kern was in Riga at the time—Lotman] and you should travel... where? To Trigorskoe? Not at all: to Mikhailovskoe! This is a magnificent project that has been taunting my imagination for 15 minutes already. Can you imagine how happy I'd be? You'll tell me: "What if word gets out? What about a scandal?" The Devil take it! When one abandons one's husband, it's already a great scandal. Everything else that happens later on makes no difference or very little difference. You must agree that my project is truly Romantic! A similarity in characters, a disdain for obstacles, a highly developed capacity for flight.

In this letter Pushkin found a formula, clearer and more individualistic than what could be said in verse, for his attraction to Kern: "Disdain for obstacles, and a highly developed capacity for flight." Following the quoted passage, Pushkin continues to jokingly describe a Romantic plot wherein Kern breaks with her aunt, starts seeing her cousin at Trigorskoe in secret, etc. All of a sudden, Pushkin adopts a prosaic tone: "Let's talk seriously, that is, coldly: will I see you again?" (13:213–214 and 546).

In all of this there is a lot of play, coloring Pushkin's attitude towards the inhabitants of Trigorskoe. The time for a simple, unpretentious expression of his feelings towards women had not yet come for Pushkin. But there is something infinitely more serious here. Pushkin's personality is so rich that his experiences cannot be expressed in just one genre or stylistic plane. He simultaneously lives not one, but many lives: his Kern is "a genius of pure beauty," and "charm itself," and "lovely, divine," and "disgusting," and "the whore of Babylon," and a woman possessing "an organ of flight"—all are true and all express Pushkin's true feelings. Such richness of experience could only exist with a view of life that has been carried over from working on a page of a poetic manuscript. In life, a completed action cuts off all unrealized alternatives: having done one thing, it is no longer possible to do something opposite at the same time. Action takes away the freedom of choice. In working on a manuscript, one can develop one variant without crossing out another; one can return to the rejected variant and restore it; one can, having made a choice, simultaneously parody it on the same sheet of paper. This gives the life of the poetic imagination greater completeness and freedom than real life. Pushkin could not reconcile himself to any lack of freedom and transferred the freedom of poetry—its capacity, in realizing itself, to maintain a multifaceted existence—into reality.

In this sense, the fun, jokes, spoofs—the almost serious, serious, and completely serious love affairs—that were frothing over in Trigorskoe were full of meaning: here stood out, through the flair and ready-made clichés of Romantic collisions, the contours of that free, uninhibited life, following the laws of art, whose sketch the poet drafted in the poetic utopia of his later lyrics, at the very end of his journey—a life that had elevated itself to art.

But life in Pushkin's Mikhailovskoe exile was least of all reminiscent of a joyful idyll of love, play, and creativity. It was still exile, and at times it became unbearable for Pushkin. It is no coincidence that he contemplated plans to escape abroad through Derpt, constructing improbable plans for an operation on a fictitious "aneurysm in his leg," disguising himself as Vulf's servant, and so on.

The connection between one's native home, which is a place of refuge from wanderings and persecutions, and prison, which is a place of enforced stay, even the slightest time away from which could be viewed as an attempt to escape, was unnatural and therefore particularly difficult. "Home exile" was a torment. The years spent in Mikhailovskoe became for Pushkin a time when the ideal of a true native home, sanctified by love, became increasingly painful in the poet's consciousness. He now attributed the features of such a native nest to the Lyceum. In the Lyceum he saw a paternal home, and in the Lyceum students, brothers, forgetting that just a few years ago he had wholeheartedly strived to break free from his Tsarskoe Selo "cell." It was in Mikhailovskoe that Pushkin created verses in which everything related to a person's most intimate and secret attachments was devoted to the Lyceum ("19 October").

Moreover, the most exciting events were the visits to Mikhailovskoe of Lyceum friends: Ivan Pushchin (January 11, 1825) and Anton Delvig (April 1825). The arrival of Pushchin, who visited Pushkin first, required courage. Alexander Turgenev strongly advised Pushchin against this dangerous venture, and the poet's uncle, Vasily Pushkin, at first issued warnings, and then rushed to embrace him, like a hero, with tears. But Pushchin was not easily frightened: he had long been a member of a secret society, and on December 14, on Senate Square, he would show himself as one of the most cool-headed and active leaders of the uprising ("by the Imperial decree" of Nicholas I, he was sentenced to twenty years of hard labor).

However, Pushchin was not only courageous, but also remarkably kind. "Whoever loves Pushchin is already undoubtedly a rare person," Ryleev said about him.* In Siberia, Pushchin was called an "Old Lady Maremyan" for the way he cared for everyone—calling this manner of behavior "Maremianstvo" (it was especially comical to call him a woman's name because Pushchin was not only manly, he was also tall, well-built, and handsome deep into his

---

* Ryleev, *Polnoe sobranie sochinenii*, 491.

elderly years). And Pushchin showed tender care for Pushkin. The meeting was short, but the conversation was intense. The conversation turned to the secret society, and Pushchin did not hide his involvement from his friend. In the evening, Pushchin left. Later he recalled: "We still clinked glasses, but it was sad to drink: it felt as if we knew it was the last time we were drinking together, and we were drinking for eternal separation!"* Twelve years later, when Pushchin was living out his exile in Nerchinsk, Pushkin, as he lay dying, would call his name.

Meanwhile, the times were troublesome in Russia. On December 13–14, 1825, Pushkin wrote the narrative poem *Count Nulin*. Three days later, the Osipovs' cook Arseny arrived in Trigorskoe with news of the revolt on Senate Square. Days of anxiety and uncertainty followed. Letters were scarce. Newspapers reported arrests sparingly. Pushkin anxiously read the names of friends on lists of those arrested. At the end of January, Küchelbecker was arrested in Warsaw. Pushkin's own situation was uncertain: he did not know what the government knew about him, and he lived in anxious anticipation. He instructed his friends in St. Petersburg (through Zhukovsky): "… I tell you decisively not to respond and not to vouch for me" (13:237).

And this was precisely a time of intense creative activity. Creative thinking goes along complex paths: in early January 1826 Pushkin finished the fourth chapter of *Eugene Onegin*, with playful verses about his preference, for some time now, for Bordeaux over Champagne Aÿ. Then, with feverish haste, the fifth chapter was written, followed by the sixth chapter of the novel, along with stanzas dedicated to Odesa that later would become part of *Onegin's Travels;* then followed a draft translation from *Ariosto* about jealousy and plans for *The Miserly Knight* and *Mozart and Salieri*.

The prevailing mood of these weeks, apparently, was a languid anticipation. Pushkin evidently understood that the great era of Russian life, the era

---

*   *Contemporaries*, 1:111.

he knew, in which he grew up, whose leaders were familiar to him, had ended. The reign of Alexander I had ended: the gentleman and liberal who waded through his father's blood, who promised much but accomplished little; the dreamy friend of Arakcheev; the conqueror of Napoleon; the Russian tsar who despised Russia; the melancholic friend of Karamzin; and the vengeful pursuer of Pushkin. The period of the legendary heroes of 1812 had ended: Raevsky, Ermolov, Wittgenstein, Miloradovich; a time when the tradition of Catherine II was still alive, when important positions were held by important personalities. The time of the Secret Society had ended, a time when civil fortitude was esteemed, when the title "carbonari" was flattering, and when independence of opinions and actions was valued in society.

What the new era would be like, no one knew. What kind of person Nicholas was, not only Russia, but also noble society did not know. In the Guard, he was not liked for his petty cruelty, and outside the barracks of the Guard Corps, they were not interested in him. The future was unknown. One thing was clear: Russia was experiencing a historical moment and it fell to contemporaries to witness what their grandchildren would read about, and Pushkin was ready to courageously face this new era, not giving in to romantic lamentations, but trying to understand the historical meaning of what was happening. In early 1826, he wrote to Delvig: "Let us not be superstitious or one-sided, like the Fr[ench] tragedians; but let us look at the tragedy with Shakespeare's gaze" (13:259).

This optimism was supported not only by faith in the truth of historical development and the pursuit of "Shakespearean" objectivity, but also by hopes for relatively lenient sentences. In the same letter to Delvig Pushkin wrote: "I firmly hope for the generosity of our young tsar." In Russia since the time of Empress Elizabeth,[16] the death penalty had been abolished. There were, of course, exceptions (Pugachev,[17] Mirovich[18]). However, throughout the entire nineteenth century there was not a single death sentence carried out (soldiers and military settlers killed in action were not considered, as they were not formally sentenced to death, firstly, and they were not nobles and "were not counted," secondly).

The large number of those accused, who belonged to the best families of Russia, who had high connections, and whose cause was sympathized with by many high officials—all this created the expectation that the triumphant government would show mercy, i.e. under the pretext of the coronation or some other solemn event, a wide amnesty and mitigation of punishments would be announced. Even Pestel, who made fatally frank confessions during the investigation, hoped that his punishment could be reduced to being demoted to a soldier. Nobody knew the petty vindictiveness of Nicholas I, nor the fact that December 14 made him endure humiliating moments of fear. He could never forget this and forgive the defeated Decembrists.

Nicholas I studied the art of grandeur to perfection. However, in reality, he was a man plagued by insecurity, suspicious, painfully aware of his mediocrity, and tormentingly envious of people who were bright, cheerful, and lucky. The repression of the Decembrists may have been dictated by political considerations, but in the vindictiveness (hard for contemporaries to comprehend), the petty persecution of no longer dangerous enemies, there was something else: the emperor still envied those once brilliant, lucky, bright, mocking officers of the previous reign, in whose intellectual light he, untalented, uneducated, and dull, disappeared into an impenetrable shadow. Nicholas knew he couldn't be loved—he wanted to be feared.

On July 24, Pushkin learned of the execution of Ryleev, Pestel, Sergei Muravyov-Apostol, Bestuzhev-Ryumin and Kakhovsky.[19] The executions and sentences shocked Pushkin. In a letter to Vyazemsky of August 14, 1826, sending a tragic response to the rumor that Nikolai Turgenev had been handed over by the English authorities and brought by sea to St. Petersburg (the rumor turned out to be false)—

> ... In our vile age
> Gray Neptune is an ally of Earth.
> On all the elements, man
> Is a tyrant, traitor, or prisoner

—Pushkin added: "I still hope for the coronation: the hanged are hanged; but the sentence of hard labor for 120 friends, brothers, and comrades is horrific" (13:290–291). Pushkin's own fate was yet unknown.

On the night of September 3–4, 1826, a courier arrived at Mikhailovskoe with an order to immediately travel with Pushkin to Moscow, where Nicholas I was present for his coronation. Pushkin was ordered to be taken "freely in his own carriage, not as a prisoner" (13:293), but the presence of a convoy officer was sufficiently striking. The Mikhailovskoe exile was over. Pushkin was heading to Moscow to meet Nicholas I.

Chapter Five

After the Exile, 1826–1829

Pushkin arrived in Moscow on September 8; straight from the carriage he was taken to Nicholas I's cabinet. The new tsar having been officially coronated a mere two weeks prior, was only three years Pushkin's senior. Nicholas was of tall stature, muscular, and had been handsome as a youth. His excellent military bearing as an officer of the Guard allowed him to conduct himself with majesty and hide the fears and insecurities that terrorized him during the first years of his reign, until flattery and a lack of restrictions gave rise to a similarly unrestricted self-assurance. He received an extremely mediocre education and had the cultural horizons of a parade commander. The ideas of unrestricted despotism and the divine right of kings to power—the paltry and archaic ideologies of miniscule German courts—were ingrained into the mind of his mother, Maria Feodorovna, who instilled them in her youngest sons—Nicholas and Michael. Multiplied by the power of an aristocratic, bureaucratic government and Russia's tremendous material potential, these ideas bore the most dreary fruit. Nicholas I was convinced that he could demand the unequivocal execution of any commands from the country under his power.

Not only was any display of personal opinion or freethinking intolerable and offensive to him, but even the simplest transgression of symmetry, of the aesthetic ideals of the military barracks. In September 1827—a year after his meeting with Pushkin—Nicholas I encountered a young gymnasiast on Nevsky Prospekt in St. Petersburg wearing an unbuttoned uniform. This matter, worthy of nothing more than a comment by the youth's tutor, became subject to inquiry as a matter of government importance. By the emperor's decree, the Military Governor-General of the capital, Golenishchev-Kutuzov[1] (the same man who administered the executions of the Decembrists) sought out the "guilty party" and reported: "His untidiness and unsightly appearance, based on my own observations, is born of his unfortunate physique; he has hunches on his chest and back, and the frock coat is so slim that he cannot button it." The Military Governor-General of St. Petersburg, an adjutant-general, personally examined a sick boy in order to ascertain that there is no sedition hiding behind his "unsightly appearance"! And the emperor, having read this, did not feel any shame; rather, he wrote up a resolution ruling that the arrestant be sent to the minister of education—and the latter subsequently received a reprimand: for "dressing [the boy] in clothes he could not wear."

This episode—minor in itself—exceptionally vividly illustrates Nicholas I of whom Benckendorf wrote: "The sovereign's entertainment with his soldiers, by his own admission, is his only true delight."

However, we would not be able to properly comprehend the nature of the relations between Pushkin and Nicholas I if we view the latter forgetting that in 1826, many negative qualities of his character were still latent, and disregarding a range of the new tsar's attractive qualities. Alexander I had been crafty and hypocritical; even those in circles close to him did not believe his words. Nicholas I, consciously cultivating an advantageous image in contrast to his predecessor, played the forthright soldier, the knight of his word, the gentleman. He demonstratively removed Arakcheev, causing all of Russia to breathe a sigh of relief. He engaged in intense and energetic activity in contrast to the administrative impotence of the last decade of Alexander I's rule. Furthermore, with his reign having begun in a time of rebellion, Nicholas I recognized the need for reforms. Thoughts of a peasant reform occupied him quite earnestly, and he would return to these notions in his later years as well. It should also be added that, despite not being intelligent, Nicholas I possessed the ability to act majestically or graciously and to appear sincere and charismatic.

Pushkin and Nicholas I's conversation was diffuse. Apparently, the conversation touched on a wide array of political issues. Nicholas I was successful in convincing Pushkin that before him stood a reformist tsar, a new Peter I. One can suppose that Pushkin received some kind of murky assurances to the effect of amnesty for his "brothers, friends, comrades." It was precisely from the time of this first meeting with the tsar that Pushkin began undertaking the role of intercessor for the Decembrists which he would highlight as one of the most important deeds of his life.

And I called for mercy for the fallen. (2:109)

Pushkin did not renounce his friendly ties with the Decembrists; on the contrary, it would seem that he hid his profound doubts regarding the Decembrists' tactics and decisively highlighted his agreement with their views, stating that if he had been in St. Petersburg, he would have gone out to Senate Square on December 14. Nicholas I, despite the pomp of his coronation ceremony, clearly understood the instability of his position. Frightened by a sprawling image of general discontent which the investigation of the Decembrists revealed, the tsar felt that it was necessary for him to make a dramatic gesture that would reconcile Russian society to him. The acquittal of Pushkin provided such an opportunity, and Nicholas I decided to utilize it. He tactfully acted out a scene of forgiveness, promising freedom for Pushkin from the regular censorship, which would be replaced with the personal censorship of the tsar. Pushkin was brought back from exile and given the right of selecting his place of residence for himself.

The true cost of these "graces" would be revealed to Pushkin later on. Naturally, it was impossible for Pushkin to trouble the tsar with every poem, and the person on whom the fate of Pushkin's work actually depended was the sovereign commander of the Third Department of His Imperial Majesty's Own Chancellery, Alexander Benckendorf. The grandson of an Estlandian civil governor, Benckendorf could certainly not have counted on such a brilliant career had his mother not been a close friend of the empress, Maria Feodorovna. Having been tethered to the court of Paul I since he was a child (at the age of 15, he was appointed aide-de-camp to Emperor Paul I) and endlessly loyal to the ruling family (Nicholas I's favorite quote is well-known: "Russian nobles serve the government, German nobles serve us"), he in no way, however, resembled Arakcheev, who had occupied a similar role under Alexander I as fell to him under Nicholas and had passed through the school of Pauline service. Unlike Arakcheev, Benckendorf was not without education. Arakcheev had been uncouth in dress, emphatically rude, and plumed himself on his illiteracy—Benckendorf acquitted himself as a man of society and was proper in his conduct. Unlike the cowardly Arakcheev who shied away from any military involvement, Benckendorf possessed a rich military past: he had participated in a range of campaigns from 1803 to 1814 and proved himself an active and bold general, but his true calling was found not in war, but rather in political investigation.

Napoleonic France had possessed the most developed political police in Europe, created by Fouché.[2] Compared to it, the political police in Russia were crude and dilettante. Under Alexander I, it had even lacked a single organizational center: the minister of police, the commander of the chambers of the guard corps, the St. Petersburg and Moscow governors-general each had their own—generally ineffective—systems of political control and espionage. There were, however, always those who were eager to privately act as agents of political surveillance at their own risk. Thus, General Witt, the commander of the southern (Odesan) military settlements, sent his agent Boshnyak to Mikhailovskoe in 1826 where he adopted the disguise of a botanist and collected information on Pushkin, being empowered to arrest the poet if needed. Benckendorf, however, took it further than anyone else. In 1821, with the help of his agent Gribovsky, a member of the Central Command of the Union of Welfare, he managed to penetrate the innermost Decembrist circles and then relay information to Alexander I. Benckendorf's activity, however, was only able to reach its full scope under Nicholas I. He distinguished himself as one of the most leading members of the Investigative Committee for Decembrist Affairs after which he was appointed as the commander of the Gendarmes corpus and then the head of the Third Section of His Imperial Majesty's Own Chancellery established by Nicholas.

The chancellery was created with the aim of encompassing Russia in a network of secret surveillance. Benckendorf was not himself without a particular kind of honesty: he never invented false accusations, did not pursue his personal rivals, and in matters which he had handled personally, we can sometimes find his disgusted remarks on people who made false denunciations for selfish purposes. He did, however, genuinely consider literature a frivolous and harmful activity and any manifestation of freethinking as dangerous sedition to be stamped out. People interested him insofar as they were objects of surveillance or potential agents to assist in investigations. Such was the person to whose "paternal cares" Nicholas I entrusted Pushkin's fate. Pushkin clearly irritated Benckendorf, and the latter did much to exasperate Pushkin's lot in the last ten years of the poet's life. But the opposition that, originating with Zhukovsky, was drawn between the tsar's mercy and Benckendorf's* persecutions of Pushkin must be apprehended critically: ultimately, it was Nicholas I who determined Pushkin's position, and Benckendorf was, first and foremost, the executor of the monarch's prescriptions and the interpreter of the tsar's will.

After leaving the tsar's cabinet in the Kremlin, Pushkin would not have been able to surmise just how difficult and humiliating his relations with the government would become in the future; he earnestly believed that it had

---

* In a fit of grief following Pushkin's death, Zhukovsky wrote an exceptionally bold letter to Benckendorf, in which he said: "Allow me to speak frankly. The emperor wanted to pacify Pushkin through his patronage and simultaneously allow for the full development of his genius; and you turned that patronage into an endlessly persecutory surveillance" (*Contemporaries*, 2:363–364).

fallen to him to witness truly historic changes at their point of genesis and that he would be able to influence their subsequent development. He was rather optimistically inclined. His lively disposition was bolstered by the unanimous ecstasy with which Muscovite society greeted the poet. Years prior, he had left the capital as an unknown youth.

Alexander I had persecuted him, but it never would have occurred to the tsar to indulge Pushkin with personal discourses. Pushkin's exile had only worried the literary circles; his friends had chided him as a youth who had made a mistake. His return was jubilant. The tsar conversed with him longer than he had with any of his noblemen; after the audience, the tsar publicly called him the wisest person in Russia. A society encumbered by repressions, afraid to voice its dissent directly, found a source of relief in the raptures that it poured upon poet returned from exile. Pushkin's jubilant reception in Moscow in 1826 was something of a counterweight to the onerous, official festivities surrounding Nicholas I's coronation. Pushkin was at the height of his glory. The elderly Vladimir Izmailov,[3] in whose journal *Russian Museum* the first poem signed with Pushkin's name was published in 1815, greeted him from his estate in the area around Moscow, somewhat archaically expressing the general ecstasy: "I'm jealous of Moscow. She has crowned an emperor and now crowns a poet" (13:297).

One of the chief cares of the returned poet was the idea of consolidating literary forces. Already during his time at Mikhailovskoe, he had considered the publication of a journal that would unify everything of literary merit. He now revisited this idea. There were myriad obstacles on his way to realizing these plans: as a result of the government repressions, Russian literature had incurred significant losses, the ranks of writers from Pushkin's generation had thinned; as such, it was necessary to cultivate ties with the literary youth. Moscow was the place to do this: St. Petersburg letters had suffered greater losses, and the center of literary activity had temporarily shifted to Moscow.

Chapter Five. After the Exile, 1826-1829 | 149

Younger literary life in Moscow in the second half of the 1820s was organized around two centers. The first was *The Moscow Telegraph* [Moskovsky Telegraf] journal, published by Nikolai Polevoi,[4] a young and lively writer, together with Pushkin's longtime friend, Prince Vyazemsky. Polevoi, a gifted autodidact from a merchant family, was a decided champion of Romanticism to which he sought to impart a radical political coloring. His literary program, however, seemed dilettante to Pushkin. There was no use in hoping that Polevoi would reject his own rigidly defined literary platform, and Pushkin wished to tie himself to a journal whose course he would primarily be charting. In this regard, association with the *The Moscow Telegraph* was a dead-end.

The second literary center of the time was comprised of a group of young writers connected to the philosophical circle of the *'liubomudry'*[5] (lovers of wisdom): Dmitry Venevitinov,[6] Stepan Shevyrev,[7] Mikhail Pogodin, Vladimir Odoevsky,[8] and Ivan Kireevsky, among others. All of them were graduates of the Moscow University, younger siblings of the Decembrists deeply engaged in the study of German aesthetic philosophy, who propounded the works of the German Romantics. They disbanded their philosophical circles following the post-Decembrist repressions. Pushkin hoped that theoretical disagreements would not prevent him from guiding these young writers in his desired direction. The liubomudry represented a novel and unfamiliar type of youth for Pushkin: politically moderate, dedicated to armchair studies, accustomed to systematic speculation, severe and taciturn; many in Moscow called them "the archival youth" (they often served in the Archive of the Ministry of Foreign Affairs). Among the liubomudry's ideas were the seedlings of the ideas that would later blossom in Belinsky and Stankevich's[9] circle, as well as the conceptions of tomorrow's Slavophiles.[10] Pushkin considered this group with interest, but remained intrinsically alien to it.

The meeting took place on October 12, 1826, at Venevitinov's apartment. There, Pushkin read his yet unpublished *Boris Godunov*, his songs on Stepan

Razin,[11] the recently written addendum to *Ruslan and Liudmila* ("By Lukomorye a green oak"). Here is how Mikhail Pogodin characterized this reading:

> It is impossible to convey what kind of effect this reading produced on us. To this day—and forty years have since elapsed—my blood is roused by the mere act of recollection. [...] One has to picture Pushkin's own figure first. The great priest of high art whom we awaited was a man of moderate height, almost short, with long hair, somewhat curly at the ends, without any pretensions, with lively darting eyes, restless, with impetuous grimaces, a pleasant voice, in a black frock coat, in a dark vest tightly buttoned, in a carelessly tied tie. Instead of Kokoshin's* language, we heard simple, clear, distinct, poetic, and entertaining speech. The first scenes we heard quietly and calmly or, better to say, in bewilderment. But the longer we listened, the stronger our impressions grew. The scene with the chronicler and Grigory simply shocked everyone. I cannot even recount what happened to me. I felt as though my dear and gracious Nestor[12] had arisen from the grave and was speaking through Pimen's[13] mouth: I heard the living voice of an ancient Russian chronicler. And when Pushkin reached Pimen's tale of how Ivan the Terrible[14] visited Kirillov monastery, of the monks' prayer—"May the Lord send peace unto his tormented and tempestuous soul"—it was as though we lost consciousness. Some grew feverish, some cold. Everyone's hairs stood on end. There was no strength for restraint. [...] The reading was over. We looked at each other for a while before throwing ourselves at Pushkin. Everyone started embracing, there was an uproar, laughter, tears shed, loud congratulations. "Evoe, come here, bring cups!" The champagne began to flow, and Pushkin became animated, having seen the effect he had on these chosen youths.**

After learning of the Moscow youths' plans for the publication of a journal, Pushkin shared his own intentions with them, and they decided to join forces. A festive dinner took place on December 24 at Khomyakov's,[15] marking the birth of the journal. Starting from the beginning of 1827, *The Moscow*

---

*　This refers to Fedor Kokoshkin, a well-known thespian and director of theatres in Moscow, who was renowned for his mastery of the high classical style of declamation.

**　*Contemporaries*, 2:27–28.

Herald [Moskovsky Vestnik] journal (a clear combination of Karamzin's two legendary Moscow journals, *The Moscow Journal [Moskovsky Zhurnal]* and *The Herald of Europe [Vestnik Evropy]*) began circulation. Pushkin had counted on the leading role in the journal, as well as on significant material earnings (the editorial board was supposed to pay out 10,000 rubles to him on a yearly basis).* Pushkin actively supported the journal, publishing in it scenes from *Boris Godunov*, excerpts from *Eugene Onegin*, and a range of poems ("The Mob," "Stanzas," "The Prophet," "The Poet" and others). His experience of cooperating with the journal was largely unsuccessful, however: the journal was geared towards an elite readership, the number of readers constantly fell, the absence of a more militant criticism hindered the breadth of its literary resonance. Its commercial success was lower than anyone could have expected. Pushkin was disappointed early on. Already on March 2, 1827, he wrote to Delvig:

> You rebuke me for *The Mosc.[ow] Herald*—and for German metaphysics. God knows how I hate and despise it, but what is to be done? These warm, stubborn lads have gotten together; the priest to his own, the devil to his own. I say, Gentlemen! Do you truly delight in pouring emptiness into emptiness? All of this is good and fine for the Germans, who have already had their fill of positive knowledge, but for us…
> (13:320)

This unsuccessful experience of cooperating with the *The Moscow Herald* revealed that there were difficulties and mutual misunderstandings arising between Pushkin and the younger generation of writers. It also emerged that the readers' demands for the journal did not correspond to the publishers' expectations. Polevoi's *The Moscow Telegraph* had an incomparably inferior literary section, compared to *The Moscow Herald*, and could not boast of major

---

*   Pushkin did not receive this amount. In the first year he was only paid 1,000 rubles. Subsequently, it would seem, he received even less.

names among its staff writers. It did, however, have a combative critical section supplied with articles by Prince Vyazemsky and Polevoi himself, and this ensured its victory over the *The Moscow Herald*. Pushkin's plans of exerting an organizing influence on literature contemporaneous to him in the second half of the 1820s terminated in failure.

The life that Pushkin led during these years was bustling and disorderly. Few who met the poet during this time could surmise that it was a time of deep and almost tragic reflections.

The main question that demanded discernment concerned the results of the Decembrist movement. Pushkin's initial and most immediate reaction was a feeling of emotional solidarity with the victims of the government terror. Pushkin did not stop emphasizing his concern for the fates of the Decembrist and did not shy away from bringing up the matter several times with the tsar. On December 26, 1826, at a dinner hosted by Zinaida Volkonskaya,[16] the proprietress of an aristocratic salon which was a particular cultural hotbed in post-Decembrist Moscow, Pushkin met Maria Volkonskaya who was heading for Siberia after her husband. Later she would remember the meeting: "During the time of self-willed exile for us, the wives of those exiled to Siberia, he was full of the most genuine admiration; he wanted to pass on to me his 'Epistle to the Prisoners' ('In the depths of Siberian mines…'—Lotman) to convey it to them, but I left that same night, and he passed it on to Alexandra Muravyova."*[17]

"Arion," the tenth chapter of *Eugene Onegin*, and a range of unfinished plans (*A Tale of a Praporshchik from the Chernigov Regiment*, a novel titled *The Russian Pelham*, and others) attest to the fact that Pushkin was constantly thinking about the Decembrists; we know of five drawings by Pushkin rep-

---

*   *Contemporaries*, 1:215.

resenting the gallows and the five hanged Decembrists.* The failure of the rebellion begged explanation, however. Already in 1823, the deep discord between the Decembrists and the people had become apparent. The notion that the government would engage in a series of decisive reform efforts with which Pushkin had left Nicholas I, naturally led the poet to consider the "path of Peter I"—the realization of progressive social aspirations through a system of transformations directly administered by the government. The parallel between Peter I and Nicholas I persistently came to mind for him during these years.

However, this question possessed a more profound, philosophical aspect. The Decembrists were Romantic in their approach to history. World events, they believed, were determined by heroic personalities destined to guide the passive "crowds," the chance of the hero's birth either quickened or completely changed the movement of historical events. In contrast to this, Pushkin arrived at the conclusion that historical development adhered to a set of laws: history crystallized in his mind as a linear movement defined by profoundly obscure objective causes. In his struggle against Romantic subjectivism, Pushkin, in the period from 1826–1829, would even be inclined to significantly depreciate the role of the individual's personal agency. If a feud were to arise between history and the individual personality, history would always be in the right in his mind. In his works from these years, his severe anti-Romantic pronouncements often became intertwined with the salutation of the triumphant movement of History, which, in his mental life, most often manifested in the image of Peter the Great.

This unequivocal privileging of the general over the particular—of history over people—a profound belief of Pushkin's during this time, often contra-

---

* See Abram Efros, *Risunki poeta* [Drawings by the Poet] (Moscow–Leningrad: Academia, 1933), 356–364; Tatiana Tsiavlovskaia, "Novie avtografi Pushkina" [New Autographs by Pushkin], in *Vremennik Pushkinskoi Kommissii* 1963 (Leningrad: Nauka, 1966), 24.

dicted the humanistic pathos of his works and could rightfully be described as, at least to some degree, the fruit of self-inflicted violence.

As far as the spiritual development of Russian thought is concerned, the development of the principles of historicism was certainly a step forward. But this step forward was purchased at the cost of a profound inner bifurcation. A "historical" point-of-view on one's surrounding life which at every step cried out injustice, degradation of people's dignity, and arbitrary used force could only satisfy one possessed of a lazy soul and an undemanding conscience. Pushkin was not such a person: his musings on the severity of historical laws, rather than muting his ethical-humanist demands, only intensified them.

Pushkin's thinking, for a long time, developed along two independent and, up to a certain point, non-intersecting lines: in his finished works, the egoism of the individual failing to measure his desires against the laws of the historical whole is cause for stark rebuke (for example, the seventh chapter of *Eugene Onegin*, *Poltava*), but in his manuscripts and sketches, ideas of the irreducible worth of the human being as such still abound. In 1826, in a draft of the sixth chapter of *Eugene Onegin* appears: "O Hero, first be human." This idea, coursing through various unfinished texts, would finally surface during the time of the Boldino Autumn.

> Leave the hero a heart! What
> Will he be without it? A tyrant… (3:253)

Such a duality in his relation towards the world was deeply uncharacteristic for Pushkin and filled him with internal trepidation and dissatisfaction with himself. An interesting paradox emerges with respect to the relation between Pushkin's life and art: while in *Poltava*, truth is equated to the stoic historical gaze cast over the temporal distance of a century ("A hundred years had passed"), or in *Eugene Onegin*, the rebellious Onegin is reproached and contrasted with the wisely obedient Tatyana (in the seventh chapter of the novel), or in his verse, Pushkin frequently dwells on the image of the Olympian poet

("The Poet and the Crowd"), in his life, Pushkin least of all approached the ideal of the wise observer. In a letter to Pogodin, Pushkin respectfully cites the authority of "the great Goethe,"[18] "our German Patriarch" (14:21), but it is difficult to find something farther removed from the life of "the Weimar Olympian" than the poet himself during these four years. Pushkin meanders and seems unable to sit still: in 1826, after his audience with the tsar and a short stay in Moscow, he travels to Mikhailovskoe in November, but already in December, he returns to Moscow from which in May 1827 he travels to St. Petersburg; in June, he makes for Mikhailovskoe; in October, for St. Petersburg anew. The year of 1828 featured a string of unsuccessful attempts at a long journey: his requests that he be allowed to travel with the acting army to the Turkish front, abroad to Europe, and to Asia were met with rejections. In October 1828, Pushkin departs for the Vulfs' Malinniki estate in the Tver region from which he travels to Moscow in December, but in the beginning of January 1829, he is once again at Malinniki and after a short stay, leaves for St. Petersburg. In the early days of March, he once again finds himself on the road: he travels from St. Petersburg to Moscow in order to court Natalia Goncharova, and then travels to the Caucasus (Orel, Kuban, Tiflis, Kars, Erzurum). On September 20, 1829, Pushkin is once again in Moscow. After which follow Malinniki, Petersburg, unsuccessful requests for a trip abroad or to accompany a diplomatic trip to China, Malinniki again, Petersburg, a request for a trip to Poltava (rejected), and Moscow. On May 6, 1830, Pushkin is betrothed to Natalia Goncharova and travels with her to her grandfather's[19] estate in the Kaluga region—then Moscow, Petersburg, Moscow... On September 3, 1830, Pushkin, at this point an engaged man, departs for his father's Boldino estate in the Nizhny Novgorod region.

It was not only his desire to always be on the road that reveals his inner turmoil (the road would calm him, make him dizzy, distract him; on the road, daily life and reality retreat into the background, one finds it easier to think and daydream; it is no wonder that Gogol, when he stayed in place, saw "pig snouts," but on the road "a trio of birds"). Pushkin plays cards frequently and with some obduracy. A direct relation arises between his gambling "benders" and his spiritual condition. We will limit ourselves to one example. On November 2, 1826, Pushkin left Moscow. He traveled "with death in his heart" (13:301, 561). The tsar commissioned a "Note on Upbringing" from him. It was a difficult and dubious commission: the authorities clearly expected information from him which could be used for an investigation; they were looking for ways to coax him into collaborating.*

Pushkin expressed his thoughts cautiously, but firmly, voicing his support for Nikolai Turgenev, and subsequently received a reply containing a threat masked by flowery politesse. Writing the "Note" was cumbersome and unpleasant. Before his departure from Moscow, he received a reprimand from Benckendorf on entirely unheard-of grounds: he would henceforth be forbidden not only from publishing works that had not passed the censor, but also from *reading* them to his friends. After coldly rebuking him for readings of *Boris Godunov*, Benckendorf reminded Pushkin of the requirement that he

---

* From 1826–1829, the government (particularly Benckendorf) intensely probed the possibility of—overtly or secretly—enlisting influential leaders from among the opposition to their ranks. Alexander Mordvinov became the director of the Third Section (second-in-command after Benckendorf)—Mordvinov was the second cousin of Nikita Muravyov, the Decembrist, and was himself not a stranger to liberal ideas: at the very least, his son would later be indicted for the Petrashevsky Affair and go on to be an active figure in the liberal circles of the 1860s, as well as a collaborator with Herzen. Moreover, Mordvinov himself would later be fired for unreliability. His successor, who took change of the gendarme corpus staff, would be Leonty Dubelt—a friend of Mikhail Orlov close to the southern Decembrists—according to the so-called "Decembrist Alphabet" (a secret document compiled personally for Nicholas I), he was cited as having "belonged to the secret gatherings in Kyiv" (see Natan Eidelman, "Posle 14 dekabria" [After December 14], in *Puti v neznaemoe* [Paths to the Unknowable] (Moscow: Sovetskii pisatel', 1978), 14). This was a pervasive intelligence operation. At this time, the government sought out (occasionally through force) the cooperation of the writers Perovsky, Griboedov, Vyazemsky. In the former half of the 1820s, Bulgarin and Grech had also been known, first and foremost, as liberals close to the Decembrist circles. It was precisely this circle of writers, along with Pushkin, that Benckendorf approached with the offer to write similar notes.

send any new works through him for the Sovereign's approval. Pushkin was forced to write a letter to Pogodin from the road requesting that he suspend all his works sent to the regular censor. This was humiliating and unprofitable. Pushkin had need to travel from Mikhailovskoe to Moscow ("she commanded," he wrote to Vyazemsky). But his relationship with "her" was also tumultuous. In Moscow, Pushkin became enamored with Alexandra Rimskaya-Korsakova,[20] a renowned beauty, and almost simultaneously a different passion arose within him for his distant relative, Sofia Pushkina,[21] to whom he even proposed. This ball of yarn needed to be unspooled in Moscow. And on his way back from Mikhailovskoe, Pushkin, pleased to have an excuse (he fell out of his sleigh and injured his chest and side), stayed in Pskov and gambled everything away to shreds (in a letter to Vyazemsky: "Instead of writing the 7th chapter of *[Eugene] Onegin*, I'm losing a fourth hand of Faro[22] in Pskov: not amusing" (13:310).

Cards and gambling attracted him for another reason as well. They contained a poetry of risk. If the philosophy of historism, as it appeared during the first stages of its formation, precluded chance and left no room for unforeseen actions, Pushkin "corrected" this theory through life, experiencing an uncontrollable need for play with fate, for the imposition of daring in the sphere of life operating according to certain laws. The philosophy of "reconciling with reality," one would have thought, would produce, on the level of personal behavior, self-renunciation before the objective laws of life, obedience and resignation. It led Pushkin, however, to the opposite: to convulsive outbursts of rebellious disobedience. Pushkin was a brave person. Liprandi, whom it had been difficult to impress with bravery, reminisced:

> the matter, in which none were greater than Pushkin, was in readiness before danger. In this regard, at least in my eyes, he was inimitable. [. . .] Alexander Sergeevich always marveled at the heroic deed in which life, as he would say, was staked on a turn of the cards. He always gave special heed to tales of military incidents; his face would become red and represent his thirst to find out some other exceptional story

of self-sacrifice; his eyes would sparkle, and sometimes he would suddenly fall into deep thought. I cannot speak to the degree of his glory in poetry, but I can firmly say that he was created for a military office; in such a capacity, he would be a noteworthy figure; but, on the other hand, it seems as though the words of the Empress Catherine II might be applied to him: "in the lowest rank I would fall in the very first battle on the field of glory."*

Pushkin was indeed brave, and gazing in the face of danger was a need for him, and ridding himself of threats through direct and decisive action was a natural impulse. However, his situation after leaving the tsar's cabinet was developing starkly differently from what he had imagined. From that point on, he would find himself entangled in petty and unending troubles, occasionally dying down or menacingly flaring up, but not ending until his very death.

Dangers would arrive from an unknown place; accusers and denunciators almost always remained anonymous. The face of the man whom one could call to answer for his actions and face across the dueling barrier faded and disappeared in the bureaucratic fog.

The relationship between Pushkin and Benckendorf (direct access to the tsar was possible only in extraordinary circumstances) quickly took the form of the heavy and humiliating relationship between a strict supervisor and a supervised child. For even the slightest misstep, the poet was forced to hear out or read written reprimands of the strictest sort, justify himself, and thank Benckendorf for his condescension and fatherly advice. One may recall how Pushkin could not abide "the shame of patronage" even from his friends in order to comprehend what it was to him to have to endure this treatment from the malevolent Benckendorf. Signs of yet greater danger, nevertheless, did not hesitate to appear.

---

* *Contemporaries*, 1:326, 330. Catherine II spoke these words to the Prince of Ligne.

Pushkin was endowed with the gift of attracting sympathy. Arkady Rodzianko,[23] a friend of Pushkin's, who himself had once allowed himself an unkind attack against the latter, wrote after the poet's death:

> His melodies were thirsted after by the ear
> His face was sought by the eyes.*

But it is precisely such people that earn numerous enemies: "wit, desiring breadth, is cramped," and talent engenders jealousy. On January 17, 1824, when Pushkin was in Tiraspol, and General Sabaneev was tantalizing him with the provocative offer of a meeting with Vladimir Raevsky, Ivan Skobelev,[24] the military general-policemaster of the First Army (he would go on to be the commander of the Peter and Paul Fortress and a famous military writer) wrote to the Supreme Commander of the First Army: "Would it not be better to [...] forbid that Pushkin from publishing his debaucherous poems? [...] If the composer of those harmful pasquils were to immediately lose a few shreds of his hide as a reward, it would be better."**

Several years had passed, and Skobelev (via his agent) came across a copy of Pushkin's poem "André Chénier," on which Andrei Leopoldov,[25] a teacher, wrote an inscription on the front that read "On the 14th of December." In August 1826, Skobelev, together with a corresponding denunciation, sent the poem to Benckendorf who then asked the former: "Who is this Pushkin? Is it the one who lives in Pskov, that famous composer of liberal poems?"*** It is probable that this was the first time that Benckendorf had registered Pushkin's surname. The tsar summoned the poet and acted out a scene of pardoning and

---

*   Vadim Vatsuro, "Pushkin i Arkadii Rodzianko (Iz istorii grazhdanskoi poezii 1820-kh godov) [Pushkin and Arkadii Rodzianko (From the History of Civil Poetry in the 1820s)]," in *Vremennik Pushkinskoi Komissii 1969* (Leningrad: Nauka, 1971), 68.

** Alexei Petrov, "*Skobelev i Pushkin*" [Skobelev and Pushkin], *Russkaia starina*, no. 12 (1871): 670, 673, quoted in *Letopis' zhizni I tvorchestva A. S. Pushkina, 1799–1826*, 387.

*** *Letopis' zhizni i tvorchestva A. S. Pushkina, 1799–1826*, 634.

reconciliation, but the surveillance would not stop. It continued of its own accord. In January 1827, Pushkin, by Benckendorf's command, was interrogated by the Moscow Ober-Policemaster.[26] He explained that the subtitle of the poem ("On the 14th of December") had been written in accidentally and not by him, and that the poem had actually been written long before the Decembrist uprising. However, the examination of the matter continued until May 1828. It led to the establishment of a system of secret surveillance over Pushkin, the result of a decree made by the Government Council (it was officially cancelled only many years after Pushkin's death).

This affair had not even reached its conclusion by the time a new, even more unpleasant affair had arisen before Pushkin. Servants of Staff-Captain Mitkov had denounced their master to the government for perverting them with readings from the *Gavriiliada*. An investigation was opened threatening Pushkin with the most dire consequences. When summoned to the governor-general of St. Petersburg, Pushkin declined having authored the poem, stating, "I saw the *Gavriiliada* for the first time at the Lyceum in [18]15 or [18]16,"* and rather equivocally named Dmitrii Gorchakov[27] as the poem's author; Gorchakov had long been in the grave, beyond the reaches of keepers of order. The Third Section was well-informed, however. It could not be so easily fooled. Pushkin was forced to personally defend himself before Nicholas I after which the matter was put to rest. It was clear that this defense had not gone easily for Pushkin.

These investigations convinced the poet as to the degree to which his freedom was fragile and how intent and vigilant the attention paid to him was. Despite this, it was not only Nicholas I and Benckendorf he had to fear. The failure of the Decembrist uprising had had a ruinous effect on Russia's social and political development. A direct consequence of Nicholas I's triumph and the fall of the best representatives of the younger aristocrats was a stark fall

---

* *Rukoiu Pushkina* [In Pushkin's Hand] (Moscow–Leningrad: Academia, 1935), 749.

in public morality. All of a sudden, an entire army of enthusiastic informers had arisen, besieging the regime with voluntary denunciations; even the Third Section occasionally complained of the most impudent of these well-wishers. One memoirist wrote: "Moscow was filled with spies. All the bankrupt sons of merchants; all the meandering louses ill-equipped for the labor of service; all the filth of human society decided to seek out good and evil, shoveling in money from both sides: from the gendarmes for their spying, and from honest people whom they threatened with a denunciation."*

Being a spy became not shameful, but profitable. In the drafts of *Onegin's Travels*, there are the following lines:

> He has been noticed—of him speaks
> Grandiloquent Rumor,
> Moscow is taken with him,
> And calls him a spy,
> Spins poems about him
> And promotes him to the rank of bridegroom. (6:479)

This incident is autobiographical. In 1829, Pushkin was the victim of hurtful gossip his acquaintance Alexander Poltoratsky[28] had spread, as Pushkin had written to Vyazemsky, "that I am a spy and receive 2500 a month for it [?] (which would really come in handy after craps**) and I've already been approached by third cousins inquiring after service posts and the graces of the tsar." (14:266)

This society of Famusovs had grown tired of being ashamed of itself, its disgrace, and backwardness and greeted this liberation from shame with relief—this expulsion of Chatskys from its midst. The number of people hanged

---

* *Vospominaniia* [Recollections] by Mikhail Dmitriev, M. 8184/2, Manuscript Collection, Russian State Library, Moscow, Russia, quoted in Arkadii Shteinberg, "Pushkin i E. L. Panova" [Pushkin and E. L. Panova], in *Vremennik Pushkinskoi Komissii 1965* (Leningrad: Nauka, 1968), 50.

** This refers to a high-stakes loss at a cards game.

or exiled compared to the general aristocratic population was insignificant. However, the removal of this minority deprived society of an ethical perspective cast back on itself. Societal immorality became the token of the era. It would be naive to limit the cause of this to Nicholas I's personal influence. Keen-eyed contemporaries were aware that a society that had lost its sense of shame was shaping its emperor just as profoundly as he was shaping this society in his image and likeness. The Decembrist Alexander Poggio[29] wrote, addressing aristocratic society: "You have welcomed a modest brigade commander into your embraces and elevated him to the throne and through your low prostration, indulging foundational, creeping-in wicked inclinations, you have allowed them to develop and fortify, and turned him into the Nicholas whom you have created, who has long oppressed Russia and yourselves. I repeat: Nicholas was your creation."*

There had been a time when Pushkin had been an exiled wanderer who craved a return to Petersburg. Now he was being kept in Petersburg as on a leash, and he wanted to escape wherever he could: to Paris or China, to the Turkish front, or to his village. Having had all his requests rejected, on March 9, 1829, Pushkin traveled to Moscow from where, in the beginning of May, without having received permission, he ventured on to the Caucasus, intending to visit the acting army. The Caucasus attracted Pushkin not only for reasons of romantic nostalgia—he had intended to meet there with the friends of his youth and with exiled Decembrists. On May 26, Pushkin arrived in Tiflis where a decree establishing secret surveillance over him had already arrived from the capital. In the beginning of June, in the acting army, he meets with Volkhovsky, a Lyceist, Nikolai Raevsky (the older Raevsky's son) in whose tent lived Pushchin's brother Mikhail,[30] and also with many exiled Decembrists. He had parted ways with Alexander Bestuzhev, and in one of the mountain passes,

---

* Aleksandr Podzhio, *Zapiski dekabrista* [Notes of a Decembrist] (Moscow–Leningrad: Molodaia Gvardiia, 1930), 20.

Pushkin encountered the coffin containing Griboedov's body, following his murder in Persia.

Pushkin did not fear danger. He had been seen armed with a lance in hand in the front ranks of the attacking Cossacks. Soldiers observed the stately figure in a top hat in bewilderment and, taking him for a priest, called him "Father." There was nothing of the former levity, however: we find in Decembrist Alexander Gangeblov's[31] memoirs the following, "during Pushkin's time in the ranks, he acquitted himself soberly, avoiding new meetings and going about only with his old acquaintances; before strangers he was taciturn and appeared perpetually in thought."*

It would seem that disagreements with Paskevich, who all too enthusiastically rose to the charge of establishing surveillance over the poet, forced Pushkin to abandon the Caucasus. In St. Petersburg, he was awaited by burdensome explanations owed to Benckendorf with respect to his unauthorized travels.

A short overview of the circumstances of Pushkin's life during the latter half of the 1820s demonstrates just how difficult and tragically contradictory it was during this time. No matter which aspect we consider: Pushkin's journalistic endeavor or his struggle with the censors, precarious political investigations, denunciations, Benckendorf's reprimands, or the intense and tangled circumstances of his personal life—any of these would have sufficed to drain a person of all his time and spiritual strength with vengeance. A striking feature of Pushkin's personality was his capacity for encompassing all these conflicts simultaneously. Yet all of this, even the breakneck trip to the Caucasus lacking official permission undertaken "the soul to freshen / and the former life to live," even his quickly successive, lightly or intensely tragic infatuations

---

*   Alexander Gangeblov, *Vospominaniia dekabrista* [Memoirs of a Decembrist] (Moscow: Universitetskaia Tipografiia, 1888), 188.

with women were a mere backdrop of his life. Its center invariably remained in poetry.

Work progressed on the seventh chapter of *Eugene Onegin*, its continuation was being contemplated, *Poltava* was written, numerous poems, ideas for drama were taking root in the poet's creative consciousness. However, arguably, of greatest importance was the turn to prose. In the summer of 1827, at Mikhailovskoe, Pushkin began writing a historical novel set in the era of Peter I (eventually, it would be published under a title not determined by Pushkin as *The Moor of Peter the Great*). The novel would remain unfinished, and in 1829, Pushkin undertook another attempt at prose—a novel set in his time (*Novel in Letters*) while simultaneously working on yet another work set in the high society of the same era (*Guests Were Arriving at the Dacha*).

Pushkin's turn to prose also illuminated his understanding of the prose of the everyday in a novel way, elevating the minutiae of daily life to the level of high poetry. At the same time, the statutes of the "poet," established by the Romantic tradition, with which Pushkin unavoidably had to reckon, defending himself from the vulgar curiosity of the crowds seeking to subordinate the living writer to a number of literary clichés, had become unbearable to Pushkin:

> The object of noisy judgements,
> It's obnoxious (you must agree)
> Among prudent people
> To be branded a simpering eccentric,
> Or a melancholic wanderer,
> Or a Satanic monster,
> Or even my own Demon. (6:170)

In 1936, Boris Pasternak[32] wrote the following in his poem "The Artist":

> To my liking is the obstinate ethic
> Of the artist in action: he has grown unaccustomed to
> The phrases, and conceals himself from their gazes…

Chapter Five. After the Exile, 1826–1829

Pushkin was an "artist in action" and the constant frivolous curiosities of others exhausted him, and their "loud rebukes" angered him. His position in society recalled that of which he wrote to Delvig from Malinniki: "The neighbors travel to come look at me like they would at a Munito dog" [a domesticated dog—Lotman]. Then he wrote about Pyotr Poltoratsky's[33] (Anna Kern's father) jig: he had convinced his children to ask to visit because "Pushkin will be there—he's made of sugar, and his behind is of apple; he'll be cut up in pieces and each of you will receive a piece—the children started crying: we don't want a plum, we want Pushkin. There was nothing to be done; they were brought to me, and when they approached me, licking their lips, and saw that I was not saccharine, but covered in skin, they completely lost their minds" (14:34).

Pushkin sought to resolve these issues by strictly delineating three different areas: the life of a professional writer, journalist, and polemicist, demanding social ties with his fellow writers, book-sellers, and other literary professionals; secondly, the life of a poet, his deeply intimate creative work which demanded isolation and calm; and thirdly, the life of a man in aristocratic society who socialized with people like himself—people in aristocratic society who were irked by any notions of professional society or interests. Pushkin did not enjoy the intermixing of these areas.

In his story *Egyptian Nights* he wrote:

> The bitterest evil, the most intolerable thing for the poet is his own title and calling with which he is marked and which never abandons him. The public gazes upon him as if he were its property; in the public's opinion, he was born for its *use and delight*. As soon as he returns from his village, the first person to see him will ask: have you brought any new little curiosities for us? As soon as the poet thinks about the paltry state of his affairs or about the illness of one dear to him, a vulgar smile comes to accompany a vulgar exclamation: ah, surely you must be composing something! If the poet happens to fall in love—his beauty buys herself an album at the English store and sits already expecting his elegies. [...] Charsky put all of his efforts towards erasing the

intolerable title from his name. He avoided the company of his fellow writers and preferred people of society to them, no matter how vain the latter were. He engaged in the emptiest conversations that never touched on literary issues. He always attended to the latest fashions in his attire with the timidity and superstition of a young Muscovite come to Petersburg for the first time. In his cabinet which was furnished like a woman's bedroom, there was nothing to hint at its being a writer's cabinet; there were no unseemly piles of books strewn over and under the tables; the couch was free of ink stains; there was a complete lack of the disorder that signifies the Muse's presence and of visible brooms and brushes.

Nonetheless, he was a poet, and his passion was unmovable: when this *rubbish* visited upon him (that was what he called inspiration), Charsky would lock himself in his cabinet and write from the early morning hours to late at night. He would confess to his true friends that it was only during such times when he was truly happy. During the rest of the time, he would stroll around, adopting this or that pose, and hearing the same old glorious question every odd minute: have you written anything new?" (8:263–264).

Of course, Charsky was not Pushkin, who had long abandoned the strategy of transforming his characters into self-portraits. Pushkin, however, did place Charsky in his position and give him the chance to extend the tendencies of his own behavior to the extreme.

However, the division of himself into different people could not have been Pushkin's ideal: it was a temporary, transitional solution. Vis-à-vis the perfect ideal of an artist's personality that Pushkin strenuously worked to formulate within himself, this strategy recalled the numerous unfinished and abandoned drafts of the time. This transitional period could not bear integrity. His designs were never brought to completion, and his behavior would not come together as a unified whole. This only intensified his desire for completeness. The inertia initially released at Mikhailovskoe beggared arrest. 1830 became the year of completions: *Eugene Onegin* was finished, the *Little Tragedies* planned already at Mikhailovskoe were written, as well as the first completed prose works—*The Tales of Belkin*.

Chapter Six

The Year Eighteen Thirty

The very consequences that Pushkin's decision to marry entailed in the tragic novel of his life are reason enough to closely consider the circumstances of the decision. Pushkin would easily get carried away. In 1828, in a variation on a theme by André Chénier, he wrote:

> I am the same now as I have been before:
> Insouciant, apt to fall in love. You know, my friends,
> Whether I can gaze upon beauty without affection… (3:143)

However, an examination of the facts allows us to see that the decision to marry was nourished by more profound impulses. It might be said that Pushkin intended to marry not because he fell in love, but rather that he would fall in love because he had intended to marry. In 1826, he was courting Sofia Pushkina; in 1828—Annette Olenina; in the latter case, he was so certain with respect to their future marriage that he would mull over the sound of "Annetta Pushkina." On May 1, 1829, he asked for Natalya Goncharova's[1] hand and did not receive an unequivocal answer. In March 1830, however, Vyazemsky informed his wife, writing from Moscow, that Pushkin was practically engaged to Ekaterina Ushakova,[2] a twenty-year-old beauty whom the poet himself called "ravishing." Finally, on May 6, 1830, Pushkin and Natalya Goncharova became formally engaged, and Pushkin—officially a groom. Much like how when one examines the chain of rushed challenges that preceded the fateful duel at Chernaya Rechka, one cannot forego the feeling that before one lay the rough drafts of a single creative plan, this string of courtships, too, impress one as a series of fittings, repetitions of a long-ago decided and firmly considered solemn act. We ought to further consider the meaning of this.

The news of Pushkin's marriage was greeted with surprise and distrust by those that were close to him. Among all the varied reactions, the chief motif was the following: Pushkin was a man of poetic nature, and marriage encapsulated something prosaic. Married life, and especially happy married life, seemed fundamentally incompatible with the Romantic aura that Pushkin, even according to people who were truly close to him, was fated to carry through his life as a poet.

Elizaveta Khitrovo[3] was the daughter of Feldmarshal Mikhail Kutuzov and Pushkin's loyal friend, who profoundly and sincerely loved him. Concealing the bitterness and jealousy that gripped her after having found out about the poet's engagement, she wrote to him, using various Romantic clichés about the idea of the poet: "I am afraid for you: the prosaic side of marriage frightens me. Furthermore, I have always believed that the genius is only empowered by complete independence and that a series of tragedies furthers his development—that complete happiness of a stable, durational, and, finally, rather monotonous nature is the death of talent and will fatten one and more likely turn one into a mediocre man, rather than a great poet! And it is perhaps precisely this—after the personal pain—that immediately struck me most of all..." (14:91, 410).*

Pushkin was well-acquainted with this Romantic cliché, and he had the bravery to challenge it, both in poetry and in life. In July 1830, Egyptologist Ivan Gulianov,[4] upon learning of Pushkin's engagement, dedicated a congratulatory poem to him. The poet responded with a poem titled "A Response to Anonymous" in which he declared the Romantic idea of poeticized suffering

---

* As far as this mix of Romantic notions and socialite wit is concerned, the following quip by Elena Ushakova regarding her sister's marriage is characteristic: "They are disgustingly happy" [literally: happy to (the point of) disgust—Transl.]

to be vulgarian and contrasted it with the poet's right to simple human happiness.

> Ridiculous is he who expects aught of high society!
> The cold throngs behold the poet,
> As a traveling buffoon: should he
> Profoundly express a heartfelt, heavy groan,
> Or if his tortured verse, piercing-bleak,
> Strikes the heart with unheard-of power,
> High society claps her hands and praises, or on occasion,
> Disapprovingly nods her head.
> Should the singer be struck by a sudden trouble,
> A mournful loss, exile, or imprisonment,
> "All the better," say the lovers of the arts,
> "All the better! He'll grasp new thoughts and sensibilities,
> And share them with us." But the poet's happiness
> Will never find itself well met amongst them. (3:229).

From the Romantic perspective, the mundane is vulgar. For Pushkin who at this point called himself a "poet of reality"—it is pretensions towards being extraordinary that are vulgar, whereas mundane life is filled with poetry. On February 10, 1831, Pushkin wrote to Nikolai Krivtsov informing the latter as to his marriage: "Hitherto I have lived as men normally live. I have not enjoyed happiness. Il n'est de bonheur que dans les voies communes.* I'm over 30. At the age of 30, people ordinarily marry—I'm behaving as people do, and likely I won't regret it" (14:150–151).

Of course, all this was not motivated by the desire to "behave as people do," in order to become one

> Who at twenty was a dandy or a dashing fellow,
> And at thirty, married advantageously. (4:169)

---

*   "Happiness only exists on the beaten path (in ordinary life)"—a quote from Chateaubriand's novel *René*. This quote was beloved and frequently repeated by Pushkin.

The "mundane" is much more demanding than Romantic exceptionality: in the realm of day-to-day life, it would express the same pursuits that fueled the sublime simplicity of Pushkin's poetry in the 1830s. In order to understand Pushkin's ideals of life and living during these years that ultimately resulted in his decision to marry, it is necessary to touch upon a serious of issues.

Pushkin's position became exceptionally precarious towards the end of the 1820s. His relationship with the regime was ambivalent and predicated on falsehood. Already in the tsar's chambers in 1826, Pushkin charted a tactical mode of acquitting himself with the government which would allow him to preserve his dignity and to which he adhered through these subsequent years. This mode consisted of maintaining the utmost frankness and candor when expressing his thoughts. Pushkin considered Nicholas I an honest man and viewed deceit and artifice as beneath them. From his end, the tsar was able to convince the poet that they were engaged in an honest and open, if not always pleasant, game. In reality the matter was different: neither the tsar nor Benckendorf trusted Pushkin, reckoning him a dangerous and crafty disturber of the peace whose every action warranted surveillance. Promised freedom from censorship* practically culminated in Benckendorf's hairsplitting police custodianship. Freedom of movement soon also proved illusory: any trip beyond St. Petersburg required official permission. Pushkin found himself entangled in a web of surveillance. The government also used professional writers, such as Faddei Bulgarin, to observe him, as well as semi-literate agents.**

---

*   Seeing as it was self-evident that the tsar could not examine every minor poem or essay written by Pushkin, the latter took his statement ("I will be your censor") to be applicable only to major cases, with the rest lying under Pushkin's personal responsibilities. This would not have been unprecedented: Alexander I had relieved Karamzin's *History of the Russian State* from having to undergo examination by the censors.

** An example of a denunciation written at the start of 1828 by an anonymous admirer of this genre is brought by Boris Modzalevsky: "Pushkin! An already famous, writer! who, despite the Emperor's favor! Has published many a writing! Both in verse and in prose!! Offensive to those in power, even to the Emperor! Is acquainted with Zhulkovsky!! Whom he visits almost daily!!! As an example of the above-mentioned take a piece

Chapter Six. The Year Eighteen Thirty | 171

The tsar's distrust, Benckendorf's reproaches and reprimands, denunciations made by secret agents, and crude attacks by critics increasingly shifting from literary accusations to muted charges of political unreliability—all this, constantly stoking the flames, had created an exceptionally acute situation for Pushkin by early 1830. Pushkin's relationships with younger writers who had achieved fame after December 14 were also strained.

After the rout of the extant political opposition, the social role of literature had sharply grown in stature: it remained, in effect, the only area in which the quickly developing political consciousness of Russian society could find expression. This was coupled with a marked growth in the number of readers and means of distributing literature; the degree to which writers were financially invested in the success of their works had also grown.

Pushkin had won the battle for the professional compensation of literary labor, and writers consequently became a recognized professional class with a distinct social status and interests with which even the government had to contend. However, this essentially progressive process was not without adverse effects: the literary atmosphere became murky, as it began to fill with unprincipled actors primarily interested in making money. A race for readers began, along with a competitive struggle for a place in the emergent literary market; people ostentatiously played at a democratism that in reality entailed a refusal to rise above the tastes of the mass consumer. Moreover, seeing as the most assured way of securing one's business interests in a feudal police state was through monopoly (with the monopoly preferably being supported by the police), certain groups of these literary businessmen began cultivating ties with the secret police, hoping to secure extra-literary support in their literary

---

called Tania! Seemingly already published in the Northern Bee!! Published thanks to Zhulkovsky's grace!! (Modzalevsky, *Pushkin under Secret Surveillance*, 77). Benckendorf's assistant, Magnus Gottfried von Fock, who considered the most illiterate and tongue-tied denunciation more useful than the best poem, used this denunciation for juridical purposes.

struggles. For its part, the system of secret surveillance actively being created by Benckendorf was in need of more agents. Such was the beginning of a pact entirely unprecedented in Russia between literary sell-outs and the secret police. In the minds of people grown accustomed to the purity of a literary atmosphere fostered by the moral authorities of Novikov, Radishchev, Karamzin, Zhukovsky, the world of Russian letters had found itself in disgrace:

> ... the roundelay
> Of the old lady muses no longer tempt us.
> And, from the lofty classical heights, we brought,
> Our campgrounds to the bustling market. (5:85)

During this period, the hitherto nearly overlooked figure of Faddei Bulgarin enjoyed swift advancement. Bulgarin was born in 1789 (meaning, he was ten years older than Pushkin and survived him, peacefully living to seventy) to a family deeply permeated with the ideas of Polish nationalism. Nonetheless, he was educated at the St. Petersburg Cadets Corpus where, by his own confession, he became a zealous follower of Russian Orthodoxy and so Russified that he took effort to forget Polish. He graduated with the rank of cornet, serving first in the Ulan Regiment and then in the infantry; he participated in military expeditions but earned an extremely poor characterization in conduct reports. After retiring from service in 1811, remarkably, he ran over to the side of the Napoleonic army and participated in campaigns against Spain and Russia. Following Napoleon's defeat, he reappeared in Petersburg and became a journalist. Endowed with the qualities of a decent journalist and critic, an easy style, and a knack for making friends in the right places, he quickly fell in with progressive writers and became well-acquainted with Griboedov, Ryleev, Bestuzhev, and others. Truth be told, Bulgarin's lack of principle already began to lead to conflicts between him and his liberal friends.

Following a tactlessly flattering review of his work in an article by Bulgarin, Griboedov found it necessary to break off their acquaintance in October

1824: "We are no longer acquainted. [...] Of course, your feeling of noble pride must also inhibit you from falling in anew with one who has rejected you."* Ryleev, half-jokingly, warned Bulgarin that after the revolution the Decembrists would cut his head off onto a page of *The Northern Bee* (Bulgarin's newspaper). Once even, they had almost fought a real duel. During about that same time, Bulgarin avoided dueling with Delvig, claiming the incipient offense as a joke. Despite Griboedov's opinion, Bulgarin completely lacked "noble pride," and he managed to quickly recover his shaky connections to the literary world: just half a year later, Griboedov, in correspondence, called him his "most gracious friend" and "my kind." His relationship with Ryleev even began to appear like true friendship—anticipating his arrest after the failed rebellion, Ryleev transferred his archive to Bulgarin. After December 14, Bulgarin had every reason to suspect impending danger to his own person. At that point, as at many others throughout his life, Bulgarin changed his allegiances.

The government, feeling out possible points of contact with writers, turned to him in 1826, assigning him the task of issuing a statement on the organization of education of Russia. A deliberately neutral pretense had been chosen: the government did not care about this or that writer's ideas about educational organization—they simply sought to determine who was prepared to work with the government and on what grounds. We have already spoken of the position in which such an assignment placed Pushkin and how unsatisfactorily, in Nicholas I and Benckendorf's opinions, he had carried it out.

Benckendorf, however, quickly found his footing: he passed along a note titled "On the Tsarskoselsky Lyceum and Its Spirit"—a calculated and noxious political denunciation.

> The young scatterbrain must, by necessity, ironically reproach all the actions of those who occupy significant positions, all manners of governance, have committed to memory or himself composed epigrams,

---

*   Griboedov, *Sochineniia*, 551.

pasquils, reprehensible songs in Russian—and know in French every impudent and insidious verse and the most explicit places from revolutionary compositions. Furthermore, he must treat upon constitutions, wards, elections, parliaments; he must make himself out to be one who rejects Christian doctrine and, above all, a philanthropist and Russian patriot.

Moreover, he contends with the need to belaugh the poise and training of the military forces, and, to this effect, they have come up with a word: *marching studies* (shagistika). Prophecies of changes, animadversions of all kinds or hateful silence when someone is praised are the distinguishing marks of these gentlemen in society. "A loyal subject" is an insult in their tongue, whereas "European" and "liberal" are noble titles.*

As Küchelbecker and Pushchin were already condemned and such Lyceum graduates as Korf and Gorchakov were beyond suspicion, the denunciation was aimed at Delvig and Pushkin: Bulgarin knew that Benckendorf was poorly predisposed to Pushkin and thus sought to play into his new master's hand. In truth, as he was handing in these secret denunciations, publicly, Bulgarin maintained perfectly amicable relations with Pushkin, unrestrainedly praising him in printed reviews and publishing his story *Esterka* with the subtitle "Dedicated to the Poet A. S. Pushkin." Even in his secret denunciations, Bulgarin avoided attacking Pushkin directly, having heard of Nicholas I's cordial talk with the poet and fearing the sympathies enjoyed by the poet amongst the former members of Arzamas whose own affairs were trending upwards during these years; instead, Bulgarin limited himself to attacks on Pushkin's friends and noxious hints.

Benckendorf was completely satisfied with his new employee's "comprehension" and provided Bulgarin with enthusiastic protection. In a note "On the Praiseworthy Literary Efforts of F. V. Bulgarin" compiled for Benckendorf, seemingly by Bulgarin himself, it is written that "Bulgarin would consider himself a happy man if he could receive an official position somewhat

---

*   Modzalevsky, *Pushkin under Secret Surveillance*, 36.

commensurate with his years and rid himself of the title of a French captain" (lacking a Russian rank, Bulgarin was forced to sign all official papers with "Former Captain of the French Service"). In the same note, Bulgarin was presented (presented himself?) as a victim of the Decembrists, allowing him to retroactively denounce his executed friend: "It is known to all who formed their circle of acquaintances the degree to which Bulgarin suffered for his thought from the party that had once held strength in society, whose fateful ideas became subsequently revealed. Bulgarin was even publicly threatened that they would cut his head off on a page of *The Northern Bee* for his proliferation of non-European ideas (as they called them). But Bulgarin was always steadfast in his principles and seeing freedom of thought among the youth and certain so-called thinkers, without knowing the source, always sought to counteract their influence on public opinion."*

Under Benckendorf's protection, as a reward for the "laudable works of the former captain of the French service Bulgarin," the latter was given a position in the Ministry of Education. His alliance with another influential journalist, Nikolay Grech (who similarly had been close to the Decembrists before 1825 and underwent an evolution akin to Bulgarin's), afforded their bloc a monopolistically dominant position in Russian journalism and literature: in their hands was the most popular newspaper in Russia—*The Northern Bee* (published three times weekly, and daily from 1831), the influential journal *The Son of the Fatherland* (published twice, and from 1829 four times a month), and *The Northern Archive* journal, later incorporated into *The Son of the Fatherland*. To this must be added that Bulgarin was experienced in matters of self-promotion and was truly able to satisfy unscrupulous literary tastes: his novels enjoyed a broad and successful readership, and, quantitatively,

---

* Mikhail Sukhomlinov, *Issledovaniia i stat'i po russkoi literature i prosveshcheniiu* [Research and Essays on Russian Literature and Education], vol. 2 (St. Petersburg: Izdanie A. S. Suvorina, 1889), 277–278.

he occupied one of the first places in Russian literature by the early 1830s, leaving Pushkin behind.

In 1829, Pushkin and his friends discovered Bulgarin's engagement as a secret agent on the government's behalf. In truth, Bulgarin exposed himself: Pushkin's tragedy *Boris Godunov* was in the hands of the tsar who was to determine whether it would see print. Nicholas I passed it over to an anonymous reviewer whose advice was then recorded in the following conclusion: he advised that the play be turned into a novel "like those of Walter Scott."[5] Pushkin refused to rewrite it, and the tragedy thus remained censored. However, Bulgarin decided to follow his own advice (seemingly, he had been the anonymous reviewer), and in 1829 published his own historical novel *Dmitry the Pretender*. Pushkin, not without reason, suspected Bulgarin's acquaintance with the text of his tragedy, and this served as apparent proof of Bulgarin's ties to Benckendorf. Pushkin considered the exposure of Bulgarin's hidden side and his dark services to the Third Section to the public his duty.

Pushkin, Delvig, Vyazemsky and others' struggle became especially heightened when, in 1830, *The Literary Gazette* [Literaturnaya Gazeta] entered circulation. Writers from Pushkin's circle had found themselves somewhat blockaded after the termination of Decembrist publications: they had nowhere to publish their own works. Delvig's almanac *The Northern Flowers* was a small book published once yearly—it could not replace a proper literary journal. Pushkin's relations with *The Moscow Herald* soured, as did Vyazemsky's with *The Moscow Telegraph*.

Such were the conditions in which *The Literary Gazette* arose; its editor was Anton Delvig, and its chief writers were Pushkin, Vyazemsky, and the minor, but not ungifted writer, Orest Somov.[6] The aims of the publication were not the propaganda of some kind of artistic doctrine or socio-political conception (amongst its managing contributors there was no consensus in these questions, and the conditions of censorship in which the publication operated, ruled out activity on issues of this kind). The chief struggle of

The Literary Gazette was for literary morality. In the 1820s, Pushkin believed that there could be no literature without professionalization. He struggled for the legal positions of writers, literary property rights, the legal defense of literary labor, and the diminishment of abuses of censorship. At this point, however, he considered himself liable to intercede on behalf of the purity of literary ethics and an ethically sound atmosphere of literary activity. Earlier, polemically accentuating his thought, he would compare the poet to the artisan, working for a salary, and demanded that their labor be compensated fairly. Now he emphasized the first part of a bipartite refrain:

> Inspiration is not for sale,
> But a manuscript can be sold. (2:330)

Naturally, a gazette centered on purely literary issues could not be directed at a mass readership (even in the limited sense that this term possessed in the literature of the time). *The Literary Gazette* could not compete with Bulgarin's publications. Still, Bulgarin was troubled. When his material interests were threatened, he rejected any remnants of literary and human decency. On their end, the writers of Pushkin's bloc were infuriated irreconcilably.

Their position was made even more precarious by the fact that Bulgarin was not the only opponent of Pushkin's group. The deep social changes that occurred in the latter half of the 1820s left their mark on the literary world as well. The new mass and significantly more democratic reader could not be satisfied with the form that literature had taken at the start of the nineteenth century. For him, such literature seemed limited to the aristocratic caste, aesthetically unacceptable, and provoked feelings of social resentment. In his view, Pushkin was at the head of this seemingly bygone period of literature. The sensibilities of this still not fully matured reader were most emphatically expressed by two journalists representing opposing camps: Nikolai Polevoi and Nikolai Nadezhdin.[7]

Nikolai Polevoi was an energetic and talented autodidact from a merchant family; he managed, in a short time, to become a famous writer. Together with his brother Ksenofont,[8] he ran *The Moscow Telegraph* which had become one of the most popular Russian publications. As far as his literary convictions went, Polevoi was a Romantic. His political opinions had been anchored in the Decembrist tradition of love of liberty, but in the latter half of the 1820s, came under the influence of ideas widespread in the contemporaneous French bourgeois democratic press. Polevoi was adept at circumventing censorship, his articles were bold and vivacious, thought-provoking for his readers, but were distinguished by a theoretical eclecticism and a heavy-handed style. Towards the end of the 1820s, Polevoi raised a campaign against the recognized authorities of aristocratic culture: Derzhavin, Karamzin, Pushkin.

Nikolai Nadezhdin, a professor at the Moscow University who had studied at Russian Orthodox seminaries, was an educated literary scholar and a talented polemicist. Like Polevoi, he was a steadfast opponent of aristocratic culture and aristocratic privileges. A monarchist according to his conviction, he had created a utopian ideal of democratic autocracy founded on the enlightenment of the folk (*narod*). He was a decided foe of Romanticism in which he perceived a lordly disregard for folk culture, a lordly refusal to accept life. The Romantic rebellion, revolution appeared to him as a form of lordly entertainment—"the coarse self-sacrifice of the Russian lordling." In his eyes, Romantic theomachy was nothing more than the cynicism of the semi-enlightened nobleman, and Romantic subjectivism—a cheap egotism and disregard for the fate of the people. Instead of Romantic literature, which he considered (like all "lordly" culture) superficial and alien to the authentically Russian national tradition, Nadezhdin wanted to see poetry that was imbued with a folk spirit, tied to the depths of Russian life. Truth be told, the positive side of his agenda was typically murky and lost in sharp and mean-spirited critical attacks. Nadezhdin's position vis-à-vis Decembrist Romantic revolutionary activity was negative (though this could not be discussed openly due to censorship: rebuking the Decembrists was as forbidden as praising them—instead, it was as though "they had never been"). Nadezhdin saw in Pushkin the brilliant leader of aristocratic literature and resolutely struggled against him.

A paradoxical position emerged. Polevoi attacked Pushkin hinting at his "treachery" towards ideals of liberty and the Decembrist tradition: understanding Pushkin-as-Romantic as an abandoned ideal, he rebuked him as a deserter who had shed the noble banners of Romantic rebellion for middling pictures of middling realism. Nadezhdin, conversely, saw Pushkin as the head of Russian Romanticism and in sharp (and occasionally politically tactless) articles accused him of "rebelliousness" and loyalty to lordly liberalism (against Nadezhdin's will, under Benckendorf's auspices this objectively became a printed denunciation). For Polevoi, the domestic, deeply ironic epic poem, *Count Nulin*, was a betrayal of mighty Romanticism; Nadezhdin, in *The Herald of Europe*, conversely, branded it as an extreme manifestation of Romantic "cynicism" and "nihilistic daintiness" (Nadezhdin's was the first use of "nihilism" in the Russian language).

In the eclectic camp uniting opponents of Pushkin and his circle, in the intense polemics that surrounded *The Literary Gazette* in 1830, there was a single formulation crafted for the offensive: Pushkin and *The Literary Gazette* were attacked for their overarching "literary aristocratism." Albeit this barb was construed in different ways: Polevoi understood "aristocratism" as anti-democratism and a rejection of social activism; Nadezhdin tied the notion of Romantic "chosenness" to rebelliousness and construed "aristocratism" as a synonym of skepticism and constant dissatisfaction with reality.

Pushkin had gone so far ahead of his time that it seemed to his contemporaries as though he trailed behind it. He could not be the "commander of thought" for the young generation, for he possessed a foresight that infinitely superseded it—he began facing accusations of conservatism and backwardness.

Most harmful were Bulgarin's barbs; in accusing Pushkin of literary aristocratism, he managed to simultaneously address two groups: demagogically, he addressed the reader, seeking to undermine the poet's popularity among the circles of democratic youth, and in denunciatory fashion, he addressed the government. Nicholas I was far less afraid of a people's uprising than he was of an aristocratic coup d'état. He earnestly believed that declaring "On your knees!" in his stentorian, well-projected division commander's voice would be enough to quell any people's uprising. However, "my friends from December 14," as he called the Decembrists, remained his nightmare until his dying days. The slightest hint of aristocratic opposition terrified him and was pursued mercilessly. Bulgarin understood this very well in calling *The Literary Gazette* a breeding ground for aristocratic conspiracy. Such was the noxious idea behind, for instance, a pasquil published by Bulgarin in *The Northern Bee* on March 11, 1830. Pushkin was depicted there under the guise of a certain French poet who "hurls rhymes at all that is sacred, struts around before the rabble with his free-thinking, but secretly cowers at the feet of the strong, hoping that they will allow him to don a woven caftan, who stains white sheets of paper with ink to sell them, only to spend the money on emblazoned paper, and whose one defining sensibility is vanity."

Pushkin could not remain silent, though his literary predecessor, Karamzin, as a personal rule, never allowed himself to be dirtied by literary squabbles and never responded to even the most offensive attacks undertaken by his adversaries. Pushkin understood, however, that the future of Russian literature directly depended on his and his friends' efforts. And if we can affirm that throughout the subsequent existence of Russian literature, it enjoyed an atmosphere of moral purity; that the name Bulgarin became pejorative and offensive; that cooperation with the Benckendorfs of the world was forever discredited and unthinkable to any self-respecting Russian writer, no matter his views or membership in this or that movement; that literature preserved its moral authority in society; and that the nineteenth-century reader viewed writers as representatives of his own conscience—all this is Pushkin's historical achievement, and in this was encompassed the meaning of his epigrams and polemical articles from 1830–1831. On the grand scale of Pushkin's legacy, these works seem insignificant, and the reader well-acquainted with the poems and stories by the author of *Eugene Onegin* and *The Queen of Spades* leaves his critical works to specialists. Nevertheless, these are not only brilliant works by Pushkin-the-artist, but also a "feat of an honest man,"* one of Pushkin's great services before the history of Russian culture. Pushkin exposed Bulgarin's police activity first by circulating an epigram where the editor of *The Northern Bee* was called "Vidocq Figliarin" (Vidocq⁹ was a French detective, criminal, and deserter, the head of the Parisian secret police whose *Memoirs* enjoyed a popular and scandalous circulation). Subsequently, in *The Literary Gazette*, Pushkin published an unsigned review of Vidocq's memoirs featuring a devastating caricature of Bulgarin in which he is unmasked as an agent of the secret police: "Who could believe it? Vidocq is ambitious! He loses his mind when he reads unfavorable reviews of his style (Mr. Vidocq's style!). As soon as this happens, he pens denunciations against his enemies accusing them of immorality and freethinking, and treats upon (without irony) of nobility of feeling and independence of thought…" (9:129).

Accusations of literary aristocratism also needed to be deflected, seeing as *The Literary Gazette*'s opponents frequently poked fun at the fact that the editorial board consisted of Vyazemsky (a prince), Delvig (a baron), and Pushkin—who was fond of recalling his family's 600-year-long history of nobility. Vyazemsky presented *The Literary Gazette*'s position in the following manner, in a letter to his friend Maksimovich,¹⁰ also a writer:

> You sure take pleasure in the employment of those liars' terminology, joining them in accusing us of literary aristocracy, of the *Gazette*'s aristocracy? It is understandable that police and tavern writers bawl

---

* Pushkin said this of Nikolai Karamzin's actions.

against aristocracy (I mean, of course, Bulgarin and Polevoi—I don't have anything against Polevoi's trade,* although he would sell church candles if given the chance—but his writing is for the tavern: judging by his style, audacity, and caprices). They feel as though well-educated and honest people have nothing in common with them—but then why should you stand alongside them? If we understand aristocracy in the feudal sense—none of us is a feudal lord; is Pushkin of better rank than Grech or Sviniin?[11] If we understand it in the sense of nobility, rather, of a spirit of politesse, education, then why would one cast it appellatively and pejoratively, following the example of the French sans-culottes who gave it the latter sense? If we understand it in the sense of an aristocracy of talent, that is a natural aristocracy, then who are we to rebuke God for giving Pushkin a great mind, Polevoi— a great forehead,** and Bulgarin—a great tongue of which the police might have use?"***

Pushkin, however, was not in agreement with such a position and did not seek to resolve it by simply disregarding the accusation entirely: it was precisely during this time that (partially out of polemical considerations) Pushkin would persistently emphasize the ancient nature of his family's nobility (for example, the poem "My Genealogy," the unfinished epic poem *Ezersky*). Pushkin's position in this regard requires further elucidation.

In the years following the Decembrist uprising Pushkin constantly mused on the idea of history. A Romantic belief in the heroes who through their great deeds determined the movement and development of the historical process, leading the passive "crowd" behind them was opposed in his mind to the

---

* The Polevoi brothers, belonging to the merchant class, owned a vodka factory, which often gave fuel to their literary foes' jokes at their expense.

** A "forehead" (or "a bronze forehead") signified shamelessness in the idiom of the time.

*** Letter by Pyotr Vyazemsky to Mikhailo Maksimovich, Archive of the National Academy of Sciences of Ukraine, Kyiv, Ukraine, quoted in Vasilii Gippius, "Pushkin v bor'be s Bulgarinym v 1830–31 gg." [Pushkin in Battle Against Bulgarin in 1830–1831], in *Vremennik Pushkinskoi Komissii*, vol. 6 (Moscow–Leningrad: Izdatel'stvo Akademii nauk SSSR, 1941), 245–246.

notion of history as a logical process ordered by rules whose iron links followed one another with relentless certainty.

Pushkin's ideas regarding history evolved, and a deeper humanistic essence began to increasingly permeate them. With respect to history, Pushkin began emphasizing not only the objectivity of its foundational processes, but also its meaning as a gradual accumulation of cultural values, leading to the enrichment and liberation of the human self. Memories of the past constituted one of the people's chief riches—its culture; and the individual's heritage—the foundation of his self-respect. A frivolous ignorance of the cultural efforts of generations past and cultural nihilism became two chief objects of Pushkin's condemnations. History was the people's memory. In Pushkin's unfinished *Novel in Letters* (end of 1829), the main character whose opinion is clearly close to that of the *Novel*'s author, writes to his friend:

> It is always with sorrow that I beheld the debasement of our historical noble houses; nobody values them, first and foremost, those who belong to them do not. But who can expect pride of a people who on their monuments writes: To the Cit[izen] Mi[nin] and Pr[ince] Pozharsky. Who is this P[rince] P[ozharsky]? Who is this Cit[izen] Mi[nin]? There was an Okolnichy Pr[ince] Dmitri Mikhailovich Pozharsky and a merchant Kozma Minich Sukhorukii, elected as the face of the government. But the fatherland has forgotten the real names of its saviors. The past is non-existent for us. A pitiful people!" (8:53).

Pushkin wrote these bitter words to be spoken by a character of non-aristocratic descent, which is meant to emphasize that he speaks not to class privileges enjoyed by the nobility, but rather to the notion of the aristocracy as the people's cultural heritage.

Deference towards the past is closely tied to self-awareness of the individual who feels as part of a whole—that of a unity of national life. Self-respect is fostered by a love of liberty. Thus, Pushkin considered the Russian nobility (not as a privileged caste, but as a cultural force) a powerful catalyst for social progress and a reserve of revolutionary energy.

Pushkin's attitude towards history had another significant feature: he treated history not as an abstraction or a discrete concept, but rather as the living connection between living people—a throughline that passed from grandfather to father and son and then to further descendants—a connection between people living in the same places, growing up and dying in one house, and finding rest in the same graveyard. One of Pushkin's most profound (albeit unfinished) poems is dated to 1830. There, two feelings are united as one—love for one's childhood home and love for the place where one's ancestors are at rest:

> Two feelings are wondrously dear to us—
> Our heart finds in them sustenance—
> Love for our native hearth,
> And love for our fathers' graves.
>
> A vitalizing shrine!
> The earth would be desolate without them,
> Like .... a desert
> And like an altar without a god. (3:242)

In earlier variants of the poem, these feelings were decoded as the connection between one's pride in one's ancestors, one's love for generations past ("love for our departed forefathers"), and one's feeling of personal dignity:

> On these is ever founded
> By God's own will
> Man's self-sufficiency
> And the guarantee of his greatness. (3:849)

History thus passes through one's Home, through one's private life. Neither titles nor medals nor the tsar's good graces, but rather "man's self-sufficiency" causes one to become a historical individual. A feeling of dignity, spiritual wealth, connection to the history of one's people are what made one a Man worthy of entering History. Home and the "native hearth," therefore, were tinged with especial deep meaning for Pushkin. They represented a sanctuary of human dignity and a link in the chain of historical life. This was a fort and crutch in the battle with the Bulgarins of the world—something left inaccessible (as Pushkin thought) neither to the tsar nor to Benckendorf—a place where one encountered love, labor, and history.

In 1829, Pushkin was working on a poem intended as a hymn dedicated to the home (it is not crucial that it is a translation of Robert Southey's[12] "Hymn to the Penates"—Pushkin never "simply" translated; he always selected texts that were personally important to him from the corpus of world poetry). The gods of the heart (the Roman Penates) are declared as the highest sanctuary and the foundation of all creation.

> Almighty gods, of everything
> You are the cause, according to the wise men,
> And great Zeus with his white-headed spouse
> Jubilantly follow behind you
> Together with the wise goddess, the mighty maiden
> Pallas Athena—praised be you.
> Accept this hymn O secret powers!

However, through their power over the universe (even the almighty Zeus "jubilantly follow[s]" them!), the gods of the hearth commit another, no less significant act—they instruct man in self-sufficiency and self-respect:

> And us they instruct in the first science—
> *Respecting oneself.* (3:192–193)

Pushkin's decision to get married, to establish his own home was dictated by many vastly different considerations: firstly, that of love, passion, a desire to possess her whom he loved, and hopes of happiness. More practical considerations also played a role: weariness over the disorderly life of a bachelor, a need for more profound, tranquil labor, which an ordered family life promised. But this decision was linked to Pushkin's ardent social and historical thinking, his search for an independent and dignified existence—for a Home. Here converged his yearnings after that which he had been deprived of in his youth—a warm home and his deep theoretical thinking that convinced him that only he who was in possession of a Home of his own was "firmly in his native land," his history, and his people.

Towards the end of 1828 or at the beginning of 1829, Pushkin met the beauty Natalya Goncharova at a ball organized by the dance-master Pyotr Iogel where families customarily brought only their young daughters (a description of such a ball can be found in Leo Tolstoy's *War and Peace*). At that point, she had just turned sixteen. On May 1, he asked for her hand in marriage, but received an uncertain response and departed for the Caucasus. In March 1830, at the height of his literary wars with Bulgarin and co., Pushkin abandoned everything and left for Moscow. There, on March 12, in a concert held at the hall of the Noble Assembly, at which Nicholas I was present, he once again encountered Natalya Goncharova. On April 5, Pushkin addressed a decisive letter to Natalya's mother.[13] Subsequently (on April 6; the same day the article about Vidocq-Bulgarin was published in *The Literary Gazette*), he paid a visit to the Goncharovs and once again proposed. This time his proposal was accepted. But there were immediate difficulties. One had to do with the fact that the bride-to-be's parents were concerned regarding their future son-in-law's dubious political reputation. Pushkin remembered how it had been these precise considerations that disrupted his engagement to Olenina and, despite how unpleasant it must have been, he addressed a letter to Benckendorf in which he divulged his desire to marry and requested that his good standing in the eyes of the government be certified. At the end of April, he received a letter from the chief commander of the gendarmes in which Pushkin was notified that the tsar accepted the news of Pushkin's incipient marriage with "favorable satisfaction." As far as the government's attitude towards Pushkin was concerned, Benckendorf wrote,

> there was never any command given to the police to establish surveillance over you [this was a lie—Lotman]. The advice which I, on rare occasions, gave you as a friend was only intended for your well-being, and I hope that with the passage of time you will become ever more convinced of this. What shadow can fall upon you in this regard? I empower you, kind sir, to show this letter to any whom you deem necessary.

This was a permit, and their betrothal took place on May 6. Pushkin officially became the groom of Natalya Goncharova.

There were other difficulties—namely, of a financial nature. A wedding and domestic life demanded large expenditures, and the bride's parents' financials were in a sorry state; Pushkin's parents were also in debt. With great difficulty, Pushkin's father managed to transfer ownership of the small village of Kistenevka with 200 peasant souls to his son; it was located in the Nizhny Novgorod Governorate, close to his father's Boldino estate.

The summer was spent in various financial tribulations. In August, Pushkin once again arrived in Moscow, where he visited his uncle, Vasily Pushkin, who was on his deathbed. There was a heavy spirit in the air: Pushkin had quarreled with his future mother-in-law and out of frustration had written a letter to his bride in which he recanted his promise to wed her. It was time for Pushkin to depart for his village, but he did not know whether he was still a groom or not. Historical woes imposed themselves on personal ones: a revolution had begun in Paris, and in Moscow—a cholera epidemic. On August 31, in a troubled mood, Pushkin left Moscow for Boldino. Autumn was approaching—the autumn of Pushkin's "season of poetry."

Chapter Seven

The Boldino Autumn

Pushkin departed Moscow on August 31, arriving at Boldino on September 3. He had reckoned that a month's time would suffice for him to enter into ownership of the village set aside by his father, foreclose it,* and return to Moscow for his wedding. He was somewhat irritated that these cares would occupy most of the autumn, his most productive season: "Autumn is approaching. It's my favorite time of year—my health usually fortifies—the time of my literary endeavors arrives—and I'm forced to go about soliciting a dowry [Pushkin's bride did not have a dowry. Pushkin was prepared to marry her without a dowry, but Natalia's vainglorious mother would not allow this, and so Pushkin was forced to himself secure funds for a dowry that he would then nominally receive from the bride's family—Lotman] and the wedding, which we will act God knows when. All this is hardly comforting. I'm traveling for the village and God only knows whether I'll have the time for my occupations and the spiritual tranquility without which one cannot produce anything, save for epigrams on Kachenovsky"[1] (14:110).

Pushkin was athletically built, though short in stature, physically strong and hardy; he was in possession of agility and strong health. He enjoyed movement, riding horseback, noisy peasant throngs, the bustling crowds of high society. But he also enjoyed complete isolation, quiet, and the absence of unwanted visitors. In the spring and summer heat, he was troubled by excessive

---

* Coming into ownership was a bureaucratic procedure executed through the local court, which formalized the transfer of a manor to a new owner; foreclosure signified a financial operation through which the bank would lend the landowner a sum of money to be repaid later, with a certain number of peasants owned by the latter indicated as collateral.

perturbation or fatigue. By his habits and physical nature, he was a man of the north: he enjoyed the cold, the fresh autumn climate, the winter frosts. He would experience an influx of strength in the autumn. Rain and sleet did not frighten him: they did not impede his horseback riding—his only source of entertainment during this busy time—and they supported the heat of poetic labor. "It is a delightful autumn," he wrote to Pletnev, "there is rain, and snow, and dirt to the knee" (14:118). The possibility that this cherished time for his work would be lost predisposed him towards frustration. It was not only that 1830 had rendered him exhausted: his Petersburg life with its commotion of literary squabbles exasperated his strength and left little time for him to flesh out his different literary ideas—and he had many of them filling his notebooks. He imagined himself an "artist at the height of his strength"—at the peak of his creative potential and maturity, but there was a lack of "time" and the "spiritual tranquility without which one cannot produce anything." Furthermore, his autumn "harvest" of poems was a chief source of sustenance for the rest of the year. Pushkin's friend and publisher, Pletnev, who managed the material side of Pushkin's publications, constantly and persistently reminded his friend of this. He needed money. It was crucial to his independence—the possibility of living without bureaucratic service—the possibility of family life. Pushkin wrote with the following joking irony to Pletnev from Boldino: "What is Delvig doing, do you see him. Please tell him to save some money for me; money is no joke; money is an important thing—just ask Cancrin[2] [the minister of finance—Lotman] and Bulgarin" (14:112). Work was imperative, work was much desired, but his circumstances were coming together such that, in all likeliness, he would not have the chance to work.

Pushkin arrived at Boldino in a dismal mood. It is no coincidence that the first poems of this autumn were one of Pushkin's most troubled and intense poems, "Demons," and his "Elegy" ("The faded happiness of mad years past…") betraying a profound weariness in which even hope for future happiness is tinged with melancholic tones. However, Pushkin's mood swiftly changed for the better. His position was improving; he received a "delightful" letter from his bride which "completely calmed" him: Natalya was prepared to be married without a dowry (it must have been a kind letter—but it has not survived). The bureaucratic rigmarole was entrusted to a clerk, Peter Kireev,[3] but departing Boldino turned out impossible: "Cholera morbus [cholera morbus was the medical term for the cholera—Lotman] swarms around me. Do you know what kind of beast it is? Just you see, it'll make its way to Boldino and bite all of us" (in a letter to Natalya, Pushkin gave it a gentler name—"that very gracious lady"—in accordance with the general tone of the letter (14:112, 111, 416)). In truth, the cholera worried Pushkin little—on the contrary, it promised to force upon him a prolonged stay in the village. On September 9, he cautiously wrote to his bride saying that he would be delayed for twenty days, but that same day, he wrote to Pletnev that he would arrive in Moscow no sooner than in a month. With every day, as the epidemic gained, the day of his departure became more and more delayed, hence leaving more time for poetic labor. He believed that the Goncharovs did not remain in a Moscow assailed by the cholera and were in their village in full safety—consequently, there was no cause for alarm or for rushing his departure. Having taken in his first fill of Boldino, he wrote to Pletnev on September 9:

> You can't even imagine how pleasant it is to steal away from my bride, to be able to sit and write poetry. A bride is far different from a wife. How different! A wife is like a man's own brother. One can write as much as one likes in her presence. But a bride is worse than Shcheglov,[4] the censor, she binds your arms and tongue [...] Ah, my dear friend! How delightful is the local village! Imagine: steppes and steppes; not a soul among the neighbors; ride horseback to your heart's content, [sit (?) and] write at home as much as you want, no one will disturb you. I'll prepare a great miscellany for you, of prose and verse (14:112).

There was another charm for Pushkin in his solitary stay at Boldino; it was not at all of a peaceful nature: death swirled around him, with cholera encircling the locale. He was electrified, entertained, and coaxed by this feeling of danger, much like the double threat (of plague and war) had roused him in his expedition with the acting army at Erzurum just two years prior. Pushkin adored danger and risk. Their presence aroused and provoked his creative forces. The cholera yoked him on to acts of mischief: "I'd like to send you the sermon on the cholera that I read to the local peasant men; you would die of laughter, but you hardly deserve such a gift" (14:113), he wrote to Pletnev. The contents of this sermon remain preserved in memoirs. Anna Buturlina,[5] the wife of the Nizhny Novgorod governor,[6] later inquired as to Pushkin's time at Boldino: "How did you occupy yourself in the village, Alexander Sergeevich? Were you bored?" "There was no time to be bored, Anna Petrovna. I even read sermons." "Sermons?" "Yes, at the church, at the altar. About the cholera. I assured them, 'And the cholera has been sent to you, my brothers, because you do not pay your dues, and booze around. And if you continue on this path, it will strike you down. Amen!'"*

It was not only the danger of disease and death that energized Pushkin. And the verses he composed at Boldino—

> All, all that threatens death,
> Surely brings to the mortal heart
> Inexplicable delights (7:180)

—although they surely concerned the "breath of plague," also mention "the rapture of battle / and the dreary abyss at the edge."

After the routing of European revolutions in the 1820s and the defeat of the Decembrist uprising in Petersburg, a static, leaden, reactionary cloud hung over Europe. History, as it were, had stopped. In summer 1830, this quiet was succeeded by feverish events.

---

* See Petr Boborykin, *Vospominaniia* [Memoirs], vol. 1 (Moscow: Khudozhestvennaia Literatura, 1965), 66.

The atmosphere in Paris had been heated ever since King Charles X[7] had given power to the fanatical ultraroyalist Count Jules de Polignac.[8] Even the moderate parliamentarians, whose power hinged on an agreement made between allies of the anti-Napoleonic coalition that restored the Bourbons[9] to power, entered into conflict with him. When he was in Petersburg, Pushkin closely followed these unfolding events. Although the proliferation of French newspapers was illegal in Russia, Pushkin received them through his friend Elizaveta Khitrovo and also obtained information through diplomatic channels, through the latter's son-in-law, the Austrian ambassador Count of Ficquelmont.[10] Pushkin's knowledge of the situation and intuition were so remarkable as to allow him to predict, with great accuracy, the subsequent course of political events. Thus, on May 2, 1830, discussing the prospects of publishing a political newspaper in Russia with Vyazemsky he brings examples of future headlines declaring that "there was an earthquake in Mexico, and the parliamentary chambers are closed until September" (14:87).

On July 26, the king and de Polignac organized a coup d'état, repealing the constitution. Six ordinances were published, all constitutional safeguards were repealed, the election laws were edited under a reactionary bent, and the next parliament was set to be assembled in September, as Pushkin had predicted. Paris responded with barricades. By July 29, the revolution had triumphed in Paris. De Polignac and other ministers were arrested, and the king fled.

Pushkin had departed for Moscow on August 10, 1830, sharing a carriage with Pyotr Vyazemsky, and, upon his arrival, stayed at the latter's house. During this time, they had one of their classic arguments over a bottle of champagne: Pushkin opined that de Polignac, through his coup d'état, had committed an act of treason which warranted the death penalty. Vyazemsky affirmed that doing this "was not necessary and not possible" out of legal and moral considerations. Pushkin left for his village without finding out how the matter had been concluded (in the end, de Polignac was sentenced to prison). On September 29, he asked Pletnev in a letter from Boldino: "What is Philippe[11] doing

[Louis-Phillipe was the king appointed by the revolutionaries—Lotman] and how is Polignac's health?" (14:113). Even in a letter to his bride, he inquired, "How fares my friend, de Polignac?" (as if Natalya was also wracking her head over the French Revolution!).

Meanwhile, revolutionary ripples made their way far beyond their Parisian source: on August 25, a revolution had begun in Belgium, and on September 24, in Brussels, a revolutionary government had been formed, declaring the separation of Belgium from the Netherlands. In September, riots had begun taking place in Dresden, later spreading to Darmstadt, Switzerland, and Italy. Finally, a few days prior to Pushkin's departure from Boldino, a rebellion took place in Warsaw. The European order established at the Vienna Congress was cracking and falling apart. The "quiet bondage" as Pushkin called the peace in 1824 prescribed by the monarchs upon triumphing over Napoleon had been succeeded by a whirlwind.

A troubled wind also blew over Russia.

In Russian history, epidemics had often coincided with troubles and folk uprisings. At that point, there were still people who possessed a living memory of the Moscow Cholera Revolt of 1771, which had been a direct prologue to Pugachev's rebellion. It is no coincidence that the theme of the peasant revolt appeared for the first time in the cholera-marked year of 1830 in Pushkin's drafts, as well as in the poetry of the then sixteen-year-old Lermontov ("The year will come, a black year for Russia").

News of the cholera prompted extensive measures to be taken by the government. Nicholas I, demonstrating decisiveness and valor, rode into the cholera-stricken city. For Pushkin, this gesture became tinged with symbolic meaning: he viewed it as a combination of bravery and humanism, a guarantee that the government would not shy away from moments of crisis, clinging to political prejudices, but would rather boldly rise to the occasion. He awaited reforms and hoped that the Decembrists would be pardoned. He wrote to Vyazemsky: "And what about our tsar? Well done! Just you wait, he might just pardon our prisoners—God grant him health" (14:122). Towards the end of October, Pushkin wrote a poem titled "Hero" that he secretly sent along to Pogodin in Moscow, requesting that the latter publish it "where you want, even in the *Vedomosti*—but I ask and demand in the name of our friendship that you not reveal my name to *anyone*. If the Moscow censor denies it, forward it along to Delvig, but without mentioning my name and not in my handwriting..." (14:121–122). The poem was dedicated to Napoleon: among his greatest triumphs, the poet considered his greatest act to be not his military victories, but the mercy and bravery that he had supposedly shown upon visiting a plague hospital in Jaffe. Both the theme and the subtitled date of the poem hinted at Nicholas I's arrival in cholera-stricken Moscow. This was the cause of the secrecy which Pushkin desired: Pushkin feared the shade cast by suspicions of flattery—while openly airing his disagreements with the government, he preferred to express his approval anonymously, carefully concealing his authorship.

The poem, however, also possessed a more general meaning: Pushkin advanced the idea of humanity as the ultimate measure of historical progress. Not every historical development was valuable—the poet only accepted ones founded on humanity. "O Hero, first be human," he wrote in 1826 in a draft of *Eugene Onegin*. Now, the poet expressed this notion in print and more explicitly:

> Leave the hero his heart! What
> Will he be without it? A tyrant... (3:253)

The combination of quiet and leisure required by thinking, as well as the turbulent and joyous tension born of a feeling of approaching, ominous events, erupted in a period of creative surge unprecedented even for Pushkin, even compared to previous "autumn-times of leisure" when it was "pleasurable to write." In September, he wrote *The Undertaker* and *The Young Lady-Peasant*; he finished *Eugene Onegin* and wrote *The Tale of a Priest and His Worker Balda*, as well as a range of poems.

In October, he wrote *The Snowstorm, The Shot, The Station Observer, The Little House in Kolomna*, two "little tragedies" (*The Miserly Knight* and *Mozart and Salieri*); Pushkin also wrote (and subsequently burned) a tenth chapter to *Eugene Onegin* and a series of poems, such as "My Genealogy," "Red-faced critic mine...," "The Spell," and several critical sketches. In November, he composed *The Stone Guest* and *A Feast in Time of Plague, A History of the Village of Goriukhino*, critical articles. During the Boldino Autumn, Pushkin's talent entered its full maturity.

At Boldino, as never before, Pushkin felt himself at liberty (paradoxically, this liberty was ensured by 14 quarantines that blocked the road to Moscow, but they also separated him from Benckendorf's "fatherly" rebukes and friendly counsel, the meddling curiosity of strangers, muddled romantic attachments, and the vanities of social entertainments). Freedom ultimately was for him the fullness of life, its richness, diversity. The freedom of his work at Boldino is striking, expressed in part in the boundless diversity of creative ideas, themes, and images.

The variety and richness of these materials were unified by a pursuit of a rigidly truthful perspective, of an understanding of the entire surrounding world. For Pushkin, to understand meant to grasp the hidden inner meaning that lay behind various events. It is not by accident that in the "Verse written during a night of insomnia," Pushkin addresses life itself with the following:

> I wish to understand you,
> I seek meaning within you. (3:250)

The meanings of events are revealed by history. Pushkin is not only surrounded by history while seated at his writing desk and not only when turning to different eras in his *Little Tragedies* or when analyzing the historical works of Nikolai Polevoi. He himself lives surrounded and permeated with history. Alexander Blok[12] viewed that to grasp the fullness of life, one had to

> Look in people's eyes,
> And drink wine, and kiss women,
> And fill the evening with the fire of one's desires,
> When the heat precludes one from day-dreaming
> And singing songs! And hearing the wind swirl through the world!
> ("On Death," 1907)*

The last line could well be chosen as an epigraph to the Boldino chapter of Pushkin's biography.

Boldino was where Pushkin's most significant work, *Eugene Onegin*, was completed after more than seven years of writing. In it, Pushkin achieved a hitherto unprecedented maturity of artistic realism. Dostoevsky[13] later called *Eugene Onegin* an epic that was "tangibly real, in which true Russian life manifests with such creative force and such finality the likes of which had never seen prior and even, perhaps, afterwards."** The typicity of the characters in the novel is coupled with an exceptionally complex depiction. This is thanks to Pushkin's flexible narratorial manner in which a one-sided point of view is principally rejected, allowing him to overcome the division of characters into "positive" and "negative" ones. This is what Belinsky had in mind, noting that thanks to the narratorial style, "the poet's personality" "seems so loving, so humane."***

Insofar as *Eugene Onegin* serves as the culmination of a certain stage in Pushkin's poetic evolution, *The Little Tragedies* and *The Tales of the Late Ivan Petrovich Belkin* heralded in a new stage. In *The Little Tragedies*, Pushkin illustrated how historical crises impact human characters in moments of heated conflict. However, both in history, and in the deepest recesses of man's individual life, Pushkin espies deadening tendencies that stand in conflict with

---

* Aleksandr Blok, *Polnoe sobranie sochinenii* [Complete Collected Works], vol. 2 (Moscow: Nauka, 1997), 208–209.

** Fedor Dostoevskii, *Polnoe sobranie sochinenii* [Complete Collected Works], vol. 26 (Leningrad: Nauka, 1984), 139.

*** Belinskii, *Polnoe sobranie sochinenii*, 7:503.

those vivifying, human forces full of passion and awe. Thus, the theme of stiffening, arrest, petrification, or turning a human being into a soulless thing—which frightens more with its movements than its stillness—is coupled with coming alive, awakening, and the triumph of passion and life over stillness and death.

The Tales of Belkin were the first completed works by Pushkin-the-prose-writer. Introducing the conventional figure of Ivan Petrovich Belkin as narrator, together with an entire system of other intersecting narrators, Pushkin paved the road for Gogol and the subsequent development of Russian prose.

After multiple unsuccessful attempts, Pushkin finally succeeded in returning to Moscow on December 5, to his bride. His impressions from the road were melancholic in nature. On December 9, he wrote to Khitrovo, "The people are crushed and frustrated; 1830 is a tragic year for us! (14:134, 422)

A consideration of the circumstances surrounding the Boldino Autumn leads to conclusions of some interest. In the 1840s, the tremendously productive ideas that one's environment impacts the fact and character of the individual began to enjoy great popularity in literature. Every idea has its reverse side, however: in the day-to-day, the average person would employ the phrase "my surroundings have consumed me," that would not only explain, but even justify, as it were, the domination of all-powerful environments over man to whom was left the passive role of the victim. A member of the intelligentsia in the latter half of the nineteenth century would occasionally justify his weakness, drinking benders, spiritual ruin by claiming a collision with insurmountable circumstances. Pondering the fates of people from the earlier nineteenth century, he would simply affirm that their environments had been kinder to the intelligent aristocrat than his to a non-aristocrat.

The fate of the Russian intelligentsia of non-aristocratic extraction was of course exceptionally difficult, but the fate of the Decembrists was no less so. Meanwhile, none of them—neither those flung into the casemates nor those who, after their exile, were dispersed around Siberia, in states of isolation and material want—none of them allowed themselves to become degraded, take to drink, not only did they not abandon their spiritual world, their interests, but they even tended to their appearance, habits, and verbal manners. The Decembrists greatly impacted the cultural history of Siberia: it was not their surroundings that "consumed" them, but rather, they reformed their surroundings, fitting them to the spiritual atmosphere to which they had previously become accustomed. To even a greater degree, the same can be said about Pushkin: regardless of whether we speak of Pushkin's southern exile or his exile at Mikhailovskoe or his prolonged isolation at Boldino; one is forced to note what a productive impact these circumstances had on the poet's creative development. There is almost a sense that Alexander I, in exiling Pushkin to the south, provided a tremendous service to the development of Pushkin's Romantic poetry, and Vorontsov and the cholera, respectively, facilitated Pushkin's immersion in folk culture (at Mikhailovskoe) and historism (at Boldino). Needless to say, everything was much more difficult in reality: the periods of exile were a difficult burden, and his isolation at Boldino and the uncertainty surrounding his fiancée's safety could break even a very strong-willed man. Pushkin was never spoiled by fate. The reason why the Decembrist's Siberian exile or Pushkin's wanderings seem less dreary to us than the financial troubles of the burgher running in poverty around the corners and basements of mid-century Petersburg lies perhaps in the former's active dispositions to his surroundings: Pushkin commandingly transformed the world in which life planted him, endowing it with spiritual richness and never allowing his "surroundings" to prevail over him. It was always impossible to force him to live contrary to his will. Thus, even the most difficult periods of his life were filled with light—one of Dostoevsky's famous quotes is applicable to Pushkin only in part: there were times when he was *insulted*, but he never allowed himself to be *humiliated*.

Chapter Eight

A New Life

On February 18, 1831, at the Greater Church of the Ascension in Moscow on Malaya Nikitskaya street, Pushkin married the beauty Natalya Goncharova. She was nineteen years old. A week later he wrote to Pletnev: "I'm married—and happy; my one wish is for nothing to change in my life; I can hardly hope for anything better. This is such a new state for me that I feel as though I've been reborn" (14:154–155).

Pushkin was happy. The word "happiness" for him in 1831 did not comprise a Romantic notion of "heavenly bliss" or "murderous passion." The intensity of his passion, rather than excluding, implied the simplicity and tranquility of domestic life. Happiness required not only love, but also a Home, a hearth of one's one, a harmonious and dignified existence, "the end of his nomadic living" (14:152), as Pletnev, who was privy to Pushkin's spiritual state, expressed it when congratulating his friend on his marriage.

However, the start of this new life was accompanied by ill forebodings. The world in which Pushkin planned to erect his Home portended little tranquility.

In May 1831, Pushkin departed Moscow, where he had spent the first few months of his married life at Khitrovo's house on Arbat street (these days, No. 53), together with his young wife. The house had been chosen on the grounds of the consonance the name of its owner shared with that of Ekaterina Khitrovo—the daughter of Fieldmarshal Mikhail Kutuzov and Pushkin's loyal friend. Losing no time in Petersburg, the Pushkins left for Tsarskoe Selo where they intended to spend the summer and autumn. It was no mere coincidence that for the start of his new life, Pushkin chose a locale tied to his Lycean memories: here he had found a substitute for his family among his school friends and it was here that he wanted to begin his new family life "in inspiring solitude," "in the company of dear memories" (14:158).

In Petersburg, things were worrying.

Already on November 17, 1830, a rebellion had flared up in Warsaw. In the beginning of 1831, the Polish Sejm declared its rejection of the Romanov dynasty and the independence of Poland from Russia. From January 24–25, Russian forces entered the territory of the Kingdom of Poland. A war began that eventually turned into a protracted conflict. Meanwhile, in Petersburg, the first signs of a cholera outbreak came to light, and largely because of the government's inaction, it quickly spiraled into a full-blown epidemic. On June 22, on Sennaya Square, a riot occurred—the people killed several doctors whom they perceived as the cause of the disease and raided hospitals. It took the arrival of the tsar and his personal involvement to quell the riots. In June, the riotous mood had spread to the Novgorod military settlements—the rebels murdered officers and doctors. Pushkin's acquaintance, Nikolai Konshin,[1] who participated in the quashing of the riots, wrote to him: "How vicious in its bitterness is the good Russian people! They express sympathy and then tear you apart; call you 'Your Excellency' and then beat you with clubs—all this simultaneously" (14:216).

Europe's general position was hardly better: the Polish rebellion and news of the Russian military's incursion in Poland provoked a wave of anti-Russian attitudes in western Europe and especially in France. Democratic and liberal deputies and other politicians demanded military involvement on Poland's side; demonstrations boomed in Paris. Pushkin feared a greater European war—a new European campaign against Russia, like in 1812.

But even in his small domestic world, the sky was overcast: a month before his wedding, Pushkin was notified as to the death of his closest friend—Anton Delvig. This loss was especially felt in Tsarskoe Selo, surrounded as he was by Lycean memories. Tsarskoe Selo was blocked off by cholera quarantines; the post traveled inefficiently and brought cheerless news of new victims of the disease. On July 17, the court arrived there, fleeing the disease; the place became noisier and more restless. Prices in the city skyrocketed. And for Pushkin, cut off from his communications with booksellers and Pletnev who managed his affairs, means were limited.

However, the onerous environment and danger, combined with activity, never managed to crush Pushkin's spirits. His letters from these days are lively and even cheerful. He is full of energy and is preparing for the autumn—the time of his poetic labors.

A lively interest in politics was always natural for Pushkin. In the 1830s, he was especially troubled by Russia's foreign affairs.

Pushkin's political views during this period were founded on ideas of historicism: he viewed society as the result of unceasing and logical historical development. On the one hand, this implied a rejection of Romantic revolutionary ideas, of hopes for an instantaneous and voluntary reformation of society; he mentally opposed the harsh truth of history to Romantic illusions. On the other hand, history itself appeared as a constantly flowing current, as opposed to a stultified mass.

As far as foreign affairs were concerned, for Pushkin, this meant a principle of non-interventionism: the historical development of a people was subordinated to internal laws and was supposed to be free from external impositions. This principle had been rejected by the Vienna Congress in 1816 with its idea of international solidarity among monarchs in their struggle against revolutions on which basis French forces crushed the Spanish revolution in 1823, and Austria sent its forces into Piedmont and Naples. When a revolution shook France and then Belgium in 1830, Nicholas I, both out of political and dynastic interests (the Dutch court was closely blood-related to the Russian court), offered to intervene in order to "straighten things out." Such plans provoked condemnation on Pushkin's end who considered both French affairs and the Dutch-Belgian conflict to be disputes between the peoples of the West.

The poem "To the Slanderers of Russia" was favorably received by Nicholas I (truth be told, it was also ecstatically received by Chaadaev who subsequently called Pushkin a "folk poet"; friends of Pushkin's, such as Alexander Turgenev and Vyazemsky regarded it coldly or even with outright hostility). Pushkin was endowed with a false belief that he could influence the government presenting opposition to Bulgarin's snitching. The chance of joining the historical power of governance to the incorruptible word of honest Russian writers was too tantalizing: Pushkin, through Benckendorf, requested of Nicholas I that he be allowed to publish an official political newspaper. In government circles, this idea was received with interest: former members of Arzamas, renegades Bludov and Uvarov, were attracted to this idea. After certain formal procedures, permission was officially given. However, Pushkin soon understood whom he would have to work alongside in this endeavor, and his interest soon cooled; he delayed the publication by a year and then, little-by-little, rejected the idea entirely.

Hopes that Nicholas I would make the right conclusions from the calamitous events of 1830–1831 and turn to the execution of long overdue reforms were not fated to come to fruition. The political incompetence of those in power manifested itself in the fact that they were more concerned with suppressing public discussions of social issues rather than the social issues themselves. In forbidding these conversations, they sacrificed a truly healthy governance for the appearance of prosperity. The yoke of censorship greatly intensified. In 1831, *The Literary Gazette* ceased its existence. On February 22, 1832, Kireevsky's journal *The European* became forbidden. Zhukovsky and Vyazemsky's imploring demarches to the tsar were pronounced in vain: they were outweighed by secret denunciations, as well as the tsar and Benckendorf's clear dislike for the unbought word and independent thought.

Pushkin abandoned all hopes of cooperating with the government. He redirected all his energy to a different field in which his emerging ideas of historism would find a direct application: the study of history. In July 1831,

Pushkin received official permission to use the government archives to pen a history of Peter the Great's rule. It was even declared that Pushkin be given a stipend as a government employee (truthfully, this "stipend" was only declared—the government would constantly forget to bring it about, and the poet, in great want of money, was forced to recall this commitment, facing various bureaucratic hurdles). A bit later, Pushkin notified the military minister as to his intentions of working on a biography of Suvorov and thus obtained access to materials connected to Pugachev's rebellion. This topic had come to interest him more and more.

However, this feeling of being engulfed in grand historical movements formed not only his political views or his research interests. It also influenced the very essence of his personality and behavior and how he conceptualized himself and his family life.

"Historism" in terms of his personal life-construction signed, first and foremost, a feeling of belonging to history, a sense of oneself as part of a single stream of life, and not an isolated being withdrawn into itself. In the 1830s, Pushkin was taken to the idea that the existence of an individual human being was nothing more than a link in the chain connecting ancestors and descendants—chain whose either end extends into infinity. Nonetheless, man was conceived of not as an abstract unit, but rather as representing a living being, *myself*, in all my lived concreteness, ancestors and descendants were to be pondered not "in general"—these were the grandfathers and great-grandfathers whose portraits, first composed by serf artists and then artists who arrived from Amsterdam and Paris, hung in the halls of a neglected manor in the village, whose graves filled their family graveyard (serfs did not have portraits in their cottages, but, like aristocrats, knew and reverentially treated the places where their ancestors were buried); his descendants would be the sons and grandsons who would occupy the rooms of the selfsame house, carouse and kiss in the shade of the same trees in the park and then give life to the next generation themselves. To enter this chain was to lead a truly historical existence.

Here, in this private life and not in the chambers of tsars or halls of parliament, history becomes a tangible reality.

The first consequence of this perspective was a sense of life's endless renewal and a constant readiness to receive its new forms. In the height of the cholera epidemic, in a sorrowful time for himself and others, Pushkin received a woeful letter from Pletnev regarding the death of the old Molchanov[2] to whom Pletnev had been truly attached. Pushkin responded:

> Your letter [...] has firmly thrust me into grief. You're sulking again. Hey, look: sulking is worse than the cholera; the latter kills the body, where the former kills the soul. Delvig is dead, Molchanov is dead; just you wait, Zhukovsky will die, and so will we. But life is still rich; we will make new acquaintance, new friends will ripen, your daughter will grow and become a bride; we will be old curmudgeons, our wives—old curmudgeonesses, but our children will be a glorious, young, and cheerful lot; the boys will romp, and the girls will sentimentalize, and we will delight in this. Nonsense, my dear friend, do not sulk—the cholera will pass, and as long as we're alive, there will come a time when we will be happy (14:197).

"New friends will ripen"—the young Pushkin had always been surrounded by elders; his friends were older mentors, his lovers were teachers. Now, he was surrounded by young people: his young wife's young unmarried sisters came to pay visits; their house was filled with increasingly more children. In 1832, Natalya gave birth to a daughter, Masha;[3] in 1833, to a son, Sasha;[4] in 1835, to a son, Grisha;[5] and in 1836, to a daughter, Natasha.[6] Pushkin's circle of friends and acquaintances in these years "becomes younger"; he was clearly drawn to young people, to a novelty of personalities and opinions. Earlier, he had looked for a substitute for his father; now, he took great pleasure in playing the role of a father and mentor for others, in life and literature.

However, Pushkin understood being "a link in the chain" in a particular way: in order to pass the torch to later generations, one had to be a brilliant personality in one's own right, possessing dignity, personal independence, a plenitude of spiritual and inner life, and a wealth of intelligence and emotions. One is only a part of history if one is also wholly an outstanding human being. It was not impersonality and subordination, but independence, the blossoming of human individuality, a brilliance of sentiment, thoughtfulness and ease, both cheer and sorrow, contributing to culture and joining it.

From this perspective, Home became the focal point and intersection of national, historical, and personal existence. It was not an abstract conception of Home, but rather something intrinsically personal—one's singular and real Home. If one multiplies the force of these ideas by the force of the true passion Pushkin felt for his wife, together with the power these ideas held for him, one easily recognizes the central place that Pushkin's wife, Natalya Nikolaevna—Natalie in society and Tasha at home—occupied in his life. Pushkin would also come to call her Tasha. She was thirteen years younger than her husband and had been raised like other Moscow aristocratic girls from intelligent, but not wealthy families; she had been dowerless. She was distinguished by her delicate, watercolor-like beauty (Pushkin called her his Madonna), a marvelous figure, and magnificent height (she was taller than Pushkin). Her slightly crossed eyes gave her a particular charm. Her manners were tactful and possessed an aristocratic simplicity; she could acquit herself with simultaneous affection and somewhat cold dignification. Passionate marriages, at that point, existed predominantly in novels. Men, it is true, could fall in love and choose their brides. More often than not, women simply consented. Their real acquaintance took place after the marriage service. In lucky cases, it would then take the form of peaceful friendship or simple habit. In less fortunate cases—that of obedient patience. Family grievances and disagreements were rarely aired.

Natalya consented to give her hand to Pushkin without much passionate attachment. Pushkin was not good-looking (as a bride, she could hardly gauge the charm of his engaging conversation, the expressiveness of his unhandsome face, and the profundity of his soul). He was not well-off and, in every regard, could not be regarded as a brilliant match. Her decision was probably conclusively prompted by her desire to be independent of her despotic mother.

Having become Pushkin's wife, Natalya adapted to this hardly facile role. Pushkin was a genius not only as a poet, but as a person: the plenitude of his life literally caused him to erupt from within: he enjoyed flowing, like a great river, with several different simultaneously flowing streams—being a poet and a socialite, a scholar and a solitary melancholic, an enjoyer of tumultuous gatherings of the folk (always involving a brawl!), a family man and a card-player; he enjoyed conversing with the tsar and the coachman alike, with Chaadaev and socialite women. There was enough of him for everything, but everything was never enough for him. He wanted the same of his wife: he liked how she was a talented homemaker, that she was also capable of haggling with booksellers, giving birth to children—one after the other—and being brilliant at balls. He wished to have her both live the life of a quiet homemaker in a little wooden house far from the capital and the life of the star of the Petersburg ball, brilliant and unapproachable. He did not stop to consider how difficult it was for her, a young lady from Moscow, to be the first beauty of the "elegant, regal Neva," the wife of Russia's prime poet, responsible for a large house—while also lacking money, facing brash servants, being in a state of unending pregnancy or just after birth. The feeling of her own "adulthood" and success sent her head spinning. But she was virtuous and not foolish. It was not without reason that Pushkin wrote to her: "Have you looked in the mirror and become convinced that there is nothing to compare with your face in the world—yet I love your soul even more than your face" (15:73).

And so, Pushkin was wed. What did he expect from family life and how did he imagine *the family life of a poet*? We have seen that those of Pushkin's friends who were adherents to Romantic ideas held domestic bliss for a prose that threatened inspiration. Karl Briullov,[7] a gifted artist, who subordinated his own personal life to the rules of artistic bohemianism, recorded his recollection of a visit to the Pushkins'. The poet wanted to show his kids to Briullov, but the kids had already gone to bed. Pushkin then carried them out, in their sleepy state, one by one to show the artist. Briullov was hardly touched by this scene—he considered it "contrived." He was deeply convinced that a poet's life was principally incompatible with domestic joys. He believed that Pushkin was as much trying to convince himself that he was happy, as he was trying to convince him. Briullov did not believe that it was really happiness.

But Nicholas I and Benckendorf responded to Pushkin's marriage "with benevolent satisfaction" (14:81 and 408). They assumed that the poet, after marriage, would "settle down" and cease being a source of troubles. From completely different perspectives, but also hoping that Pushkin would enter a calmer period of his life, a few other close friends approved of Pushkin's marriage. What kind of ideal family life did Pushkin have in mind himself?

He was forced to invent this ideal himself: the existing cultural tradition abounded with models of both happy and tragic love, as well as even (albeit in smaller numbers) poetic images of domestic "heaven in a tent," but it was silent insofar as the combination of the prosaic and poetic sides of family life were concerned. Everyone knew how a Romantic poet was to acquit himself in life. But what were the behavioral norms for a "poet of real life"? How was realism as an artistic worldview to manifest in the poet's daily life?

In the third chapter of *Eugene Onegin*, Onegin ironically characterizes the Larin family as a "simple Russian family." Now, Pushkin could deploy similar language in describing *his own* ideal of family life. This ideal was by no means simple and incorporated a host of Pushkin's hopes and cherished beliefs. Above all, it was opposed to notions of stylish marriage and the socialite open house. This ideal was generally difficult to reconcile with life in Petersburg.

In order to properly comprehend the spirit that Pushkin sought to elevate in his Home, let us closely examine the style of his letters to his wife.

Firstly, notably, they were written in Russian.

In Pushkin's era, the question of whether to write a particular letter in Russian or in French was of tremendous significance. Correspondence was not only a means of conveying certain information to a certain addressee: it also established the nature of the relationship between the letter's writer and its recipient. This was demonstrated by the form of address (in Russia there were rigid formulae for official correspondence, as well as strict modes of address for everyone from the tsar himself to the minor bureaucrat and the nobleman without position and rank; transgressing these norms was completely out of the question) and by the signature. There is a famous story regarding an important nobleman from the early nineteenth century who, writing a letter to someone approximately equal to him in standing and rank, addressed him "My kind sir" (instead of simply "kind sir"). The letter's recipient was offended: he felt that the mode of address was overly familiar and degraded his dignity—he responded by addressing the writer: "My, my, my kind sir!"

In light of this sensitivity for written etiquette, the language in which a letter was written received particular significance. Oftentimes, it did not correspond to the language that two correspondents would use to communicate upon meeting. Thus, for instance, it would be perfectly natural for a Russian aristocrat to speak to the tsar in French, but, under Nicholas I, one had to write letters to the tsar in Russian: to address the tsar in writing in French would have compromised the character of this address as one made by a loyal subject to his lord, which was heavily reinforced by requisite formulae and clichés; French was reserved for the freer correspondence between two aristocrats. Pushkin only wrote to Benckendorf in French. With this he avoided the need to employ a humiliating bureaucratic tone and instead established a style signifying social equality as the norm for their interactions.

Judging by the norms of day-to-day discourse accepted in the social circles to which Pushkin belonged, it can be presumed that Pushkin typically spoke to his wife in French at home. It is thus all the more surprising that he wrote to his wife exclusively in Russian. By virtue of this he established, as it were, a stylistic norm for familial discourse. This was not a neutral, stylistically unadorned Russian. We can be sure that he spoke to no one in Petersburg in such a Russian—except, perhaps, with Arina Rodionovna. Here is how he addressed Natalya: "my little wife," "my little soul," "what a fool you are, my angel," "you're a smart and kind shrew." He did not call his kids *Marie* or *Alexandre*, as was the norm in his circles, but rather Mashka or Sashka or "red-headed Sashka"; later Grishka appears in his letters (letters to his wife mentioning the name of his youngest daughter Natasha have not been preserved, but it is typical that even in a letter to his closest friend he calls her by her full name, as opposed to calling her in the laconic manner with which he called his other children in letters to Natalya: the wife "has successfully given birth to a daughter, Natalya"). He instructed his wife in a markedly patriarchal tone: "Don't you dare go swimming—have you gone mad?!"; "Quit telling lies; let's speak of business; ple-ase, be safe" (the archaic usage of "telling lies"* meaning "speaking nonsense" that was still extant in the eighteenth century, as well as the demotic division of the word "ple-ase"** to imply a folksy intonation are indicative). Here is how Pushkin describes his "day-to-day": "Ah, wifey! The post gets in the way [that is, the stranger reading intimate correspondence gets in the way—Lotman], otherwise I'd tell you three packs of lies,"*** "the only benefit of your absence is that I don't have to snooze away my time at balls and guzzle down ice cream." He expects his wife's letters to come "from Novagorod" (and not from Novgorod);**** on the topic of his efforts on behalf of his parents' and sister's financial troubles he writes: "It's easy for them, I'll suffer the worst of it."*****

---

*   *vrat'* (Translator's note).

** The Russian word for "please" consists of two historically morphologized lemmes—(*pozhalui* + *sta*). Pushkin's usage deliberately harkens back to the archaic and folksy form in which this word would still have been understood as combining two separate words (Translator's note).

*** Here too Pushkin employs a folksy idiom (Translator's note).

**** Another archaism (Translator's note).

***** Pushkin employs an untranslateable idiom from the Russian word for "gypsy," meaning "to beg." Literally: "It'll be me who'll be gypsied to." (Translator's note).

If the language of the salon was distinguished by a demure elegance, in his letters to his wife, Pushkin was, by contrast, not only pronouncedly simple—he was demotically rude, calling things by their simple names. When Alexandra Smirnova,[8] a close friend of the Pushkins, herself a brilliant, intelligent woman who combined beauty with taste, became pregnant, Pushkin wrote to his wife: "Smirnova does not appear at the Karamzins; she can't carry her gut up those stairs." Pushkin did not mean this as rudeness—this was a conscious turn to the simplicity and truthfulness of folk language. At the end of his letters, he would invariably pass along a patriarchal blessing to his kids and to his wife, wishes such as: "Ozerov[9] arrived yesterday from Berlin with his wife who's as wide as three arm-lengths. A grand shrew; I looked at her, thought of you, and desired that you come back as such a dame from Zavod.* Long enough you've been as thin as a match! Goodbye, wifey."

The language of Pushkin's letter was a completely new phenomenon: it implied a realism that went beyond writing, seeping into one's own life—a pursuit of simplicity and truth as the foundation of one's daily living. Pushkin only had but a single model to emulate in this regard—that of Ivan Krylov.[10] Krylov was a professional writer and one of the most popular Russian poets, welcome in any aristocratic household, who nevertheless spoke the same tongue to the soldier in the street and the tsar in the palace alike; he had earned an extraordinary right in the Petersburg of Nicholas I—to be himself. He spoke a simple folk tongue and slept soundly at social receptions without being ashamed of his loud snoring. He was known as an eccentric in society, but had thus garnered the right to live without reckoning with "that which Princess Maria Alekseevna would say" (Griboedov). Not a single critic dared to chastise his fables and not a single socialite dandy dared to poke fun at his

---

* This refers to the Polotnyany Zavod—the Goncharovs' manor which Natalya traveled to with the children in summer of 1834.

manners. In slavish Petersburg, he was free, if one equates freedom with personal independence.

When Pushkin wrote to his wife and with the style of these letters, like an architect through his designs, sketched out the outlines of his Home, Krylov's mode and style came in the depths of Pushkin's soul. There are specific figures of speech that betray this fact. Thus, in a letter from July 11, 1834, he wrote to his wife: "You, my little wife, are careless . . . Think about everything, and you will see that before you, I am not only correct, but almost saint-like." It is unlikely that Natalya, reading this letter, would have recalled Krylov's fable, "The Pestilence of Animals":

> And all those who here were wealthy
> Whether in little claws or little teeth, turned out
> To be all around,
> Not only correct, but almost saint-like.

Pushkin, moreover, probably did not expect that the quote would be discovered—Krylov served rather as a teacher of language—the source of "Russisms" in Pushkin's speech.

We have no record of Natalya's responses: they have been lost and have yet to be found. In all likelihood, she responded to her husband in French.

The poetry of familial patriarchalism, idyllic images of the homely nest were not without their foundation in culture. A direct line can be drawn from Pushkin's conceptualizations in the 1830s to the poetic imagery of *War and Peace* and Leo Tolstoy's own self-image. These were less theoretical formulations than they were deep sensibilities that had taken root in one's personality. They were fed by a general thirst for freedom.

Personal behavior concluded its existence as a personal preference, and family was no longer viewed as the final bastion—the place of refuge for the morose and fatigued poet who had given up on socio-political objectives. Rather, it was the bulwark.

In order that family could fulfill this grand role that Pushkin, in his thought, ascribed to it—to become a true citadel of personal independence and human dignity—it needed to be safeguarded from police incursions and to become a sanctuary in which no external power—from that of the soldier to that of the emperor—could step foot. In Pushkin's mind, the government managed the political existence of its subjects, whereas their private lives were their own business.

These ideals, however, summarized by the English expression "My house is my castle" were difficult to reconcile with the reality of life in Russia under Nicholas I. The idea that his power could be at all limited was alien and incomprehensible to Nicholas I. The Gendarmes corpus organized under his purview was given an exceptionally extensive and deliberately ambiguous mandate. When examining the records of the Third Section and the gendarmes' denunciations, one finds that their fields of inquiry not only concerned political crimes, but also crimes against morality—and not only crimes, but even intentions, opinions, words, and thoughts. The gendarmes might concern themselves with the reading habits of this or that person, the contents of his private correspondence; they did not shy away from printing love-letters and eavesdropping on conversations between friends. Alexandra Smirnova wrote from abroad: "In mother Russia, you can write in Chaldean, and they'll still make out the meaning at the post office. [...] I sometimes receive letters in envelopes simply cut open at the sides." In these circumstances, hopes for a family life safeguarded from government power were fraught, and Pushkin soon became convinced of this.

At the end of April 1834, Pushkin penned a letter to his wife in which he confessed that he feigned illness so as not to have to congratulate the heir to the throne (the future Alexander II[11]) with his coming-of-age. The letter contained an ironic evaluation of the courtly responsibilities forced on Pushkin by Nicholas I. The letter was opened at the post office, given over to Benckendorf who passed it on to the tsar. Pushkin, having found out about all this from a frightened Zhukovsky, was extremely worried. In his diary on May 10, 1834, he wrote: "What profound immorality lies in the habits of our government! The police open letters from husband to wife and bring them to the tsar to read (a man of good education and honesty), and the tsar is not ashamed to admit this—allowing intrigues to take root that are worthy of Vidocq and Bulgarin! Say what you will, autocracy is a tricky business" (12:329).

This entry contains the chief features of Pushkin's attitude to the government at that point: he sought to divorce the tsar as a person whom he regarded with deference and in whom he still recognized worthy traits ("an honest man!") from the principles of absolutism that he saw as the root of evil—regardless of the man behind it. Of utmost importance here is that Pushkin highlights immorality as the essence of this governance. The police practice of opening letters for the sake of political surveillance had been in place since the days of Catherine II (it was introduced by Postmaster Ivan Pestel[12]—the Decembrist's father). Under Nicholas I, it was systematized and completely normalized; the character of Shpekin in Gogol's *The Government Inspector* was a principally contemporary figure.* In 1827, upon finding out that his correspondence was thus illegally read, Zhukovsky wrote an outraged letter to Alexander Turgenev: "Who will trust the post now? What have they gained by destroying sanctity, faith, and possibility of respect for the government? This is infuriating! How can they expect respect for the law from private persons when the government permits itself such illegality?"**

Pushkin was aware that his letters were perused already during his period of southern exile. Then, however, he regarded this with humor: he proposed to Vyazemsky that they organize a private correspondence that avoided the post: "I would send something too intense for the post. It would be better if we

---

*　Belinsky wrote to Gogol in his renowned letter: "The Shpekins open others' letters not only for purposes of delight, but out of the duty of service, for the sake of denunciations."

**　Vasilii Zhukovsky, *Pis'ma k A. I. Turgenevu* [Letters to A. I. Turgenev] (Moscow: Russkii Arkhiv, 1895), 232.

corresponded through Asia on occasion" (13:82). Now, however, his outrage knew no bounds: police surveillance penetrated an area of his life where he hoped to spiritually settle—into his Family and Home. He wrote to his wife of the "secret of family relations disrupted in a most evil and dishonest manner." "No one is supposed to know what happens between a husband and wife; no one must be accepted into our bedroom. Without discretion, there can be no family life" (15:150). A few days later, he wrote again: "The thought that someone is eavesdropping on us brings madness *à la lettre* upon me [*literal madness*—Lotman]. One can get along without political freedom; however, once the inviolability of family (*inviolabilité de la famille*) is threatened—it's impossible: imprisonment is incomparably better" (15:154).

These letters were not simply complaints: it was not in Pushkin's nature to consign himself to helpless complaint. They are the start of a struggle. First and foremost, Pushkin defined the legal basis of his position: by means of analogy to the legal term comprising the foundation of western European juridical norms, that of "the inviolability of the individual's rights," he introduced his own term—"the inviolability of the family" (the translation of the phrase into French was meant to lend it an air of juridical terminology). Later developing this line of thought, Pushkin distinguished two kinds of freedom in his writing—political freedom which lay in the possibility of

> disputing taxes
> Or making it difficult for tsars to fight one another (3:420)

and spiritual freedom, based on the inviolability of family (at this point, Pushkin was only laying the foundations of these ideas; they would come to their complete fruition in his work, and especially lyrics from 1835–1836). His mention of imprisonment has a clear sense: he contrasts himself (struggling for spiritual freedom) with the Decembrists (who struggled for political freedom—imprisonment, in Pushkin's case, could only point to them).

The nature of the struggle determined its tactics as well. Having become convinced of the fact that his letters were being read, he, first and foremost, responded by rejecting the idea that such actions were normal. Demonstratively ignoring this fact, he began to write letters to his wife significantly more severe in nature than earlier. In the space of these letters, he first gave the legal grounds for his idea of the inviolability of family (the fact that it encompassed the right to private correspondence demonstrated the breadth that Pushkin conceptually accorded it). These rights were founded not on political, but moral grounds. Secondly, he undertakes a struggle against those whom he considered guilty of infringing upon his rights as a husband and head of a family. Knowing that they were the ones who were reading his correspondence and that they could never admit it, he included extremely offensive passages directed at them in his letters.

Thus, Pushkin, not without grounds, suspected that the first link in the chain through which his private correspondence passed was the Moscow Postmaster General Alexander Bulgakov.[13] Sashka Bulgakov, as Pushkin hatefully called him in his diary, combined, in his own person, the traits of both Shpekin and Zagoretsky: he was a skillful, gracious, "all-general lender," as Pushkin's friends called him. First and foremost, he was a living chronicle of social rumors, the bearer of news and conveyer of hearsay. Having become the Moscow postmaster in 1832, he, in Vyazemsky's words, found his place in the world: "He received letters, wrote letters, sent letters: in a word, he bathed and swam in letters like a sturgeon in the Oka."*

He not only "bathed and swam," however, but also practiced an art unknown to sturgeons: he opened and read other people's letters, subsequently spreading juicy gossip throughout his circles. He did this of his own accord, "out of love for the literary arts." However, an examination of the records of the

---

* Petr Viazemskii, *Polnoe sobranie sochinenii* [Complete Collected Works], vol. 7 (St. Petersburg: Tipografiia M. M. Stasiulevicha, 1882), 189.

Third Section reveals less innocuous entertainments: copies of letters read by him regularly reached Benckendorf.

Pushkin started his campaign by directly and sharply offending "Sashka Bulgakov." Knowing that his letter would fall into the hands of the Moscow Postmaster General, in one letter, he warned his wife to be more careful seeing as in Moscow, "operates the Postmaster General, that v[illai]n Bulgakov who considers it no sin to open others' letters and sells his own daughters."*

Pushkin not only sent this letter to the post, but also showed it to his friends (this is how we know of its content despite the original having been lost). There is a clear meaning and deliberate strategy behind Pushkin's choice of whom he showed the letter. For instance, Pushkin showed the letter to the minor poet Mikhail Delarue.[14] Delarue was not a close friend of Pushkin's, but he was a close friend of Pavel Miller.[15] Miller, in turn, was a Lyceum graduate and an admirer of Pushkin's work—moreover, he was Benckendorf's personal secretary, and Pushkin could thus count on information of his conflict would come to light not only through Bulgakov's eyes (Pushkin believed that the conflict over the contents of the aforementioned letter had stemmed from the fact that it was improperly expounded to the tsar; there is an entry from Pushkin's diary that states: "The Police [read: "Benckendorf"—Lotman], without having fully understood the meaning, presented the letter to the tsar who hastily also misunderstood it" (12:329).

The force of the offensive strike was concentrated in the mention of the fact that Bulgakov "sold his own daughters." Bulgakov's youngest daughter, who had married Prince Alexander Dolgorukov[16] three weeks before Pushkin's marriage, was famous in Moscow for her beauty. There were also scandalous rumors regarding her intimacy with Nicholas I. Pushkin wrote in his diary that Nicholas I, in Moscow, "courted the young Princess D.[olgorukaya]."[17] When

---

* "D. M. Delariu i A. S. Pushkin" [D. M. Delariu and A. S. Pushkin], *Russkaia Starina* 29, no. 9 (1880): 219.

she gave birth to her first daughter, Nicholas I was the godfather. By hinting at this rumor, Pushkin precluded the possibility that Bulgakov would show a copy of the letter to the administration.

Pushkin did not plan to confine himself to branding the postmaster's person. He needed to ensure that the tsar knew what such actions were called in the language of honest people. After having found out that his letters were read, he began writing more harshly. The most audacious of these passages were accompanied with such ambiguous phrases as: "This is not for your eyes"; "Do you not think that swinish Petersburg is abominable to me? What joy is it to live from pasquil to denunciation?" (15:154). While foregoing any caution himself, he constantly called on his wife to exercise caution, emphasizing that he did not for one minute forget the alien eyes that looked upon their correspondence: "be careful, it is likely that your letters are opened as well: Government Security demands this" (15:157). The bitter irony of the latter phrase is directed towards the same ambiguous addressee. The tsar liked to present himself as a gentleman: he was impeccably polite with the ladies and enjoyed the occasional act of gallantry. Pushkin puts forth a noxious caricature—a gentleman who reads strangers' letters—and then with insulting generosity forgives the tsar for using this as means of "government security." "I am no longer angry at him because *toute réflexion faite*,* he's not at fault for the swinishness of his surroundings." He then writes that "when one lives in a latrine," one grows accustomed to the stench, "and the stench ceases to be repulsive, albeit you're a *gentleman*. Oh how I would love to breathe some clean air" (15:159). This unique assessment of Nicholas I's reign was intended for a readership among government circles.

The case of the opened letters was imbued with symbolic meaning in Pushkin's eyes: it signified the powerlessness of the individual under an autocratic regime. Pushkin's moods were apparently closely in line with a favorite

---

* In essence (French).

expression of Sergei Saltykov's,[18] a famous eccentric and original, whose "Tuesdays" in his house on Malaya Morskaya Pushkin frequented in 1833–1836. In his early childhood, he had a quarrel with the future Alexander I having been the latter's playmate. His career was subsequently beyond repair, and he had retired early on, isolating himself in demonstrative opposition to the government. A friend and companion of Saltykov's thus recalled one of his favorite topics for discussion: "Often Saltykov addressed his wife with the following which often provoked surprise in me: 'I saw today *le grand bourgeois*—it is not difficult to guess whom he meant with these words—I assure, *ma chère*, he *can* whip you with a rod, if he *wishes*; I repeat: he *can*.'"*

It would be topical to recall here Leo Tolstoy's reaction to the police search of his Yasnaya Polyana estate in 1862, which psychologically echoes Pushkin's feelings of frustration. Leo Tolstoy wrote to his aunt, Alexandra Tolstaya,[19] on August 7, 1862: "I shan't hide, I will loudly declare that I am selling my estate so as to leave Russia where one cannot be sure that a minute hence, he, his sister, his wife, his mother will not be bound and whipped—I am leaving."**

The fact that Tolstoy and Pushkin's positions are so congruous is no coincidence: it was Tolstoy who continued the tradition of Pushkin's ideas with his cultivation of notions of the family as a sanctuary of "one's self-dignity." The foundation of Pushkin's ideological program was personal independence. This was the thing that was most hard to come by in the "swinish Petersburg" of Nicholas I.

---

* By calling the tsar a "tradesman," Saltykov expresses aristocratic disdain for the emperor. *Ma chère*—"my dear" [French]. The quote belongs to Wilhelm von Lenz. (Aleksander Pushkin, *Dnevnik. 1833–1835* [Diary. 1833–1835] ed. Boris Modzalevsky (Moscow–Petrograd: Gosizdat, 1923), 145.

** Tolstoi, *Sobranie sochinenii*, 18:589.

Nicholas I was wary of taking his eyes off Pushkin. Benckendorf advised him to this effect: "It would do well that he served, as opposed to being left to his own devices."*

On January 1, 1834, Pushkin made the following entry in his diary: "On the third, I will be granted the office of Gentleman of the Bedchamber (which is rather unbecoming to my years)"** (12:318). This "office" would create all sorts of troubles for the poet, and ultimately would contribute to his tragic death. Pushkin found himself tethered to Petersburg and the court. Henceforth he would have to appear at every official ceremony in a courtly uniform, bear the lessons of not only Benckendorf, but also those of the Court Oberchamberlain, the Count Litt.[20] Nicholas I, in his soul, was a petty tyrant: even in church he would rebuke his courtiers and straighten out the great princes and princesses like soldiers before a parade. Pushkin was forced to endure petty complaints as to his mistakes in different courtly rituals. Pushkin's pride was damaged for an additional reason as well: the office of Gentleman of the Bedchamber was a minor one. It was typically given to young men who had not yet made a name for themselves. The appearance of a thirty-year-old poet and head of a family in their company was cause for jokes and laughter, simultaneously demonstrating that in the eyes of Nicholas I, to be a poet was to be no one.

Pushkin was unable to reject the "graces" of the tsar, though he openly demonstrated his dissatisfaction: he refused to sew a uniform befitting

---

* *Starina i novizna* [The Old and the New], vol. 6 (St. Petersburg: Tipografiia M. M. Stasiulevicha, 1903), 10.

** Pushkin was relieved of his duty in 1824, having reached the rank of collegial secretary (a rank "of the tenth class"). Pushkin did not serve subsequently, and when Nicholas I returned him to government service, Pushkin was given a rank of the ninth class (the classes were arranged in descending order). At court, where the tsar registered the poet, this corresponded to the rank of Gentleman of the Bedchamber. Strictly speaking, this was fair on the tsar's part—he did not want to contradict the regular order of elevation through the ranks for Pushkin. In fact, however, this was insulting: Gentlemen of the Bedchamber were almost always young men in their teenage years.

a Gentleman of the Bedchamber, and his friends had to nearly force him to purchase a used uniform. Pushkin also regularly skipped official ceremonies, much to the tsar's frustration. After receiving this post, Pushkin met the tsar at a ball given by the Countess Bobrinskaya.[21] Despite what etiquette absolutely demanded, Pushkin neglected to thank the tsar for the post given to him, rather speaking about Pugachev on whose history he was working: he spoke with the tsar in a manner befitting a poet and historian, not as a gentleman of the bedchamber.

Natalya had a different attitude towards her husband's appointment. She had hardly turned twenty-two. She wanted to enjoy herself, delighting in balls at which her beauty always shone most brightly. It was as though she considered these pleasures a reward for a joyless childhood and an adolescence spent in a miserable house dominated by a half-mad father[22] (who soon after became *fully* mad) and a mother who was predisposed to heavy bouts of drinking. As the wife of a Gentleman of the Bedchamber, her presence was always expected not only at the glamorous balls and receptions held at the Winter Palace, but even the more prestigious courtly balls and parties held at the Anichkov Palace, reserved for only the most carefully chosen people close to the royal family. She was flattered that her beauty impressed the tsar himself who platonically courted her. Pushkin had no reason to doubt her faithfulness, as he was fully convinced of her loyalty, but this courting was torturous, as it spawned rumors in society.

Society and the court had quickly become a force that pretended towards Natalya's heart and interest, threatening to do away with Pushkin's ideals of home and family. Pushkin limited himself to jokes, aiming to diminish the charms that "the vanity of society" held for Natalya. Informing her as to rumors that were spreading around Moscow regarding her, he wrote: "It's clear that you forced someone into a state of such despair with your coquettishness and harshness that, in order to console himself, he found himself a harem of young theater students. This is no good, my anger: humility is the greatest flower of your sex" (16: 112-113). "Someone" refers here to Nicholas I.

The struggle with society over Natalya's heart invariably occupied Pushkin's thoughts. While building his home, he sympathetically recalled a line from a poem by Kantemir: "A pot of cabbage stew, the biggest one, I'm the master of my house."*

When he was yet pondering his ideals for family life, he understood that a prerequisite in realizing his plans was a conception of the Mistress. Like Leo Tolstoy later, he planned on "marrying a young lady" (an expression out of Leo Tolstoy's book, when the latter was planning his own family life) and turn her into a mistress of the house. He characteristically reworked Kantemir's line:

> My ideal is now a housewife
> My desire is but peace
> And a pot of cabbage stew, the biggest one. (6:201)

He steadily led Natalya towards this ideal: in his letters he instructed "What kind of helpers or workers are you? You only work with your little feet at the balls and help husbands spend their money." So, on one side of the opposition is the mistress, the helper, and even the worker; on the other, the woman of society, the frequenter of balls.

Pushkin and Tolstoy's ideas were strikingly similar: they conceived of their ideals of Family and Home not as something genteel and Petersburgian, but rather as something national and even demotic. However, even for *Anna Karenina*'s Levin, "marrying a peasant girl" remains a fantasy. Pushkin, like later Tolstoy and Levin, arrives at the idea of marrying a noble girl and raising her to be a Mistress. Pushkin's relationship towards Natalya was a system of instruction. But Tolstoy, in order to "instruct" Sofia Andreevna[23] according to his ideals, took her to his Yasnaya Polyana estate; Pushkin was tethered to

---

*   Kantemir, *Sobranie stikhotvorenii*, 137.

"swinish Petersburg" and all his attempts to flee to his rural estate were met with Benckendorf's malevolence and the tsar's suspicions.

While drafting one of his most touching poems, "'Tis time, my friend, 'tis time! The heart demands calm," addressed to his wife, Pushkin included on the same sheet a summary of his thoughts and feelings at the time:

> Youth has no need of the *at home*,* and maturity is horrified at its solitude. Happy is he who finds a companion—that means he's found a home.
>
> O will it be soon that I shall bring my hearth and home to the countryside—fields, gardens, peasants, books; poetic labors—family, love, etc.—religion, death. (3:941)

However, Pushkin and Tolstoy's domestic ideals only enjoyed a partial intersection: Pushkin's worldview was entirely free of notions of asceticism. He desired a full life; he was attracted not to self-limitation, not to thoughts of "how much man needs on earth," but to a life, rather, that boiled over the edge, bursting out in every possible colors. Thus, the disgust that "swinish Petersburg" provoked did not signify a rejection of the poetic beauty of the white nights of Petersburg, the rich cultural life in all its manifestations: from his labors in publishing a journal (which was only possible in the capital) to intellectual and lively conversations with writers close to him, to the disputes and exchanges of opinions he engaged in with diplomats, or the inspiring conversations he participated in with the women of society in possession of good taste and poetic feeling.

It would be a mistake to think that neither genteel life nor the image of the woman of society held any charm for Pushkin. It is hardly accidental that at the same time that he was declaring the mistress as his ideal, he described his beloved Tatyana as a "commander of the hall." The social salons of Elizaveta Khitrovo, Dolly Ficquelmont,[24] or Sofie Karamzina[25] were oases of cultural life

---

* Pushkin uses this English expression in his letter (Translator's note).

in "swinish Petersburg." For Pushkin, they had little in common with the salons of the hateful gossiper Maria Nesselrode[26] or those of d'Anthès'[27] patron, Sofie Bobrinskaya, with balls held at the Anichkov Palace.

A thirst for a fullness of existence, peaceful happiness and a desire for rest and willpower, rather than precluding, supplemented Pushkin's ideal of an existence replete with creative intensity. When Pushkin pondered a life in society that, instead of excluding, added to "familial independence," he would think of the circles that echoed the cultural life of the Decembrist era.

After the Decembrist movement had been routed, women were the chief guardians of the spirit of freethinking. Men during Nicholas I's reign, terrified of the gendarmes and trapped in their service uniforms, spoiled by the spirit of the servile pecking order, fell much more easily under the sway of the degenerating influence of the government machine. Aristocratic women were largely removed from this. A type emerged, among families steeped in the cultural tradition, of a proud and independent, freedom-loving, educated, and nuanced woman. The social circles of *such* women, who preserved the spirit cultivated by their brothers and childhood friends sent by Nicholas to the depths of Siberia, did not disrupt the world of independent family living. Natalya was attracted to a different kind of a society—the kind that was more closely tied to the official face of Nicholas I's monarchy. There, Pushkin was the object of antagonistic curiosity, and his wife—the object of hypocritical pity and noxious rumors. Slaves disdain independence in others. Pushkin, who allowed himself to condemn the acts of the government and, moreover, to have an opinion of his own; Pushkin, who through his appearance and behavior negated the trivial differences between a gentleman of the bedchamber and noblemen of any other possible rank and level; Pushkin, with whom foreign diplomats spoke with deference, having heard of his fame as it spread through Europe, whom they valued not for his rank, but for the depth of his political acumen and his disposition as a man of governance—Pushkin, as such, provoked the jealousy and hatred of the latter circles.

Pushkin's relationship with the governing bureaucracy was also becoming increasingly strained. Sergei Uvarov must surely be named among Pushkin's most irreconcilable enemies of the mid-1830s. Uvarov's own character is notable, and his conflict with Pushkin was not by chance.

Sergei Uvarov was an influential public figure during Nicholas I's reign who is famous for his ill-fated phrase "Orthodoxy, Autocracy, Nationality"; he was a person of great talents and possessed a brilliant albeit superficial education. In his youth, he had been a member of the Karamzinists' literary camp and become one of the founders and driving forces behind Arzamas. His friendships with Karamzin, Zhukovsky, Turgenev and his magnificent skill at declaring his own opinions guaranteed him the glories he would enjoy as a future critic and man of letters. In the 1810s, a certain group from among the Karamzinists was close to the "liberal" government bureaucracy and quickly made careers for themselves. Bludov, Dashkov,[28] the Turgenev brothers, Severin,[29] and Zhukovsky occupied influential government, diplomatic, and court positions. Griboedov, who regarded the Karamzinists with humor, presciently showed in his Molchalin how sentimentality, Romantic dreaminess, playing the flute, and platonic affairs with the daughters of noblemen went excellently hand-in-hand with careerism, intellectual equivocation, and bureaucratic soullessness. There are grounds for presuming that Uvarov had been something of a prototype for Molchalin.

Uvarov had been poor and of a minor family. However, he managed to force his way into the house of Alexei Razumovsky,[30] the minister of enlightenment, and, as if acting out a sentimental novel, married an unattractive but incredibly wealthy daughter[31] of his who was much older than Uvarov and had already given up hopes off being married. Thanks to his marriage, Uvarov's star ascended: at the age of only thirty-two and despite being little more than a talented dilettante, he became the president of the Academy of Sciences. The Molchalin-like traits he exhibited already worried his former Arzamas companions; Turgenev wrote the following regarding Uvarov's service in the

Ministry of Finance (like many other successful bureaucrats, he occupied several posts simultaneously): Uvarov "knows all of Cancrin's wet-nurses and feeds oatmeal to the children."*

1825 was the year that sealed the fates of the Karamzinists. Though most of them found themselves, more or less, in opposition to the new regime, Bludov and Uvarov abruptly switched to the victors' sides and took active part in investigations conducted on their erstwhile Decembrist friends and also actively contributed to the ideological formation of the new regime.

Historian Sergei Solovyev[32] gave a notable characterization of Uvarov:

> Uvarov was a man, needless to say, of brilliant talent [...] but the capabilities of his heart did not in any way correspond to the capabilities of his mind; conversely, he was a servant who had learned good manners in the house of his honest master (Alexander I), but remained, in his core, a servant; he spared no expenses in appeasing his master (Nicholas I); he flattered the latter with notions that he, Nicholas, was the creator of some kind of new education based on new fundamentals: Orthodoxy, Autocracy, Nationality; he promoted Orthodoxy despite being godless himself; autocracy despite being a liberal, and nationality despite not having read a single Russian book in his life.**

Solovyev then writes that "there was no baseness too low for him to grasp."

Renegades always exert themselves beyond every measure. A former liberal, Uvarov informed Nicholas I that the measures taken by Benckendorf in bringing literature under rein were insufficient. Thus, it was he who, overcoming Benckendorf's resistance and the latter's dissatisfaction with an incursion into "his" field, was able to attain the prohibition of Polevoi's *The Moscow Telegraph*. The rivalry between Uvarov and Benckendorf—between the ideological apparatus and the police apparatus in the literary field—must be

---

*   *Ostaf'evskii arkhiv kn. Viazemskikh* [The Ostafyev Archive of the Princes Vyazemsky], vol. 3 (St. Petersburg: Tipografiia M. M. Stasiulevicha, 1899), 33.

** Sergei Solov'ev, *Zapiski* [Notes] (Petrograd: Prometei, 1915), 58–59.

understood in order to grasp the meaning of one of Pushkin's most dramatic conflicts with the government in the 1830s.

Uvarov hoped to use Pushkin's tremendous authority for his own careerism. In 1831, he actively requested to be placed in the role of Pushkin's patron: he took haste in translating Pushkin's "To the Slanderers of Russia" into French; he presented himself as an intermediary between Pushkin and Benckendorf. He genuinely could not understand that nobility, human dignity, and the pursuit of independence *existed*, and thus saw in Pushkin a proud man aiming to raise his stock, someone with whom an agreement could be reached. He promised Pushkin that he would give him "the first open spot" in the Russian Academy, and, taking him to the halls of the Moscow University, presented him to the students, introducing him with a premeditated, flattering phrase.

When Pushkin coldly rejected these attempts and then fastidiously distanced himself from Uvarov, the latter's ire knew no bounds. Uvarov undertook a campaign of social slander against Pushkin, affirming in salons that *The History of Pugachev* was a harmful and dangerous work (though it had received the tsar's approval and was being printed in the Third Section's typography with Benckendorf's support—the latter had even given Pushkin credit from the government in order to finance it). Pushkin wrote the following in his diary in February 1835: "Uvarov is a great scoundrel. He bemoans my book as an outrageous composition" (12:337). At the same time, Uvarov was making Pushkin's service difficult. Following 1826, the censorship procedures of Pushkin's works, though nominally conducted by the tsar himself, were de facto undertaken by Benckendorf's department, but still avoiding the usual censor. Oddly enough, this was something of a relief: Benckendorf was the master, and the censors his lackeys. They were systematically terrorized at work and fired from their posts (these people were, as a rule of thumb, not wealthy and highly valued their posts), and were even occasionally arrested for a small error. Seeing as there were no regulatory standards for censorship and nobody had possessed an exact notion of what was permitted and what was not (for instance, *The Moscow Telegraph* became prohibited after publishing an article that had passed the censor), the brunt of the censorship fell on the censors' cowardice. Uvarov managed to set up the censorship process in such a way that Pushkin's journal *The Contemporary* [Sovremennik], aside from having to pass Benckendorf's censorship, also had to pass the regular censorship process, and Uvarov deliberately gave it to the stupidest and most cowardly censors to peruse. Pushkin's position as a writer became unbearable: Uvarov slowly and persistently tightened the noose around Pushkin's neck.

Pushkin, however, was capable of standing up for himself. It is no wonder that he admired Lomonosov[33] for the fact that "it was unwise to joke with him." He landed a marvelous retaliatory strike on Uvarov—lightning-fast like the swipe of a saber and sharp like a slap in the face. Pushkin made use of a scandalous story that was spreading like wildfire among members of society: Sheremetev,[34] a renowned rich man who lacked direct heirs became dangerously ill, and Uvarov, who was his cousin-twice-removed's husband and expected to receive part of the inheritance, began counting Sheremetev's money in hurried and unseemly fashion. Sheremetev's health improved, however, and Uvarov found himself in a disgraced position. In September 1835, in *The Moscow Observer* [Moskovsky Nabludatel], Pushkin's poem titled "On Lukulla's Recovery" was published. It was subtitled "An Imitation of the Latin" though this could not mislead anyone—it only accentuated the irony.

In the spirit of a Horatian satire and brilliantly imitating the style of the Latin poet, Pushkin described the illness of a young wealthy man and featured a repulsive caricature of the impatient heir. Capably weaving Uvarov's biographical features into the caricature, Pushkin attained a great comic effect, unifying the "Roman" spirit of the narrative with the realities of Uvarov's biography, who, pondering his future inheritance, says:

> "Now then I won't have to
> Nurse my nobleman's little children
> [...]

> I won't shortchange my wife
> And I won't have to steal
> Government firewood!" (3:405)

The poem achieved its desired effect. Nikitenko,[35] a censor, wrote in his diary: "the piece has caused an uproar in the city. Everyone, without doubt, recognizes Uvarov in it."* Pushkin was forced to explain himself before Benckendorf. He used this opportunity to innocently express his shock that Uvarov would identify with this caricature of "a lowly, miserly villain, who steals government firewood, shortchanges his wife with false bills, a sycophant turned wet-nurse in noble houses" (16:251). In the eyes of society, Uvarov was disgraced. He responded to Pushkin in kind, with limitless hatred and noxious slander.

Aside from these various unpleasant occurrences, disappointments, and cares that Pushkin experienced during the 1830s, there was another major one: a lack of money. Supporting his family, life in society into which Pushkin had been forced against his will, financial support of his parents, sister, and completely financially incompetent brother required money, money, and more money. Pushkin did not have it. Troubled reflections on the fact that in the event of his untimely death, his children would be left penniless, appear more and more frequently in his correspondence with his wife. Pushkin counted on the publication of *The History of Pugachev* to remedy his financial circumstances somewhat and borrowed 10,000 rubles from the government. The publication did not live up to his expectations, and the debt remained. In the future, he would have to ask for another loan from Nicholas I, hedged on his future salary. In 1836, according to his own calculations in a letter to Cancrin, the minister of finances, he had racked up debts to the government totaling a stupefying 45,000 rubles. This debt inexorably tied Pushkin to the court, his service post, and Petersburg. And there was still no money. Without new literary ventures, there could be no hope that these financial troubles could be alleviated, and the bustle of Petersburg life prevented him from reaching the "quiet and freedom" he required to work. In the autumn of 1835, during his favorite time for literary work, he traveled to Mikhailovskoe, "to earn money." From there he wrote to his wife: "You have no idea how lively the imagination is when one sits alone between four walls or strolls through the woods, and nobody inhibits your thinking—you can think until your head hurts. And what do I think of? I think of this: what will we live on?" (16:48).

Pushkin's heavy mood was intensified by his feeling that he had lost touch with readers. The reader was becoming more democratic, and the years-long campaign in the journals that declared Pushkin an aristocrat bore its fruits. This was certainly aided by news of Pushkin's appointment as Gentleman of the Bedchamber, a position whose real responsibilities were unknown to the public. Pushkin received an anonymous satire accusing him of treachery towards the ideals of his youth and servility before the government.

It was a difficult time for Pushkin.

Chapter Nine

The Final Years

Knowing Pushkin's circumstances during his last years, it is perfectly natural that one would imagine him tired, tortured, and in low spirits. Weariness really does permeate his letters from this time. A few of his contemporaries recall him as lost and crestfallen during this time. They are correct insofar as these judgments reflect impressions gleamed by eyewitnesses who, unlike us, were able to see him. They are, however, incorrect with respect to what we know about Pushkin that they could not have known. Thus, his contemporaries believed that Pushkin abandoned writing except for the odd journalistic piece written with the express intent of earning money. Only his death, which revealed his manuscripts, initially to narrow circles of people, would show just how untrue these assumptions were. Even people as close to Pushkin as Baratynsky were forced to subsequently admit how obscure Pushkin's inner life had been to them. In a letter to his wife,[1] Baratynsky wrote the following regarding the discovery he had made "when rifling through Pushkin's unpublished new poems" (in 1840, had Baratynsky visited Zhukovsky when the latter was examining Pushkin's papers): "There are incredible beauties, completely new in spirit and form. All his late compositions are distinguished by what, would you think? By their force and depth! He was only coming into maturity."*

Onlookers saw Pushkin at balls of which he had grown weary, where he, in his own words, was "forced to snooze by the time and guzzle down ice cream." They also saw him engaged in literary discussions where he was

---

*   Evgenii Baratynskii, *Stikhotvoreniia. Pis'ma. Vospominaniia sovremennikov* [Poems. Letters. Contemporaries' Recollections] (Moscow: Pravda, 1987), 270.

frustrated by his interlocutors' stupidity, in financial troubles, and in the heat of literary conflicts. Nobody had the chance to see him, however, when he sat, by his own expression, alone "between four walls" or strolling through the woods, when nobody prevented him from "thinking, thinking until your head hurts." Yet this was where his real life was concentrated. Pushkin's creative life during these troublesome years does not carry any marks of spiritual dejection, as might be expected. Alexander Turgenev, who frequently met Pushkin, wrote on December 21, 1836, in a letter: "He is full of ideas."* After all, this was one of the most dramatic moments in the poet's life: this was when Pushkin challenged d'Anthès to a duel for the first time, and d'Anthès, either in order to avoid it (in Pushkin's opinion) or responding to a demand made by Nicholas I (also a plausible version of what transpired), proposed marriage to Ekaterina, Natalya Goncharova's sister. It is easy to imagine what tempests stormed in Pushkin's soul during these days. Yet it was chiefly during this time that he was "full of ideas." His creative thinking did not stop for a minute. It endowed Pushkin's entire existence with sublime meaning and gave him astonishing strength. Life tried to crush him, and in his soul, he would transform it into a world permeated with dramatism and harmony and enlightened by the wise clarity of its author's eye. Only a day-by-day reconstruction of the reality of Pushkin's existence during these final years, full as it was of tragedy and hopelessness, affords a true appreciation of the lucidity, simplicity, and serenity of his writing from these years.

There was no "calm and freedom," and it appears as though everything was conspiring against Pushkin, but the drive of creative energy was more powerful than any external circumstances and transformed them.

In the difficult years of 1833–1836, Pushkin's writing achieves its upper limit of intensity. He writes the epic poems *Angelo* (1833), *The Bronze*

---

* *Moskovskii pushkinist*, ed. Mstislav Tsiavlovskii, vol. 1 (Moscow: Nikitinskie subbotniki, 1927), 270.

Horseman (1833); his best prose compositions, *Dubrovsky* (1832–1833), *The Queen of Spades* (1833), *Egyptian Nights* (1835), *The Captain's Daughter* (1833–1836); and his most significant poetry, "Autumn" (1833), "'Tis time, my friend, 'tis time! The heart demands calm…" (1834), "Songs of the Western Slavs" (1834), "The Commander," "Once again I visited…," "The Feast of Peter the Great," "When the Assyrian ruler…" (1835), "Secular Power," "From Pindemonte," "Desert Fathers and Women Without Fault," "When, outside the city, in thought I wander," and "I erected a monument for myself, not built by hands" (1836). In 1836, he began publishing a journal called *The Contemporary* whose critical section was largely filled with his own articles. Pushkin was also intensively engaged in historical work: he wrote *The History of Pugachev*, he was also working on a history of Peter the Great's rule. (He considered this work especially important: when Pushkin petitioned to resign his post with the intention to finally cut ties with Petersburg and leave for the countryside, it sufficed for Nicholas I to threaten to revoke his access to the archives which would have made the continuation of Pushkin's work impossible; Pushkin then immediately recanted his request. All the suffering he endured in Petersburg was worth, in his mind, the chance to continue his work.)

The intensity of Pushkin's creative work manifested not only in its pure quantity, but also in the dynamic nature of his thought. During periods of creative uplift, "when thoughts tremble in valor," Pushkin's mind operated with fabulous speed. During this periods, new ideas swiftly replaced old ones, with plans continuously outrunning the possibility of their implementation. There are numerous remaining plans, sketches, ideas for large works and drafts of unfinished works serving as monuments to these intense streaks in Pushkin's creative life. They could not be finished because Pushkin's mind ran too far ahead, leaving them behind like uncompleted palaces whose creator became drawn to newer, even grander plans. Pushkin's inspired state during these years can be attested by the sheer quantity and ambition of these unfinished works.

He becomes possessed with the idea of writing a long novel with a complex adventure plot that would allow him to illustrate the different classes of Russian society—he planned a *Novel at the Caucasian Waters*, a work that perhaps could have been a precursor to *A Hero of Our Time*. In 1834–1836, he sketched out a long psychological adventure novel (its tentative title in the draft papers was *The Russian Pelham*) in which he was to present all of Russia—from the Decembrist Union of Welfare to the dens of forest bandits. At the same time, he began working on a story with a plot from Roman life (perhaps this mysterious idea should be connected to a long-ago conceived idea of writing a work on Christ). Pushkin was interested in the fate of European civilization: he read French historians who had treated upon class struggle during the feudal era and the roots of the French Revolution; he was interested in writing a history of the French Revolution himself and began work on two compositions which were to encompass the bourgeois era from its roots to the present-day. The first was as a collection of scenes from a grand historical drama (after Pushkin's death it was published under the title *Scenes from Chivalric Times*); Nikolai Chernyshevsky[2] considered it Pushkin's greatest work. The second was a story titled *Maria Schoening*, a tragic story of poverty and humiliation. He was also working on a drama about Russian folk life, *Rusalka*. He was quite literally overrun with creative ideas, and so he generously shared them. Thus, he had sketched out a plan for a comedy about a man who was confused for an important bureaucrat in a provincial town; he gave this plan over to Gogol. Gogol wrote *The Government Inspector*. Later, he ceded to Gogol a plan from which *Dead Souls* would emerge.

This sprawling list—which extends beyond what is catalogued here—of things planned, begun, considered, set aside, abandoned in favor of works newly rushing up is a testament to Pushkin's inspired state as a writer during these years. And needless to say, the old Romantic cliché that there are two personalities embodied in the poet's soul, one that is involved in ordinary life and crushed under its burden and the genius that hovers over his own existence, will not explain anything in Pushkin's inner life for us. No, Pushkin was a human being in his poetry and a poet in his life.

Contemporary archaeology knows the following method: aerial surveillance and aerial photography. Oftentimes a wonderful metamorphosis occurs with the objects that the archaeologist works with on the ground: that which, on ground level, appears as nothing other than a disorderly pile of rocks or the remnants of scattered disjointed buildings is suddenly transformed into parts of a unified whole from a bird's eye view, acquiring rhythm and a singularly designed meaning.

When examining the completed and unfinished works from Pushkin's final three years, we are struck, on the one hand, by their richness, and on the other, by their diversity and, one might even say, eclecticism. It is difficult to unify a drama with scenes from folklife, *Rusalka*, and the beginning of a fantasy adventure epic poem with Spanish scenes based on the plot of Jan Potocki's[3] novel *A Manuscript found in Saragossa* (Pushkin's fragment "Alfons mounts his horse"), or scenes from the European Middle Ages and a contemporary novel whose action takes place in the Caucasus. This is where one must employ the method of "aerial photography," so that these fragments come together as a whole, unified by a single deliberate design. This design is a grandiose conception of world civilization as a certain singular stream. Pushkin was interested in moments of historical cataclysm, tragic conflicts through which the idea of humanity paves its way. He esteemed progress as a humanization of history—the triumph of the cultural and spiritual foundations of human existence over the violence and crude materiality of power.

Ideas of historism preoccupied Pushkin as long back as the mid-1820s. At that time, history as a vessel of progressive essence manifested in state governance and in its ideal representative—Peter I. The individual's pretensions towards happiness and an existence independent of the general historical process were reckoned as a form of Romantic egotism and fervently rejected. In *Poltava*, positive characters, like Kochubei and Iskra, and villains, such as

Mazepa,⁴ are condemned alike by history to oblivion due to their having both been driven by personal, human impulses:

> A century has passed, and what is left
> Of these proud and hardy men. (5:63)

History only preserves the memories of those that entirely merge with it, leaving no trace. By relinquishing their autonomous individuality, they acquire historical immortality:

> Amidst the citizenry of the northern power,
> In its bellicose fate,
> You alone, hero of Poltava,
> Erected a massive monument to yourself. (5:63)

At this point, however, Pushkin treated history not as something opposed to the individual, but as a living chain of real human lives. History is understood as a generation of simply "non-historic" individuals, a chain in which ancestral graves, a roundelay of living people joined hand-in-hand, and cradles full of children comprise a single ring of immortality. Progress consists of humanity's accumulation of memory, that is, culture, and in the spiritual progress of the individual. Therein lay the older Pushkin's interest in a history reflected in the diaries of private people, in episodes of lives lived in different eras. Pushkin collected historical anecdotes from Russian life in the eighteenth century and assembled in his own diary a domestic chronicle of life at the court and in Petersburg. The pathos of culture in all the richness of its historical existence and the pathos of the spiritual significance of the individual are what unifies Pushkin's manifold plans and sketches of this late period.

Pushkin's proud cognizance of the idea that spirit and culture accord immortality, and not power and force, served as the foundation of his "I erected a monument for myself not built by hands"—his poetic final will and testament.*

---

* For an overview of scholarship and interpretations of this text see Mikhail Alexeev, *Stikhotvorenie Pushkina "Ia pamiatnik sebe vozdvig...": Problemi ego izhucheniia* [Pushkin's

Two central themes become intertwined in Pushkin's works from the 1830s: the theme of Peter I and the theme of peasant rebellion. Their complex interaction reveals the idiosyncrasy of the Pushkin's attitude towards history. The theme of peasant rebellion appears in draft sketches for *A History of the Village of Goriukhino* and later becomes the chief theme of his novella *Dubrovsky*.

Further developing the ideas of aristocratic revolution, Pushkin opined that the leading aristocrat was a natural ally of the folk, and that the Russian nobility, which with every decade was losing its social privileges while maintaining a centuries-long experience of resisting absolutism, was a revolutionary force by its very nature. In 1834, he entered the following in his diary regarding the Russian aristocracy: "There is no such dire rebellious element in Europe. Who was at the square on December 14? Only aristocrats. How many will appear with the next troubles? I'm not sure, but I think many will" (12:335). The government leaned on sycophants and minions, a pseudo-aristocracy, a "miserable crowd standing by the throne" (Lermontov), and also on a faceless bureaucratic machine. An exemplary nobleman, the descendent of an ancient house, Dubrovsky becomes a folk leader, and Troerukov—a relative of Princess Dashkova,[5] a friend of Catherine II and a participant in the coup d'état of 1762—"leaves for the mountains" (8:162). A single chain stretches from Catherine II who usurped power, through Dashkova, to the foolish feudal lord, and the Shabashkins of the world.

The idea of a nobleman who joins the side of the people was initially placed at the heart of a novel about Pugachev's era. However, the closer Pushkin got to fleshing out this plan, the more he became disillusioned with the possibility of such an alliance.

Poem "I erected a monument for myself...": Issues of its Study] (Leningrad: Nauka, 1967).

The notion that irreconcilable struggle between different social forces is always historically justifiable and unavoidable lay at the heart of several historical works (*The Captain's Daughter, Scenes from Chivalric Times*); it is completed by that humanity in which, according to Belinsky, was encompassed the chief pathos of Pushkin's works. When humanity incurs upon a world of merciless social conflict, the heroes of *The Captain's Daughter* are able to elevate themselves above the "cruel age"; thus, in *The Bronze Horseman*, the historical mercilessness of Peter I's reforms becomes a cause for rebuke of reform as a whole. Describing Pushkin's pathos, Belinsky wrote: "Ethical instruction makes us simply 'human beings', that is creatures who reflect the brilliance of Divinity and thus loom over the living world. It is good to be a scholar, a poet, a warrior, a giver of laws etc., but it is lousy when one stops being a 'human being' at the same time; to be 'human' means to possess a complete and perfect right to existence without having to be anything but 'human.'"*

This pathos also serves to explain Pushkin's predisposition to featuring "simple" heroes (the objective of Pushkin's historical novels becomes the depiction of the fates of the "simple man" in the tragic circumstances of historical conflicts), which is one of the defining features of Pushkin's realism:

> Exclaim: "what nonsense!" or "*bravo*"
> Or say nothing at all
> I am resolved—I had the right
> To elect my own neighbor
> As the hero of this humble tale,
> Though he is no military man,
> No [second-rate] Don Juan
> No demon—not even a gypsy,
> But just a citizen of the capital
> Such as we encounter in multitudes. (5:103)

Pushkin's creative position was tied to his psychology of living. The idea that human beings have a "complete and perfect right to existence without be-

---

*   Belinskii, *Sobranie*, 7:391.

ing anything other than human" defined the poetry of private existence, "calm and freedom" which, for Pushkin, became the foundation not only of how he organized his poetry, but his life as well.

However, during this time, in a gradual swell, tragic notes began to sound in Pushkin's life. There were many reasons for this, but they all had a single common denominator. The ebullient lifestyle of writing and play, filled with diverse interests, required by Pushkin, demanded a correspondingly "playful," effervescent, and creative milieu and era. The genius personality, when placed within a dynamic situation full of inexhaustible possibilities, multiplies its riches, gaining more and more new, unexpected aspects of life. Living is turned into art, and such a person derives the joy of an artist from life itself. The creative glimmer of Pushkin's personality did not find a fitting interlocutor in his milieu and era. In Pushkin's conditions, every new acquaintance became a new chain tying him down; every situation, rather than compounding, limited his freedom more greatly. Instead of swimming in a rugged sea, Pushkin was treading in quickly hardening cement.

Pushkin was not capable of limiting himself to a kind of "passivity" that would have, in these circumstances, singularly preserved some semblance of inner freedom—the kind that was the lot of Mikhail Orlov or Chaadaev, after the latter had been deemed insane. Meanwhile, his own activity only increased his cumbersome ties, removing his "separateness" from a world in which he found no happiness, freedom, or respite. Attempts at participating in the historical life of the era culminated in humiliating and fruitless conversations, rebukes, dressings-down carried out by Benckendorf or the tsar. Whenever Pushkin attempted his hand at poetry in any public measure, it brought conversations with censors, struggles for freedom of expression and thought; other attempts at participating in literary life led to literary conflicts, unavoidable contacts with thick-headed and treacherous "colleagues," as well as a growing disconnection and lack of understanding from his readers; activity in society engendered gossip and slander. Even the family life that had been so crucial to Pushkin revealed its stereotypical, rigid core: financial troubles, jealousy, mutual alienation.

Pushkin, by his deepest nature, was incapable of creating a small, isolated world *of his own*. Rather, he entered into a hopeless and heroic struggle with the world around him, trying to stir it up and to arouse spirit and life within it—but in every such attempt, Pushkin would be greeted not by a warm handshake, but rather by the cold outstretched hand of a corpse. Hence emerge two opposite pursuits: on the one hand, Pushkin felt the need to carve himself out a new position, find new people ("new friends will appear to us"), new connections; on the other hand, Pushkin felt impelled to "spit on everything and run" (3:422)—to resign his position and leave for the countryside with his wife and children, or even to leave without them for the Orenburg steppe, for Boldino, for the road.

The theme of the peasant rebellion still very much interested Pushkin, and at the end of summer 1833, he obtained permission to travel for four months around the sites of the Pugachev Rebellion in the Orenburg and Kazan Governates. Pushkin's desire to leave Petersburg had also apparently played a not insignificant role in his decision to travel: Pushkin would muse on plans of buying a house with land between Mikhailovskoe and Trigorskoe (even entering the necessary negotiations with the help of Osipova); he also planned on traveling to Ekaterina Karamzina in Derpt (Tartu). The latter project went so far as to be permitted by Nicholas I; Pushkin's subsequent abrupt change in intentions—his idea of traveling to the Ural, instead of Derpt—provoked confused questioning on Nicholas I's end.

Pushkin traversed the sites of the Pugachev Rebellion, collecting materials and interviewing elderly people who had borne witness to the rebellion themselves. Afterwards, he traveled to Boldino. There he worked on *The History of Pugachev, The Bronze Horseman, Angelo, A Story of a Little Fish and a Fisherman, A Story of a Dead Tsarevna*.

On October 20, Pushkin returned to Petersburg.

The History of Pugachev was finished. It needed to be printed. Pushkin had great expectations for the book's publication. It was not only the first scholarly treatment of the "Russian rebellion"; the 1830 waves of unrest among the peasants and military settlers once again enlivened debates around serfdom.

Certain government circles were already inclined towards reforming peasant law. Nonetheless, even discussions of the issue provoked stark resistance from conservatives; Pushkin's book was a fearsome reminder that the clock of history was ticking. Pushkin needed to receive permission for publication. He sent the manuscript to the tsar via Benckendorf, adding a short analysis dedicated to the behaviors of different social groups during the Pugachev Rebellion, written specially for the tsar and not for publication. In a section titled "General Remarks," Pushkin provided an exceptionally deep and insightful sociological analysis, indicating that "the plain folk were all for Pugachev," and "the aristocracy was openly on the government's side" because the "interests" and "benefits" for the aristocrats and the folk "were too far opposed" (9:375). The precision of this sociological analysis revealed both Pushkin's exemplary knowledge of the historical material and his ponderings on the role of "interests" in social struggle, inherited from readings of Restoration-era historians François Guizot[6] and François-Auguste Mignet,[7] as well as his thinking on the general movement of Russian and world history. If we recall that not long prior Pushkin believed that the progressive aristocrat, the vessel of the historical tradition of liberalism, Dubrovsky, was the natural ally of the people, then the development of Pushkin's thought and the unsettling nature of his conclusions regarding the prospects of a "Russian rebellion" become self-evident. The precarity of this position was intensified by the fact that doubts as to the feasibility of an alliance between the progressive aristocracy and the rebelling people was coupled with a growing feeling of alienation from those in power. Both historical hopes for a "new Peter" and his personal relationship with the government were reaching a critical point.

Pushkin's literary relationships grew no less exasperated: the prohibition of *The Literary Gazette*'s publication, along with Delvig's death, had completely done away with the remnants of the literary atmosphere that had thrived prior to December 14. The very spirit of literature itself had decisively shifted.

Pushkin grasped the apex of his art. His stature as a person was simultaneously growing. His brilliance, wit, charm, and genius were joined by a depth, liberty, and significance that are only supplied by a rich inner life. This power was gratified by calmness—Pushkin was cognizant of his power. On a bookmark inserted into a volume from his library he wrote:

> Deep waters,
> Flow smoothly,
> The wisest people
> Live quietly. (3:471)

However, in recognizing himself as a deep current, he still felt as though he possessed strength and a capacity for new changes and tempests—

> …the current of my days, murky for so long,
> Has now grown quiet

—and immediately interrupted himself with the question: "Will this last long?" (3:329). This was an indicator of maturity: a balancing point between a youth that had not fully passed, and experience which was advancing with time. Wisdom.

In his art, this translated as *realism*. It was necessary to find an accordance between one's creative principles and one's daily living—a realism of everyday behavior.

Romanticism, which had been discovered by the poetic geniuses of the early nineteenth century, had become entirely vulgarized and was practically worthless at this point. Every Petersburg bureaucrat, young merchants, army sergeants, and students amid their studies were Romantics. In November 1835, Pushkin received a letter from a certain Nikanor Ivanov, who informed him that "he had hardened his heart, darkened his mind with doubts, his youth, that costly pearl of life—he stained with vices, stubbornness, and crimes—and fell like an angel separated from the brilliant heavens by a throng of demons." Nikanor Ivanov compared himself to Prometheus and Pushkin (whom he was quick to address with the informal *you*) he called "my comrade in this miserable, tragic life." All of this was concluded with a request for "monetary support, no higher than 550 rubles" (14:59–61), a very significant sum at the time.

In Pushkin's mind, the vulgarized Romantic phrase and pose were opposed to the bitter truth—in life, as well as in art. In a review written in 1836, he addressed the following question to lovers of Romantic phraseology: what does it mean to be "prosaic"? Does it mean being "calm, intelligent, and reasonable? Is that it?" (12:93). The ideal of a practical life, a life that Pushkin took pains to obtain for himself was rich and complex in and of itself. It encompassed mental forces that, in the next generation, parted from each other to the point of irreconcilability. It involved liberty and independence, and life with the family and in the countryside. This ideal, however, also implied active participation in literary and political life: the work of a poet, historian, and journalist.

As a historian, Pushkin aimed to preserve a tranquil belief in truth, untainted by prejudiced thought—a position he believed imperative to the work of the playwright as well: "What does a dramatic writer need? Philosophy, impartiality, the governmental thought of a historian, intuition, an animated imagination, a lack of prejudice or recurring thought. *Freedom*" (11:419). As a journalist, Pushkin wanted to immerse himself in the "moods of the day." As early as 1825, he wrote to Pletnev from Mikhailovskoe: "My brother Pletnev! Do not write *kind* criticism! Show your teeth" (13:154). Both the position of the historian and the journalist advanced a single demand, a common psychological imperative: as opposed to feuding with life or bitterly turning away from it, like a Romantic, one ought to deeply peer into it—with curiosity, horror, hope. The psychology of realism demanded, in particular, that one accept the fact that the reading public had grown in number, that financial considerations had penetrated the literary and journalistic sphere, transforming these activities into a profession and even a means for growing personal wealth. Pushkin did not fear the approaching era and had the boldness to employ such phrases as "business venture" not only in a negative, but even in a positive sense, challenging the Romantics who cursed the persistent approach of a pragmatic "iron age."

In an exceptionally important review of French poet François-René Chateaubriand's translation of John Milton's[8] *Paradise Lost*, written during the last months of Pushkin's life, Pushkin declared:

> The translation of *Paradise Lost* is a business venture. The greatest living French writer, the teacher of an entire generation of writers, a former prime minister, and many-times ambassador—Chateaubriand, in his old age, translated Milton *to earn his bread*. Regardless of the quality with which he conducted this work, the work itself and its objective honors its author. He could have easily, after negotiating with himself, found it possible to quietly enjoy the generosities of a new government, its power, honors, and riches—yet he preferred an honest poverty to these. Retreating from the chambers of many quills where his eloquent voice long resounded, Chateaubriand has arrived at the bookstand with a manuscript for sale and a conscience unbought" (12:144–145).

The words "with a manuscript for sale and a conscience unbought" could have been inscribed on the banner of Pushkin the journalist, the creator of the *The Contemporary*, which would become the greatest Russian journal, destined for a glorious place in the history of Russian political life following the poet's death.

In 1834, in St. Petersburg, *The Reader's Library [Biblioteka dlya Chteniya]* began to circulate: it was a monthly journal published by Osip Senkovsky[9] and funded by publisher Alexander Smirdin.[10] *The Reader's Library*, which invited a variety of the best Russian writers (among them Pushkin) widely employed advertisements, paid writers unprecedented fees, was published unfailingly on the promised date, quickly won the loyalty of its readership, and became the most popular Russian journal. Senkovsky, however, having approached the journal's publication as a business affair of the bourgeois type, provoked the ire of leading writers with his cynicism and exploitation of a retrograde readership. The journalistic alliance set forth between Senkovsky and the party of Bulgarin and Grech conclusively inhibited all writers with any worth and of any group from participating in it. *The Moscow Observer* journal, which arose in 1835 (its publishers were writers at one point connected to *The Moscow Herald*), though it aimed to rival Senkovsky, could not handle the battle: their narrow-minded Romantic-aristocratic position prevented them from seriously contending with the lively and flexible *Library* mired into a mass readership's tastes.

It was in these circumstances that Pushkin received permission to publish his own journal. The journal was called *Sovremennik (The Contemporary)*. It began circulating in 1836, at four volumes a year. Gogol cooperated most closely with the publication, having grown close to Pushkin during these years.

From the journal's very inception, Pushkin encountered difficult limitations: the journal was forced to exclude any and all political information from its program, which obviously made its competitive position precarious; the number of volumes it could have yearly was also limited—*The Contemporary* was practically not a journal, being published as something more similar to a trimonthly almanac, which largely impeded its capacity for participating in the literary polemics of the day. Its censorship conditions were also extremely harsh: the journal's censorship was given over to Alexander Krylov,[11] an exceptionally dull and cowardly censor; soon thereafter, Pushkin was also required to receive visas from military and religious censors. Pushkin wrote to Davydov: "It's difficult, what can I say. You'll dance plenty around one censor; how can one be dependent on four whole censors?" (16:160).*

Despite all this, the journal was a dear and important endeavor to Pushkin; even when he was departing for his fatal duel, he was thinking of the next volume of the journal: he was ordering articles and organizing meetings with potential authors. Pushkin accepted the responsibility not only of general direction, but also over the entire technical and financial organization of *The Contemporary*—he was practically the journal's sole owner and head. Pushkin viewed himself as the head of Russian literature and felt a personal responsibility for its future; he treated the journal as a means of manifesting his influence on the development of letters in Russia.

Pushkin's journal was distinguished by the independence of its contributors' opinions—though it declined to engage directly in polemics, as well as by the exceptional artistic maturity of the works placed therein (among works published there were Pushkin's *The Captain's Daughter, A Journey to Arzrum, The Feast of Peter the Great, The Miserly Knight, My Hero's Genealogy, The Commander* etc., Gogol's *The Nose, The Carriage, The Busy Man's Morning*, as well as poems by Tiutchev,[12] Zhukovsky, Baratynsky, Vyazemsky, and Koltsov). It also featured exceptional scholarly materials. Pushkin was deliberately orienting the journal towards burgeoning literary forces. Gogol's classic article "On the Movement of Journal Literature in 1834 and 1835" was published in *The Contemporary*, and in the last months of Pushkin's life, the poet (without notifying his literary friends) began talks with Belinsky regarding the latter's possible collaboration with the journal—he was then a young and hardly known critic and, moreover, had coldly reviewed *The Contemporary* in print.

---

*   Pushkin's journal was forced to undergo review by the general censor, the spiritual (church) censor, the military censor, and the censor of the court ministry—until being finally reviewed personally by Benckendorf.

Pushkin was full of energy and historical optimism—it was no coincidence that the journal was called *The Contemporary*. In its rivalry with *The Reader's Library*, Pushkin accounted for the latter's experience: he established generous fees for writers and sought precision in the performance of his responsibilities before subscribers. The journal, however, was unsuccessful: the number of its subscribers fluctuated between 600 and 700 (compared to *The Reader's Library*'s typical print run of 5,000 and *The Northern Bee*'s print run which also numbered in the thousands.). The rift separating Pushkin from the contemporary reader was growing. Even Belinsky—an impassioned proponent of Pushkin's talent, who would go on to write a remarkable group of articles on Pushkin, declared in 1834: "with 1830 the *Pushkin* period ended or, better say, was abruptly interrupted, because Pushkin himself has ended and with him—his influence; since then, hardly a sound worthy of those past has his lyre released."*

Social ties occupied an important position in Pushkin's personal life. Courtly responsibilities were wearisome at this point. Pushkin wrote to his wife: "It would be good if I am able to live another twenty-five years; but if I fold after ten, I really don't know what you will do, what Mashka will say—not to mention Sashka. They will be hardly consoled by the fact that their dear little father was buried like a fool [that is, in a courtly tuxedo; two and a half years later, his friends would lower him into his grave wearing a civilian tailcoat—Lotman] and that their little mother was terribly pretty at the Anichkov [that is, court—Lotman] balls" (15:180). Pushkin dreamed of resignation, of life in the countryside. It would be incorrect, however, to presume that nothing was attractive for him in society: he loved "the cramped spaces, and the brilliance, and the joy" (6:17), he enjoyed engaging in lively conversations with intelligent, educated, and beautiful women, historical recollections by old men and women who could recall the reigns of Empress Elizabeth and Catherine II,

---

* Belinskii, *Polnoe sobranie sochinennii*, 1:87.

dances, conversations with diplomats on European politics. He was an expert at the art of conversation—his intercourse was untiring and brilliant.

At the salons, he preferred to present himself as something of a socialite, as opposed to a poet (he regarded the mask of the disillusioned poet at the ball as intolerably trite); he never spoke to women about poetry and strictly distinguished between his social acquaintances and his literary friends. Pushkin considered that he by right belonged to society—a world which he never idealized, discerning its vulgarity, a depravity obscured by manners, and its slavishness, but in which he also encountered havens of fine culture such as the salons of Ekaterina Khitrovo or Dorothea de Ficquelmont, or Prince Vladimir Odoevsky—a poet, writer, musician, and friend of Pushkin's. Pushkin, however, stuck out like a sore thumb in society. The combination of inner slavishness and superficial gloss was deeply alien to him: Pushkin was independent and awkward.

We have seen that disaster was creeping up on Pushkin from all sides, but the decisive, final blow was dealt precisely here.

On January 26, 1834, Pushkin recorded in his journal: "The Baron d'Anthès and the Marquis de Pinas,[13] two Chouans, will be accepted into the Guard immediately as officers. The Guard grumbles" (12:319). George d'Anthès, the son of a poor Alsatian aristocrat, was forced to abandon France following the July Revolution, seeing as he was an ultraroyalist. He found himself in Germany without a cent to his name and any prospects for the future. Fate brought him together with the Dutch ambassador in St. Petersburg, the Baron Heeckeren.[14] The comely and tall d'Anthès—endowed with a handsome smile—was aptly suited to the role of the "kind lad," though in reality, he was wry, self-interested, and calculating. Together with Heeckeren, with whom he had a dubious relationship, he disembarked from the "Nicholas I" steamship in St. Petersburg on October 8, 1833. D'Anthès was able to secure effective patronage and was enlisted as a cornet in the Cavalry Guard Regiment—one of the most prestigious regiments in Russia. Heeckeren adopted the young man who had in an instant been transformed from a homeless, penniless wanderer into a well-established person and a wealthy inheritor, and a fashionable hero of the Petersburg salons welcome in the highest echelons of aristocratic society. In order to solidify his position in Petersburg, d'Anthès was demonstratively successful with women—a success he earned through the unsophisticated art of social gallantry. However, the strangeness of his relationship with Heeckeren had stained his good name and threatened to destabilize a career that had gone off to a brilliant start. He devised a simple solution: a publicly visible affair with any well-known socialite lady would have simultaneously distanced him from the rumors and endowed him, in accordance with the values of the time, with a certain "brilliance" in society's eyes.* All of d'Anthès behavior indicated that he was interested simply in scandal—there was no search for love to speak of, but rather a calculated move made out of ignoble, careerist pretensions. D'Anthès chose Pushkin's wife as the object of his amorous pursuits: she was at the height of her success in society, and d'Anthès undertook a crude and persistent chase consisting of confessions of apparent passion.

Pushkin was enraged that his personal life had become an object of dirty play and the cause of explosive rumors in society. Neither Pushkin's feelings nor his principles could reconcile him to the fact that his Home, his human dignity, his wife's honor—the world which was the very grounds of his existence and poetry—were opened wide by prying policemen who opened others' letters and socialite gossipers playing with others' lives. There was only one solution—Pushkin decided to duel. The brilliant cavalry-guardsman had no stomach for it, however: d'Anthès declared that the object of his pursuits was not Pushkin's wife, but her sister Ekaterina,[15] a foolish girl who had fallen in love with the handsome Frenchman. His proposal was accepted, and Pushkin recanted his challenge. D'Anthès, now married to an unloved and

---

* Compare the opinion of Vronsky's mother in Tolstoy's *Anna Karenina* that nothing quite "gave a brilliant young man a finishing touch like an affair in high society."

unattractive wife, found himself in an awkward position, seeing as Pushkin had decisively rejected the prospect of familial contact between his own household and his new relative.

D'Anthès understood that his game had gone too far and that he made out a fool. But, like a true gambler, he could not forfeit the game and was inclined to raise the stakes. Now he was forced to demonstrate that his marriage was not an act of cowardice, but rather an act of self-sacrifice made for the honor of his beloved—with new-found strength, d'Anthès renewed his pursuits of Natalya, aiming to breathe life into the legend of his "great passion."

Pushkin had many enemies. It would be admittedly erroneous to imagine the world that the poet inhabited during his last years as a den of criminals or theatrical villains. However, the corrupting reverberations of Nicholas I's victory at Senate Square would only come to their full fruition in the latter half of the 1830s. A few months prior to his duel, Pushkin wrote Chaadaev: "Our contemporary society is just as hateful as it is stupid." Pushkin observed "the absence of public opinion," "a cynical hatred for thought and human dignity" (16:261, 422). Pushkin, who could not imagine a life without a feeling of personal dignity, provoked the frustrations of others who lacked it or had lost it through various compromises with their consciences. These same people, charged with malevolent curiosity, observed and stoked the flames of these events, hoping to savor the spectacle of the poet's humiliation.

A true social conspiracy enveloped Pushkin in which participated a host of do-nothings, gossipers, carriers of petty news, as well as experienced schemers and merciless enemies of the poet: Minister of Enlightenment Sergei Uvarov, who had been humiliated by Pushkin and despised him, Nesselrode, the Minister of Foreign Affairs, together with his wife, an avowed foe of Pushkin's, and, needless to say, the Dutch ambassador, the Baron Heeckeren. There are no grounds for considering Nicholas I a direct participant in this conspiracy or even as being sympathetic to its devices. He is, however, directly responsible for something else—for the creation of an atmosphere in Russia in which Pushkin could not survive, the humiliating position that damaged the poet's nerves and made him painfully sensitive to insults to his honor, and for the lack of freedom that drop for drop tormented Pushkin.

Even Pushkin's friends thought that he was acting unwisely: they considered his behavior to be overly aggressive and hostile to notions of compromise and reconciliation. There was some truth to their assessment, if we go by normal standards. But Pushkin had a different set of criteria. According to the rules of society, Pushkin was conducting himself inappropriately and awkwardly. In Edward Bulwer-Lytton's[16] *Pelham*—a novel beloved by Pushkin—the hero, who adheres to highest standards of dandyism, says, "I have observed that the distinguishing trait of people accustomed to good society, is a calm, imperturbable quiet, which pervades all their actions and habits, from the greatest to the least: they eat in quiet, move in quiet, live in quiet, and lose their wife, or even their money, in quiet; while low persons cannot take up either a spoon or an affront without making such an amazing noise about it."* Pushkin loved emphasizing his 600-year-old aristocratic lineage, but internally he was entirely devoid of aristocratism. It would be proven to him time and again that in Russia, "aristocratism" fatally became enjoined with slavishness, and personal dignity only existed for those who were never safe from insult. Only in those who could not tolerate insult, who were incapable of not "raising an unruly fuss about it" truly dwelled an aristocratic spirit and a respect for "thought and human dignity." Pushkin's friends treated his behavior as a consequence of unjustified jealousy, perhaps poor upbringing, and blamed the African blood that flowed through his veins. In reality, it was a long-simmering pain stemming from his injured dignity, which was defended by nothing, save for pride and a preparedness to die.

---

* Edward Bulwer-Lytton, *Pelham, or Adventures of a Gentleman* (Boston: Little Brown & Company, 1899), 42. [Lotman quotes a Russian translation—Transl.]

Pushkin was not a person who could be conquered by his circumstances. Later, when he was dying and suffering from unbearable pain (the bullet had shattered his pelvis and torn his intestine), he refused to allow himself to moan: "it would be funny were this nonsense to overpower me!" he told Vladimir Dahl.*[17] He chose one-on-one combat with his opponent—face-to-face, cutting through the webs spun by his enemies and schemers. He made his final decision and on January 26, 1837, sent Heeckeren a frightfully insulting letter which firmly precluded any hopes for reconciliation, leaving the duel as the only possible outcome. After making the decision, Pushkin immediately, according to recollections by his contemporaries, calmed down and became "especially joyous." He expected to live—he was filled with literary ideas and, when departing for the duel, wrote to Alexandra Ishimova,[18] an author of children's literature, commissioning translations for *The Contemporary* from her. The letter written a few hours prior to that fateful duel ended with the following words: "Today I accidentally discovered Your Story among other tales and accidentally became engrossed in its reading. That's how one should write!" (16:227). These were the last lines written by his hand.

Around 4 o'clock, Pushkin, together with his second, his Lyceum friend, Konstantin Danzas,[19] left a bakery on the corner of Nevsky and the Moika River for the place of the duel. Two hours later, he was brought home fatally wounded.

On January 29, 1837, at 2:45, Pushkin died.

In *A Journey to Arzrum*, Pushkin wrote about Griboedov's death which, in many ways, fatally recalled Pushkin's own: "…a death that had befallen him amidst a bold, unequal fight, was not at all terrible or torturous for Griboedov. It was instantaneous and wonderful" (8:461–462). A line higher, Pushkin wrote that the death of Griboedov who had "married her whom he loved" and

---

*   *Contemporaries*, 2:231.

found death in battle provoked his jealousy. These words could be applied to Pushkin as well.

For one for whom life is more valuable than honor, death is purely tragic. Preserving one's own life becomes one's chief objective. Pushkin cannot be understood from this point of view. Pushkin for whom "the first science" remained *"respecting oneself,"* (3:193) who based his "love for one's native hearth" and a right to a place in the history of his people on a feeling of proud self-respect, had loftier goals than the preservation of his life, though he aspired to death least of all: he pursued victory and liberty. He earned victory by defending his honor, having humiliated and branded d'Anthès and Heeckeren who, after subsequently facing universal disdain, were forced to abandon Russia. An instance of the highest liberty was bestowed upon him by a "death that had befallen him amidst a bold, unequal fight."

Pushkin died not as the defeated, but as the victor.

Examining Pushkin's behavior during the final months of his life, we come to discover, at first glance, a contradiction: it seems as though his actions were dictated by bursts of passion, as though they were often undeliberated and unreasonable. This is what even his friends and loved ones observed. However, after endlessly reconstructing the chain of events, one cannot but discover a deliberate strategy behind Pushkin's behavior, as well as a decisive will towards its performance.

I would like to dispute two common views on Pushkin's tragedy. According to the first, Pushkin was a victim (already in Lermontov's renowned poem, Pushkin was equated to Lensky, which formed the basis for the Romantic legend of the poet's death). Downtrodden, persecuted, and tormented, Pushkin was murdered by the powerful forces of social evil—by enemies whom the lonely poet could only oppose through his death. This view is tied to the second—that "Pushkin actively sought out death." Both views are reasonable at their core. The forces that were anticipating the poet's downfall were indeed powerful. The malevolence of their power consisted of the fact that there was no conscious plan to destroy Pushkin. However, the matter is ultimately different: poetry, human dignity, art, and genius were deeply incompatible with the world that Pushkin inhabited, and this world was rejecting Pushkin as an alien body, simultaneously rejecting him from life itself. This world could have offered life to the poet but on conditions that the poet could not have accepted. This latter idea frequently involuntarily came to mind to Pushkin's contemporaries (for instance, to Vladimir Sollogub[20]), who would observe that, in his last years, Pushkin feverishly sought out grounds for duels long before his conflict with d'Anthès. A whole sequence of "repetitions" preceded the fateful duel—duels that did not take place, challenges, sometimes completely without grounds.

Nonetheless, these views are inscribed with a profound falsehood: Pushkin did not permit himself to become a toy in others' hands, the victim of rumors, devices, and others' schemes. Victimhood was entirely foreign to him.

During his final years, Pushkin would become more and more firmly convinced that Petersburg was hostile to him. No enemy could frighten the poet, who in his early youth had written

> A battle is familiar to me—beloved is the sound of swords;
> An admirer of abusive Glory,
> I love the bloody whims of war,
> And the thought of death is dear to my soul.
> In the color of my years, a true warrior of freedom,
> He who has not seen death unfold before him
> Has not tasted complete happiness
> And is unworthy of the caresses of beloved maids. (2:138).

The poem is devoid of the flat autobiographical quality that is often sought out in lyric poetry: as opposed to reproducing the real conditions of Pushkin's biography, it reflects features of his psychology. Struggle—Freedom—Love were parts of an unbreakable whole: battle is the lot of a man, only the joyous fortitude of the "true warrior of freedom" makes him worthy of women's love. Pushkin relished battle. Gogol's words could be applied to him: "He saw something festive in battle." The political conspiracy of the Decembrists and the actions that plunged him into the midst of battle during the Erzurum expedition (on horseback in tailcoat and top coat!), the intensity of journal polemics, the ardor of card games, the cold-blooded resilience at the duel barrier on the battlefield of honor—all of this stemmed from a common psychological source: "There is delight in battle..."

Battle, however, presupposes an opponent, a live opponent who possesses a face, as opposed to a faceless and anonymous force. However, facelessness and anonymity were the chief features of society in Nicholas I's Russia. Pushkin felt as though he were always under surveillance: even his personal, family letters, love-letters, were all read. Even in conversations with the closest of friends, he could not brush off the impression that there were others listening. Pushkin had even developed a strategy for counteracting this: for the most intimate of conversations, Pushkin would reserve a private bath at the Moscow bathhouse. Thus, it was precisely there that he first met Vyazemsky after his exile at Mikhailovskoe (they had not seen each other from 1819 to 1826: the death of Alexander I, the events of December 14, 1825, Pushkin's rendezvous with the new tsar, the fates of the Decembrist—all this left much for them to discuss without witnesses). Later, also in the bathhouse, Pushkin "relieved his soul" conversing with Pavel Nashchokin whose good-natured wife would later recall: "As was later explained to me, they lay there, giving themselves over to a most spirited discussion fully assured that there, no one would be listening."*

This surveillance was agonizing, but it was entirely impersonal—Pushkin could not discuss this issue with Benckendorf who, in an official letter, had assured Pushkin that nobody would ever dare think of establishing any surveillance over him. Anonymous were also the censors' pretensions—the censors themselves could not be blamed for them, for if they were guilty of something, it was only cowardice; faceless and intangible was social gossip, anonymous

---

* *Contemporaries*, 2:204.

were unsigned lampoons that Pushkin received in the mail; denouncers and whisperers who concealed their identities operated in the dark. There was an enemy, but he was faceless and refused to embody an "opponent."

Finally, the enemy showed his face. It was a simple, cynical cavalry guard who had brilliantly grasped the science of life in the petty world created by the European aristocracy during the Restoration era, in a world where originality was considered illness, and talent was persecuted as a crime. He was brazen and self-assured. He believed that an entertaining adventure awaited him— a meeting with an angered lion. It was not only the incursion of an impudent popinjay cavalry guard into the holy home that provoked Pushkin's anger. Sollogub was right in declaring that "he [Pushkin] in d'Anthès' face searched . . . for revenge on all of high society."*

To his friends' horror and to his enemies' delight, Pushkin had found himself increasingly wound in a web of intrigues and rumors, with his name ever more damagingly tied to harmful gossip, and noxious hearsay flooding his household. Even Vyazemsky, Pushkin's old friend, declared a few days prior to the duel that he is "covering his face and turning it away from the Pushkins' house." With a single action, Pushkin tore through these shackles. The moment of the duel was his victory: he showed that it was "foolish to joke with him," that only life and death were commensurate with the sanctity of his home and hearth. Instead of the light vaudeville which the socialite gossipers and young do-nothings from the "jolly band" of the golden youth prepared, he dragged them out onto the tragic stage upon which the merciless misery of these worthless pygmies became apparent.

Pushkin knew that he was no Gentleman of the Bedchamber or an ugly husband of a famous beauty—he was the first Poet of Russia, and his name belonged to History. Casting down the card of life and death on the table, he summoned the spirit of History for this terrible price, which would set

---

* *Contemporaries*, 2:302.

everything in its proper place. Pushkin had not yet breathed his last breath, when it became clear that he had been born for a new, legendary life, that the scale on which his name and actions would be measured was one on which all the Heeckerns, d'Anthèses, all the Uvarovs and Nesselrodes, and even Benckendorfs and Nicholases were nothing. Pushkin's wound—and later his death—caused an uproar in Petersburg the likes of which had never been seen. Petersburg had witnessed the death of Peter I and later several natural and many "over-natural," as they said in the 18th century, deaths of emperors. Petersburg had also buried Lomonosov and Derzhavin, witnessed the death of Suvorov, and, in hushed tones, recalled the deaths of the five condemned Decembrists. It had known nothing comparable to that provoked Pushkin's duel. One contemporary recalled that "the wall in Pushkin's apartment was broken down to accommodate visitors."* Pushkin's grave was visited by an unprecedented amount of people. Zhukovsky conservatively estimated it (speaking to the frightened Benckendorf) at 10,000 people, but other sources put it at 20,000 (Sofia Karamzina) or 50,000 (the Prussian ambassador von Liebermann[21]). Even Pushkin's friends, who had known him since childhood and just the day prior had seen his human frailty, who disciplined him, rebuked him, "turned away their faces," had suddenly felt that Pushkin, through his death, had been transformed into a bronze monument of Russia's glory. This is what Alexander Turgenev called him—the selfsame Turgenev who arranged for his place at the Lyceum, who called him "Firefly" in Arzamas, who taught him and defended him—and always regarded him slightly from above. Now he would write in his diary, appalled at the shamelessness of the salons who attempted to defend Pushkin's killer: "Our nobility knows nothing of the Russian glory personified by Pushkin."**

---

*   *Contemporaries*, 2:317.
** *Contemporaries*, 2:177.

Pushkin emerged triumphant. His foes were not only humiliated—Pushkin revealed their nothingness. It was this impression that Koltsov expressed, having called him a "sun that had been shot through":

> Thus, dark forest,
> Knightly Bova!
> All your life
> You flailed in battle.
> The powerful
> Could not overpower you,
> So you were finished
> By the dark autumn.
> <...>
> They removed your head
> From your knightly shoulders
> Not by a great mountain,
> But with a little straw...*

The terrified gendarmes were in turmoil, hoping to prevent the spontaneous outpour of honor from the people given to the poet's body. When the body was being carried out of the church, according to Alexander Turgenev, "gendarmes, police and spies appeared."** By the tsar's personal instruction, the body was covertly transported to the Sviatie Gori near Pskov,*** where it was buried without any honors.

This was irrelevant to Pushkin, however: a new life had begun for him—a life in the immortality of Russian culture. Pushkin's biography in life had come to a close, and his second, posthumous biography had begun.

---

*   Alexei Koltsov, *Polnoe sobranie stikhotvorenii* [Complete Collected Poems] (Leningrad: Sovetskii pisatel', 1952), 135.
** *Contemporaries*, 2:177.
*** The name of the place means "Holy Mountains." This locale is now known as "Pushkinskyie Gory" (Pushkin Mountains) in Russia. [–Trans.]

Pushkin entered Russian culture not only as a Poet, but as a genius master of life, a person who was endowed with an unprecedented gift at finding happiness even in the most tragic of circumstances. Alexander Blok used to say:

> Our memory, from its early days, treasures a joyous name: Pushkin. This name, this sound fills the many days of our lives. The murky names of emperors, military commanders, inventors of new means of killing, the tormentors, and martyrs of life. And alongside them—that airy name: Pushkin.
>
> Pushkin was able to carry the burden of his art with such ease and joy despite the fact that the role of the poet is neither light nor joyous—it is tragic.*

Such is the source of the endless charm of Pushkin's personality—and the reason for the boundless fascination with his biography.

---

* Alexander Blok, *Sobranie sochinenii* [Collected Works], vol. 6 (Moscow, Leningrad: Khudozhestvennaia Literatura, 1962), 160.

Endnotes

Endnotes to Introduction

1 **Napoleon Bonaparte** (1769–1821), general, First Consul of the Republic from 1799, Emperor Napoleon I in 1804-1815 At the height of his power in 1812, Napoleon ruled Europe from the Baltics Rome, and his relatives ruled Italy, Spain, and parts of Germany. The rest of Germany, Switzerland, and Poland were also under French control; Denmark, Austria, and Prussia were allies. Only Portugal, Sweden, Britain, and Russia were independent. Napoleon attacked Russia in June 1812, with an army of more than 500 thousand men. The Russian troops retreated, drawing Napoleon's forces deeper into the country. Napoleon captured the capital, Moscow, but was forced to retreat because he could not supply his army. The harsh winter claimed the lives of many soldiers as they returned to France. Napoleon was defeated when the British and Prussians routed his forces at the Battle of Waterloo in 1815, subsequently, he was exiled from France to St. Helena in the South Atlantic, where he lived out the remaining six years of his life.

2 **Paul I (Pavel Petrovich)** (1754–1801), Emperor of Russia from 1796, son of Peter III and Catherine II. As Paul I's behavior grew increasingly erratic leading to his increasing unpopularity. This culminated in a coup d'etat in 1801, when he was assassinated. From 1799 till his assassination Paul I was also de facto Grand Master of the Knights Hospitaller of the Order of Malta.

3 **Alexander I (Aleksandr Pavlovich)**, the Blessed (1777–1825), prince, Emperor of Russia (from 1801), the eldest son of the Emperor Paul I and his second wife Maria Feodorovna (née Duchess Sophie Dorothea von Württemberg). From 1809 he also was the Grand Duke of Finland, and from 1815—first King of Congress Poland.

4 **Ypsilantis, Alexander (Alexandros)** (1792–1828), Prince of the Danubian Principalities, son of the Moldovan ruler, cavalry general during the Napoleonic Wars. Along with his younger brother Dimitry (Demetrios), he was a leader and hero of a secret organization Filiki Etaireia that drove the Greek War of Independence against the Ottoman Empire.

5 **Volkova, Maria Apollonovna** (1786–1859), Moscow socialite, Maid of Honor by the court of Russian Empress Maria Fyodorovna. Volkova's letters to Varvara Lanskaia, her St. Petersburg friend and relative, occupy a prominent place in Russian epistolary literature.

6 **Lanskaia, Varvara Ivanovna** (1790–1845), born Princess Odoevskaia, wife of Sergei Lanskoi. In St. Petersburg she held a literary salon frequented by Vasily Pushkin (the poet's uncle), Ivan Dmitriev, Vasily Zhukovsky, Pyotr Vyazemsky, Alexander Pushkin, Vladimir Odoevsky, Sergei Sobolevsky. Her correspondence with Maria Volkova was printed in *The Herald of Europe* (Vestnik Evropy) in 1874–1875 as a record of Moscow high society during the reign of Alexander I.

7 **Balashov, Aleksandr Dmitrievich** (1770–1837), general and statesman, the chief of police in Moscow (1804), and later in St. Petersburg (from 1806), Military Governor

of St. Petersburg (1809). In 1812 as a general–aide–de–camp of Emperor Alexander I, Balashov delivered the Emperor's letter to Napoleon after La Grande Armée crossed the Russian frontier. During the Napoleonic Wars, Balashov organized the people's militia, later he became a diplomat, member of the State Council and Minister of Police.

8   **Arakcheev, Alexei Andreevich** (1769–1834), count, general and statesman, he served under Emperors Paul I and Alexander I as Inspector of Infantry, Army commander, Chief Inspector of Artillery, Minister of War. Arakcheev reorganized the Russian army and supervized the creation of a system of military settlements. His harsh reforms and violent disciplinary measures alienated officers serving in the military. During the reign of Alexander I he dominated in the administration of Russia's internal affairs, carrying out his bureaucratic functions with brutal and ruthless efficiency. The period is known as Arakcheevshchina. He was mentioned in Leo Tolstoy's novel *War and Peace*.

9   **Bock (Bok), Timotheus Eberhard von** (1787–1836), baron, Livonian nobleman, colonel, who married an Estonian peasant woman. In 1818 he developed a draft for a national constitution. His note was intended to be read in the Livonian Landtag. Tsar Alexander I ordered the arrest of the letter's author. Timotheus von Bock was declared insane, imprisoned and spend 9 years in the Shlüsselburg fortress; he was released only in 1827, already under Nicholas I.

10 **Biron (Bühren), Ernst Johann von** (1690–1772), courtier of Duchess Anna in Courland, later becoming Chief Chamberlain in St. Petersburg during the reign of the Empress Anna. From 1737 he was Duke of Courland and Semigallia and under Ivan VI served as Regent of the Russian Empire from 1740. Biron was unpopular among the Russian nobility. In 1740 after a palace coup led by Anna Leopoldovna, Ivan VI's mother, Biron was arrested and sentenced to death, and subsequently pardoned, exiled to Pelym, and then to Yaroslavl. Tsar Peter III returned Biron to St. Petersburg; Empress Catherine II restored him to the ducal throne of Courland.

11 **Griboedov (Griboyedov), Alexander Sergeevich** (1795–1829), diplomat, playwright, poet, and composer, author of the verse-comedy *Woe from Wit*. As ambassador to Qajar Persia he participated in the ratification of the Treaty of Turkmenchay after the Russo–Persian War in 1828 after which he was sent to Tehran as the Minister Plenipotentiary and murdered there when a mob assaulted the Russian embassy, as a result of widely spread anti–Russian sentiment. Buried in Tiflis (now Tbilisi).

12 **Bestuzhev–Ryumin, Mikhail Pavlovich** (1801–1826), officer, one of the organizers of the Decembrist uprising. Bestuzhev was the most extreme republican among the comrades, author of the Decembrists' Proclamation. He was the youngest of the five Decembrists sentenced to quartering, later this sentence was replaced with hanging.

13 **The Union of Salvation** ("Sojuz spaseniya"), also known as the **"Society of True and Loyal Sons of the Fatherland"** ("Obshchestvo istinnykh i vernykh synov otechestva") was formed in 1816 as the first secret political society of the Decembrists. In 1816, at the initiative of Alexander Nikolaevich Muravyov, a group of young officers of the Russian army founded the "Union of Salvation" (UoS). The first members had taken part in the War of 1812 and in the foreign campaigns of 1813–1814. The UoS numbered some 30 members, including Nikita Muravyov, Sergey Muravyov–Apostol, Matvey Muravyov–Apostol, Prince Sergey Trubetskoy, Ivan Yakushkin, Pavel Pestel, Evgeny Obolensky, Ivan Pushchin, Mikhail Lunin and others. In 1817 they approved the UoS charter, written by

Pavel Pestel, and changed the society's name to "Society of True and Loyal Sons of the Fatherland." The UoS aimed at the abolition of serfdom and at the introduction of constitutional monarchy by means of armed revolt at the time of next Emperor's succession to the throne. While preparing for the seizure of power, UoS members sought to expand the society's influence, secure key military and civil posts in government structures, and form public opinion. UoS members each belonged to one of three categories. The conspiracy operated in such a manner that only the first two categories of members knew the final purpose of the society. Low–ranking members had to obey high–ranking members without question. The admission of new members, as well as internal promotion, could only take place with the consent of the supreme council. Initiations and promotions were accomplished in strict accordance with a complex system of rituals and vows adopted from freemasonry. Members of the UoS differed in terms of radicalism as to both the means and ends of the society. Regicide was frequently invoked as a plan of action, but each time it was ultimately rejected. In light of this, more radical members decided to vote for to dissolve the UoS and to establish a new organization, which would have more members and be more competent. They first created a transitional organization called "Military Society" ("Voennoe obshchestvo") and then in 1818 formed the Union of Welfare ("Soyuz blagodenstviya").

14 **Pestel, Pavel Ivanovich** (1793–1826), officer, colonel, studied in Hamburg, Dresden, and St. Petersburg, participated in the military campaigns of 1812–1814, honored with 6 orders. He joined various masonic lodges and clandestine societies. From 1821 became the leader of the Southern Society of Decembrists. His plans for the abolition of serfdom and inequality, for social and political reorganization of Russian society into a Republic, were elaborated in a constitution called *The Russian Truth*. Pestel was hanged along with other leaders of the Decembrist revolt in the Peter and Paul Fortress.

15 **The Union of Welfare ("Soiuz blagodenstviia")** was a larger secret society of the Decembrists, established in early 1818 on the basis of the dissolved "Union of Salvation" the "Green Lamp" was a sister-society. Members of the Union of Welfare (UoW) included Alexander Nikolaevich Muravyov, Nikita Muravyov, Sergey Muravyov–Apostol, Matvey Muravyov–Apostol, Pavel Pestel, Ivan Yakushkin, Mikhail Lunin and others. The first part of its charter was drawn up by Alexander and Mikhail Muravyov, Pyotr Koloshin and Prince Sergey Trubetskoy, in part adapting the charter of the German "Tugendbund" secret freemason society. The Korennaia Uprava was the governing body of the UoW and the six–member Soviet, or Duma, was the executive body of the society. The UoW was divided into upravas (regional branches), located in Saint Petersburg, Moscow, Tulchin, Chisinau and other cities. Most members of the UoW were nobles. The organizational structure and legal activities of the UoW are given formulation in the first part of the charter titled *The Green Book*. The second part of the charter, written for the eyes of only a small inner of members, expressed the ultimate purpose of the UoW: the abolishment of autocracy and serfdom and the introduction of constitutional government in Russia. These goals were to be reached by relatively peaceful means. The UoW members strived to overcome the internal reserve and conspiratorial tactics of the "Union of Salvation" by attempting to exert influence on public opinion. A number of literary and pedagogical societies, Masonic lodges, and journals sided with the UoW. In their works and speeches, UoW members criticized serfdom, despotism, Arakcheev's military reforms, the lawlessness characterizing the activities of the tsarist court, authorities and censorship. In 1820,

members of the Korennaia Uprava argued for the introduction of a republican system of government in Russia following a speech given by Pavel Pestel at a meeting in St. Petersburg. Meanwhile, there were others in the UoW who suggested a "military revolution" amidst increasing disagreements over the UoW's program and tactics. In order to shed several unreliable members, as well as those representing its more radical factions, and furthermore, to mislead the tsarist authorities, the Moscow section of the Korennaia Uprava voted for the dissolution of the UoW in early 1821. Its most active members formed the basis for the establishment of the Northern and Southern Decembrist Societies.

16 **Katenin, Pavel Aleksandrovich** (1782–1853), poet, dramatist, and literary critic, who translated many French tragedies for the Russian stage, and authored the neo-classical *Andromache*. Katenin participated in the War of 1812. In 1818 he reached the rank of colonel. Katenin was one of the leaders of the clandestine Decembrist Military Society, which preceded the Southern Society of Decembrists. In 1820 Katenin was temporarily dismissed from the army for "freethinking." Later he served in the Caucasus from 1833–1838.

17 **Northern Secret Society, The** (1822–1825), a political society, formed in St. Petersburg from two small Decembrist groups, led by Nikita Muravyov and Sergei Trubetskoy. The Northern Society was created after the dissolution of the Union of Welfare at the Moscow Congress in 1821. Some of the Decembrists, led by Pestel, did not recognize the decision of the Moscow Congress and entered the Southern Secret Society. The structure of the Northern Society was formed in 1822. The governing body was the "Supreme Duma" (Nikita Muravyov, Nikolai Turgenev and Evgeny Obolensky, and later Sergei Trubetskoy, Kondraty Ryleev, Alexander Odoevsky, and Alexander Bestuzhev (Marlinsky)). Other members of the Northern Society included Pyotr Kakhovsky, the guards officers Ivan Gorstkin, Mikhail Naryshkin, naval officers Nikolai Chizhov, and the brothers Boris and Mikhail Bodisko. The Northern Society was more moderate in its goals than the Southern Society. The chief document reflecting the Northern Society's objectives was the *Constitution* authored by Nikita Muravyov. However, the radical wing headed by Kondraty Ryleev, Alexander Bestuzhev, Evgeny Obolensky, and Ivan Pushchin shared the principles of Pavel Pestel's *Russian Truth*. Members of the Northern Society rebelled on Senate Square in December 1825.

18 **The Southern Secret Society** was created in March 1821 on the basis of the Tulchyn Council of the "Union of Welfare." The Society was headed by a directory consisting of Pavel Pestel, Alexey Yushnevsky and Sergey Muravyov–Apostol. Other members included Vasily Davydov, Sergey Volkonsky, Kondraty Ryleev, Mikhail Bestuzhev–Riumin, Alexander Poggio. Together they formed the so-called "Root Duma." At the congress of 1823, the society was divided into 3 councils (branches): Tulchynskaya, headed by Pestel (later Baryatinsky), Kamenskaya, headed by Davydov and Volkonsky, and Vasylkovskaya, headed by Sergey Muravyov–Apostol. The participants of the 1824 congress discussed and approved the program of the society "Russian Truth," written by Pestel. At the congress in 1825, they discussed the possibility of organizing an uprising in the army. The leaders of the Southern Society tried to unite with the Northern Society of Decembrists, but this unification never took place. In 1824, Pestel negotiated in St. Petersburg with the leadership of the Northern Society, but he failed to persuade them to unite on the basis of *The Russian Truth*, although the Northern Decembrists were ready to adopt

republican principles, and Pestel was prepared to accept the idea of a Constituent Assembly as opposed to a dictatorship of the Provisional Supreme Government. An agreement was reached on the grounds of unified action in the event of an uprising and on the convocation of a unification congress. In 1823–25, negotiations were held between the Southern Society and the Polish Patriotic Society on the possibility of a joint opposition to tsarism. In September 1825, the Society of United Slavs became part of the Southern Society, which was transformed into the Slavic Council. The revolt, scheduled for the summer of 1826, was accelerated by the death of Alexander I. The atmosphere of "interregnum" and the threat of exposure forced the Decembrists to change the date of the uprising to December 14, 1825. After the defeat of the Decembrist revolt in St. Petersburg, the Southern Society organized the Chernigov Regiment revolt, which, however, was also quickly defeated. The Society's leaders, including Pestel, were arrested, and the Southern Society ceased to exist, its members were exiled to Siberia or executed.

19   **Nicholas I** (Nikolay Pavlovich) (1796–1855), Emperor of Russia, King of Congress Poland, and Grand Duke of Finland. He was the third son of the Emperor Paul I and the younger brother of his predecessor, Alexander I. Nicholas I strived to achieve stability in Europe, to preserve and strengthen Russia's old and new borders, to subordinate Poland, the Baltic states and Finland to the interests of the Empire. His main goal was to suppress and unroot revolutionary sentiments in Russia and other countries. The functions of His Imperial Majesty's Own Chancellery expanded, that led to creation of the Secret Police, centralization and bureaucracy. During his reign a complete set of laws of the Russian Empire was compiled under Mikhail Speransky's supervision. In 1837, first public railway road was built from St. Petersburg to Tsarskoe Selo, Emperor's summer residence. In 1851 another railroad connected St. Petersburg and Moscow. His reign culminated in the disastrous Crimean War (1853-1856).

20   **Benckendorf, Alexander Khristoforovich von** (1783–1844), count, born in Reval (now Tallinn, Estonia) in a noble family. His father, once military commandant of Riga, was an infantry general, and his mother held a privileged position as Senior Maid of Honor at the Romanov court, close to Emperor Paul I's second wife, the Empress Maria Feodorovna. Benckendorf fought in the Caucasus (1803), during the Turkish campaign (1809), and in the War of 1812, headed Cossack irregular partisan units, became a cavalry general and statesman though he was not a favorite of Tsar Alexander I. In 1821 Benckendorf collected information about the Union of Welfare, one of the Decembrist organizations, submitted a memorandum to Alexander I and called for urgent measures, but the report was ignored. Under his successor, Nicholas I, Benckendorf was appointed head of the Third Section of His Imperial Majesty's Own Chancellery, chief of the Gendarmes' armed corps and Secret Police, and widely engaged in political investigations. He managed and established surveillance over indivudals deemed politically unreliable or precarious.

21   **Dubelt (Dubbelt), Leonty Vasilyevich** (1792–1862), fought as a soldier at the Battle of Borodino, then achieved the rank of colonel during the reign of Tsar Nicholas I. In 1828 Dubelt joined the Gendarmes Corpus becoming an assistant of Benckendorf, who headed of the Third Section of His Imperial Majesty's Own Chancellery (in 1839–1856). Dubelt was familiar with future Decembrists Sergei Volkonsky and Mikhail Orlov, and even was suspected of involvement in the Decembrists' uprising. He specialized in

censorship and took part in secret-service cases involving writers and intellectuals, such as Pushkin, Lermontov, Saltykov–Shchedrin and Nikolay Turgenev.

Endnotes to Chapter One

1   **Pushkin, Sergei Lvovich** (1770–1848), the poet's father, a retired major, secular wit and amateur poet. In 1811 he was awarded the Order of St. Vladimir. In 1814, while in Warsaw he joined the Order of Free Masons, and later the Northern Shield freemason-lodge.

2   **Pushkina, Nadezhda Osipovna (née Hannibal)** (1775–1836), granddaughter of Abram Hannibal. Married Sergei Pushkin in 1798. The couple lived together for 40 years and had eight children, four of whom survived: Olga, the eldest, Alexander, as well as Nikolai and Lev. The other children (Sofia, Pavel, Mikhail, Platon) died in infancy.

3   Throughout this edition, italics, unless otherwise specified, belong to the pen of the quoted work's author.

4   **Nevsky, Alexander Yaroslavich** (1221–1263), prince, Saint (monastic name: Aleksiy), Prince of Novgorod (1236–1240; 1241–1256; 1258–1259), Grand Prince of Kiev (1246–1263) and Grand Prince of Vladimir (1252–1263). Commonly regarded as a key figure in medieval Russian history, Alexander was a grandson of Vsevolod the Big Nest and rose to legendary status on account of his military victories over Swedish invaders, specifically at the Battle on the Neva and the Battle on the Ice. He preserved a form of sovereignty and Orthodoxy, while agreeing to pay tribute to the powerful Golden Horde. Metropolitan Macarius of Moscow canonized Alexander Nevsky as a saint of the Russian Orthodox Church in 1547.

5   **Hannibal, Abram Petrovich** (1896–1781), an Ethiopian, son of an African prince, who was a vassal of the Turkish Sultan. In 1703 Abram was captured and sent to the Sultan's palace in Constantinople. In 1704, an Istanbul merchant, Savva Raguzinsky, brought Hannibal to Moscow, and a year later the boy was baptized. He became a servant, godson, pupil and close associate of Emperor Peter I, and later a chief military engineer and general. Married twice, had many children. He was Pushkin's great-grandfather.

6   **Peter I (Pyotr Alexeevich), the Great**, (1672–1725), the last Tsar of All Rus' (since 1682) and the first All–Russian Emperor (since 1721). Peter I is considered to have determined the direction of Russia's development in the eighteenth century. He founded St. Petersburg, proclaimed it the capital of the Russian Empire, opened the first shipyards, and created the Russian Navy. Under his reign, Russia emerged victorious against its major rival, Sweden, in the twenty-one-year-long Northern War. Peter was married twice: his first wife in 1689–98 was Evdokia Fedorovna Lopukhina with whom he had the Tsarevich Alexei. In 1712 he married the future Catherine I.

7   Pushkin's ancestor was actually not a negro, but a Moor, that is, an Ethiopian. His arrival at Peter I's court was, perhaps, prompted by more significant causes than just widespread European fashion of Moorish pages: in Peter I's designs against the Turkish empire, ties to

Ethiopia, a Christian country located in a strategically vital region, in the rear of the often troubled Egyptian flank, played a certain role.

8   **Rzhevskys, family,** an ancient Russian noble family, from the Smolensk princes, descended of Prince Rurik. The genus is included in the Velvet Book and in the genealogical books of the Voronezh, Kostroma, Kursk, Moscow, Oryol, Ryazan, St. Petersburg, Tambov and Tver provinces.

9   **Cherkasskys, family,** a Russian princely family, originating from the patriarch Inal Svetly, who ruled in Circassia in the 15th century. His descendants, relatives of the Kabardian princes of the house of Idar (Idarov), upon moving to Russia, after the conquest of Astrakhan by Ivan IV the Terrible in the 16th century, were called the Princes of Cherkassy.

10 **Vyazemsky, Pyotr Andreevich** (1792–1878), prince, poet, literary critic, historian, translator, publicist, memoirist and statesman. Close friend and life-long correspondent of Alexander Pushkin. Co-founder and first chairman of the Russian Historical Society (1866–78), Full Member of the Russian Academy (1839) and after its abolition, a member of the St. Petersburg Academy of Sciences (1841). Chamberlain (1831), Privy Councilor and Senator (both from 1855), Chief Chamberlain (1861), Obershenk (senior cupbearer) of the court of His Imperial Majesty (1866). In 1811 he married Princess Vera Gagarina (1790–1886) with whom he had eight children most of which died in childhood and adolescence from tuberculosis, except for one son, the future literary historian and archaeologist Pavel Vyazemsky.

11 **Pushkin, Lev Sergeevich** (1805–1852), major, Court Councilor, and the poet's younger brother. During Pushkin's exile Lev was his literary secretary, though he managed his brother's financial and publishing affairs poorly. In 1825, as the result of his error, the publication of the first collection of Pushkin's poems was greatly delayed. Realizing that his brother was unable to conduct publishing business, losing money and accumulating debt, Pushkin handed the task over to his friend Pyotr Pletnev. Lev Pushkin carried on a range of affairs (Anna Kern, Natalya Goncharova, Maria Osipova), but later married Elizaveta Zagryazhskaya.

12 **Pushkin, Vasily Lvovich** (1766—1830), the poet's paternal uncle, a minor poet from Nikolai Karamzin's circle, and a member of Arzamas literary circle. He was Alexander Pushkin's first literary mentor.

13 **Karamzin, Nikolai Mikhailovich** (1766–1826), historian, poet, critic and journalist, representing the sentimentalist school in Russian literature. Having resigned from the army in 1781, he translated Luís Vaz de Camões and Shakespeare, published the first Russian journal for children and The Moscow Journal [Moskovsky Zhurnal]. After visiting Europe, in 1802 and 1803 Karamzin edited his new journal *The Herald of Europe* [Vestnik Evropi], where some of his poems and novels were published, such as *Poor Liza, Letters of a Russian Traveler,* and *Martha the Mayoress.* Karamzin enriched the Russian language with new words and semantic usages, and even introduced the letter "ё" to the Russian alphabet. He is best remembered for his fundamental work *The History of the Russian State,* a comprehensive summary of Russian national history in 12 volumes. A reformer of literature and language, Karamzin is sometimes considered a founding father of Russian conservatism in politics. Following his appointment as state historian, Alexander I valued Karamzin's advice on political matters. His conservative views were expounded in *The Memoir on Ancient and Modern Russia,* written for Alexander I in 1812. This attack on the

liberal reforms proposed by Mikhail Speransky formed a cornerstone to official ideology of imperial Russia for many years.

14   **Aksakov, Sergei Timofeevich** (1791–1859), writer, novelist, known for his semi-autobiographical tales of family life, his books on hunting, shooting, fishing, butterfly-collecting, and memoirs chronicling interactions with Nikolai Gogol. Aksakov studied at the University in Kazan, became a translator in the legislative commission of the civil service, served in the military, participated in the Napoleonic wars, married in 1815, and retired to the family estate (1816). Later he became literary censor in the civil service in Moscow, inspector, and director of the college of land surveying. His friends were mainly writers and members of Slavophile circles. In 1834 his first successful novel *Blizzard* was published. Aksakov's writings were emblematic of somewhat outmoded literary tastes. He also translated works by Nicolas Boileau and Molière, and wrote poems and articles on the theatre. His Slavophile sons Ivan and Konstantin Aksakov inspired him to set down the story of his grandfather, his parents, and his own childhood. His personal new genre was a cross between memoir and novel.

15   **Tolstoy, Leo (Lev Nikolaevich)** (1828–1910), count, writer, publicist and playwright, publisher, sculptor and philosopher, who received nominations for the Nobel Prize in Literature every year from 1902 to 1906 and for the Nobel Peace Prize in 1901, 1902, and 1909. His most famous works are the novels *War and Peace* (1869) and *Anna Karenina* (1878). In the 1870s, Tolstoy experienced a profound moral crisis, followed by "a spiritual awakening," as outlined in his *Confession* (1882). He became a Christian anarchist and pacifist. His ideas on nonviolent resistance, expressed in such works as *The Kingdom of God Is Within You* (1894), had an impact on Mahatma Gandhi, Martin Luther King Jr. and Ludwig Wittgenstein. Influenced by the economic philosophy of Henry George, Leo Tolstoy wrote the novel *Resurrection* (1899).

16   **Lermontov, Mikhail Yuryevich** (1814–1841), Romantic writer, poet and painter, sometimes called "the poet of the Caucasus," a central figure of Russian Romanticism. His prose founded the tradition of the Russian psychological novel. After his mother died, Lermontov was raised by his grandmother, Elizaveta Arsenyeva. The poem "Death of the Poet," written after Pushkin's death, gained Lermontov significant fame, but led to his first exile to the Caucasus due to its controversial content. While in exile, Lermontov continued to write, producing some of his most famous works, including the novel *A Hero of Our Time*. His experiences in the Caucasus provided rich material for his poetry and prose. He returned to St. Petersburg briefly, but after another duel was exiled to the Caucasus again. In 1841, Lermontov was killed in a duel with fellow officer Nikolai Martynov.

17   **Lermontov, Yuri Petrovich** (1787–1831), father of Mikhail Lermontov, an educational officer, who retired in 1811 with the rank of captain due to health reasons, later participated in the War of 1812. In 1810 he married Maria Mikhailovna, née Arsenieva (1795–1817), the only daughter from an aristocratic family. Their marriage was unhappy, Maria's health deteriorated, and she died of tuberculosis. A family dispute ensued over Lermontov's custody, resulting in worsening relations with Yuri's mother-in-law, who did not approve her daughter's choice. Yuri left Tarkhany, leaving his son to be raised by his grandmother Elizaveta Arsenieva (1773–1845).

18   **Arina Rodionovna (Yakovleva, Arina Rodionovna)** (1758–1828), nanny of Alexander Pushkin, serf peasant, who raised children of the Hannibal family, including Pushkin's

mother, Nadezhda Osipovna, and later the poet and his siblings. Her husband Fedor Matveev and their four children lived in Kobrino, near Gatchina. She accompanied Pushkin while in exile 1824–1826 to Mikhailovskoe. He dedicated poems to her, and she is frequently mentioned in his correspondence.

19 **Michael (Mikhail Pavlovich)** (1798–1849), Grand Duke, the tenth child and fourth son of the Emperor Paul I and his second wife, Empress Maria Feodorovna (née Duchess Sophie Dorothea von Württemberg), The younger brother of two Emperors, Alexander I and Nicholas I, and the disputed Emperor Konstantin I. In 1824 the Grand Duke obeyed his mother's wishes and married Elena Pavlovna (née Princess Charlotte of Württemberg), a granddaughter of the Empress Maria Feodorovna's brother.

20 **Speransky, Mikhail Mikhailovich** (1772–1839), count, State Secretary of the Emperor of the Russian Empire, a reformist during the reign of Alexander I. Honorary member of the Free Economic Society and the St. Petersburg Academy of Sciences. He later served under Emperor Nicholas I and held the rank of Active Privy Councilor. During the reign of Nicholas I a complete set of laws of the Russian Empire was compiled under Mikhail Speransky's supervision.

21 **Konovnitsyn, Peter Petrovich** (1764–1822), count (from 1819), Russian military leader, participant of the Russo–Swedish War (1788–1790) and Russo–Turkish War (1791), Polish campaigns (1792 and 1794). As a lieutenant-colonel he was appointed adjutant to Grigory Potemkin. In 1797 Konovnitsyn was promoted to the rank of major-general. Under the command of Kutuzov, he advanced against the Napoleonic army until the occupation of Vilna by Russian troops. Konovnitsyn became an infantry general (1817), Minister of War of the Russian Empire (1815–1819), a member of the State Council, the Committee of Ministers and the Senate. He was married to his relative, Anna Korsakova (1769–1843).

22 **Maria Feodorovna (née Duchess Sophie Dorothea von Württemberg)** (1759–1828), princess, Empress, and second wife of the Grand Duke Paul, the future Emperor Paul I. She was mother to 10 children, and two of her sons became emperors (Alexander I and Nicholas I). In spite of her German origins she was popular among the people. She founded the Office of the Institutions of the Empress Maria.

23 **Malinovsky, Vasily Fedorovich** (1765–1814), diplomat and publicist, with excellent knowledge of modern Greek, ancient Greek, Latin, Turkish, French and English. Worked in diplomatic missions in England, then Yassi. In 1800 he was sent as consul to the Moldavian principality. After 1802 he returned to Moscow, published the journal *Fall Evenings*, where he printed his essays. His "Thoughts on War and Peace" were published under the pseudonym "V. M." He appealed to Count P. Kochubey with a project for the serfs' emancipation, one of the first proposals of the kind in Russia. He married Sophia Samborskaya. Until the Napoleonic War of 1812 Malinovsky was the first director of the Lyceum in Tsarskoe Selo and for 3 years after his death the Lyceum was without a director. His son, Ivan Malinovsky, was Pushkin's schoolmate.

24 **Kunitsyn, Alexander Petrovich** (1783–1840), Pushkin's teacher at the Lyceum, a lawyer, professor, and State Councilor. Kunitsyn studied in Russia and Germany and later compiled several political and philosophical works influenced strongly by Rousseau and Kant, where he expounded the idea of the necessity of limited power, both in state and familial matters, as a means of preventing tyranny and injustice. He taught the basics of

political economy and an overview of various social systems, including an analysis of the evils of the serfdom. As Pushchin stated, Kunitsyn never mentioned the name of the tsar in his opening speech at the Lyceum in the presence of Alexander I. Pleasantly surprised by this lack of flattery, the tsar sent the professor the Order of St. Vladimir. In 1811–1820 Kunitsyn taught moral, political and legal sciences at the Lyceum, at the St. Petersburg University, and at other institutes. The course of sciences included 12 subjects: logic, psychology, ethics, natural law, Russian civil law, criminal law, financial law, and so on. Printed in 1000 copies Kunitsyn's book was subsequently confiscated both from its author and from all education institutions. He became the subject of intense persecution until the publication of the University Charter in 1835. Dismissed from the university after accusation of "godlessness," Kunitsyn served in the commission for drafting laws, gave lectures on the rights of the elected representatives of theological academies, preparing for the title of professor of jurisprudence. From 1838 he was an honorary member of St. Petersburg University, and in 1840 he was appointed director of the Department of Spiritual Affairs.

25   **Galich, Alexander Ivanovich** (1783–1848), Pushkin's teacher at the Lyceum (in 1814–1815), writer and philosopher, one of the first followers of German philosopher Friedrich Wilhelm Joseph Schelling in Russia. His real name was Alexander Govorov. He taught Latin and Russian literature, history and logic at various institutions, and was a professor at St. Petersburg University. In 1821 he was accused of "godlessness" by the famous freemason Dmitry Runich and suspended from teaching. Galich's lessons in Russian and Latin literature turned into casual and cheerful conversations with the Tsarskoe Selo students. They visited him in a friendly manner in his room after classes. He enjoyed an excellent reputation among his pupils. He prompted Pushkin to write the poem "Recollections at Tsarskoe Selo" for a public reading before Derzhavin. Later in life, Pushkin would both write poems addressed to Galich and poems mentioning his beloved teacher.

26   **Bulgarin, Faddei Venediktovich** (1789–1859), born as Jan Tadeusz Krzysztof Bułharyn in a family of a Polish rebel exiled to Siberia. He became a Russian writer, critic, journalist and publisher, actual state councilor (1857). As an officer of the guard, upon graduating from the Cadet Corps, he participated in the Napoleonic and Russian–Swedish wars. Dismissed from the army for disciplinary offenses in 1811, he left for Warsaw and enlisted as a private in the Polish Legion of the army of Napoleon I. As a legionary, he took part in the Napoleonic campaigns in Italy and Spain (1811). In 1812 he fought in the corps of Marshal Oudinot, who operated in Lithuania and Belarus against the Russians under Count Wittgenstein. Taken prisoner in France in 1814 he was sent to Prussia. After the exchange of prisoners with the end of the war Bulgarin returned to Warsaw, pardoned by the manifesto of Tsar Alexander I, and collaborated with a number of periodicals, entering the circles of liberal Polish writers. He began appearing in print in 1816 with small stories, historical and geographical notes, and published a selection of translations from Horace's *Odes*. In 1819 Bulgarin moved to St. Petersburg and began publishing the *Literary Leaflets* [Literaturnye Listki] journal (1823–24), *The Northern Archive* [Severnyi Arkhiv] (1822–1828) and *The Son of Fatherland* [Syn Otechestva] (1825–1839). In 1820–1840 he wrote a number of novels of moral description and historical content: *Ivan Vyzhigin, Dmitry the Pretender*, and *Mazepa*. Later he opposed the realistic trend in art and writers like Dostoevsky, Turgenev, Goncharov, Herzen, Nekrasov. He also published the anthologies

almanac *Russian Talia* [Russkaya Taliya] (1825), *Children's Interlocutor* [Detskiy Sobesednik] (1826–27) and *The Economist* [Ekonom] (1841). For over 30 years he headed the only private daily newspaper in Russia *The Northern Bee* [Severnaya Pchela] (1823). It was the unofficial counterpart of the Third Section, supporting the serf nobility, bureaucracy, and conservative circles. Bulgarin acquired great literary acquaintances, moved in the best literary circles, supported various political and social ideas. He met with Griboedov, Alexander Bestuzhev, Ryleev, and Pushkin, but was also connected with officials, Arakcheev's circle. Though he was connected with progressive-minded youth, Bulgarin stood apart from the Decembrists' uprising. According to Nikolay Grech, Bulgarin assisted the police in arresting Küchelbecker, but was not brought to the investigation and the trial. Apart from literary pursuits, Bulgarin served in the Ministry of Public Education. He was appreciated by the chief of the gendarmes Benckendorf, achieved significant ranks and a large fortune, and enjoyed the patronage of General Dubelt, the head of the The Third Section of the Imperial Chancellery, and called himself "Faddei Dubeltovich" in honor of the Gendarme General.

27 **Delvig, Anton Antonovich** (1798–1831), baron, of German origin, Romantic poet, literary critic and publisher, one of the first graduates of the Lyceum and a close friend of Pushkin's. His poem "Six Years," written at the graduating from Lyceum, was published, set to music, and sung for many years by students. Delvig's first poems appeared in print in 1814, in the *The Herald of Europe*. Later he published his poems in various almanacs and magazines: *Russian Museum* (1815), *News of Literature* [Novosti literatury], *Literary Leaflets*, *The Well-Intentioned* [Blagonamerennyi], and *Competitor of Enlightenment* [Sorevnovatel' Prosvescheniya]. In 1825–1830, together with Orest Somov, Delvig published seven books of the almanac *The Northern Flowers* [Severnye Tsvety], and then the almanac *Snowdrop* [Podsnezhnik] (1829). From 1830 he issued *The Literary Newspaper* [Literaturnaya Gazeta], which continued after his death. Already during the poet's lifetime, his poems were set to music by Dargomyzhsky, Varlamov, Glinka, Alyabyev. His famous romance "The Nightingale," dedicated to Alexander Pushkin and set to music by Alexander Alyabyev, later supplemented by variations by Mikhail Glinka, has been alive for about two centuries and is still performed today. His career started in the Department of Mining and Salt Affairs, and followed to the office of the Ministry of Finance. From 1821 to 1825 he was an assistant librarian of the poet Ivan Krylov at the Imperial Public Library. Later Delvig worked in the Ministry of Internal Affairs. In 1825 he married Sofia Saltykova (1806–1888), daughter of Senator Mikhail Saltykov. Pushkin, Baratynsky, Zhukovsky, Pletnev, Yazykov visited their literary salon.

28 **Gogol, Nikolay Vasilyevich** (1809–1852), born Gogol-Yanovsky, writer, critic, publicist, and playwright of Ukrainian origin. After leaving high school in Nezhin, where he studied law, Gogol tried to become an actor in St. Petersburg, but was unsuccessful. Thanks to the patronage of Faddei Bulgarin, he obtained an ill-paid government post in the Third Section. In 1831 Gogol met Zhukovsky and Pushkin. These acquaintances changed his future fate and literary activity. Pushkin even suggested the plot of *The Government Inspector* to Gogol. In 1836 Gogol travelled and lived in Europe, where some of his early works were written. He became famous with his stories collection *Evenings on a Farm near Dikanka*, a celebration of Ukrainian customs and traditions. In addition to his heroic historical novel *Taras Bulba*, Gogol's short stories *The Overcoat* and *Nevsky Prospekt* formed the groundwork for the nineteenth-century tradition of Russian

realism. He often explored the grotesque in his writings (*The Nose, Viy*). His greatest novel *Dead Souls* deeply influenced Russian literature, but the second volume was burned by the author, who died soon after.

29 **Illichevsky, Alexei Demyanovich** (1798–1837), poet, State Councilor. One of the first students of the Lyceum, graduated in the same year with Alexander Pushkin. Pushkin's "Song," one of his earliest juvenilia, was corrected and completed by Illichevsky. At the Lyceum, Illichevsky was one of the most active writers of fables, messages and epigrams (especially on Küchelbecker). In 1825 he became collegiate assessor, served in the Department of State Property of the Ministry of Finance. Later he became a state councilor and headed the Fifth Section of the Department of State Property.

30 **Pushchin, Ivan Ivanovich** (1798–1859), Pushkin's classmate and friend from the Lyceum, officer, later civil servant. As a member of several secret circles and a Decembrist, he was sentenced to death. This death penalty was replaced by twenty years exile to Siberia.

31 **Küchelbecker, Wilhelm Ludwig von** (1787–1846), Romantic poet, friend of Alexander Pushkin, Anton Delvig and Evgeny Baratynsky, Pushkin's classmate at the Lyceum, Collegiate Assessor, served in the Ministry of Foreign Affairs, a freemason and Decembrist. Küchelbecker fought in the Caucasian War under General Alexei Ermolov. During the Decembrist revolt, Küchelbecker tried to assassinate the Grand Duke Michael, but was arrested, sentenced to corporal punishment, imprisoned in Sveaborg, and exiled to Kurgan. He died in Tobolsk from tuberculosis. In 1925, Yury Tynyanov published *Kyukhlya*, a biographical novel about him.

32 **Volkhovsky (Valkhovsky), Vladimir Dmitryevich** (1798–1841), Pushkin's friend from the Lyceum, major-general, Captain of the Guards General Staff. Volkhovsky was a member of the Sacred Artel, the Union of Salvation, and the Union of Welfare. Volkhovsky fought in the Russo–Persian and Russo–Turkish Wars, and was still in service during the campaigns in Poland and Georgia. In 1834, he married Maria Malinovskaya (1809–1899), daughter of the Lyceum director.

33 **Muravyov, Alexander Nikolaevich** (1792–1863), Russian statesman and political figure, fought in the War of 1812 and other foreign campaigns of the Russian army (1813–1814), one of the founders of the Decembrist movement. After the uprising, he was arrested and exiled to Siberia. Later he was military governor of Irkutsk and Tobolsk and returned to the army, becoming a major-general, lieutenant-general, and senator.

34 **Burtsev, Ivan Grigoryevich** (1794–1829), major-general (1829), member of secret Decembrist organizations the Sacred Artel and the Union of Salvation. Burtsev was one of the leaders of the Union of Welfare and knew about the existence of Southern and Northern societies. He did not take part in the uprising, but was arrested and imprisoned, then sent to the Caucasus, where he served in the Kolyvan, Tiflis, and Mingrel regiments. He participated in the Russo–Turkish War in 1828–1829 and was the commandant of Tabriz.

35 **Matiushkin, Fedor Fedorovich** (1799–1872), navigator, admiral (from 1867), Pushkin's classmate. In 1817 he graduated from the Lyceum. In 1817–19 he participated in Vasily Golovnin's circumnavigation on the "Kamchatka" sloop. In 1820–1824, he took part in an expedition led by Ferdinand von Wrangel, where he explored Chetyrekhstolbovoy Island (the Bear Islands), the tundra northeast of Kolyma, Chaunskaya Bay and

collected valuable ethnographic material. From 1825-27 he assisted in a circumnavigation also led by Wrangel.

36 **Derzhavin, Gavriil (Gavrila) Romanovich** (1743-1816), court poet and statesman. He was one of the most highly esteemed Russian poets working before Alexander Pushkin. Derzhavin's works are traditionally considered emblematic of Russian classicism, though his best verse is rich with antitheses and conflicting sounds, in a manner reminiscent of John Donne and a more Baroque poetics. He rose from the rank of a common soldier during Pugachev's rebellion to the highest offices of state under Catherine II. He was Governor of Olonets (1784) and Tambov (1785), Personal Secretary of the Empress (1791), President of the College of Commerce (1794), and finally Minister of Justice (1802). Dismissed from his post in 1803, he spent much of the rest of his life at his country estate near Novgorod, writing idylls and Anacreontic verse. His St. Petersburg house played host to an influential conservative literary society called "The Lovers of the Russian Word."

37 **Schiller, Friedrich (Johann Christoph Friedrich von)** (1759-1805), a German Romantic poet and playwright, polymath, historian, philosopher, physician, lawyer and humanist. In 1788-1805 he was a friend of Johann Wolfgang von Goethe.

38 **Rousseau, Jean-Jacques** (1712-1778), a philosopher, composer, writer, and political theorist. His philosophy and novels inspired the leaders of the French Revolution and the Romantic generation. He influenced the progress of the Enlightenment throughout Europe, as well as the development of modern political, economic, and educational thought.

39 **Batyushkov (Batiushkov), Konstantin Nikolaevich** (1787-1855), Romantic poet, a literary predecessor of Alexander Pushkin. Batyushkov was one of the founders of the Russian Romantic tradition and gained fame as a satirist, prose writer, and translator. He was a member of the Arzamas group since 1815 (under the penname Achilles). His great uncle, Mikhail Muravyov, helped him gaina footing in in St. Petersburg society. Batyushkov was acquainted with Gavriil Derzhavin, Nikolai Lvov, Vasily Kapnist, Alexei Olenin, Ivan Pnin, Nikolai Gnedich, Alexander Voyeykov, Pyotr Vyazemsky, Vasily Zhukovsky, Nikolai Karamzin. For about a year Batyushkov worked in the Public Library as an assistant curator of manuscripts. He fought in the War of 1812, served in the Russian embassy in Naples. In 1822, he was placed in a mental hospital following a fit of insanity.

40 **Chaadaev, Pyotr Yakovlevich** (1794-1856), Russian philosopher, who wrote eight *Philosophical Letters* about Russia, which circulated among intellectuals in Russia in manuscript form in French for many years. They comprise an indictment of Russian culture for its lagging role behind the leaders of Western civilization. His writings cast doubt on the greatness of the Russian past and ridicule Russian Orthodoxy for failing to provide a sound spiritual basis for the Russian mind. He extolled the achievements of Europe, especially in Enlightenment thought, its progressive spirit, its leadership in science, and indeed its leadership on the path to political freedom. The Russian government saw his ideas as dangerous and unsound. After some letters were published, they were all banned by the censorship. In lieu of concrete legal charges, Chaadaev was declared insane and put under constant medical supervision, though this was largely a formality rather than a real administrative abuse.

41 **Kaverin, Pyotr Pavlovich** (1794–1855), Russian military leader, colonel, participant in the foreign military campaigns of 1813–1815. He had a notorious reputation as a reveler and a dashing rake. He was a close friend of Pushkin's from 1816 until the poet's exile to the south. In 1817 Pushkin penned two poems addressed to Kaverin. Like many other veterans of the foreign campaigns, Kaverin expressed liberal views. In 1818–1821, he joined the Union of Welfare. Following the Decembrist Revolt, Kaverin evaded conviction and fought in the Turkish War and suppressed the uprising in Poland. He retired again in 1836 with the rank of colonel.

42 **Orlov, Mikhail Fedorovich** (1788–1842), major–general, participant in the Napoleonic Wars, who drew up the conditions for the surrender of Paris to the anti-Napoleonic forces. In the 1820s, Orlov was a liberal public figure, a Decembrist, and a frequent interlocutor of Pushkin. Mikhail Orlov was an illegitimate son of Count Fedor Orlov and Elizaveta Gusyatnikova (1757–1791), Mikhail's elder brother was Prince Alexei Orlov. Their father, Fedor Orlov was one of the Orlov brothers who helped Catherine II ascend the throne during the coup d'etat. By decree of Catherine II all his children were legitimized. Orlov married Ekaterina Raevskaya (1797–1885), the daughter of General Nikolai Raevsky. Following the Decembrist Revolt, he was arrested, spent six months in the Peter and Paul Fortress, and then was exiled to his estate with a ban on appearing in the capitals.

43 **Turgenev, Nikolay Ivanovich** (1789–1871), economist and publicist, participated in the Decembrist movement, member of the Union of Welfare, one of the key figures of Russian liberalism. He proposed a tax reform, various solutions for the potential reforms of peasantry, and the abolition of serfdom. After the Decembrist Revolt, he emigrated to France and was convicted in absentia.

44 **Molostvov, Pamfamir Khristoforovich** (1793–1828), a cornet; from 1817 he was captain of the Life Guards Hussar Regiment, from 1823 retired with the rank of colonel. An eccentric, cheerful and witty person, he was a friend of Pushkin during the latter's final years at the Lyceum.

45 **Krivtsov, Nikolai Ivanovich** (1791–1843), a famous Anglophile of Pushkin's time, Governor of Tula (1823–1824), Voronezh (1824–1826) and Nizhny Novgorod (1827). A friend of Pushkin's and the addressee of several of his poems. In the battle of Borodino, Lieutenant Krivtsov was wounded and captured. Returned to Moscow, where during the liberation of the capital he saved some wounded Frenchmen from an angry crowd, for which he was later awarded the French Order of the Legion of Honor. During a foreign campaign, in the battle of Kulm, he lost a leg and was forced to retire from military service and embark on a career in civil service. In 1814–1817 he attended lectures on technology, physics, political economy, literature, law, and education in Geneva and Paris. He arrived in St. Petersburg in 1817, where entered the literary circle of Karamzin, Zhukovsky, Vyazemsky, Pushkin, although he was not a member of the Arzamas group. From 1818 he served at the embassy in London, where he became close to Dmitry Bludov. In 1820 he married Ekaterina Vadkovskaya (1798/1801–1861), a Maid of Honor at the court, daughter of Senator Fedor Vadkovsky; two of her brothers participated in the Decembrist movement. Their daughter Sofia (1821–1901) married the ethnographer Pompey Batyushkov, the younger brother of the poet Konstantin Batyushkov. Krivtsov's

younger brother Sergey was later among the Decembrists; the other, Pavel, was the leader of a group of Russian artists sent by the Academy of Arts to Rome.

46   **Gnedich, Nikolai Ivanovich** (1784–1833), Pushkin's patron and publisher, a Russian writer, critic, poet and translator of Ukrainian descent. He is best known for his translation of the Homer's *Iliad* and as the author of the idyll "The Fishers." His poetry, plays, and prose works contain elements of classicism and sentimentalism.

47   **Pletnev, Pyotr Alexandrovich** (1792), writer, poet and critic, professor of Russian literature, the rector of the St. Petersburg University (1840–1861), member of the St. Petersburg Academy of Sciences (1841). Recommended by Vasily Zhukovsky, from 1828 Pyotr Pletnev taught literature to the then-heir to the throne Alexander II and the Grand Duchesses. His first poems were influenced by Karamzin, Zhukovsky, and Batyushkov. He wrote elegies, epistles and ballads. From 1824, Pletnev helped Anton Delvig with the publication of *The Northern Flowers*. Pletnev was a close friend of Pushkin and published almost all the collected works of the poet, who, in turn, dedicated the novel-in-verse *Eugene Onegin* to his friend. In 1838–1846 Pletnev edited Pushkin's magazine *The Contemporary* [Sovremennik].

48   **Ryleev, Kondraty Fedorovich** (1795–1826), poet and public figure, fought in France and Germany, was member of the Free Society of Lovers of Russian Literature. In 1820 he became famous as the author of the satire "To the Temporary Man," directed against Count Alexei Arakcheev. He was also the author of poems' collection *Meditations* and the narrative poem *Voinarovsky*, his narrative poem *Nalivaiko* remained unfinished. In 1823–1824, Ryleev published the magazine *The Polar Star* [Polyarnaya Zvezda] together with Alexander Bestuzhev. From 1823 he was a member and then the leader of the Northern Society; he was one of five Decembrists sentenced to death.

49   **Bestuzhev, Alexander Alexandrovich** (1797–1837), Decembrist, writer, critic, whose writings were contemporaneously known under the pseudonym Marlinsky. He published poems and short stories in *The Son of the Fatherland* and *The Competitor of Enlightenment* in 1819, and in 1820 he was elected a member of the St. Petersburg Society of Lovers of Russian Literature. In 1821, his *Trip to Revel* was published as a separate book, and in 1823–1825 he published the almanac *The Polar Star* together with Ryleev. Bestuzhev was the brother of Mikhail, Nikolay and Pyotr Bestuzhev, also Decembrists. Alexander was accepted by Ryleev into the Northern Society in 1824. During the Decembrist uprising he led a battalion of the Moscow Regiment to Senate Square. After the rebels were scattered, Bestuzhev managed to escape, but the next day appeared at the guardhouse of the Winter Palace and confessed. He was exiled to Yakutsk, and later transferred to the Caucasus as a soldier (a private in the Tenth Black Sea Battalion). Participating in the Caucasian War, he received the rank of non-commissioned officer and the St. George Cross and later was promoted to ensign. He was killed in action.

50   **Baratynsky, Evgeny Abramovich** (1800–1844), a philosophical poet and writer, who combined an elegant, precise style with spiritual melancholy in poems tending towards abstraction. His poems appeared in The Polar Star. He was lauded by Alexander Pushkin as the finest Russian elegiac poet. For a long period Baratynsky's poems were often overlooked. His works were later reappraised by the Russian Symbolist poets. He married Anastasia Engelhardt.

51 **Yazykov, Nikolai Mikhailovich** (1803–1847), Romantic poet, collector of Russian folk poetry, a member of the Society of Lovers of Russian Literature (1834). He was one of the brightest representatives of the golden age of Russian poetry. His sister, Ekaterina Yazykova, later became the wife of the philosopher and poet Alexei Khomyakov. In the 1820s Yazykov rivaled Alexander Pushkin and Evgeny Baratynsky as the most popular poet of the generation. Yazykov engaged with members of Moscow Slavophile circles, becoming friendly with Pyotr Kireevsky, Nikolai Gogol and Nikolai Stankevich.

52 **Kireevsky, Ivan Vasilyevich** (1806–1856), religious philosopher, literary critic and publicist, editor of the *The European* [Evropeets] journal, one of the main theorists of Slavophilism, brother of Pyotr Kireevsky. Through his mother, he was closely related to the poet Vasily Zhukovsky, who influenced both brothers' literary future. In 1823, Kireevsky entered the service of the Moscow Archive of the Collegium of Foreign Affairs and was one of the "archival youths," who organized the Society of Lovers of Philosophy, which dissolved in 1825 after the Decembrist Revolt. In 1834 Kireevsky married Natalia Arbeneva (1809–1900). Together with the elders of Optina Pustyn, he prepared an edition of the works of the Orthodox Church Fathers for publication.

53 **Pogodin, Mikhail Petrovich** (1800–1875), historian, writer, journalist, publisher of journals *The Muscovite* [Moskvityanin] and *The Moscow Herald* [Moskovskii Vestnik], Privy Councilor (1871), Professor and Honorary Member of Moscow University. His conservative views on Russian history brought him close to the Slavophiles. In 1818–1821 Pogodin was a member of The Society of Lovers of Philosophy. After 1820 he became secretary and chairman of the Society of Lovers of Russian Literature, developed the ideas of Pan-Slavism; he was well-acquainted with many of the era's writers and poets.

54 **Koltsov, Alexei Vasilyevich** (1809–1842), poet who collected Russian folklore, which strongly influenced his poetry. His poems stylize peasant songs and idealize agricultural labor and simple village lives. Many of his verses were set to music. Koltsov was close to Belinsky and Stankevich, as well as Zhukovsky, Vyazemsky, Odoevsky, and Pushkin, who published one of Koltsov's poems in his journal *The Contemporary*.

55 **Belinsky, Vissarion Grigoryevich** (1811–1848), literary critic, theorist, journalist, publicist, employee of *The Telescope* [Teleskop] journal, de facto editor of *The Moscow Observer* [Moskovskiy Nabludatel]. He worked in the journals *Notes of the Fatherland* [Otechestvennye zapiski] and *The Contemporary*. As a literary critic, Belinsky put forward and substantiated the theory and poetics of literary realism in the Russian tradition. He authored articles on the works of Pushkin, Gogol, Griboedov, and Lermontov. Belinsky was a symbol and banner of the liberal intelligentsia in Russia, and especially since the Soviet period, his works are considered exemplary in the Russian critical tradition.

56 **Nashchokin, Pavel Voinovich** (1801–1854), art collector and philanthropist. In 1814–1815 he studied at the Lyceum and in 1819–1820, served in the Life-Guards Izmailovsky Regiment, then as a cadet, cornet and lieutenant in the Life Cuirassier Regiment. He knew Karl Briullov and was friendly with Pushkin and Gogol. Nashchokin was the godfather of Pushkin's first son, Alexander, and a close friend of Pushkin's younger brother.

57 **Sobolevsky, Sergey Alexandrovich** (1803–1870), bibliophile and bibliographer, author of epigrams and comic poems, a friend of Lev and Alexander Pushkin, Mikhail

Lermontov, Evgeny Baratynsky, and many other writers of the "golden age" of Russian literature. In 1820 Sobolevsky prepared Pushkin's *Ruslan and Liudmila* for publication; in 1825–1826 he was an intermediary between Pushkin and *The Moscow Telegraph* [Moskovsky Telegraf]. After Pushkin's return from exile (1826), Sobolevsky introduced him to the Moscow literary public. He also brought Pushkin to the works of Adam Mickiewicz, whose works, though banned in Russia, he retrieved from France. He was also an intermediary in Pushkin's contacts with Prosper Mérimée.

58   **Zhukovsky, Vasily Andreevich** (1783–1852), poet, translator, and a leading figure in Russian literature in the first half of the nineteenth century. His vast body of work includes lyrics and odes, including the patriotic poem "The Bard in the Camp of the Russian Warriors" (1812), and translations. It was his translations that especially solidified his poetic reputation. He translated many English, French, and German poets and gave a new quality of flexibility, subtlety, and grace to Russian verse. He held a high position at the Romanov court, as tutor to the Grand Duchess Alexandra Feodorovna and later to her son, the future Emperor Alexander II.

59   **Karamzina, Ekaterina Andreevna**, née Kolyvanova (1780–1851), in 1804 she became the second wife of historian and sentimentalist writer Nikolai Karamzin. She was half-sister of the poet Prince Pyotr Vyazemsky, an illegitimate daughter of Prince Andrey Vyazemsky and the Countess Elizaveta Sivers. As an illegitimate child, she received the surname Kolyvanova, derived from the ancient Russian name of the city Kolyvan (later Reval), in which she was born. Karamzina hosted a renowned literary salon visited by Pushkin, Vyazemsky, Lermontov, Tyutchev, Turgenev and others. According to Alexander Koshelev, it was the only salon during this in St. Petersburg which did not play host to card-games and in which conversations were held in Russian, as opposed to French. Karamzina assisted in her husband's work on *The History of the Russian State*, proofreading and conducting inspections of copies brought from the printing house. After Karamzin's death, she helped Bludov and Serbinovich finish and publish the final 12th volume. Karamzina gave birth to 9 children, and also raised Sofia Karamzina (1802–1856), the only daughter of Nikolai Karamzin from his first marriage to Elizaveta Protasova (1771–1802).

60   **Tynianov (Tynyanov), Yury Nikolaevich (Nasonovich)** (1894–1943), a Soviet scholar, writer, literary critic, translator, and screenwriter. He was an authority on Pushkin and an important member of the Russian Formalist school. In 1928, together with the linguist Roman Jakobson, Tynianov published a famous work titled *Theses on Language*, a predecessor to structuralism. His works also included popular biographies of Alexander Pushkin and Wilhelm Küchelbecker and notable translations of Heinrich Heine and other authors. In 1916, he married Leah Abelevna Zilber, the elder sister of his friend and well-known Russian author Veniamin Kaverin.

61   **Voltaire (Arouet, François-Marie)** (1694–1778), French Enlightenment writer, philosopher, satirist, and historian, famous for his wit and criticism of slavery, censorship, government, and the Roman Catholic Church. Voltaire advocated civil liberties, freedom of thought, speech and religion, separation of church and state, campaigned to eradicate priestly and aristo-monarchical authority, supported a constitutional monarchy, for protecting people's rights. His body of writing comprises more than 20,000 letters and

2,000 books and pamphlets, as well as scientific expositions, essays and historical studies, plays, novels, stories and poems.

62 **Ariosto, Ludovico** (1474–1533), Italian poet, son of a count, and a scholar influenced by the ideas of the humanist Luca Ripa. Ariosto studied law at the University of Ferrara, served at the court of Cardinal Ippolito D'Este, where he fulfilled a variety of roles, among them diplomatic journeys to other courts in Italy. Later was he was employed by the cardinal's brother, Alfonso I, who was then ruler of the Duchy of Ferrara. Ariosto was the author of the romance epic *Orlando Furioso*. In 1528 he secretly married Alessandra Benucci.

63 **Tasso, Torquato** (1544–1595), an Italian poet, writer, playwright and philosopher. His 1591 poem *Jerusalem Delivered* depicts military battles between Christians and Muslims at the end of the First Crusade, during the Siege of Jerusalem of 1099. His works were widely translated and adapted, and until the beginning of the twentieth century, he remained one of the most widely read poets in Europe.

Endnotes to Chapter Two

1 **Klokachev, Alexey Fedotovich** (1768–1823), vice-admiral and statesman. In 1820 he was appointed Governor of the Arkhangelsk, Olonets and Vologda provinces. His father Fedot Alekseevich Klokachev (1732–1783) was also a vice-admiral and commanded the Russian Black Sea Fleet; he was the first naval officer to receive the Order of St. George.

2 **Pavlishcheva, Olga Sergeevna (née Pushkina),** (1797–1868), the poet's older sister. In 1828 she married Nikolay Pavlishchev, a historian and state councilor. Her memoirs were recorded by her husband at the request of nineteenth-century Pushkinist and literary scholar Pavel Annenkov; they provide a chronicle of relationships within the Pushkin family. Annenkov also used Pavlishcheva's oral testimonies regarding the poet's earlier years in his biography of Alexander Pushkin.

3 **Kantemir, Antioch (Antiochus) Dmitryevich** (1708–1744), statesman, ambassador to England, then France, poet, translator, philosopher, scholar, and one of the leading writers of in the Russian neo-classical tradition. His poems, satires and fables frequently attacked opposition to Peter the Great's reforms and enjoyed wide circulation in manuscript form. His works were first printed posthumously in 1762.

4 **Saburov, Yakov Ivanovich** (1798–1858), essayist, Tambov landowner and leader of the Tambov district nobility. In 1818 he was an officer in the Life-Guards Hussar Regiment, located in Tsarskoe Selo. He enjoyed a close relationship with Pushkin during the latter's Lyceum years.

5 **Yakushkin (Iakushkin), Ivan Dmitryevich** (1794–1857), Decembrist, author of autobiographical notes, a cousin of Griboedov and the folklorist Pavel Yakushkin. Yakushkin fought in Napoleonic Wars, became a member of Semenovskaya Artel (1815) and was one of the founders of the Union of Salvation (1816). He was a proponent of regicide, but other members of society rejected the notion. Yakushkin left the society, but later

re-joined his friends in the Union of Welfare. In 1822 he married Anastasia Sheremeteva, Arrested in 1826, Yakushkin was kept in solitary confinement and then exiled to Siberia, where he engaged in meteorology and teaching, compiled and wrote textbooks, and built local schools.

6   **Grabbe, Pavel Khristoforovich** (1789–1875), count (from 1866), military leader and statesman, fought in the Napoleonic, Russo-Turkish and Russo-Polish Wars, member of the Union of Salvation, and then the Union of Welfare, memoirist, adjutant-general (1839), General of the Cavalry (1855), one of the most successful commanders of the Caucasian War (1838–1844). In 1862–1866 he was a military ataman of the Don Cossack Army, later a member of the State Council. He married twice. Two of his sons from his second marriage died in battle.

7   **Plutarch**, born in the first century, was a Greek Middle Platonist philosopher, author, historian, biographer, essayist, and priest at the Temple of Apollo in Delphi. He is known primarily for his work *Parallel Lives*, a series of biographies of illustrious Greeks and Romans, and *Moralia*, a collection of essays and speeches arranged in pairs to illuminate their common moral virtues and vices. His works exerted a profound influence on the development of the essay, the biography, and historical writing in modern European literature.

8   **Livy (Titus Livius)** (59 BC–17 AD), a Roman historian. Livy wrote a monumental work on history of Rome and the Roman people, from its foundations through the reign of Emperor Augustus. The last event covered by Livy is the death of Drusus in 9 BC. His work titled *Ab Urbe Condita* is a chronicle of the attitudes and culture of Rome during his time. His history of Rome set new standards of literary style and exercised a profound influence on the philosophy of historical writing down to the eighteenth century. About a quarter of his works are still extant.

9   **Cicero (Marcus Tullius Cicero)** (106 BC–43 BC), Roman statesman and politician of the Republican period, orator, writer and poet, critic philosopher, scientist. He entered the Senate in 73 BC and became consul in 63 BC, played a key role in defeating the Catiline conspiracy. During the Civil Wars, he was a supporter of the republican system. Cicero was executed by members of the Second Triumvirate, who sought unlimited power. A significant part of his extensive literary heritage has survived to this day. His works are considered exemplary in terms of rhetorical style, and are the most important source of information about all aspects of life in Rome in the first century BC.

10 **Tacitus, Publius Cornelius** (56–120) was a Roman orator and public official. Among his works are the *Germania*, describing the Germanic tribes, the *Historiae* (Histories), concerning the Roman Empire from AD 69 to 96, and the later *Annals*, dealing with the Empire in the period from AD 14 to 68.

11 **Brutus, Marcus Junius** (85 BC–42 BC), adopted as Quintus Servilius Caepio Brutus, was a Roman politician, orator, and one of the assassins of the Emperor Julius Caesar. During the Second Civil War in Rome, the Caesarians, headed by Mark Antony and Octavian fought and defeated the Liberatores led by Marcus Junius Brutus and Gaius Cassius. Soon after Brutus committed suicide. His figure has been condemned for betrayal of Caesar, his longtime friend and benefactor, so as to become synonymous with treachery, or alternately praised in other accounts, as a committed republican who fought for freedom and against tyranny.

12   **Octavius (Gaius Octavius)** (died 59 BC), ancient Roman Senator. He came from a rich equestrian family of the Octavians, and was the first in the family to reach the rank of Senator. Father of Emperor Augustus (Octavianus Augustus).

13   **Orlov, Alexei Fedorovich** (1786–1862), count (from 1825), prince (from 1856), adjutant-general (1820), cavalry general (1833), led the Third Section and the Separate Corps of the Gendarmes (1844–56). Alexei Orlov signed the Treaty of Paris (1856) which ended the Crimean War. He was an honorary member of the St. Petersburg Academy of Sciences (1856). He was an illegitimate son of Count Fedor Orlov, brother of Mikhail Orlov. In 1826 married Olga Zherebtsova (1807–1880).

14   **Chernyshov (Chernyshev), Alexander Ivanovich** (1786–1786), prince, cavalry general (1827), diplomat and statesman whose career began in the Napoleonic Wars. After the Battle of Austerlitz (1805), he carried out successful diplomatic missions to France and Sweden and served with distinction in battles throughout 1812 and 1813. Chernyshov rose through the ranks to occupy the positions minister of war (1827–52), chairman of the State Council and Cabinet of Ministers (1848–56), and acquired the official styles of count (1826) and later, prince (1849). Chernyshov paid great attention to the logistics of the Russian Army, carried out a number of reforms that consolidated the army's recruitment system (The Charter of 1831).

15   **Kiselyov (Kiselev), Pavel Dmitryevich** (1837–1841), general, commander of Russian troops in the Danube principalities during the Russian–Turkish War of 1828–1829. In 1829–1834 he administered the Danube principalities, which were under the protectorate of Russia, and under his leadership the first constitutions of Moldavia and Wallachia were adopted. In 1837–1841, Kiselyov headed the Ministry of State Property, carried out a reform targeted at state-owned villages. In villages on state lands, peasants were given self-government rights. His reform strengthened the peasant community and gave the state more control over the peasants, aiming at the elimination of land shortages, the introduction of new crops, and the creation of grain reserves in case of crop failure.

16   **Muravyov, Nikita Mikhailovich** (1795–1843), officer, captain of the Guards General Staff, one of the main ideologists of the Decembrist movement, member of the Three Virtues lodge, one of the organizers of the first secret Decembrist society (the Union of Salvation), and a member of Arzamas. He was the main organizer and ideological leader of the Northern Society, the author of a drafted constitution. Muravyov was exiled to Siberia in 1826.

17   **Davydov, Denis Vasilyevich** (1784–1839), poet, one of the prominent representatives of "hussar poetry," memoirist, member of the Society of Lovers of Russian Literature, a member of Arzamas. In 1819 he married Sophia Chirkova (1795–1880), the daughter of General Nikolai Chirkov. Davydov, as a former adjutant of Prince Bagration, was one of the commanders of the largescale partisan movement during the War of 1812 and armed peasants with weapons taken from the French invaders; his troops often took action in conjunction with the serfs. His last military campaign was against the Polish rebels in 1831, which earned Davydov the rank of lieutenant–general.

18   **Turgenev, Ivan Petrovich** (1752–1807), Director of Moscow University, Actual Privy Councilor, and freemason, member of the masonic Friendly Society, a friend of Nikolai Novikov, Mikhail Kheraskov, Ivan Dmitriev and Nikolai Karamzin. Father of the famous Turgenev brothers: Andrei, Alexander, Nikolai, and Sergei.

19 **Turgenev, Alexander Ivanovich** (1784–1845), historian, publicist, official, Privy Councilor, brother of the Decembrist Nikolay Turgenev and poet Andrey Turgenev, a member of the Arzamas circle, a friend of Pushkin's. He was also a writer in his own right, writing letters, notes and essays published in Pushkin's journal *The Contemporary*. After Pushkin's death Alexander Turgenev accompanied the coffin with the poet's body to its burial place in the Svyatogorsk Monastery.

20 **Turgenev, Sergey Ivanovich** (1792–1827), diplomat, embassy advisor in Constantinople. After the Decembrists' uprising of 1825 he became seriously ill and died in Paris.

21 **Miloradovich, Mikhail Andreevich** (1771–1825), count, infantry general (1809), one of the military leaders of the Russian army during the War of 1812. In 1818–1825 Miloradovich became Military Governor-General and a member of the State Council in St. Petersburg. In 1820 he interrogated Pushkin about his anti-government poems and actually saved the poet from exile to the Solovetsky Monastery or Siberia. He was mortally wounded during the Decembrist uprising in 1825.

22 **Nechkina, Militsa Vasilyevna** (1899–1985), Soviet historian, professor, member of the USSR Academy of Sciences (1958) and the Academy of Pedagogical Sciences of the RSFSR (1947). Winner of the Stalin Prize (1948) and amateur poet. Nechkina was a prominent researcher of the life and works of Alexander Griboedov, and an author of many history textbooks for secondary and high schools in the USSR.

23 **Gorstkin, Ivan Nikolaevich** (1798–1877), Decembrist, public and cultural figure of the era of peasant reform, active state councilor, officer of the Life-Guards of the Jaeger Regiment, member of the Union of Welfare, the Northern Society and the Practical Union. He was a member of Pushkin's social circle. In 1825 Gorstkin was arrested and imprisoned in the Peter and Paul Fortress, sent to Vyatka, and later to the Penza Province, where he was known as a theatergoer and founder of the first permanent theater in Penza. His first wife was Elizaveta Lomonosova, sister to Pushkin's Lyceum comrade, the diplomat Sergei Lomonosov.

24 **Dolgorukov (Dolgoruky), Ilya Andreevich** (1797–1848), prince, second lieutenant (1815), adjutant to Count Arakcheev, captain (1824), colonel and adjutant to Grand Duke Michael (1828), major-general (1833), lieutenant-general (1847), adjutant-general (1848), who fought in the Russo-Turkish War and assisted in the suppression of the Polish Rebellion (1831). He was a freemason, a member of the United Friends lodge, as well as the Three Virtues Lodge. He later became a member of the Union of Salvation and Union of Welfare, but left them after 1821. After the defeat of the Decembrist uprising, he denied his having participated in the movement. His brother Vasily Dolgorukov was the chief of the Gendarmes Corps. In 1824 Ilya Dolgorukov married Princess Ekaterina Saltykova (1803–1852).

25 **Lunin, Mikhail Sergeevich** (1787/1788–1845), aristocrat, Decembrist, lieutenant-colonel of the Life-Guards (1822). He was the son of Actual State Councilor and wealthy Tambov-Saratov landowner, the aristocrat Sergei Lunin (1760–1817). In 1816, Lunin joined the Union of Salvation and was one of the founders of the Union of Welfare, later a member of the Northern Society. After 1822, he shifted away from the ideas of the movement, but he remained assured in the need for political changes and, above all, the liberation of the serfs. He rejected the methods proposed by members of secret societies as unacceptable. Lunin was the last Decembrist to be arrested and exiled to Irkutsk. In

1837, Lunin created a series of political letters addressed to his sister: he was intending to write a history of the Decembrist movement. He was arrested again in 1841 and died in the Akatuy Prison.

26 **Raevsky, Vladimir Fedoseevich** (1795–1872), poet and publicist, major, who fought in the War of 1812, a friend of Pushkin's. In 1819 Raevsky was accepted into the Union of Welfare. He was arrested before the uprising, in 1822. He was kept under surveillance in Chişinău, then transferred to the Tiraspol Fortress, where he spent four years in solitary confinement. Later he was sent to other fortresses, deprived of his rank and orders, exiled to Irkutsk province, where he built a school for peasant children. In 1829, Raevsky married a baptized Buryat woman, Evdokia Seredkina (1811–1875).

27 **Robespierre, Maximilien François Marie Isidore de** (1758–1794), a French lawyer and statesman, a radical Jacobin leader, principal figure of the French Revolution. His vision was centered on forging a unified and indivisible France, establishing equality under the law and eradicating aristocratic privileges. In the latter months of 1793, he came to dominate the Committee of Public Safety of the Revolutionary government during the Reign of Terror, but in 1794 he was overthrown and executed in the Thermidorian Reaction.

28 **Herzen, Alexander Ivanovich** (1812–1870), writer and political thinker known for originating the theory of "agrarian populism," foundational to future Russian leftist thougth. Renowned for his memoir titled *My Past and Thoughts*. In 1834, Herzen and his friend Nikolai Ogaryov; Herzen was found guilty, and in 1835 banished to Vyatka. In the early 1840s Herzen was a leading member of the Westernizer group, which claimed, against the so-called Slavophiles, that Russia's historical evolution could not be understood apart from western European politics and culture.

29 **Golitsyna, Evdokia (Avdotya) Ivanovna (née Izmailova)** (1780–1850), princess, known by the nicknames "Princesse Nocturne" ("princess of the night") and "Princesse Minuit" ("princess of midnight"). She was renowned for her beauty in society and operated a literary salon. In 1799 she married Prince Sergei Golitsyn, owner of the Kuzminki estate. In 1800, they left for Dresden, but in 1801, Golitsyn returned to Russia, and Evdokia remained in Dresden and lived abroad for several years together with her sister and her young son. She never returned to her husband living separately from him both in Naples and in St. Petersburg.

30 **Vsevolozhsky, Nikita Vsevolodovich** (1799–1862), vaudeville performer and translator, amateur singer, , founder of The Green Lamp society. Vsevolozhsky was a major landowner, industrialist, and an Acting State Councilor. Initially a wealthy man, Vsevolozhsky gradually lost all his fortune, was declared bankrupt and finally died in a debtor's prison.

31 See Tomashevskii, *Pushkin*, 1:192–234.

32 **Trubetskoy, Sergei Petrovich** (1790–1860), prince, son of Prince Pyotr Trubetskoy (1760–1817). Sergei Trubetskoy participated in the War of 1812 as a Guard colonel and later became a staff-officer of the 4th Infantry Corps (1825). He authored several memoirs. Trubetskoy was a member of The Green Lamp society, a master and honorary member of the Masonic Lodge of the Three Virtues in 1818–19, a member of Semenovskaya Artel, the Union of Salvation, and the Union of Welfare. In 1823, Trubetskoy became one

of the chairmen of the Northern Society. After the revolt he was arrested, sentenced to death (beheading), pardoned, and exiled to Irkutsk province.

33   **Tolstoy, Yakov Nikolaevich** (1791–1867), poet, theater critic, chairman of The Green Lamp society (1819–1820), member of the Union of Welfare and the Northern Society. He fought in the War of 1812 and in foreign campaigns, retired in 1823, and went abroad. After the Decembrist revolt he decided to stay in France. Vyazemsky published Tolstoy's works in The Moscow Telegraph. While in Paris, Yakov Tolstoy wrote articles and reviews about the Russian literary life in French journals, such as *Revue Encyclopédique*. Prince Elim Meshchersky convinced Benckendorf to invite Tolstoy to St. Petersburg, where Yakov met with Pushkin shortly before the fatal duel. In subsequent years, Tolstoy "defended Russia" in French magazines and reported to St. Petersburg on the state of affairs in France. He served in the Ministry of Public Education and in the Third Department. He was a Privy Councilor and secret agent of the government of Nicholas I.

34   **Mansurov, Pavel Borisovich** (1794–1881), lieutenant of the Life-Guards Horse Regiment, official of the Ministry of Finance, participant in the War of 1812. Mansurov was a relative of Nikita Vsevolozhsky, member of The Green Lamp society. In 1819, Mansurov was sent to the Novgorod Province. Later he became actual state councilor, and married Princess Ekaterina Khovanskaya (1803–1837).

35   **Gorbachevsky, Ivan Ivanovich** (1800–1869), Decembrist, member of the Society of United Slavs, participant in the uprising of the Chernigov Regiment. Gorbachevsky was a supporter of the idea of regicide and volunteered himself for the task. During the days of the uprising of the Chernigov Regiment, led by Muravyov-Apostol, Gorbachevsky tried to convince neighboring military units to join the cause. Exiled to Siberia, he corresponded with Nikolai and Mikhail Bestuzhev, Pushchin, and others. Several chapters of Gorbachevsky's *Notes*, written in Siberia after his release to the settlement, are devoted to the uprising.

36   **Muravyov-Apostol, Sergei Ivanovich**, (1795–1826), military serviceman, lieutenant-colonel, one of the leaders of the Decembrist movement, one of the first members of the Union of Salvation and the Union of Welfare, and also one of the leaders of the Southern Society together with Pavel Pestel and his close friend Mikhail Bestuzhev-Ryumin. He had contacts with the Polish Patriotic Society and the Society of United Slavs. Muravyov-Apostol led the uprising of the Chernigov regiment. After the rebels were defeated, their commander, seriously wounded, was arrested. Convicted "out of rank" he was sentenced to quartering, but was ultimately hanged.

37   **Bestuzhev, Mikhail Alexandrovich** (1800–1871), captain of the Life-Guards Regiment in Moscow, Decembrist, writer, member of the Northern Society. Brother of Alexander, Nikolai and Pyotr Bestuzhev, also Decembrists. After the Decembrist, he was deprived of rank and nobility, sentenced to 20 years of hard labor, and exiled to Siberia. While in solitary confinement, Mikhail Bestuzhev searched for a way to communicate with his brother Nikolai. Attempts to tap out letters by their serial number in the alphabet were not successful, and he composed his own alphabet on a principle, familiar to sailors, based on the ringing of ship clocks, where bells or bottles strike a double, short-term ring. This prison alphabet spread widely throughout the dungeons of Russia, was improved and used by several generations of political prisoners. Mikhail Bestuzhev published stories and memoirs on the history of the Decembrist movement.

38   **Raevsky, Nikolai Nikolaevich Sr.** (1771–1829), commander, cavalry general (1813). During his thirty years of service, he participated in many of the most significant battles of the era and became one of the most popular generals in the Russian army. The fight for the Raevsky battery was one of the key episodes of the Battle of Borodino. He was a participant in the Battle of the Nations and the capture of Paris. Raevsky later became a member of the State Council (1826). He was closely acquainted with many Decembrists. In 1794 Raevsky married Sophia Konstantinova, granddaughter of the major eighteenth-century poet, Mikhail Lomonosov.

39   **Korf, Modest Andreevich** (1800–1876), baron (from birth), count (from 1872), statesman, historian and bibliographer, one of the first graduates of the Tsarskoe Selo Lyceum, Pushkin's classmate. He was director of the Imperial Public Library (1849–61), Chairman of the Buturlin Committee, Chief Manager of the Second Department (1861–64), Chamberlain (1827), State Secretary (1834), Acting Privy Councilor (1854). In the 1840s–1860s, Korf taught legal sciences to the sons of Tsar Nicholas I (Grand Dukes Konstantin, Nicholas, and Michael) and the sons of Alexander II (Tsarevich Nicholas, Grand Dukes Alexander and Vladimir). He is also the author of memoirs published with Alexander II's notes.

40   **Luginin, Fedor Nikolaevich** (1804–1884), colonel of the General Staff, landowner of the Vetluzhsky district of the Kostroma province. Luginin had studied at the Muravyovsky School in Moscow; in 1822 he was sent to conduct a military topographical survey of Bessarabia. Two days after his arriving in Chişinău, the young officer met Pushkin whom he had already heard about as the author of the "Ode to Liberty." Luginin's arrival in Chişinău coincided with the destruction of the Bessarabian branch of the Southern Secret Society. Pushkin was increasingly drawn to the independent community of officers of the General Staff. Luginin married Varvara Poludenskaya (1813–1891).

41   **Shcherbatov, Mikhail Mikhailovich** (1733–1790), prince, figure of the Russian Enlightenment, historian, publicist, philosopher, major-general, senator, Actual Privy Councilor.

42   **Vasilchikov, Illarion Vasilyevich** (1776–1847), count (since 1831), prince (since 1839), a favorite of Emperor Nicholas I, major-general, adjutant-general, lieutenant-general. In 1817–22 Vasilchikov was in command of a separate Guards Corps and later earned the rank of Cavalry General (1823), Chairman of the Committee Ministers (1838–47), Chairman of the State Council (1838–47). He convinced Emperor Nicholas I to take severe measures against the Decembrists and was a member of the Supreme Criminal Court in the case.

43   **Cassius (Gaius Cassius Longinus)** (86 BC–42 BC), Roman senator and general, elected as plebs' tribune in 49 BC. He opposed Caesar and eventually commanded a fleet against Caesar during the Civil War. After defeating Pompey in the Battle of Pharsalus, Caesar overtook Cassius and forced him to surrender. Cassius was a leading instigator of the plot to assassinate Julius Caesar. His brother-in-law Brutus became another leader of the conspiracy. After Caesar's death, Brutus and Cassius fled to the Roman East. Cassius was supported and made governor by the Senate, amassing an army of twelve legions. In late 42 BC they marched west against the allies of the Second Triumvirate and met the combined forces of Mark Antony and Octavian, Caesar's former supporters, in two Battles at Philippi. Cassius committed suicide after being defeated in the first battle.

44 **Raevsky, Alexander Nikolaevich** (1795–1868), son of General Nikolai Raevsky, Chamberlain, participant in the War of 1812, colonel (1817), Odesa friend and rival of Pushkin, understood to be the addressee of Pushkin's "The Demon," at least in the poem's contemporaneous reception.

45 **Karazin, Vasily Nazarovich** (1773–1842), educator and scientist, intellectual, inventor, publisher, founder of the Ministry of National Education in the Russian Empire, and of the Imperial Kharkiv University. He was the author of liberal projects for transforming the state system and the national economy. Wrote many works on meteorology, agronomy, design of agricultural machines. Karazin was a major figure of the Russian Enlightenment.

46 **Tolstoy, Fedor Ivanovich** (1782–1846), traveler and adventurer, raider, duelist, and gambler, a prototype for many characters in Russian literature. In 1803, he set off on a circumnavigation attempt as a member of the crew aboard the *Nadezhda*, but was put ashore in Kamchatka and returned to St. Petersburg by land.

47 **Inzov, Ivan Nikitich** (1768–1845) lieutenant-general, later, infantry general, who took part in the Turkish, Polish, Italian and Napoleonic Wars. In 1818 he was appointed Chief Trustee and Chairman of the Committee on the Colonists of Southern Russia. From 1820 he was Minister Plenipotentiary (Viceroy) of the Bessarabia Region and member of the Chişinău Ovid Masonic Lodge. Pushkin was under the command of Inzov during his southern exile. Inzov provided his St. Petersburg superior with flattering assessments of Pushkin's behavior during the period.

Endnotes to Chapter Three

1 **Kapodistrias, Ioannis Antonios (Ivan Antonovich)** (1776–1831), count, Greek statesman, liberal minister, politician and diplomat of the Russian Empire. He became the first president of the newly-formed Republic of Greece in 1827.

2 **Trubetskoy, Nikolai Nikitich** (1744–1820), prince, writer and translator of the Enlightenment, one of the prominent Moscow Freemasons, member of many masonic lodges. He was banned from the capitals after Nikolai Novikov's arrest, but pardoned by Paul I and appointed Senator (1796), Actual Privy Councilor (1800).

3 **Novikov, Nikolai Ivanovich** (1744–1818), educator, journalist, publisher, critic and public figure, collector of antiquities, a major figure of the Russian Enlightenment. He published journals, textbooks for schools, and composed numerous translations of works by major continental thinkers. In 1792, on Catherine II's orders, Novikov was arrested, accused of harming Orthodoxy, and placed in solitary confinement in the Schlüsselburg Fortress. In 1796 Paul I released Novikov, but did not grant him permission to continue his previous activities.

4 **Suvorov, Alexander Vasilyevich** (1730–1800), Count Suvorov-Rymniksky and Prince of Italy, general, commander, military leader. Suvorov commanded the Russian Army during the Seven Years' War, the War of the Bar Confederation, and in two Russo-

Turkish Wars. Apart his achievements on the battlefield, Suvorov was also a talented engineer. In 1778 soldiers under his command built the Kuban defensive line, which included fortresses and redoubts along more than 500 km long from the Black Sea to Stavropol. After the construction of fortifications, Suvorov advised to populate the territory with Cossacks from the Zaporozhye Sich. In 1797, Suvorov fell out of favor with Tsar Paul I and was exiled to his Konchanskoe estate. In 1799, however, the tsar reinstated Suvorov as a field-marshal, and he was given command of the Austro–Russian army. After a series of victories, he captured Milan and Turin, and nearly reversed all of Napoleon's Italian conquests of 1796–97. Later, the Austro–Russian army was defeated in Switzerland, cut off by André Masséna and surrounded in the Swiss Alps where Suvorov made the famous Alps crossing. His successful extraction of the Russian army was rewarded by a promotion to Generalissimo.

5   **Golenishchev-Kutuzov, Mikhail Illarionovich** (1745–1813), count, commander, Field-Marshal-General of the Russian Empire. Kutuzov served as a military officer, diplomat and statesman under the reigns of three Romanov monarchs: Catherine the Great, Paul I, and Alexander I, and was the first full holder of the Order of St. George. During the Battle at Izmail Fortress Kutuzov received high praise from then Fieldmarshal-General Suvorov. While engaged in battle against Ottoman forces (1774 and 1788) Kutuzov survived two separate bullet wounds to the head. Kutuzov commanded the Russian forces during the War of 1812. One of his key strategic decisions was the surrender of Moscow to Napoleon without a fight, only to engage in a counter-offensive culminating at the Battle of Borodino, which led to the complete expulsion of Napoleon's army from Russia. Kutuzov married Ekaterina Bibikova, a pupil of his uncle.

6   **Radishchev, Alexander Nikolaevich** (1749–1802), writer, jurist and social critic, arrested and exiled to Siberia under Catherine the Great, following the publication of his novel *Journey from St. Petersburg to Moscow* (1790). The harsh treatment Radishchev received dampened his liberal contemporaries' hopes for reform, the abolition of serfdom or increased civil rights. Influenced by the writings of sentimentalists and especially Jean-Jacques Rousseau, Radishchev was, during his time, a radical innovator of Russian critical thought and literature.

7   **Pnin, Ivan Petrovich** (1773–1805), poet and political writer. In accordance with a Russian Illegitimacy custom, Pnin's surname was the abbreviation of that of his father, Prince Nicholas Repnin, who was also rumored to be the father of Poland's Prince Adam Jerzy Czartoryski. Pnin was the author of a controversial essay on the Enlightenment in Russia (1804) which attacked the instititon of serfdom and was subsequently banned in the Russian Empire.

8   **Yakovlev, Mikhail Lukyanovich** (1798–1868), studied at the Tsarskoe Selo Lyceum and was a close friend of Pushkin, Küchelbecker and Delvig. Yakovlev became a statesman, privy councilor, and senator of the Russian Empire. In 1840–1843 Yakovlev headed the Committee of the Second Department, supervised the publication of a complete set of laws. He was awarded the Order of St. Stanislav and appointed a member of the Council of the Ministry of Internal Affairs. Yakovlev was known for his singing, violin-playing, and he also wrote poetry and composed music, becoming a famous salon composer. Musical works attributed to him include romances or adaptations of folk songs with lyrics from poems by Pushkin, Delvig and Derzhavin. Yakovlev's romance "Winter Evening" ("The

storm covers the sky with darkness...") with lyrics from Pushkin's eponymous poem is still widely performed today.

9   **Kozlov, Nikita Timofeevich** (1778–1858), Pushkin's servant, Boldino footman from a serf family owned by the Pushkins. After Pushkin graduated from the Lyceum, Nikita entered his service. He followed Pushkin Pushkin into the poet's southern exile, but when the latter was transferred to Mikhailovskoe, Nikita moved to live with the poet's father, who lived in St. Petersburg. In 1820, the gendarmes offered him 50 rubles to obtain his owner's papers, but he refused. Nikita witnessed Pushkin's death, and together with Alexander Turgenev he accompanied the coffin with the poet's body to the burial place in the Svyatogorsk Monastery. In the last years of his life he still served Pushkin's family, even assisting with the publication of *The Contemporary*.

10 **Timkovsky, Ivan Osipovich** (1768–1837), censor, director of gymnasiums and schools in the St. Petersburg province; actual state councilor, awarded with the Order of St. Anne and the Order of St. Vladimir. Timkovsky was in charge of hospitals in both capitals, translated medical works from French and published articles in medical journals. His sentimental poems were printed in the magazine Ippokrena. As Pushkin's censor in 1804–21, he did not allow the publication of the poem "Mermaid," though he allowed seventeen of Pushkin's poems to be printed in 1817–1820, as well as *Ruslan and Liudmila*. As a censor Timkovsky was known for his severity and petty pickiness; Pushkin mentioned him in the poems "Friend Delvig, my Parnassian brother..." (1821), "Second Message to the Censor" (1824), and the epigram: "Timkovsky reigned..." (1824).

11 **Descartes, René** (1596–1650), French philosopher, scientist, and mathematician. His mathematical innovations pioneered the field of analytical geometry. Descartes' break with Aristotelian philosophy and his articulations of new concepts such as the mind-body opposition signify a rupture in history of philosophy.

12 **Byron, George Gordon** (1788–1824), lord, English poet, satirist and peer. Byron's poetry and biography captivated the imagination of Europe. Byron was associated with radical reform throughout his life. As a young man he aspired to a career in parliament serving as an outspoken member of the House of Lords. Born into wealth and privilege, Lord Byron gained notoriety in literary circles with his early success, followed by earning a reputation for extravagance and amorous exploits. His epic poems *Childe Harold's Pilgrimage* (1812–18) and the satirical *Don Juan* (1819–24) earned him vast fame throughout Europe. Byron supported liberal causes, national independence and peoples› rights. He joined the Greek war for independence from the Ottoman Empire, training troops in the town of Missolonghi. He eventually died from malaria in Greece.

13 **Raevsky, Nikolai Nikolaevich Jr.** (1801–1843), lieutenant-general from the Raevsky family, participant in the Caucasian Wars, commander of the Black Sea coastline, founder several North Caucasian fortresses, one of the founders of Novorossiysk (1838).

14 **Grech, Nicholas (Nikolay Ivanovich)** (1787–1867), writer, publisher, editor, journalist, publicist, philologist, teacher, translator, memoirist, creator of Russian grammar manuals. He was a freemason, with ties to several Decembrists, and a member of the Free Society of Lovers of Literature, Science and the Arts (1810). From 1831, together with Bulgarin, Grech published and edited the literary and political newspaper *The Northern Bee*. Grech published articles in *Son of the Fatherland*, and later edited the journal.

15   **Catherine II (Ekaterina Alexeevna), the Great** (1729–1796), Empress, born Sophie Auguste von Anhalt–Zerbst, Catherine II came to Russia in 1744, on the invitation of the Russian Empress Elizabeth and was baptized with the name of Ekaterina Alexeevna. In 1745 she married the Grand Duke Peter, the future Emperor Peter III. After his accession to the throne, Catherine's relationship with her husband—as well as his political fortunes–continued to deteriorate resulting in a coup d'etat, supported by the Orlov brothers, Count Panin, and Count Razumovsky. In 1762 Catherine was declared Empress. Catherine II carried out many reforms in the military, navy, social, and financial spheres, reformed the Senate (1763), secularized church lands (1764), and executed several measures towards centralizing governance throughout the Russian Empire. During her reign, Russia emerged victorious in two wars against the Ottoman Empire (the Russo-Turkish Wars of 1768–1774 and 1787–1791), resulting in Russia's stable position on the Black Sea. Leading the alliance with Austria and Prussia, Catherine participated in the three partitions of Poland and annexed Courland. Catherine II also ended the Russian–Swedish war. In 1792, the Jassy Treaty was concluded, which recognized the influence of Russia in Bessarabia and the Caucasus and allowed for the annexation of Crimea. Catherine II became a supporter of the Enlightenment: she initiated the creation of a national system of public education, as well as construction of public libraries in Russia.

16   **Chénier, André Marie de** (1762–1794), French poet, journalist and politician, author of many political articles. He was born into the family of a diplomat and French consul, and his mother was a Greek woman from Cyprus. His lyrics became significant for the subsequent development of French Romanticism. From 1787 Chénier worked at the embassy in London. With the beginning of the French Revolution he joined the Society of 1789 and composed anti-Jacobin poems. Arrested in Paris as an "unknown person" and put in Saint-Lazare Prison, the poet wrote his famous "Iambs" on paper strips and secretly passed them on to his father. Chénier was executed by guillotine, 48 hours before the fall of the Jacobin dictatorship.

17   **Sobańska (Sobanskaya), Karolina Adamovna (née Rzewuska)** (1795–1885), countess, born as Karolina–Rosalia–Tekla, a Polish and Russian agent, the mistress of the General de Witt (1781–1840) and a reputed lover of Polish poet Adam Mickiewicz. Sobańska was the sister of Ewelina Hańska and the wife of Honoré de Balzac. Karolina's first spouse was a Russian officer, Stefan Cerkovic. In 1814, she married Hieronim Sobański, who was more than twice her senior. During the November Uprising of 1831, General Witt ruled Poland under martial law and gave Karolina the task to act as a spy in Russian service among the Polish rebels in Dresden and Saxony. She sent several useful reports to the Russian government. Considered a traitor in Russia and not quite trusted by the Russian Emperor regardless of her service as a spy, she settled in Paris in 1836. Her third spouse was Jules Lacroix.

18   **Volkonskaya, Maria Nikolaevna (née Raevskaya)** (1804/05–1863), princess, daughter of General Raevsky. In 1825 married Decembrist Sergei Volkonsky. In 1826, despite the resistance of her relatives and leaving her one-year-old son behind, she left for Siberia to follow her husband into exile. She spent about 30 years in Siberian exile and wrote *Mémoires de La Princesse Marie Wolkonsky*.

19   **Veresaev, Vikenty Vikentyevich** (pseud) (1867–1945), Smidovich, Vikenty Vikentyevich, Russian and Soviet writer, literary scholar, critic, publicist, translator and military

doctor of Polish descent. He wrote novels, novellas and short stories, essays, poems and plays, literary and philosophical articles, biographies (works on Pushkin, Dostoevsky, Tolstoy, Nietzsche), and translated ancient Greek poetry. Veresaev received the Pushkin Prize for his adaptation of Homer's *Odyssey* and *Iliad* into Russian.

20 **Ovid** (43 BC–17 AD), born Publius Ovidius Naso, a Roman poet. Ovid wrote elegies, epic works and dramas. His best-known work is *The Metamorphoses*, a Latin narrative poem which collected mythological and legendary stories, told in longue-duree fashion, from the creation of the universe to the death and deification of Caesar. He was a friend of the prominent Roman poets, Horace and Propertius. At the age of 50 Ovid was exiled by Emperor Augustus to Tomis on the Black Sea (now Constanta in Romania) for an uncertain reason.

21 **Augustus** (63 BC–14 AD), emperor, born Gaius Julius Caesar Octavian Augustus, also known as Gaius Octavius Thurinus, the founder of the Roman Empire. His great-uncle was Julius Caesar, who had appointed Augustus as heir to his political and personal fortune in his will. In 27 BC Augustus nominally restored the republic of Rome and reigned as the first Roman Emperor until his death. He carried out constitutional and financial reforms that culminated in the birth of the principate. His reign initiated an imperial cult, as well as an era of imperial peace ("Pax Romana") in which the Greco-Roman world was largely free of armed conflict.

22 **Madame de Stael** (pseud), *Staël-Holstein, Anne Louise Germaine de (née Necker)* (1766–1817), philosopher, political theorist, author of numerous novels, plays and literary critical articles. Influenced by the ideas of Rousseau and Montesquieu, she is considered a major founder of the Romantic thought in France.

23 **Vorontsov, Mikhail Semenovich** (1782–1856), count (from birth), prince (from 1845), His Serene Highness Prince (1852), statesman and military leader, Chamberlain (1798), adjutant-general (1815), field-marshal general (1856). In 1815–1818 Vorontsov was commander of the Russian corps in France and later served as Novorossiysk and Bessarabian Governor–General (1823–54). In this position, he contributed greatly to the economic development of the region, the construction of Odessa and other cities. In 1844–1854 he was the Governor of the Caucasus. Pushkin's exile coincided with Count Vorontsov's governorship in Chișinău, and then in Odesa (1820–24). His relationship with Vorontsov was strained, and the count became the object of numerous caustic epigrams from Pushkin.

24 **Bonivard, François** (1493–1570), nobleman, historian, and patriot at the time of the Republic of Geneva. His life inspired Lord Byron's *The Prisoner of Chillon* (1816).

25 **Tomashevsky, Boris Viktorovich** (1890–1957), Russian Formalist literary critic, poetic theorist, academic editor, historian of Russian literature and Russo-French literary ties, Pushkinist, translator, and writer. A mathematician and engineer by education, he pioneered a new quantitative approach to the study of verse. He was a member of the Moscow linguistic circle, the OPOJAZ and the Union of Soviet Writers.

26 **Orlova, Ekaterina Nikolaevna (née Raevskaya)** (1797–1885), the eldest daughter of General Raevsky. In 1821 Ekaterina married Major-General Mikhail Orlov, a Decembrist. After the Decembrist revolt he was arrested, spent six months in the Peter and Paul

Fortress, and was exiled to his estate with a ban on appearing in the capitals. Ekaterina stayed with her husband.

27 **Tumansky, Vasily Ivanovich** (1800–1860), official and poet of Pushkin's time, a son of the retired General Ivan Tumansky (1763–1812), member of the Free Society of Lovers of Literature, Sciences and Arts, a friend of Krylov, Izmailov, Ryleev, the Bestuzhev brothers and other famous writers of the time.

28 **Kozlov, Vasily Ivanovich** (1792–1825), journalist, literary critic, translator, and minor poet.

29 **Petrarch, Francis** (1304–1374), born Francesco di Petracco, was a scholar and poet of the early Italian Renaissance, one of the earliest humanists. His sonnets were admired and imitated throughout Europe during the Renaissance and became a model for lyrical poetry. He was also a celebrated classical scholar.

30 **Wittgenstein, Pyotr Christianovich** (1769–1843), count, general, who fought in Poland during the Kosciuszko Uprising and later in the Caucasus, participated in the Napoleonic Wars, Russo-Turkish Wars and Sweden Campaign. In 1818 Wittgenstein was the commander of the Second Army, in 1826 he earned the rank of Field-Marshal, in 1834 he became Prince Ludwig Adolf Peter zu Sayn–Wittgenstein.

31 **Vladimiresco, Theodore (Vladimirescu, Tudor)** (1780–1821), Romanian revolutionary hero, the leader of the Wallachian Uprising of 1821 and of the Pandur militia.

32 **Leonidas I**, ancient Spartan ruler, killed in 480 BC with his 300 soldiers in the three-day Battle by Thermopylae during the second Persian invasion of Greece during the period of Greco-Persian Wars. On the one side was Achaemenid Persian Empire under Xerxes I and on the other—an alliance of Greek city-states, led by Sparta under Leonidas I.

33 **Phemistoclus (Themistocles)**, Athenian leader in command of the Greek naval force at Artemisium, when he received news that the Persians had taken the pass at Thermopylae. He won the Battle of Salamis (480 BCE) and thus saved Athens from subjection to the Persian Empire.

34 **Paskevich, Ivan Fedorovich** (1782–1856), military officer and statesman. He fought against the Ottoman (1806–12) and French forces (1812–14) and became one of the Emperor Nicholas I's associates. After the Decembrist revolt Paskevich participated in their trial. Later he was appointed governor and military commander-in-chief of the Caucasus (1827), treating the Decembrist exiles under his jurisdiction with particular severity. In 1827 he captured the fortress of Erivan (Yerevan) for which he was rewarded with the title of count of Erivan. Paskevich annexed the provinces of Nakhichevan and Erivan to Russia (1828; Treaty of Turkmenchay). During the Russo–Turkish War (1828–29), Paskevich captured strategic Turkish strongholds that led to the Treaty of Adrianople with the Ottomans (1829) and helped to annex territory around the mouth of the Danube River and in eastern Asia Minor. Later he became Field-Marshal (1829), was transferred to Poland and suppressed the Polish rebels and was rewarded with the title Prince of Warsaw (1831), then Viceroy of Poland (1832–1856). He also commanded the Russian troops that invaded Hungary in 1849, suppressed another Polish uprising (1849), and in 1854 headed the Russian army in the Crimean War.

35 **Ermolov, Alexei Petrovich** (1777–1861), general, who commanded Russian troops in the Caucasian War. He served in all the Russian campaigns against the French, except

for the 1799 campaigns of Alexander Suvorov in northern Italy and Switzerland. As a commander Ermolov distinguished himself during the Napoleonic Wars at the Battles of Austerlitz, Eylau, Borodino, Kulm, and Paris. Accused of conspiracy against Emperor Paul I, Ermolov was sentenced to exile, but later pardoned and brought back into service by Emperor Alexander I.

36 **Landa, Semen Semenovich** (1926–1990), Soviet historian and scholar of the Decembrist movement, literary critic, Pushkin scholar and polonist, museum worker, professor.

37 **Dmitriev-Mamonov, Matvei Alexandrovich** (1790–1863), count, son of Lieutenant-General Alexander Dmitriev-Mamonov who was a favorite of Catherine the Great. Dmitriev-Mamonov was a public figure and writer, organizer and chief of the Mamonov Regiment during the Napoleonic Wars, major–general (1813), and founder of the proto-Decembrist Order of Chivalry. He possessed a significant estate, including the manor Dubrovitsy near Moscow. In 1825 he refused to swear allegiance to Tsar Nicholas I and was declared insane. For the rest of his life he lived at his Vasilevskoe manor, which became known as Mamonov's Dacha.

38 **Minin, Kuzma** (Minich, Kozma or Minich-Kosoruky, Kuzma or Minich-Sukhoruky, Kozma Zakharovich) (?–1616), organizer and one of the leaders of the Second People's Militia (Zemsky Militia) of 1611–12 in the period of Polish–Lithuanian and Swedish military interventions into Russia.

39 **Pozharsky, Dmitry Mikhailovich** (1577–1642), prince (1613), governor, military and political leader. His service lasted through the reigns of Tsar Boris Godunov, False Dmitry I, Tsar Vasily Shuysky, and Tsar Mikhail Romanov. In the Interregnum period Pozharsky participated in the organization of the First People's Militia (1611).

40 **Dmitry Ivanovich, the Tsarevich** (1582–1591), the youngest son of Ivan IV the Terrible. After Ivan's death in 1584, his son Fyodor became Tsar, with Boris Godunov acting as the true power behind the throne. Because Dmitry was the only other surviving member of the Rurik dynasty, Godunov exiled him and his mother to Uglich, a town some 140 miles (230 km) north of Moscow. It was there that the young tsarevich was found dead with his throat slashed. An investigation headed by the boyar Vasily Shuysky concluded that the boy killed himself while playing with a knife, because he had suffered an epileptic seizure. His death cast suspicion on imperial adviser Boris Godunov, but there was no direct evidence that he had ordered Dmitry's murder. After Tsar Fyodor's death in 1598, Godunov was elected Tsar outright, but he was soon forced to deal with the first of three pretenders pretending to be Dmitry and claiming the Muscovite throne. In 1605 False Dmitry I succeeded Godunov as tsar, but he was soon ousted by Shuysky, who was subsequently himself proclaimed tsar. Shuysky ordered the Tsarevich Dmitry's remains taken to Moscow, and the boy was posthumously canonized as a martyr by the Russian Orthodox Church. Shuysky's reign was threatened by False Dmitry II in 1610, and a third in 1612. Dmitry's death and Godunov's possible connection to it serve as a central theme in Pushkin's play *Boris Godunov* (1831).

41 **Rurik dynasty** (Rurikids/Riurikid dynasty), one of Europe's oldest royal houses, with numerous existing branches. As a ruling house, the Rurikids held their own for a total of 21 generations in male-line succession, from Rurik (d. 879) to Fyodor I of Russia (d. 1598), a period of more than 700 years, following which they were eventually succeeded by the House of Romanov (the Romanovs).

42   **Romanov dynasty** (the Romanovs or The House of Romanov), the reigning imperial house of Russia from 1613 to 1917. The last Emperor of Russia, Nicholas II, and his family were executed in 1918, but there are still living descendants of other members of the imperial house. The previous reigning Rurik dynasty became extinct upon the death of Tsar Feodor I in 1598. The Time of Troubles, caused by the succession crisis, saw several pretenders and imposters lay claim to the Russian throne during the Polish occupation. The Romanovs achieved prominence after Anastasia Romanovna married Ivan IV the Terrible, the first crowned tsar of all Russia. In 1613, the Zemsky Sobor elected Mikhail Romanov as tsar, establishing the Romanovs as Russia's second reigning dynasty.

43   **Philemon, Ioannis** (1798–1874), a Greek historian and publisher, historiographer and participant of the Greek Revolution, member of the secret revolutionary organization Filiki Eteria. He joined the corps of Demetrios Nailantis and became his secretary. As an expert in the Turkish language, Philemon negotiated with the defeated Ottomans.

44   **Raevsky, Vasily Andreevich** (1768/71–1829/35), son of Andrey Raevsky, cousin of General Nikolai Raevsky. In 1802 Vasily Raevsky married Baroness Olimpiada Vladimirovna von Rosen (1789–1861). They had three children: Evdokia (1803–1857), Andrey (1804–1850), Alexander (1806–1850).

45   **Okhotnikov, Konstantin Alexeevich** (1785/89–1824), son of a retired major and Kaluga landowner, Alexei Orlov and Princess Natalya Vyazemskaya. Okhotnikov studied at the Tsarskoe Selo Lyceum, became an officer, participated in three wars, was awarded orders for bravery in battles. He was an adjutant of Major Raevsky and an adjutant of General Mikhail Orlov, eventually earning the rank of captain. He was a member of the Union of Welfare. He led the divisional schools of training for lower ranks, created by Orlov in Chișinău. There he met Pushkin, who trusted him to convey his confidential messages and poems to Vyazemsky.

46   **Pushchin, Pavel Petrovich** (1768–1828), lieutenant-general, fought in the Russo-Swedish (1788–1790) and Napoleonic wars. Later he was a major-general, the governor of Kazan (1800–1801), and a senator (1818). He was an uncle of Ivan Pushchin.

47   **Dolgorukov, Pavel Ivanovich** (1787–1845), prince, member of the Committee of Trustees for Foreign Colonists of Southern Russia, Active State Councilor since 1842. He is known as an amateur composer and pianist, as well as memoirist. In 1821, he was sent on official duties to Chișinău, where he met Pushkin. In 1821–22, they repeatedly met in the house of the Plenipotentiary Governor of the Bessarabia region, Inzov. Dolgorukov married Princess Elizaveta Golitsyna (1800–1863).

48   **Ferdinand I** (1751–1825), King of the Two Sicilies from 1816 until his death. Before that he had been, since 1759, King of Naples as Ferdinand IV and King of Sicily as Ferdinand III.

49   **Frederick William III** (Friedrich Wilhelm III.; 1770–1840), king of Prussia from 1797 until his death in 1840. He was concurrently Elector of Brandenburg in the Holy Roman Empire until 1806 when the Empire was dissolved.

50   **Ferdinand VII** (1784–1833) was king of Spain during the early nineteenth century. He reigned briefly in 1808 and then again from 1813 to his death in 1833.

51   **Smirnov, Dmitry**, titular adviser. Smirnov met with Alexander Pushkin at Inzov's residence.

52 **Davydov, Vasily Lvovich** (1780–1855), officer, poet, Decembrist, who participated in the War of 1812 and in foreign campaigns. Davydov had fought in the battles of Lützen and Bautzen, was captured near Leipzig, and released from captivity by Prussian troops. In 1822 he retired with the rank of colonel. Vasily Davydov was a freemason, a member of the Alexander Lodge of Triple Salvation and of the Decembrist Union of Welfare (1820), as well as the Southern Society. Together with Sergei Volkonsky, he headed the Kamensk administration of the Southern Society and sought to unite the Southern and the Northern Societies. Arrested and exiled to Siberia, he lived in Krasnoyarsk with his children and wife, Alexandra Ivanovna, née Potapova (1802–1895).

53 **Vigel, Philip Philipovich** (1786–1856), statesman, Actual State Councilor (1830), one of the most famous memoirists of the Pushkin era, a collector of portraits (engravings and lithographs). Vigel started his career in the Moscow archive of the Collegium of Foreign Affairs. His patrons were Dmitry Bludov and later Mikhail Vorontsov. In 1836 Vigel informed Metropolitan Seraphim about Chaadaev's *Philosophical Letters* in The Telescope. He stood in long-term correspondence with Pushkin and was a member of Arzamas. Vigel wrote the widely known and popular "Notes," which were printed in the *The Russian Herald* journal in 1864.

54 **Nepenin, Andrei Grigoryevich** (1782–1845), colonel (1818), Decembrist, member of the Union of Welfare. After the Decembrist revolt on Senate Square, he was arrested, taken from Tiraspol to St. Petersburg, placed for six months in the Peter and Paul Fortress, and thereupon banned from the capitals to the estate of his brother-in-law in the Tula Province.

55 **Gribovsky, Mikhail Kirillovich** (1786–1833), publicist and translator; Collegiate, then Actual State Councilor, Simbirsk vice-governor, Sloboda-Ukrainian governor. He worked in the office of the Disabled Committee, later in the library of the Guards General Staff headed by Benckendorf. Gribovsky managed the office of the Committee and led the creation of the secret military police. He was a secret government agent from 1820. In 1821, being a member of the Central Command of the Union of Welfare, Gribovsky informed Alexander I regarding the Decembrist societies. He participated in arrests; lists of conspirators were compiled largely on the basis of his denunciations.

56 **Sabaneev, Ivan Vasilyevich** (1770–1829), military leader, infantry general. After graduating from the Faculty of Philosophy of Moscow University he fought in the Russo-Turkish War (1787–1791), in actions against the Polish Confederates near Warsaw (1794), and in the Italian and Swiss campaigns of Suvorov. He was wounded and spent more than a year in captivity in France, then returned to Russia and took part in further battles. Sabaneev met Pushkin in 1822 (during the period of the poet's southern exile in Chisinau). In the same year, Pushkin accidentally overheard Sabaneev's words about the looming arrest of Vladimir Raevsky and managed to warn his friend.

57 **Vadkovsky, Fedor Fedorovich** (1800–1844), son of a wealthy senator from Elets, cornet, ensign, Decembrist, poet, and musician. In 1923 he became a member of the Northern Society. For satirical poems against the monarchy, in 1824, he was transferred to Kursk, where he joined the Southern Society of Decembrists. His secret letter to Pestel fell into the hands of the gendarmes. Arrested before the uprising, Vadkovsky was convicted, sentenced to death, but this sentence was later commuted to exile and hard labor. His

older brother Alexander was also convicted in the Decembrist case. Together with Ivan Pushchin, he led a community of exiled Decembrists in Siberia.

58   **Sherwood (Shervud), John (Ivan Vasilyevich)** (1798–1867), son of an English mechanic, colonel of the Armed Forces of the Russian Empire. In 1819 Sherwood entered the 3rd Ukrainian Lancer Regiment as a volunteer private, served bravely, and earned awards for participation in military campaigns. He is known for his denunciation personally addressed Alexander I regarding the Southern Society and the impending Decembrist revolt. He continued his service as a military man and as an agent of the secret police. Later he was given the surname Sherwood-Verny by Nicholas I.

59   **Mayboroda, Arkady Ivanovich** (1798–1845), military leader, captain, known mainly as the author of the denunciation against Pavel Pestel and other Decembrists. In August 1824 he was admitted to the Southern Society of Decembrists. On November 25, 1825, he wrote a denunciation which, through Lieutenant–General Roth, was sent to Taganrog; on December 20, Mayboroda compiled a list of members of the secret society; then gave detailed testimony during the trial against the Decembrists.

60   **Krupensky (Krupyansky), Matvey Egorovich** (1775–1855), Bessarabian vice-governor in 1816–23, state councilor (1822). In the rank of vice-governor under two governors, Bakhmetev and Inzov, Krupensky carelessly made government loans, but after the arrival of Vorontsov Krupensky had to leave the service and paid the loans with almost all of his inherited estate. Pushkin often visited him and his wife in Chişinău.

61   **Bologovsky, Dmitry Nikolaevich,** (1780–1852), lieutenant–general, later Governor of Vologda (1836–1840), and senator. As a sergeant of the Izmailovsky regiment, he was on duty as an orderly at the office of Catherine II on the morning when she died of a stroke in her dressing room. He stood guard at the Mikhailovsky Palace on the night of March 11, 1801, when Emperor Paul I was assassinated. Bologovsky also took part in the murder. Bologovsky was one of Pushkin's Moscow acquaintances and had been well-acquainted with the poet's father and uncle. During his southern exile, Pushkin often dined at the Bologovskys' house in Chişinău.

62   **Lamartine, Alphonse Marie Louis de Prat de** (1790–1869), French author, poet, and statesman who was instrumental in the foundation of the French Second Republic. He is famous for his semi-autobiographical poem, "Le lac" ("The Lake") and "Histoire des Girondins" (1847) written in praise of the Girondists, as well as *Les Méditations Poétiques* (1820). Lamartine was made a chevalier of the Legion of Honor in 1825. He worked for the French embassy in Italy (1825–28) and was elected a member of the Académie française (1829) and member of the Chamber of Deputies (1833). A former monarchist, Lamartine came to embrace democratic ideals and opposed militaristic nationalism and liberalism. In 1833 he quickly founded his own political party and established himself as a prominent critic of the July Monarchy. Later he served as minister of Foreign Affairs (1848) and in the Provisional Government.

63   **Riego y Flórez, Rafael del** (1784–1823), Spanish General, liberal politician, and revolutionary leader, who revolted in the port of Cádiz in 1820 and played a key role in the establishment of the Liberal Triennium.

64   **Liprandi, Ivan Petrovich** (1790–1880), military historian, major-general, officer of the secret police. He was a friend of Pushkin's.

65 **Liprandi, Pavel Petrovich** (1796–1864), the younger brother of Ivan Liprandi, adjutant to General Sabaneev, with whom he soon became friendly and through whom he became known to Count Vorontsov and Kiselyov. Pavel Liprandi was a military leader, infantry general (1860), Commander of the Semenovsky regiment (1842–48). He fought in the Polish campaign of 1831 and in the Crimean War, proposed and successfully carried out a plan for the Battle of Balaklava.

66 **Baryatinsky, Alexander Petrovich** (1799–1844), prince, adjutant to Count Wittgenstein, staff-captain of the Hussar Regiment, Decembrist. Baryatinsky was a member of the Union of Welfare, Northern and Southern Decembrist societies, friend of Pavel Pestel. Established first contacts between secret societies and negotiated on the union of the Southern and Northern secret societies in 1823. In November 1825, a few days before the death of Alexander I, on behalf of Pestel, headed the Tulchynsky council of the Southern Society of Decembrists. He was arrested, sentenced to hard labor, exiled to Siberia, and died in Tobolsk.

67 **Begichev, Stepan Nikitich** (1785–1859), colonel, memoirist. Begichev was a member of the Union of Welfare, though he left it prior its dissolution and therefore evaded investigation in the aftermath of the rebellion. Begichev's house was one of the centers of cultural life in Moscow. He was a close friend of Alexander Griboedov, who worked on his comedy *Woe from Wit* in the Begichev estate in the Tula Province.

68 **Maturin, Charles Robert** (1782–1824), also known as C. R. Maturin and under the pseudonym Dennis Jasper Murphy, was an Irish Protestant, clergyman and a writer of Gothic plays and novels. Sir Walter Scott recommended Maturin's work to Lord Byron. Maturin's best-known work is the novel *Melmoth the Wanderer*, published in 1820; it appeared in French translation in 1821 and spawned numerous imitations.

69 **Hańska, Ewelina (née Contessa Rzewuska)** (1805–1882), muse and–briefly–wife of the writer Honoré de Balzac. From 1832 she engaged in a decades-long correspondence with Balzac. They met for the first time in Switzerland in 1833. In 1850 Ewelina Hańska finally married Balzac, but her husband died six months after she moved to Paris. In 1851, Evelina met the artist Jean Gigou, their relationship lasted thirty years until her death.

70 **Chateaubriand, François–René de** (1768–1848), vicomte, peer of France, French Romantic writer, poet, politician and statesman of the Restoration era, major figure of French Romanticism, minister of state (1815); minister of foreign affairs of France (1823–24) and ambassador in Berlin, London and Rome. Chateaubriand authored a range of historical sketches, pamphlets, novels, stories, and memoirs. He was a proponent of constitutional monarchy, representative political system and democratic freedoms. His philosophical and political views influenced the development of the traditionalist and conservative movement in French political thought.

71 **Mickiewicz, Adam Bernard** (1798–1855), Polish writer, poet, playwright, teacher, political publicist, essayist, translator and political activist, leader of the Polish and Belarusian national movements, member of the Philomath Society. He is regarded as a national poet in Poland, Lithuania, Ukraine and Belarus. In Russia Mickiewicz was close to members of the Decembrist movement (Ryleev and Bestuzhev), Prince Vyazemsky, and other Russian writers and poets.

72 **de Witt, Ivan Osipovich (Iosifovich)** (1781–1840), count of Dutch–Polish origin. He fought in the Napoleonic Wars (1805–1814) and the Polish Campaign (1831). Witt was a general and the commander of the southern military settlements in Odesa.

73 **Boshnyak (Boshniak), Alexander Karlovich** (1786–1831), botanist, writer, friend of Zhukovsky's, who acted as a secret agent behalf of Count de Witt.

74 **Balzac, Honoré de** (1799–1850) was a highly influential French novelist and playwright, one of the founders of realism in European literature. His magnum opus was the novel sequence *La Comédie humaine*, which presents a panorama of post-Napoleonic French life. In 1850, Balzac married Ewelina Hańska, a Polish aristocrat and his longtime love.

75 **Riznich, Amalia** (1803–1824/25), daughter of an Austrian banker, wife of Odesa merchant of Serbian origin Ivan Riznich. She lived in Odesa from the spring of 1823 to May 1824. During the first period of Pushkin's southern exile, Riznich was the subject of his ardent and painful passion, the addressee of his poems: "Night," "For the shores of a distant fatherland…," "Under the blue sky of your native country…." Riznich died shortly after returning to Italy with her young son Alexander.

76 **Vorontsova, Elizaveta Ksaveryevna (née Branicki or Branitskaya)** (1792–1880), countess, Maid of Honor, Cavalry Lady of the Order of St. Catherine, honorary trustee in the management of women's educational institutions. She was the younger sister of Count Wladyslaw Branicki, a major-general. In 1819 she married Count Mikhail Vorontsov, who was later Novorossiysk Governor-General. Vorontsova was an addressee of many poems written by Pushkin.

77 **Vyazemskaya, Vera Fedorovna (née Gagarina)** (1790–1886), princess, the eldest daughter of Major-General Fedor Gagarin. In 1811 married Prince Pyotr Vyazemsky (1792–1878). She was a friend of Zhukovsky and was related to the Karamzin family. In 1824, in Odesa, she Pushkin with whom she upheld friendly and trusting relations until the end of the poet's life.

78 **Vorontsov, Semen Romanovich** (1744–1832), count (from 1797), diplomat, infantry general (1796), Russian ambassador to Great Britain (1784–1806). A chief representative of the Russian Anglophiles, he lived in London for half a century. He was the younger brother of Princess Ekaterina Dashkova and Chancellor Alexander Vorontsov. Vorontsov participated in extensive correspondences with prominent figures of his time.

79 **Volkonsky, Sergey Grigoryevich** (1788–1865), prince, Decembrist, major-general, Brigade Commander of the 19th Infantry Division (1825).

80 **Nesselrode, Karl Vasilyevich** (1780–1862), count (born Karl Robert Reichsgraf von Nesselrode-Ehreshoven), Russian statesman of German origin, son of the diplomat Count Maximilian Wilhelm Karl Nesselrode and Baroness Louise Gontar. Karl Nesselrode was the penultimate chancellor of the Russian Empire. He held the post of minister of Foreign Affairs for almost 40 years (including the years of joint management of foreign affairs with Kapodistrias). Nesselrode opposed revolutionary movements and liberal reforms, supported the union of Russia with Austria and Prussia, and was one of the organizers of the Holy Alliance.

81 **Paulucci, Philip (Filippo) Osipovich** (1779–1849), marquis, infantry general of the Russian and Sardinian armies, diplomat, Commander-in-Chief in Georgia (1811–1812), Livonia (Liflandia), Courland, Estland (Estlandia), and Pskov Governor-General.

Endnotes to Chapter Four

1. **Gershenzon, Mikhail Osipovich (Meilikh Iosifovich)** (1869–1925), cultural historian, publicist and translator. He is best known as the author of works about Pushkin (*The Wisdom of Pushkin*, 1919), Turgenev (*The Dream and Thought of I. S. Turgenev*, 1919), Chaadaev, and the era of Nicholas I.

2. **Olenina, Anna (Anette) Alexeevna** (1807–1888), daughter of President of the St. Petersburg Academy of Arts Alexei Olenin. Pushkin's beloved in 1828–1829, later wife of the President of Warsaw Teodor Andrault de Langeron. The addressee of Pushkin's poems "Her eyes," "You are empty with your heart...," "Don't sing, beauty, before me."

3. **Lobanov–Rostovsky, Alexei Yakovlevich** (1795–1848), prince, major-general, participant in the War of 1812 and Russo-Turkish War, confidant of Emperor Nicholas I. His wife died in childbirth, leaving him a widower with three young children. Beginning in 1838, Prince Lobanov often traveled abroad to carry out assignments from Nicholas I at foreign courts.

4. **Zakrevskaya, Agrafena Fedorovna** (née Countess Tolstaya) (1799 – 1879), daughter of the famous bibliophile Count Fedor Tolstoy and Stepanida Tolstaya. Agrafena was the wife of Minister of Internal Affairs General Zakrevsky, who later became the governor of Moscow.

5. **Ge, Nikolai Nikolaevich** (1831–1894), artist, painter, famous for his works on historical and religious subjects. He influenced the development of Russian symbolism. In 1857 Ge graduated with a gold medal from the Imperial Academy of Arts in Saint Petersburg, where he studied under master painter Pyotr Basin. The gold medal gave him the opportunity to study abroad: he visited Germany, Switzerland and France. He eventually settled in Ukraine.

6. **Propertius (Sextus Propertius)** (50 BC–15 BC), Roman poet. The first and best known of his four books of elegies, *Cynthia* was published in 29 BC, the year he met its heroine who became his mistress. Her real name was Hostia. Propertius was a younger contemporary of Tibullus and a member of Maecenas's circle, as well as a friend of Ovid.

7. **Báthory, István (Batori, Stephen)** (1533–1586), Voivode of Transylvania (1571–1576), prince of Transylvania (1576–1586), King of Poland and Grand Duke of Lithuania (1576–1586), the third elected king of Poland. Báthory became the ruler of Transylvania defeating another challenger for that title, Gáspár Bekes. In 1576 Báthory married Queen Anna Jagiellon. He worked closely with chancellor Jan Zamoyski. The first years of his reign were focused on establishing power, defeating a fellow claimant to the Polish throne, Maximilian II, Holy Roman Emperor, and quelling rebellions (the Danzig revolt). He is considered one of the most successful kings in Polish history, particularly in the military realm. His signal achievement was his victorious campaign in Livonia against Russia, as he repulsed a Russian invasion of Commonwealth borderlands and secured a highly favorable peace treaty (the Peace of Jam Zapolski).

8. **Osipova, Praskovya Alexandrovna (in her first marriage Vulf, née Vyndomskaya)** (1781–1859), Pskov landowner, mistress of the Trigorskoe estate. Praskovya Osipova is known as Alexander Pushkin's neighbor on the Mikhailovskoe estate and a close friend of the poet. She was also friendly with poets Delvig, Baratynsky, Ivan Kozlov, Vyazemsky.

9   **Vyndomsky (Vindomsky), Alexander Maximovich** (1750–1813), retired colonel, leader of the district nobility, second owner of the village of Trigorskoe, father of Praskovya Osipova-Vulf. Alexander Vyndomsky traded timber, sending it abroad. He set up a linen factory, a brick factory and a distillery on the estate. The estate was extensive, much larger than the neighboring Mikhailovskoe, and included numerous outbuildings, a large orchard, a park, flower beds and an extensive landscape park in the English style. In Trigorskoe Vyndomsky collected an excellent library, which was later used by Pushkin.

10 **Vulf, Nikolai Ivanovich** (1771–1813), son of Oryol Governor Ivan Vulf and maternal uncle of Anna Kern (née Poltoratskaya). At the age of 12 (in 1783) he was assigned to the Life-Guards Preobrazhensky Regiment and in 1784 transferred to the Semenovsky regiment as a sergeant, eventually working towards the rank of lieutenant. In 1797, he resigned and retired as a titular councilor. In 1798, Nikolai Vulf worked the State Assignation Bank. Having received the next rank, in 1799 he left the office. Retired in the rank of collegiate assessor, he lived with his father in a village near Tver. In 1799 he married Praskovya Vyndomskaya with whom he had seven children five of whom survived.

11 **Vulf, Alexei Nikolaevich** (1805–1881), memoirist, a close friend of Yazykov and Pushkin. For a while Alexei Vulf was in love with Anna Kern (née Poltoratskaya), who was his cousin, and later he also courted her sister, Lizaveta Poltoratskaya. From 1819, Vulf lived in Dorpat, studying military science at the Faculty of Physics and Mathematics of the University of Dorpat in 1822–1826. During his holiday visits to his grandfather's Trigorskoe estate, Alexei regularly met with Pushkin, who was in exile at the neighboring Mikhailovskoe estate. Pushkin regularly interfaced with him regarding various creative plans—and in 1825, had the idea of fleeing abroad while posing as Vulf's servant.

12 **Vulf, Anna Nikolaevna** (1799–1857), daughter of retired Collegiate Assessor Nikolai Vulf. Vulf was never married and lived in the family estates of Trigorskoe and Malinniki.

13 **Vrevskaya, Evpraksia (Eupraxia) Nikolaevna (née Vulf)** (1809–1883), baroness, Pskov noblewoman, daughter of retired Collegiate Assessor Nikolai Vulf, wife to Baron Boris Vrevsky (1805–1886), retired officer of the Life-Guards Izmailovsky Regiment. She was Pushkin's neighbor on the Mikhailovskoe estate and a close friend of the poet's. Under her nickname "Zizi" she was mentioned by the poet in the fifth chapter of *Eugene Onegin*.

14 **Osipova, Alexandra (Alexandrina) Ivanovna** (1805/6–1864), stepdaughter of Praskovya Osipova, daughter of Ivan Osipov from his first marriage. Pushkin met Alexandra Osipova in 1824 in Trigorskoe and dedicated the poem "Confession" to her. They would later frequently correspond. In 1833 she married Pyotr Beklešov, who was then the chief of police in Pskov. The couple had two sons and a daughter. For some years Alexandra worked as a music teacher at the Pskov Mariinsky School.

15 **Kern, Anna Petrovna (née Poltoratskaya)** (1800–1879), noblewoman, translator, and author of memoirs, perhaps Pushkin's most famous muse. Her maternal grandfather was Oryol Governor Ivan Vulf. Her first husband, General Ermolay Kern was about 52 years old when he married Anna. She remarried in 1842.

16 **Elizaveta Petrovna (Elizabeth of Russia)** (1709–1762), Empress from the Romanov dynasty, the youngest daughter of Peter I the Great and Catherine I of Russia. Elizabeth lived through the confused successions of her father's descendants following her

half-brother Alexey's death in 1718. The throne first passed to her mother Catherine I of Russia (r. 1725–1727), then to her nephew Peter II, who died in 1730 and was succeeded by Elizabeth's first cousin Anna (r. 1730–1740). After the brief rule of Anna's great-nephew, Ivan VI, Elizabeth seized the throne with the military's support and declared her own nephew, the future Peter III, her heir. Her reign (1741–62) was marked by the restoration of the Governing Senate, the establishment of Moscow University and Academy of Arts, and the emergence of the first bank in the Russian Empire. She modernized Russia's roads and financed grandiose baroque projects of her favorite architect, Bartolomeo Rastrelli, particularly in Peterhof Palace. The Winter Palace and the Smolny Cathedral in St. Petersburg are among the chief monuments of her reign. The death penalty was not applied during her reign. Furthermore, the exploration and development of Siberia continued. The Russian Empire emerged victorious in the Russo-Swedish War of 1741–1743. Elizabeth ruled the Russian Empire during the two major European conflicts of her time: the War of the Austrian Succession (1740–1748) and the Seven Years' War (1756–1763). She and her diplomat Alexei Bestuzhev-Ryumin weathered the first conflict by forming an alliance with Austria and France, but indirectly caused the second. Russian troops enjoyed several victories against Prussia and briefly occupied Berlin, but when Frederick the Great was finally considering surrender in January 1762, the Russian Empress died. She was the last agnatic member of the House of Romanov to reign over the Russian Empire.

17 **Pugachev, Emelyan Ivanovich** (1742–1775), Don Cossack, fugitive, leader of the Peasant War of 1773–75. Pugachev had spread rumors among the Yaitsky Cossacks that he was Tsar Peter Fedorovich (Peter III) who managed to save himself from the coup d'état undertaken by Catherine II. He gathered a large army and took several cities and fortresses by storm, deception or siege. Russian peasants and Cossacks were joined by Bashkirs leaded by Salavat Yulaev. Eventually his forces were defeated. Pugachev was betrayed, handed over to government forces, convicted, sentenced to death. The execution of Pugachev and his assistant Afanasy Perfilyev was the last official quartering in Russia. After Pugachev's death his two wives and children were imprisoned in a northern fortress.

18 **Mirovich, Vasily Yakovlevich** (1740–1764), second lieutenant of the Smolensk Infantry Regiment, best known for his attempted but ultimately unsuccessful rescue of Tsar Ivan VI (Ioann Antonovich) from his imprisonment at the Shlisselburg Fortress during the reign of Catherine the Great. Prior to this, Mirovich had repeatedly requested Catherine to return his hereditary estates to no avail. Mirovich was executed on September 15, 1764.

19 **Kakhovsky, Pyotr Grigoryevich** (1799–1826), officer, retired since 1821, Decembrist. In 1825 Kakhovsky was introduced by Kondraty Ryleev to the Northern Society, and later established a cell of the organization in the Grenadier Life-Guard Regiment. He had actively participated in the preparation of the insurrection at Senate Square, where he shot and killed St. Petersburg Governor-General Mikhail Miloradovich and Colonel Nikolas Stürler of the Grenadier Life-Guard Regiment. He was wounded, arrested, sentenced to death by hanging and executed in 1826 on the wall of the Kronverk of Peter and Paul Fortress.

Endnotes to Chapter Five

1 **Golenishchev-Kutuzov, Pavel Vasilyevich** (1772–1843), count (from 1832), general, fought in the Napoleonic War of 1812 and other foreign campaigns, served as St. Petersburg military governor-general in 1825–30. Golenishchev-Kutuzov took the post after his predecessor, Count Miloradovich, was murdered during the Decembrist revolt.

2 **Fouché, Joseph**, 1st Duc d'Otrante, 1st Comte Fouché, French statesman, revolutionary, and minister of police under Napoleon.

3 **Izmailov, Vladimir Vasilyevich** (1773–1830), writer, poet, journalist, and censor. He was the son of a colonel and a relative of Vasily Pushkin. Izmailov translated the works of Rousseau, Chateaubriand, Genlis, Florian, and Millvois. In 1814–15 he edited *The Herald of Europe* and *The Russian Museum*. In 1827, he published the *Literary Museum* almanac.

4 **Polevoi, Nikolai Alexeevich** (1796–1846), writer and autodidact from a merchant family. In a short time he managed to become a noted literary figure. Together with his brother Ksenofont and Prince Vyazemsky, Nikolai Polevoi published *The Moscow Telegraph* journal.

5 **The Society of Lovers of Wisdom (Obshchestvo liubomudriya)** was a literary and philosophical circle that met in Moscow in 1823–1825. "Liubomudirie" is a Russification of the word "philosophy" (lit. "love of wisdom.") Its participants were Prince Vladimir Odoevsky (chairman), Dmitry Venevitinov (secretary), Ivan Kireevsky, Mikhail Pogodin, Stepan Shevyrev, and others. Members of the society called themselves "liubomudry" (lovers of wisdom). They studied German idealistic philosophy: the works of Friedrich Schelling, Baruch Spinoza, Immanuel Kant, Johann Gottlieb Fichte, Lorenz Oken, Friedrich Schlegel and German natural philosophers.

6 **Venevitinov, Dmitry Vladimirovich** (1805–1827), Romantic poet, translator, prose writer, philosopher. Venevitinov was distantly related to Pushkin, who was his fourth cousin. Together with Prince Vladimir Odoevsky, Venevitinov organized the secret Society of Philosophy Lovers (liubomudry) and participated in the publication of *The Moscow Herald* journal.

7 **Shevyrev (Shevirev), Stepan Petrovich** (1806–1864), literary critic and historian, poet, important figure in the broader Slavophile movement, professor and dean of Moscow University, member of the St. Petersburg Academy of Sciences. Shevyrev served in the Moscow archive of the Collegium of Foreign Affairs, was a member of The Society of Lovers of Wisdom, and participated in the organization and publication of the *Moscow Herald* (1827–1830). In 1835–37 Shevyrev was a leading critic of the *Moscow Observer* and together with Mikhail Pogodin, he published and edited *The Muscovite* journal in 1841–56. In 1834 Shevyrev married Sofia Borisovna, née Zelenskaya (1809–1871).

8 **Odoevsky, Vladimir Fedorovich** (1804–1869), prince, poet, writer and thinker of the Romantic era, and musician. Odoevsky took part in many journals and almanacs. From 1846 he was the director of the Rumyantsev Museum, and on the bureaucratic end, he earned appointments as Chamberlain (1836), Privy Councilor (1858), and finally, Senator (1861). His writing was influenced by contemporaneous developments in German Romantic thought. He worked in numerous different genres and is perhaps most noted for his philosophical novel *Russian Nights* (1844). His work typically appeared

under a range of pseudonyms. In 1826, Odoevsky married Olga Stepanovna, née Lanskaya (1797–1873).

9   **Stankevich, Nikolay Vladimirovich** (1813–1840), prominent philosopher, writer, poet and publicist of the 19th century, organizer and head of a circle, known in the history of Russian social thought as "Stankevich's Circle." The circle included Mikhail Bakunin, Vasily Botkin, Konstantin Aksakov, Vissarion Belinsky, Ivan Obolensky, and Ivan Turgenev.

10 **Slavophiles**, members of a broadly-defined social movement which opposed the influence of western Europe in Russia and argued that Russia was to follow a special path of historical development.

11 **Razin, Stepan Timofeevich** (Stenka Razin), (1630–1671), a Don Cossack, leader of a folk uprising in southern Russia in 1670–71. In 1670 Razin claimed, he was going to fight not against the tsar (Alexei Mikhailovich), but against the boyars who negatively influenced the sovereign. Prior to the uprising, in 1667–1669, Razin's troops blocked the Volga River, captured Russian and Persian merchant ships and the Yaitsky Cossack town, and devastated the Persian coast of the Caspian Sea. In 1670 his army captured Tsaritsyn and approached Astrakhan, which was also surrendered. They executed the governor and nobles and organized their own government led by Vasily Us. The march of Razin's army to the Volga was accompanied by massive serf uprisings. Many ethnic minorities dwelling along the Volga River joined the uprising. Many towns, including Tsaritsyn (now Volgograd), Kamyshin, Astrakhan, Cyvilsk, Alatyr, Saransk, and Penza were captured. The largest battle of the rebels with the tsarist troops took place near the villages of Baevo and Turgenevo (Mordovia). The rebels were commanded by the Mordovian Murza Akai Bolyaev (Murzakaika or Murza Kayko), the tsarist army was headed by the Governor, Prince Yuri Baryatinsky and V. Panin, who was sent to help by Yuri Dolgorukov. A group led by the ataman of the Don Army, Kornil Yakovlev, attacked Razin's headquarters in the Kagalnitsky settlement. Stepan Razin and his brother Frol, were captured and handed over to the tsarist authorities. In June 1671, Stepan and Frol Razin were brought to Moscow. Stepan Razin was quartered on Bolotnaya Square.

12 **Nestor the Chronicler** (1056–1114), Kyivan Rus monk who is known to have written two saints' lives: "the Life of the Venerable Theodosius of the Kyiv Caves" and the "Account about the Life and Martyrdom of the Blessed Passion Bearers Boris and Gleb." Traditional historiography has also attributed to him the Primary Chronicle, though this has since been disputed.

13 **Pimen** (Pimen Cherny), (about 1571), Archbishop of Novgorod, supporter of Ivan the Terrible, canonized by the Russian Orthodox Church as a saint. Pimen provided many important services to the tsar during the Oprichnina period. Later Ivan IV accused Pimen of treason, and this reprisal against the disgraced Archbishop made a great impression on his contemporaries and foreigners.

14 **Ivan IV, the Terrible** (1530–1584), Tsar, Grand Prince of Moscow and All Russia from 1533 to 1547, and the first tsar and grand prince of all Russia from 1547 until his death in 1584. His reign was characterized by Russia's transformation from a medieval state to an empire, but at an immense cost to its people and long-term economy. Ivan IV was the eldest son of Vasily III by his second wife Elena Glinskaya, and a grandson of Ivan III. He succeeded his father after his death when he was three years old. A group of reformers

united around the young Ivan, crowning him as tsar in 1547 at the age of 16. In the early years of his reign, Ivan ruled with the group of reformers known as the Chosen Council and established the Zemsky Sobor, a new assembly convened by the tsar. He also revised the legal code and introduced reforms, including elements of local self-government, as well as the establishment the first Russian standing army, the streltsy. Ivan conquered the Khanates of Kazan and Astrakhan and significantly expanded the territory of Russia. After he had consolidated his power, Ivan rid himself of the advisers from the Chosen Council and triggered the Livonian War of 1558 to 1583, which ravaged Russia and resulted in territorial losses, but allowed him to establish greater autocratic control over the Russian nobility, which he violently purged using Russia's first political police force, the *oprichniki*. The later years of his reign were marked by the massacre of Novgorod and the burning of Moscow by the Tatars. Ivan began several processes that would continue for centuries, including deepening connections with other European states, particularly England, fighting wars against the Ottoman Empire, and the gradual conquest of Siberia. Historians generally believe that in a fit of anger, he murdered his eldest son and heir, Ivan Ivanovich; he might also have caused the miscarriage of the latter's unborn child. This left his younger son, the politically ineffectual Feodor Ivanovich, to inherit the throne, a man whose rule and subsequent childless death led directly to the end of the Rurik dynasty and the beginning of the Time of Troubles.

15 **Khomyakov, Alexei Stepanovich** (1804–1860), theologian, philosopher, poet and amateur artist. He was a cornerstone of the Slavophile movement along with Ivan Kireevsky and became one of its most distinguished theoreticians. His writings, printed posthumously by his friends and disciples, exerted a profound influence on the Russian Orthodox Church and Russian philosophers and thinkers, such as Fedor Dostoevsky, Konstantin Pobedonostsev, and Vladimir Solovyov. Khomyakov's ideals revolved around the term sobornost, which can be loosely translated as "togetherness" or "symphony." Khomyakov died from cholera, infected by a peasant he had attempted to treat. He was buried next to his brother-in-law, Nikolay Yazykov in the Danilov Monastery.

16 **Volkonskaya, Zinaida Alexandrovna** (née Beloselskaya-Belozerskaya) (1789–1862), princess, daughter of Prince Alexander Beloselsky-Belozersky and Varvara Tatishcheva. In 1811 she married Prince Nikita Volkonsky, brother of the future Decembrist Sergey Volkonsky. Volkonskaya was Maid of Honor, a poetess and writer, singer, composer, who held notable literary salons in Moscow, St. Petersburg, and Rome.

17 **Muravyova, Alexandra (Alexandrina) Grigoryevna** (née Countess Chernyshova) (1804–1832), sister of the Decembrist Count Zakhar Chernyshov, wife of the Decembrist Nikita Muravyov. In 1826 followed her exiled husband to Siberia, leaving three young children with her mother–in–law in Saint Petersburg.

18 **Goethe, Johann Wolfgang von** (1749–1832), German poet, polymath and writer, philosopher, thinker, natural scientist, statesman, who exerted a profound influence on the development of European letters and thought. His plays like *Faust* and novels, such as *The Sorrows of Young Werther*, were foundational texts for various Romantic movements throughout Europe.

19 **Goncharov, Afanasy Nikolaevich** (1760–1832), nobleman, Court Councilor, second major, holder of the Order of St. Vladimir, 4th degree, leader of the nobility of the Me-

dynsky district of the Kaluga province, grandfather of Natalya Nikolaevna Pushkina (née Goncharova).

20 **Rimskaya-Korsakova, Alexandra Alexandrovna** (1803–1860), daughter of Chamberlain and Tambov landowner Alexander Rimsky-Korsakov (1850–1814). In 1832 Alexandra married Prince Alexander Vyazemsky (1804–1865). They had three sons: Nikolai, Lev and Alexei.

21 **Pushkina, Sofia Fedorovna** (1806–1862), noblewoman from the Pushkin family, a distant relative of the poet Alexander Pushkin and the addressee of his poems. She was the daughter of Fedor Pushkin and Maria Ivanovna (née Obolenskaya). After her parents' death, she and her sister Anna were raised by a wealthy aristocrat, Ekaterina Vladimirovna Apraksina. In 1827 Sofia married Valerian Aleksandrovich Panin with whom she had 3 sons and a daughter.

22 **Faro** (Pharaoh, Pharao, or Farobank), a late 17th–century French card game.

23 **Rodzianko, Arkady Gavrilovich** (c. 1793–1846), poet and critic, political satirist, Poltava landowner, retired captain, and one of Pushkin's close friends. Rodzianko published many poems in *The Son of the Fatherland*, *The Well-Intended* and *The Polar Star*, he was also member of the Green Lamp and the Free Society of Lovers of Literature, Sciences and Arts (1817). He married Nadezhda Akimovna, née Klevtsova.

24 **Skobelev, Ivan Nikitich** (1778–1849), military leader, engaged in military campaigns on Prussian soil during the Napoleonic wars and also participated in the Swedish campaign under the command of Nikolai Raevsky and was wounded. For a while he also served as a police bailiff. Then again fought in Bulgaria against the Turks under Field-Marshal Prince Kutuzov, who soon made him his senior adjutant. Skobelev became major0general (1817), then infantry general (1843). Lost his left arm in battles. As a writer he was known under the pseudonym "Russian Invalid" and wrote exclusively on military topics.

25 **Leopoldov, Andrei Filippovich** (1800–1875), historian, writer, ethnographer, journalist, teacher. Leopoldov published articles in *The Herald of Europe*, *The Moscow Telegraph*, *The Northern Bee*, and *The Son of the Fatherland*. He was arrested and convicted by the Novgorod district court for possessing Pushkin's banned elegy "André Chénier." Having been released in 1828, he entered service in the Novgorod Chamber of the Criminal Court.

26 **Shulgin, Dmitry Ivanovich** (1784–1854), major-general, infantry general, member of the State Council. In 1847–54 he was Military Governor-General of St. Petersburg. He took part in numerous foreign campaigns. In 1825 he was transferred to Moscow and became the Ober–Policemaster), then he surrendered the rebellion in Poland and became a lieutenant-general (1833) Shulgin was appointed St. Petersburg commandant (1846), St. Petersburg military Governor General (1847) and Infantry General (1848). He also was a member of the State Council (1848), member of the Board of Trustees of public charity institutions in St. Petersburg (1847–55). Vice-President of the Prison Trustee Committee (1848).

27 **Gorchakov, Dmitry Petrovich** (1758–1824), prince, poet and playwright, father of Generals Peter and Mikhail Gorchakov. Gorchakov served in the army, was adjutant of Prince Pavel Gagarin, and participated in campaigns near Khotyn, Wallachia, Kuban and

in the Crimea. He eventually retired with the rank of second major (1782), but returned to fight as a volunteer near Izmail (1790). Under Tsar Alexander I, Gorchakov became the provincial prosecutor in Pskov (1807) and in the Tauride Province (1807–10) and later served in the Ministry of Public Education in St. Petersburg (1811). In 1811-1812 he served under Mikhail Kutuzov in the Moldavian army. In 1813 Gorchakov was appointed Vice-Governor of Kostroma.

28 **Poltoratsky, Alexander Alexandrovich** (1792–1855), Pushkin's friend, retired captain. In 1834 he married Ekaterina Bakunina (1795–1869). She was a maid of honor, artist, sister of Pushkin's Lyceum friend, Alexander Bakunin, an early love of Pushkin's and the addressee of several early poems poems. In 1837, Alexander Poltoratsky was elected leader of the nobility in the Tambov district.

29 **Poggio (Podzhio), Alexander Viktorovich** (1798–1873), Decembrist, younger brother of Joseph Poggio (1792–1848), companion of Pavel Pestel. In 1820 he was a mediator between the Northern and Southern societies. In 1823 he became a member of both groups. Poggio did not participate in the Decembrist revolt of 1825, but was arrested, sentenced to death, commuted to lifelong hard labor, and sent to Siberia, where he worked at the Petrovsky plant. In 1851 he married Larisa Andreevna, née Smirnova (1823–1888). Poggio returned from Siberia in 1859. Later Poggio travelled to Switzerland, where he met Alexander Herzen in Geneva. He wrote *Notes of the Decembrist*, published in Moscow in 1930.

30 **Pushchin, Mikhail Ivanovich** (1800–1869), a younger brother of Ivan Pushchin, also a Decembrist, exiled to Siberia, then sent as a private to the Caucasian Army, fought in the Russo-Persian War (1827) and the Russo-Turkish War (1828–29), headed the engineering corps in Paskevich's army and took part in military councils with his commanders. He was a long-time acquaintance of Pushkin, Delvig, Küchelbecker and Volkhovsky.

31 **Gangeblov (Gangeblidze), Alexander Semenovich** (1801–1891), officer from a noble Georgian family, lieutenant of the Life-Guards Izmailovsky Regiment. For a while he was a member of the Northern Society. Arrested as a Decembrist, he spent three months in a fortress, then was sent to the Caucasus and later fought in the Russo–Turkish War. He authored memoirs depicting in detail the years of his studies in the Corps of Pages, his service in the Life-Guards, the history of his involvement into the Decembrist movement, and his ultimate imprisonment in the fortress and service in the Caucasus.

32 **Pasternak, Boris Leonidovich** (1890–1960), modernist poet, novelist, and translator. He translated stage plays and poems by Goethe, Schiller, Calderón de la Barca and Shakespeare. Pasternak's novel *Doctor Zhivago* (1957), rejected for publication in the USSR, was smuggled to Italy and published there in 1957. Pasternak was awarded the Nobel Prize in Literature in 1958, but the Communist Party forced him to decline the prize

33 **Poltoratsky, Pyotr Markovich** (1775–1851), Anna Kern's father, Poltava landowner and court councilor, Pyotr Poltoratsky married Ekaterina Ivanovna, née Wulf (1781–1832).

Endnotes to Chapter Six

1 **Goncharova, Natalya Nikolaevna** (1812–1863), wife of Alexander Pushkin in 1831–1837. Seven years after his death, she married General Pyotr Lanskoi (1799–1877), who was a friend of her brother's. Goncharova's role in the Pushkin's and the events preceding his last duel is the subject of scholarly debate to this day.

2 **Naumova, Ekaterina Nikolaevna (née Ushakova)** (1809–1872), daughter of Nikolai Ushakov (1779/80–1843) and Sofia Andreevna (née Gesse) (1775–1867). Ekaterina was the acquaintance and one of Pushkin's final muses. In 1836 she married Dmitrii Naumov.

3 **Khitrovo, Elizaveta Mikhailovna** (née Golenishcheva-Kutuzova), daughter of Feldmarshal Kutuzov and Ekaterina Bibikova. Khitrovo held a renowned St. Petersburg salon. After her first marriage she became Countess Tiesenhausen. Theodor von Tiesenhausen (Theodor Ferdinand from the count family of Tiesenhausen), who was General Kutuzov's aide-de-camp, died in the Austerlitz Battle in 1805. A witness of his death, composer Fedor Glinka, described this event to Leo Tolstoy, who later used this story in his epic novel *War and Peace* as an inspiration behind Prince Andrei Bolkonsky's wounding. Elizaveta Khitrovo had two daughters from her first marriage. In 1811 she remarried to Major-General Khitrovo. Count Nikolay Khitrovo was Russian special envoy to the Grand Duchy of Tuscany.

4 **Gulyanov, Ivan Aleksandrovich** (1789–1842), diplomat, historian, Egyptologist. Gulyanov's first work was the analysis of the Rosetta Stone (1804). Gulyanov was an opponent of Champollion, and the creator of an original hieroglyphic alphabet. Gulyanov used the pseudonyms "Th. Ausonioli" (F. Avzonioli) and "Naiv Lugovian."

5 **Scott, Walter**, 1st Baronet (1771–1832), Scottish novelist, poet, historian, collector of antiquities and lawyer, the founder of the historical novel genre. Travelling around the country, he collected folk legends and ballads about Scottish heroes of the past, translated and published German poetry. Outside of his literary work, Walter Scott was engaged in various legal, political and social activities. He worked as a secretary of the court of session (since 1806), and as a deputy sheriff of Selkirk County. Sir Walter Scott was a permanent member of the Conservative Party, a member of the Society of the High Lands, (1820–32), President of the Royal Society of Edinburgh, Vice-President of the Society of Scottish Antiquaries (1827–29).

6 **Somov, Orest Mikhailovich** (1793–1833), writer, literary critic and journalist. In 1824–1826, he headed the staff of the Russian-American Company. Somov was a member of the Free Society of Lovers of Russian Literature (1820). Together with Delvig, he published the *Northern Flowers* (1825–1832) and *Snowdrop* (1829) almanacs, participated in the publication of The Literary Gazette which he edited. He was briefly detained following the Decembrist revolt. As a critic Somov formulated a program of Russian romanticism, based on national identity. He insisted upon the use of folk materials and language. His own novels and short stories were based on Ukrainian folklore.

7 **Nadezhdin, Nikolai Ivanovich** (1804–1856), scientist, philosopher, literary critic, journalist, and polemicist, ethnographer, and ecclesiastical historian. Acting State Councilor, Professor at Moscow University. In 1831, Nadezhdin founded The Telescope journal.

In 1836, following the publication of Pyotr Chaadaev's "Philosophical Letters" in the journal, the publication was closed, and Nadezhdin was exiled to Ust–Sysolsk, then to Vologda.

8   **Polevoi, Xenofon (Ksenofont) Alexeevich** (1801–1867), writer, literary critic, journalist, memoirist, publisher and translator. He was the younger brother of the writers Ekaterina Alexeevna Avdeeva (née Polevaya) and Nikolay Polevoy. *The Moscow Telegraph*, created by Polevoy brothers, was thick journal, where Pushkin, Baratynsky, Vyazemsky, Zhukovsky, Krylov, and Vladimir Dal published their works.

9   **Vidocq, Eugène François** (1775–1857), detective, head of the Paris Secret Police. He was a French criminal, who turned criminalist and then first private detective, and became known for his innovations in the field of criminology. His life story inspired several writers, including Victor Hugo, Edgar Allan Poe, and Honoré de Balzac. Vidocq was the founder and first director of France's first criminal investigative agency, the Sûreté Nationale, as well as the head of the first known private detective agency.

10 **Maksimovich, Mikhailo Aleksandrovich** (1804–1873), scholar, philologist, folklorist, translator, historian, poet, botanist, Corresponding Member of the St. Petersburg Academy of Sciences, dean of the Faculty of History and Philology and, promoted by Count Uvarov, became the first Rector of the Imperial Kyiv University. Honorary member of Moscow University (1871). He was a friend of Pogodin and Gogol. In 1830, Maksimovich published the almanac *Dennitsa*, he where published the works of Pushkin, Venevitinov, Prince Vyazemsky, Delvig, Khomyakov, Baratynsky, Yazykov, Merzlyakov, Ivan Kireevsky. In 1857 Maksimovich headed the editorial office of the Russian Conversation journal. In 1858 he became secretary of the Society of Lovers of Russian Literature. He edited and published the *Kyivian* and *Ukrainian* anthologies.

11 **Sviniin, Pavel Petrovich** (1787–1839), writer, publisher, journalist and editor, artist, historian and geographer, collector of Russian antiquities. Svinyin raduated from the Imperial Academy of Arts (in 1806), then entered the diplomatic service. He published the *Notes from the Fatherland* journal.

12 **Southey, Robert** (1774–1843), English poet of the Romantic school, and Poet Laureate from 1813 until his death. Like the other Lake Poets, William Wordsworth and Samuel Taylor Coleridge, Southey's politics gradually transitioned from radicalism to a moderate or even conservative institutionalism. He is remembered especially for the poem "After Blenheim" and the original version of "Goldilocks and the Three Bears."

13 **Goncharova, Natalya Ivanovna (née Zagryazhskaya)** (1785–1848), maid of honor from the Zagryazhsky family, owner of the Yaropolets estate near Moscow. Natalya Ivanovna was the illegitimate daughter of Ivan Zagryazhsky and Baroness Euphrosinia Ulrika von Posse (née von Liphart). Natalya Ivanovna married Nikolay Goncharov (1787–1865). Together they had seven children: Dmitry, Ekaterina, Ivan, Alexandra, Natalya, Sergey and Sofia.

Endnotes to Chapter Seven

1   **Kachenovsky, Mikhail Trofimovich** (1775–1842), publisher and editor of the journal *The Herald of Europe* (periodically 1807–1830), critic and translator, professor of fine arts and archeology at Moscow University, who also taught Russian history, statistics, geography and Russian literature. Kachenovsky was a literary opponent of Karamzin and other poets from Karamzin's circle. Before the full edition of *Ruslan and Liudmila* was edited, *The Herald of Europe* published a review against the poem and its author. Later, Kachenovsky often opposed Pushkin and provided the pages of his magazine for attacks on Pushkin and his literary associates (Zhukovsky, Vyazemsky and others). Pushkin wrote eleven epigrams against him.

2   **Cancrin, Egor Frantsevich (Georg Ludwig)** (1774–1845), count, Infantry General, statesman, economist, Senator (1823), Minister of Finance (1823–44). He was a strong conservative voice, opposing industrial development and the construction of railway systems. He closed the State Commercial Bank, which provided loans for their construction, and transferred the funds to the State Loan Bank, to finance loans for landowners.

3   **Kireev, Pyotr Aleksandrovich**, a serf of the poet's father, Sergey Pushkin, who was a clerk on the Boldino estate in the 1830s. Alexander Pushkin came to Boldino three times, while Kireev was the clerk of the family. As serfs serving in the court of the manor, the Kireevs did not have their own land, and clerking became a family profession for them. Two sons and a grandson of Pyotr Kireev also served as clerks.

4   **Shcheglov, Nikolai Prokofyevich** (1794–1831), professor, physicist and mineralogist. From 1827 he was a corresponding member of the St. Petersburg Academy of Sciences. In 1828 Shcheglov was elected permanent secretary of the Free Economic Society. He was also a censor of the St. Petersburg Censorship Committee. Starting in 1824 he published the journal *Index of Discoveries in Physics, Chemistry, Natural History and Technology* in which he placed almost exclusively his translations, and from 1830 edited the industrial *Northern Ant* newspaper.

5   **Buturlina, Anna Petrovna (née Shakhovskaya)** (1793–1861), princess, daughter of Prince Pyotr Shakhovsky. Anna Petrovna married Mikhail Buturlin in 1815. The family was acquainted with Pushkin, who visited them in September 1833 on his way to Orenburg.

6   **Buturlin, Mikhail Petrovich** (1786–1860), officer and statesman, Nizhny Novgorod Governor in 1831–1843, lieutenant-general.

7   **Charles X (Charles Philippe)** (1757–1836), count of Artois, then king of France and Navarre (1824–30). He was the younger brother of reigning kings Louis XVI and Louis XVIII, an uncle of the uncrowned Louis XVII. Charles became the leader of the ultra-royalist faction and heir-presumptive after the Bourbon Restoration in 1814. He married Marie Thérèse of Savoy (1773–1805) and was the last of the French rulers from the senior branch of the House of Bourbon. He reimbursed former landowners for the abolition of feudalism at the expense of bondholders and increased the power of the Catholic Church. To distract his citizens from domestic problems, he approved the French conquest of Algeria, then lifted Haiti's blockade and recognized its independence, but forced the newly independent nation to pay a hefty indemnity. He appointed a conservative government under the premiership of Prince Jules de Polignac, who was defeated in the 1830

French legislative election. He responded with the July Ordinances where he disbanded the Chamber of Deputies and also reimposed press censorship. His actions led to the July Revolution of 1830 which resulted in Charles's abdication and exile to the Austrian Empire, and the election of Louis Philippe I.

8   **Polignac, Jules Auguste Armand Marie de** (1780–1847), count, then prince of Polignac, and 3rd duke of Polignac. Polignac was a French statesman and politician forced by the French Revolution into exile in England. On his return, he was arrested for conspiring against Napoleon and imprisoned. Following the Bourbon Restoration, he was made a peer. In 1829 Charles X appointed Polignac foreign minister and prime minister. Polignac was responsible for the restrictive ordinances causing the July Revolution (1830), that overthrew the senior line of the House of Bourbon. He was imprisoned, then pardoned, but exiled from France for 20 years. In 1816 Polignac married Barbara Campbell (1788–1819). In 1824–32 he was married to Charlotte Parkyns (1792–1864), widow of Count Cesar de Choiseul. The second marriage was annulled.

9   **Bourbons, dynasty** (home of Bourbon), a dynasty that originated in the Kingdom of France as a branch of the Capetian dynasty, the royal House of France. Bourbon kings first ruled France and Navarre in the 16th century. and were one of the most important ruling dynasties in Europe. At various times they ruled France, Spain, Naples, Sicily, and Parma. In France, the Bourbons ruled as absolute monarchs in 1589–1792. Bourbon kings returned to the French throne after the Revolution, ruling in 1814–1848. Today, Spain and Luxembourg have monarchs of the House of Bourbon.

10 **Ficquelmont, Charles–Louis (Karl Ludwig)** (1777–1857), count, officer, general, field-marshal of the Austrian Imperial army of French noble origin, later a diplomat and statesman. After the fall of Napoleon, Count de Ficquelmont was appointed Ambassador to Tuscany and Lucca, then to Russia during the reign of Emperor Nicolas I. As husband of Daria Khitrovo, Count de Ficquelmont became the son-in-law of Elizaveta Khitrovo. After the marriage Ficquelmont was appointed ambassador to the Court of King Ferdinand I of Two Sicilies in Naples.

11 **Philippe I (Louis–Phillipe)**, (1773–1850), king of France from 1830 to 1848, duke of Orleans under the name Louis–Philippe III in 1793–1830; representative of the 4th House of Orleans – the junior branch of the Bourbon dynasty, eldest son of Duke Louis–Philippe II of Orleans. His spouse in 1809–1850 was Maria Amalia of Naples.

12 **Blok, Alexander Alexandrovich** (1880–1921), poet, writer, publicist, playwright, translator and literary critic, the principal representative of Russian Symbolism.

13 **Dostoevsky, Fedor Mikhailovich** (1821–1881), novelist, short story writer, essayist, translator and journalist/. His most acclaimed novels include *Crime and Punishment* (1866), *The Idiot* (1869), *Demons* (1872), and *The Brothers Karamazov* (1880). Dostoevsky was arrested in 1849 as a member of the Petrashevsky Circle, a radical literary group. He was sentenced to death, then pardoned at the last moment, spent four years in a Siberian prison camp, followed by six years of compulsory military service in exile. He returned to Russian literary life, largely aligned with the conservative and anti-Western voices of the time.

Endnotes to Chapter Eight

1. **Konshin, Nikolai Mikhailovich** (1793–1859), writer, poet, translator, publisher, historian, participant in War of 1812. Together with Baratynsky, he composed satirical couplets (1823) critical of the government, which led to his forced resignation from military service. In 1824-28 he served in the Kostroma and Tver state chambers, in 1829 in at Tsarskoe Selo. As a historian, he discovered and published the oldest list of the complete edition of "Domostroy." He wrote memoirs about Delvig, Zhukovsky, Baratynsky, Pushkin and Krylov. Konshin was director of a gymnasium in Moscow (1849) and of the Demidov Lyceum in Yaroslavl (1850–56). Upon retirement, he received the rank of active state councilor.

2. **Molchanov, Pyotr Stepanovich** [1770/72–1831], state secretary of Alexander I, captain (1793), privy councilor (1810), Senator (1812), writer, poet, translator. In 1780–90 he wrote prose sketches, poems, epigrams, translated from German and French for various journals. He translated "The Moor of Venice" by Giraldi Cinthio and "Orlando Furioso" ("The Furious Roland") by Ludovico Ariosto. Later Molchanov withdrew from literary activity, though he maintained connections with writers, was a member of the Society of Lovers of the Russian Literature and a member of the Free Economic Society (1809). In 1814-1815, misdeeds were discovered in the activities of the Committee of Ministers, Molchanov was arrested, put on trial, forced to leave his posts. He went blind, finally retired (1828) and died of cholera 3 years later. His wife was Avdotya Ivanovna, née Kusheleva (1786–1823).

3. **Pushkina, Maria Alexandrovna** (1832–1919), a maid of honor at the court of Empress Maria Alexandrovna (wife of Alexander II), and then a trustee of the city reading room. She married Leonid Hartung.

4. **Pushkin, Alexander Alexandrovich** (1833–1914), chamberlain, military leader, cavalry general, who participated in the Crimean and Russo–Turkish Wars.

5. **Pushkin, Grigory Alexandrovich** (1835–1905), officer, lieutenant-colonel (1865), state councilor (1866), then magistrate.

6. **Pushkina, Natalia Alexandrovna** (1836–1913), Pushkina–Dubbelt after her first husband and countess of Merenberg after her marriage Prince Nikolaus Wilhelm of Nassau of the House of Nassau–Weilburg.

7. **Briullov, Karl Pavlovich** (1799–1852), born Charles Bruleau, in a family of a sculptor, descended from French Huguenots, became a famous Russian painter artist. Educated at the St. Petersburg Academy of Fine Arts (1809–21), he won several awards from the Academy of Arts for his paintings and received a Gold medal at the Paris Salon 1834, for his monumental work "The Last Day of Pompeii." He is regarded as a key figure in transition from the Russian neoclassicism to romanticism.

8. **Smirnova, Alexandra Osipovna (née Rosset)**, (1809–1882), also known as Smirnova–Rosseti, maid of honor at the Russian imperial court, memoirist, acquaintance, a close friend and interlocutor of Pushkin, Vyazemsky, Odoevsky, Zhukovsky, Lermontov, and especially Gogol. In 1832, Smirnova married Nikolai Smirnov (1807–1870) without a dowry. She was also friendly with Karamzin's daughter Sofia and frequented a salon

held by her stepmother Ekaterina Karamzina, the center of St. Petersburg cultural life in the 1820–40s.

9   **Ozerov, Ivan Petrovich** (1806–1880), diplomat, chamberlain (1834), active state councilor (1849), privy councilor (1862), actual privy councilor (1879). In 1831 Ozerov was assigned to the diplomatic mission in Berlin out of the staff, and from 1836 he became the senior secretary of this mission. In 1846–1854 he was chargé d'affaires in Baden. In 1854–1863 he was sent as an envoy to Portugal, in 1863–1880 to Bavaria. In 1832 Oserov married the Countess Rosalia Vasilyevna, née Schlippenbach (1808–1871). Rosalia Ozerova was maid of honor at the Prussian court, daughter of Count Karl Schlippenbach (1768–1939), knight dame of the Bavarian Order of Theresa (1868).

10 **Krylov, Ivan Andreevich** (1769–1844), writer and poet, journalist, publisher of satirical and educational magazines, bibliographer. Member of the Russian Academy (1811), academician of the St. Petersburg Academy of Sciences (1841). Krylov wrote more than 200 fables, borrowing several plots from Aesop and La Fontaine, although many are original. Several expressions from his fables entered the Russian language as idioms.

11 **Alexander II (Aleksandr Nikolaevich)** (1818–1881), prince, heir to the throne, later Emperor of Russia. His most significant reform was the emancipation of Russia's serfs in 1861, for which he is known as Alexander the Liberator. He fulfilled many liberal reforms, reorganized the judicial system, setting up elected local judges, abolished corporal punishment, promoted university education and local self-government (zemstvo), imposed universal military service, cut privileges of the nobility. After the first (of seven in total) assassination attempt in 1866, Alexander adopted a somewhat more conservative stance. His foreign policy was mainly pacifist, supportive of the United States, and opposed to Great Britain. Alexander backed the Union during the American Civil War and sent warships to New York Harbor and San Francisco Bay to deter attacks by the Confederate Navy. He sold Alaska to the USA in 1867, fearing the remote colony would fall into British hands in a future war. He sought peace, moved away from bellicose France when Napoleon III fell in 1871, and in 1872 joined with Germany and Austria in the League of the Three Emperors. He was assassinated in 1881.

12 **Pestel, Ivan Borisovich** (1765–1843), postmaster-general in Moscow, in 1798 he was transferred to the same position to St. Petersburg. Ivan Pestel was the third of the Pestel family, who headed the Moscow postal office, replaced on this post by his younger brother Nikolay Pestel (1768–1825). Both Pestels lost their positions in the postal department due to court intrigues in 1799. Later Ivan Pestel was sent to Siberia where he became governor-general, and his brother Nikolai followed him there. Ivan's son, the Decembrist Pavel Pestel (1793–1826) was sentenced to death and executed in St. Petersburg.

13 **Bulgakov, Alexander Yakovlevich** (1781–1863), diplomat, privy councilor, senator, Moscow postmaster-general. Bulgakov was friendly with many members of the Arzamas group: Pushkin, Zhukovsky, Turgenev, Dashkov, Prince Vyazemsky, He also corresponded with Count Rastopchin, Vorontsov, and Count Zakrevsky, Count Kapodistrias, the Turgenev brothers and Volkonsky. His extensive correspondence, published in three volumes, provides a detailed picture of the daily life of the Russian aristocracy in the nineteenth century.

14 **Delarue, Mikhail Danilovich** (1811–1868), poet, friend of Pushkin and Delvig, Lyceum graduate, collegiate assessor (1833). Trained in classical languages, he debuted in

print in 1829 with a translation of Ovid's poem "The Metamorphosis of Daphne." Delarue published his works in Delvig's almanac *Northern Flowers* and *The Literary Gazette*. In 1834, he translated Hugo's poem "La Belle," which displeased the Emperor. Reprimanded by Count Chernyshev, Delarue resigned and left for Kazan. He participated in meetings of Lyceum students, corresponded with the director of the Lyceum Engelhardt, and received the rank of state councilor in 1841.

15 **Miller, Pavel Ivanovich** (1813–1885), Lyceum graduate, actual state councilor. Miller served as Benckendorf's personal secretary and later worked in the Post Department. Through the poet Delarue, Pavel Miller warned Alexander Pushkin that the secret police was reading his letters.

16 **Dolgorukov (Dolgoruky), Alexander Sergeevich** (1809–1873), prince, son of Prince Sergei Dolgorukov, general (1769–1829). Dolgorukov began his service in the chambers of the Ministry of Foreign Affairs. He worked through the ranks of chamber cadet (1832), active state councilor and master of ceremonies (1856). In 1831 he married the favorite of Nicholas I, maid of honor Olga Alexandrovna, née Bulgakova (1814–1865), daughter of Alexander Bulgakov, who was the Moscow postmaster-general.

17 **Dolgorukova (Dolgorukaya), Olga Alexandrovna, née Bulgakova** (1814–1865), princess, wife of Prince Alexander Dolgorukov, daughter of Alexander Bulgakov.

18 **Saltykov, Sergei Vasilyevich** (1778–1846), a famous wealthy collector and bibliophile of Pushkin's time. He would organize dances on Tuesdays at his St. Petersburg mansion, where a small ballroom orchestra played. Saltykov called his evenings "Les mardis europeens" ("European Tuesdays"). Pushkin and his wife often visited him. It was in November 1836, at one of these dances, D'Anthès's engagement to Ekaterina Goncharova was announced.

19 **Tolstaya, Alexandra Andreevna** (1817–1904), countess, memoirist, friend of many Russian writers and poets, philanthropist, cavalry lady (1874), maid of honor (since 1881), teacher of the royal children, and the oldest court lady at the Russian imperial court by the reign of Emperor Nicholas II. She was a great-aunt and close friend of writer Leo Tolstoy, and engaged in extensive correspondence with him.

20 **Litta, Julius Pompeevich** (1763–1839), born Giulio Renato de Litta-Visconti-Arese, count (1797), statesman, governor chamberlain, first chief of the Cavalry Regiment, major-general (1782), vice-admiral of the Russian Imperial Fleet (1789), the highest-ranking court official of the Russian Empire from 1826 to 1839. He was brother of Cardinal Lorenzo Litta and Napoleon's grand chamberlain Duke Antonio Litta and became a high-ranking representative of the Order of Malta in Russia. Acted as a conductor of Catholic influence in Russia. At the request of Emperor Paul I, the Pope released Litta from his vow of celibacy. In 1798 he married Countess Catherine Skavronskaya, née Engelhardt (1761–1829), niece of Prince Grigory Potemkin.

21 **Bobrinskaya, Sofia Alexandrovna (née Countess Samoilova)** (1797/99–1866), countess, maid of honor to Empress Maria Feodorovna, friend of Empress Alexandra Feodorovna. Sofia Bobrinskaya was the youngest daughter of Count Alexander Samoilov from his marriage to Princess Ekaterina Trubetskaya. In 1821 Sofia married Count Alexey Bobrinsky, who was a cousin of Emperors Alexander I and Nicholas I. She held a popular literary salon in St. Petersburg, was in friendly relations with Countess

Khitrovo, Dolly Ficquelmont, Pushkin and his wife. The poet's ill-wishers were also received: Baron Heeckeren, his adoptive son George d'Anthès, Count Nesselrode and his wife.

22   **Goncharov, Nikolai Afanasyevich** (1787-1861), Natalya Goncharova's father, husband of Natalya Ivanovna, née Zagryazhskaya. He came from a family of merchants and industrialists, who received nobility during Elizabeth's reign. In 1789, by a special decree issued to Afanasy Nikolaevich, who was Nikolay Afanasyevich's father, Catherine II reaffirmed the Goncharovs' right to hereditary nobility.

23   **Tolstaya, Sofia Andreevna (née Bers)** (1844-1919), countess, wife of Count Leo Tolstoy with whom she had thirteen children. In 1884, Tolstoy renounced his rights of ownership and transferred to his wife both the property and the right to manage his estate as well his publishing affairs. For many years she was his faithful assistant and preserver of his legacy: she rewrote manuscripts, translated letters, acted as his personal secretary and the publisher of his works. She also wrote her own novels, children's stories, and memoirs, and kept a diary.

24   **Ficquelmont, Daria Fedorovna (Dorothea/Dolly)** (1804-1863), née Tiesenhausen, countess, writer and salonist, daughter of Elizaveta Khitrovo and her first husband, Count Ferdinand von Tiesenhausen. She was a granddaughter of Fieldmarshal General Kutuzov and sister of Ekaterina Khitrovo. Her father, Kutuzov's aide–de–camp, died in the Battle at Austerlitz. Countess Dolly was famous for her beauty and letter-writing. She is noted also for her diary, published in Italian and Russian in 1950, which provides an invaluable portrait of aristocratic life in nineteenth century Europe. Her husband was Charles–Louis (Karl Ludwig), Count de Ficquelmont (1777–1857).

25   **Karamzina, Sofia Nikolaevna** (1802–1856), the eldest daughter of Nikolai Karamzin, and the only child from his first marriage to Elizaveta Ivanovna, née Protasova (1771–1802), who died soon after giving birth to her daughter. Sofia Karamzina became maid of honor at the court, she was a close friend of Pushkin and Lermontov. She never married and lived with her step-mother, Ekaterina Karamzina, née Kolyvanova, the second wife of Nikolai Karamzin. Together both women held a literary salon.

26   **Nesselrode, Maria Dmitryevna (née Guryeva)** (1786–1849), countess, maid of honor (1802), lady of state (1836), cavalry-lady of the Order of St. Catherine (1816). She was the eldest daughter in the family of Dmitry Guryev and Countess Praskovya Saltykova. Maria Nesselrode married Karl Robert von Nesselrode–Ehreshofen in 1812, and held a salon. According to the memoirs of Prince Pavel Vyazemsky, Pushkin did not like Countess Nesselrode as "the last representative of the cosmopolitan oligarchic Areopagus." The hostility was mutual: the Countess could not forgive Pushkin for the epigram on her father, attributed to the poet's pen, as well as anecdotes and epigrams about herself. Maria Nesselrode accepted Baron Heeckeren into her circle, and also patronized George d'Anthès.

27   **D'Anthès, Georges Charles (de Heeckeren)** (1812–1895), baron, Alsatian aristocrat, cornet in the Cavalry Guard Regiment, adopted son of the Dutch diplomat Louis Heeckern. Being adopted d'Anthès bore the surname of Baron Heeckeren (in Russian documents; Baron George Karl de Heeckeren), French cavalry officer, monarchist, Catholic by religion. In the 1830s he served in Russia in the Cavalry Regiment. In 1837 he married Ekaterina Goncharova, the elder sister of Pushkin's wife, Natalya Goncharova. After the

duel with Pushkin, d'Anthès was deprived of his ranks and expelled from Russia. Subsequently, he was involved in politics and was a senator of the Second French Empire.

28 **Dashkov, Mikhail (Kondrat) Ivanovich** (1736–1764), prince, diplomat, known mainly as the husband of Countess Ekaterina Romanovna, née Vorontsova. After Peter III's accession, Prince Dashkov was sent as ambassador to Constantinople to inform the Sultan. Back in St. Petersburg, he participated in the preparations of the palace coup of Catherine II (1762). On her coronation day he was appointed the rank of chamber cadet and became a member of a commission on St. Petersburg and Moscow for the construction of stone buildings. In 1763, as vice-colonel of the Life Guards Cuirassier Regiment, Dashkov was sent to Poland to support the accession of Stanislav Poniatowski.

29 **Severin, Dmitry Petrovich** (1792–1865), diplomat and statesman, writer, and member of the Arzamas literary society. Severin had studied with Prince Pyotr Vyazemsky at the St. Petersburg Jesuit boarding school of Father Chizh and embarked on a diplomatic career. In 1809, after Dmitriev's appointment as Minister of Justice, Severin came under his leadership, and in 1811 to the College of Foreign Affairs. He entered Karamzin's circle, was acquainted with Prince Vyazemsky, Zhukovsky, Dashkov, Bludov, Batyushkov and was admired for his witty impromptu verses and short poems. In 1808–1811 he wrote for *The Herald of Europe*, where his translations from French, articles and two short fables "Mouse" (1808) and "Arrow" (1809) were also published. In 1815 at the seventh ordinary meeting, Severin was admitted to the Arzamas literary society under the nickname Frisky Cat. The circle ceased its activities in 1818 due to the departure of some Arzamas residents from St. Petersburg. Among those who left the capital was also Severin. As a member of the retinue of Emperor Alexander I, Severin took part at congresses in Troppau and Laibach in 1820–1821, supervised by Count Nesselrode. Since 1825 he became chamberlain and active state councilor, since 1826 – chargé d'affaires. In April 1836 he was promoted to the rank of privy councilor, then sent as envoy extraordinary to Switzerland, and from 1837 he held the same position at the Bavarian court. He was promoted to actual privy councilor in 1856.

30 **Razumovsky, Alexei Kirillovich** (1748–1822), count, who studied at the University of Strasbourg and earned the ranks of acting chamberlain (1775) and Senator (1776–1807). In 1795, he refused to pass a law favored by Catherine the Great and resigned in protest, but later re-entered service as Senator, a trustee of Moscow University, actual privy councilor (1807) Minister of Public Education (1810–1816) and a member of the State Council. In these positions, Razumovsky patronized the Society of Nature Experts, on whose behalf he formed an expedition to study the Moscow Governorate, where he opened many schools, gymnasiums and other educational institutions and scientific societies, improved teaching, increased supervision over foreign educators, established the first Department of Slavic Literature at Moscow University. In 1812 he was appointed Honorary Member of Moscow University. With the personal assistance of Razumovsky the Tsarskoselsky Lyceum near St. Petersburg was opened, but the traditional curriculum was purged of Greek, archaeology, natural history, astronomy, chemistry and the history of philosophical systems. He introduced theology as the main discipline in all educational institutions. A freemason and follower of Osip Pozdeev, with whom he had a long correspondence, Razumovsky fell under the influence of the Jesuits and, mainly, the famous Count Joseph de Maistre. Under this influence, Razumovsky introduced new censorship

restrictions and began a struggle with the Vilna Trustee Adam Czartoryski for the Russification of the Western Region of Russia. The failure in the fight against Czartoryski and the government's mistrust of the Jesuits forced Razumovsky to ask for resignation from the post of Minister and member of the State Council, in 1816. As a child of Count Kirill Razumovsky from a marriage with Ekaterina Naryshkina, Alexei Razumovsky was related to many noble and influential people in Russia. He was brother of Andrey Razumovsky, son-in-law of Count Peter Sheremetev (from 1774), father-in-law of Sergei Uvarov (from 1811), the ancestor of the Perovsky nobles: father of Antony Pogorelsky, grandfather of Alexei Tolstoy, great-grandfather of Sophia Perovskaya.

31 **Uvarova, Ekaterina Alexeevna, née Razumovskaya** (1781-1849), countess, the youngest daughter of Count Alexey Razumovsky. She became a Maid of Honor at Empress Elizabeth's court, became involved in various charity work, and was elected a member and later chairman of the Women's Patriotic Society. From 1811 she was married to Count Sergei Uvarov, then a trustee of the St. Petersburg educational district and future Minister of Public Education. They had four children.

32 **Solovyov, Sergei Mikhailovich** (1820-1879), historian. His works influenced the next generation of Russian historians (Vasily Kliuchevsky, Dmitri Ilovaiskii, Sergei Platonov). Solovyov was the founder of a separate direction in Russian historiography, the so-called "state school," Professor (1848), Emeritus Professor (1859) and Rector (1871-77) of the Imperial Moscow University, Ordinary Academician of the Imperial St. Petersburg Academy of Sciences in the Department of Russian Language and Literature (1872), Privy Councilor. Solovyov published many works concerning Peter I the Great and Alexander I, and acted as tutor to the Tsarevich Nikolay Aleksandrovich (1859) and to the future Emperor Alexander III (1866). Solovyov married Polixena Vladimirovna, née Romanova. Their eldest son Vsevolod Solovyov was a historical novelist; the other son Vladimir Solovyov was famous Russian philosopher; their daughter Polyksena Solovyova became a noted poet and illustrator.

33 **Lomonosov, Mikhail Vasilyevich** (1711-1765), natural scientist, polymath, inventor, poet, artist, historian, developer of national education, science and economics in Russia. Lomonosov innovated modern Russian poetic diction and helped found Moscow State University.

34 **Sheremetev, Dmitry Nikolaevich** (1803-1871), count, Actual State Councilor, Chamberlain and Chief Chamberlain from the wealthy Sheremetev family, known for his charitable activities. He was a member of various societies: the Free Economic Society (from 1825), the Imperial Moscow Society of Naturalists (from 1833), the St. Petersburg Philharmonic Society (from 1846). For half a century he maintained a choir chapel in his St. Petersburg Fountain House, provided financial assistance to artists, singers, and musicians. Sheremetev gave money to many Moscow churches, monasteries, gymnasiums, orphanages, and the St. Petersburg University. In 1837 Sheremetev married Anna Sergeevna, née Sheremeteva (1811-1849). In 1857 he remarried with Aleksandra Grigoryevna, née Melnikova (1824-1874).

35 **Nikitenko, Alexander Vasilyevich** (1805-1877), former Ukrainian serf of Count Nikolai Sheremetev, received his bill of freedom with the help of Vasily Zhukovsky and Kondraty Ryleev. Nikitenko was a literary historian, censor, editor, Professor at St. Petersburg University, Full Member of the Academy of Sciences. For many years he kept

a detailed diary, which is considered a important primary source regarding the literary and social life of the mid-19th century. In 1833, Nikitenko was appointed censor and soon spent 8 days in the guardhouse for missing Victor Hugo's poem "Enfant, si j'étais roi" (translated by M. Delarue). He edited the magazine *Son of the Fatherland* in 1839-41, and *The Contemporary* in 1847-48.

Endnotes to Chapter Nine

1 **Baratynskaia, Anastasia Lvovna** (née Engelhardt) (1804-1860), the eldest daughter of Lev Engelhardt, a retired major general. Baratynskaia married Evgeny Baratynsky in 1826. They had seven children and lived together for 18 years, until the poet's death.

2 **Chernyshevsky, Nikolai Gavrilovich** (1828-1889), literary critic, translator, publicist and writer, democratic revolutionary, theorist of utopian socialism, materialist philosopher. His works influenced the views of Vladimir Lenin, Emma Goldman and other revolutionaries and socialists. The Serbian socialist Svetozar Markovic was close to Chernyshevsky. Karl Marx spoke positively about Chernyshevsky's work. In the USSR, Chernyshevsky became a cult figure in the history of the revolutionary struggle.

3 **Potocki, Jan** (1761-1815), count, Polish Romantic writer, archaeologist, traveler from the wealthy Potocki magnate family, compiler of the Chechen Dictionary, author of the novel *The Manuscript Found in Saragossa*. His first wife (since 1783) was Princess Julia Lubomirska (1764-1794), daughter of Grand Marshal Stanisław Lubomirski (1722-1783) and Isabella Czartoryska (1736-1816). His second wife (from 1798) was the Countess Constance Potocka (1781-1852), daughter of Crown Artillery General Stanisław Szczesny Potocki (1751-1805) and Josephine Amalia Mniszech (1752-1798).

4 **Mazepa, Ivan Stepanovich** (1639-1709), Ukrainian military and political leader, Hetman of the Zaporizhian Host and Left-Bank Ukraine in 1687-1708. The historical events of his life have inspired many literary, artistic and musical works.

5 **Dashkova, Ekaterina Romanovna (née Countess Vorontsova)** (1743-1810), Princess, daughter of a Senator, Count Roman Vorontsov, wife of Prince Mikhail Dashkov. Dashkova was an influential noblewoman, a major figure of the Russian Enlightenment and part of the coup d'état that placed Catherine II on the throne. Dashkova founded the Russian Academy, and was its President. She published original and translated works on many subjects, and was invited by Benjamin Franklin to become the first female member of the American Philosophical Society. A former close friend of Catherine II, Dashkova was exiled from the court in 1795.

6 **Guizot, François (François Pierre Guillaume)** (1787-1874), French historian, critic, orator, statesman, ideologist of liberal conservatism, a dominant figure in French politics prior to the Revolution of 1848. He opposed the attempt by King Charles X to usurp legislative power and worked to sustain a constitutional monarchy. He served the "Citizen King" Louis Philippe, as Minister of Education (1832-37), ambassador to London and Foreign Minister (1840-47), and Prime Minister of France (1847-48). In 1848 his cab-

inet of ministers refused to change the election law. Political discontent sparked the Revolution of February 1848 and brought down the July Monarchy. In 1841 Guizot issued a law banning the exploitation of children under eight years of age in factories; but due to the lack of labor inspectors, the law was never implemented. He raised the issue of abolishing slavery in the colonies many times. His preliminary work was used by Republicans when they voted to abolish slavery in 1848.

7   **Mignet, François-Auguste** (1796-1884), French historian, orator, journalist, critic, editor in the journal *Courrier Français*, prominent author of numerous lectures and books on history. Together with Thiers and A. Carrel, Mignet founded the famous opposition newspaper *National* before the July Revolution. Mignet was one of the first journalists to sign a protest against the July ordinances. Refusing to join the new government, he became the Director of the the Ministry of Foreign Affairs Archive. Mignet was also a member of the Academy of Moral and Political Sciences (1832), a member of the French Academy (1836).

8   **Milton, John** (1608–1674), English poet and writer, author of political pamphlets and religious treatises. During the English Civil War, he was a prominent supporter of the revolution, an enemy of the monarchy, his political pamphlets advocated for a radical republicanism. He is best known for his epic poem *Paradise Lost*.

9   **Senkovsky, Osip Ivanovich** (1800–1858), real name Józef Julian Sękowski, best known by his pseudonym Baron Brambeus, was a Russian and Polish orientalist, polyglot, writer, critic, editor, journalist, editor of the first Russian popular journal *The Reader's Library*, State Councilor, Honored Professor (1847), Corresponding Member of the Imperial Academy of Sciences (1828). He is considered the founder of the theory of "Litvinism." In 1829 he married Baroness Adelaide Alexandrovna, née Rahl (1806–1859).

10 **Smirdin, Alexander Filippovich** (1795–1857), publisher and editor. Smirdin pioneered the sale of cheap consumer editions in Russia, and developed a standard set of financial criteria for compensating authors. He had strong links with the literary elite and, in retrospect, played a key role in the development of Russian literature in the early 19th century. He published all the best-known works by Nikolai Karamzin, Vasily Zhukovsky, Alexander Pushkin, Ivan Krylov, numerous textbooks and seminal books on history and science. In 1834 he launched *The Reader's Library*, the most popular magazine of the time. In 1838 he took over as a the publisher of *The Son of the Fatherland*. Though supported by the Russian government, in the mid–1840s he was declared bankrupt, lost all of his property (including the vast library, bought eventually by Pyotr Krasheninnikov, another prominent Russian bookseller) and spent the rest of his life in poverty.

11 **Krylov, Alexander Lukich** (1798–1853), professor, censor, Full State Councilor since 1850. He taught ancient and medieval history, Greek and Latin, modern history and geography, and edited the *Journal of the Ministry of Internal Affairs*.

12 **Tiutchev, Fedor Ivanovich** (1803–1873), poet and diplomat, studied in Moscow, then spent 22 years abroad. Tiutchev had met the poet Heinrich Heine and the philosopher Friedrich Schelling, and his poetics was influenced by the German Romanticism. Prince Ivan Gagarin convinced Tiutchev to publish selected poems in Pushkin's *The Contemporary*. He also wrote poems on political topics, which were published only posthumously. Some political articles of Tiutchev were printed in *Revue des Deux Mondes*. In 1826, Tiutchev married the Bavarian widow of a Russian diplomat Eleonore Peterson, née

Countess von Bothmer. After her death in 1838, he married another widow, Baroness Ernestine von Dörnberg, née von Pfeffel. Upon his return to Russia, Tyutchev served as a censor, became Chairman of the Foreign Censorship Committee and earned the rank of Privy Councilor.

13 **De Pinas, Emmanuel Ivanovich**, marquis, French royalist and emigrant; was accepted into Russian military and in 1834 received the rank of ensign. He belonged to an old French family, was the Chamberlain of the Duchess of Berry, who recommended him and D'Anthès to Emperor Nicholas I. Accepted into the Young Guard, an Austrian regiment, de Pina went on to serve in the Caucasus, where he died in battle.

14 **Heckern (Heeckeren), Louis** (born Jacob–Derk–Burchard–Anne) (1792–1884), Baron van Heeckeren tot Enghuizen or van Heeckeren van Beverweerd, a Dutch diplomat, from 1823 the Dutch ambassador in St. Petersburg. A Protestant by birth, Heckern converted to Catholicism, took the name Louis and may have been baptized under this name. In 1836 he received the title of Baron of the First French Empire. He was recognized as adoptive father of George d'Anthès; the adoption agreement was signed by the King of Holland in 1836. After d'Anthès's duel with Pushkin Heckern was recalled from St. Petersburg. His role in the events preceding the duel is not fully understood. In 1842–75 he was Ambassador Extraordinary and Minister Plenipotentiary to the court in Vienna. From 1872 he served as Minister of State (Secretary of State) of the Netherlands. Heckern was never married.

15 **Goncharova, Ekaterina Nikolaevna (Baroness Heckern)** (1809–1843), sister of Natalya Pushkina, née Goncharova, wife of Georges D'Anthès. Ekaterina received D'Anthès' marriage proposal in October 1836. This betrothal delayed the duel between D'Anthès and Pushkin. Following her husband, who was expelled from Russia in 1837 after the duel with Pushkin, she left Russia for France.

16 **Bulwer-Lytton, Edward George Earle Lytton** (1803–1873), 1st Baron Lytton, Privy Councilor, an English writer and politician. He was named Baron Lytton of Knebworth in 1866. He served as a Whig member of English Parliament in 1831–1841 and a Conservative in 1851–1866, was the Secretary of State for the Colonies in 1858–1859. In 1862, after King Otto abdicated, Bulwer-Lytton was offered the Crown of Greece, but he declined.

17 **Dahl, Vladimir Ivanovich** (1801–1872), lexicographer, Turkologist, founding member of the Russian Geographical Society. During the Russo-Turkish Wars he worked in a field hospital, then served as a military doctor and epidemiologist. He spoke many languages. compiled and documented the oral history of Russian regions. Published under the pseudonym Cossack Lugansky these works became part of modern folklore. His famous and voluminous *Explanatory Dictionary of the Living Great Russian Language* took about 53 years to compile.

18 **Ishimova, Alexandra Osipovna (Iosifovna)** (1804/1805–1881), translator, one of the first professional Russian children's authors. She was acquainted with Pyotr Vyazemsky, Vasily Zhukovsky and Alexander Pushkin. Ishimova was the last correspondent of the poet. Pushkin wrote her a letter with an enthusiastic response to her stories, and sent a book for translation before the last duel. Ishimova published monthly journals: *Little Star* (1842–63) for children, and *Rays of Light* (1850–60) intended for a female reader-

ship. Her book *History of Russia in Stories for Children* (1841) was awarded the Demidov Prize in 1852.

19   **Danzas, Konstantin Karlovich** (1801–1870), officer, Lyceum friend of Pushkin, second in Pushkin's duel with D'Anthès. Danzas became close to Pushkin and Pushchin during their Lyceum years. Together with Delvig, he published the handwritten journal *The Lyceum Sage*. Danzas participated in the Russo-Persian and Russo-Turkish Wars. He was the direct superior of Lermontov in the Tenginsky regiment. In 1844 Danzas was promoted to the rank of colonel and retired as major-general in 1856.

20   **Sollogub, Vladimir Alexandrovich** (1813–1882), count, Privy Councilor, prose writer, poet, playwright, and memoirist. The younger brother of diplomat Lev Sollogub. Sollogub's early works depicted the high society of Pushkin's time. Under the influence of Nikolai Gogol, Sollogub shared the artistic principles of the so-called "naturalist school." He also wrote dramatic works and vaudevilles. In 1840 Vladimir Sollogub married Sofia Mikhailovna Vielgorskaya (1820–1878).

21   **Liebermann, August Freiherr von** (1791–1847), baron, Prussian diplomat, member of diplomatic mission of Prussia in Russian Empire, in the 1820s he was the secretary of the mission in St. Petersburg. In 1825–1835 von Lieberman was sent as a Minister to Madrid, in 1835–1845 returned as envoy to St. Petersburg, in 1845–1847 worked in Paris.

Index of Pushkin's Works Cited in the Book

Poetry

"A Dream" (1816), XVIn11, 12n
"*André Chénier*" (1825), 128, 131, 159, 301
Angelo (1833), 231, 239
"A Response to Anonymous" (1830), 168
"Arion" (1827), 152
A Story of a Dead Tsarevna (1833), 239
A Story of a Little Fish and a Fisherman (1833), 239
"Autumn" (1833), VII, 232
"Bacchic Song" (1825), 128
Boris Godunov (1825, published 1831), drama, VIII, XXIII, 131–33, 149, 151, 156, 176, 289
"Conversation of a Bookseller with a Poet" (1824), 81, 127, 177
Count Nulin (1825), 131, 139, 179
"Demons" (1830), 120, 189
"Desert Fathers and Women Without Fault" (1836), 232
Elegy (1820; Pogaslo dnevnoye svetilo…), 33, 64, 71, 80
Elegy/Gurzuf Elegy (1820, published 1824; Redeyet oblakov letuchaya gryada…), 63, 76–77
Elegy (1830; Bezumnykh let ugassheye vesel'ye…), 76, 189
Epistle to General Pushchin (1821), 91
Epistle to Iudin (1815), 12
Epistle to Orlov (1819), 38
"Epistle to the Prisoners". *See* "To Siberia"
Eugene Onegin (1823–1831), novel in verse, XVIII–XIX, XXII, 18, 23, 35, 43–44, 59, 61, 70, 72, 92–93, 105, 107–8, 111, 113, 120–21, 123, 127, 129, 131, 139, 151–52, 154, 157, 162, 164–65, 177, 181, 194–96, 296
   Fragments of Onegin's Travels (1829–1830), poem, 74, 11, 113, 118
Ezersky (1832–1833), 84, 182
"For the shores of a distant fatherland…" (1830; Dlya beregov otchizny dal'noy…), poem, 112

"From Pindemonte" (1836), 232
Gavriiliada (1821), 70, 161
"Hero" (1830; Da, slava v prikhotyakh vol'na. Kak ognennyy yazyk, ona…), 154, 194
"I do not regret you, the years of my spring…" (1820; Mne vas ne zhal', goda vesny moyey…), 125
"I erected a monument for myself, not built by hands" (1836; Ya pamyatnik sebe vozdvig nerukotvornyy…), 232, 235–36
"Imitations of the Koran" (1824), 131
Little Tragedies (1830–1832), 166, 195–96
   A Feast in Time of Plague (1830), 191, 195
   Mozart and Salieri (1830), 139, 195
   The Miserly Knight (1830), 139, 195, 245
   The Stone Guest (1830), 195
Madrigal to Golitsyna (1817), 46
"My Genealogy" (1830), 182, 195
My Hero's Genealogy (1836), 245
"Napoleon" (1821), 70, 88, 91, 106, 128
"Napoleon on the Elba" (1815), 105
"19 October" (1825; Ronyayet les bagryanyy svoy ubor…), XVI–XVII, XXIn21, 13, 17, 20, 125n, 131, 138
"19 October" (1831; Chem chashche prazdnuyet Litsey Svoyu svyatuyu godovshchinu…), 1
"19 October" (1836; Byla pora: nash prazdnik molodoy Siyal, shumel i rozami venchalsya…), 3, 24
"Ode to Liberty" (1817), 41–42, 46, 282n40
"Of freedom the solitary sower…" (1823; Svobody seyatel' pustynnyy…), 105
"O loyal Greek wife, cry not, he died a hero…" (1821; Grechanka vernaya! ne plach', – on pal geroyem…), 91
"Once again I visited…" (1835; Vnov' ya posetil…), 232
Poltava (1828), 154–55, 164, 234–35
Quatrain on Friendship (1824, Chto druzhba? Legkiy pyl pokhmel'ya…), 26–27
"Recollections at Tsarskoe Selo" (1829), 30, 32, 268n25
"Red-faced critic mine…" (1830; Rumyanyy kritik moy…), 195
Ruslan and Liudmila (1820), XV, 57, 80, 150, 275, 285, 305
"Scorning both the voice of reproach, And the calls of sweeter hopes…" (1824; Prezrev i golos ukorizny, I zovy sladostnykh nadezhd…), 33
"Secular Power…" (1836; Mirskaya vlast': Kogda velikoye svershalos' torzhestvo…), 232
"Songs of the Western Slavs" (1834; Korol' khodit bol'shimi shagami…), 232
"Stanzas" (1827), 151
"The Black Shawl" (1820), 70, 107
"The Bridegroom" (1825), 131

The Bronze Horseman (1833), 33, 231–32, 237, 239
"The Commander," (1835), 232, 245
"The Dagger" (1821), 70, 91
"The Demon" (1823), XXIII, 105, 107–9, 283
"The Feast of Peter the Great" (1835), 232, 245
The Fountain of Bakhchisarai (1821–1823), 70, 75–76, 78–79, 82, 117, 129
The Gypsies (1824–1825), 70–71, 117, 131
The Little House in Kolomna (1830), 33, 172, 195
"The Mob" (Chern'), later renamed "The Poet and the Crowd" (1829), 151, 155
"The motionless sentinel slumbered at the royal threshold…" (1824; Nedvizhnyy strazh dremal na tsarstvennom poroge…), 88, 105
"The Poet" (1827), 151
The Prisoner of the Caucasus (1820–1821, published 1822), 64, 70, 79, 81, 117, 122
"The Prophet" (1826), 151
The Robber Brothers (1821–1822), 70, 117
"The Song of Prophetic Oleg" (1822, published 1825), 70
"The Spell" (1830), 195
The Tale of a Priest and His Worker Balda (1830), 194
"The Village" (1819), 41
"'Tis time, my friend, 'tis time! The heart demands calm…" (1834; Pora, moy drug, pora! pokoya serdtse prosit…), 222, 232
"To ***" (1825; Ya pomnyu chudnoye mgnoven'ye…/I remember a wonderful moment…), 125, 135, 137
"To a Grandee" (1830), 106
"To Chaadaev" (1818; Lyubvi, nadezhdy, tikhoy slavy…/ Love, hope, quiet glory…), 53
"To Chaadaev" (1821; V strane, gde ya zabyl trevogi prezhnikh let…/ In a country where I forgot the worries of previous years…), 52, 55, 70, 132
"To V. L. Davydov" (1821), poem, 70, 91
"To Gnedich" (1821), 73, 87
"To *Licinius*" (1815), 128
"To Ovid" (1821), 70
"To Saburov" (1824), 35
"To Siberia" (1827), 21, 152
"To Sister" (1814), 15–16, 33
"To I. I. Pushchin" (1826), XVII–XVIII
"To the Sea" (1824), 131
"To Vyazemsky" (1826), 142
"To Zhukovsky" (1816), 28
Translation of Robert Southey's "Hymn to the Penates" (translated by Pushkin in 1829), 185
"Under the blue sky of your native country…" (1825–1826; Pod nebom golubym strany svoyey rodnoy…), 112

"Verse written during a night of insomnia" (1830; Mne ne spitsya, net ognya...), 195
"Vidocq Figliarin" (1830), epigram, 181
"War!..." (1821; Voyna! Pod"yaty nakonets, Shumyat znamena...), 89
"When, outside the city, in thought I wander" (1836; Kogda za gorodom, zadumchiv, ya brozhu...), 232
"When the Assyrian ruler..." (1835; Kogda vladyka assiriyskiy...), 232
"Why where you sent here and who sent you?" (1824; Zachem ty poslan byl i kto tebya poslal?..), 24, 105
"Winter evening" (1825; Burya mgloyu nebo kroyet...), 285

Prose

A History of the Village of Goriukhino (1830), 195, 236
A Journey to Arzrum (1829), 245, 251
A Tale of a Praporshchik from the Chernigov Regiment (1826, first published in 1855), 152
Beginning of autobiography (published in 1840), 9
Draft of a comedy about a gambler (1821), 3
Dubrovsky (1832–1833), 232, 236, 240
Egyptian Nights (1835), 165, 232
Fatam, or Human Reason (1815), 17
Guests Were Arriving at the Dacha (1828), 164
"Note on Upbringing" (1826), 156
Notes on the Don and Black Sea Cossacks (1829–1830), 64
Novel in Letters (1829), 164, 183
Scenes from Chivalric Times (1835), 233, 237
The Captain's Daughter (1833–1836), 232, 237, 245
The History of Peter the Great's rule (1835), 203, 232
The History of Pugachev (1834), 226, 228, 232, 239–40
The Moor of Peter the Great (1827, published in 1837), 164
The Queen of Spades (1833), 30, 106n, 181, 232
The Russian Pelham (1834, published 1841), 152, 233
The Tales of the Late Ivan Petrovich Belkin (The Tales of Belkin), (1829–1830), 166, 194–97
  The Shot (1829), 195
  The Snowstorm (1830), 195
  The Station Observer (1829), 195
  The Undertaker (1830), 194
  The Young Lady-Peasant (1829), 194

Letters

letters to A. Benckendorf, 186–87, 208
letters to A. Bestuzhev, 76–78
letters to A. Buturlina, 191
letters to brother Lev Pushkin, 16, 63–64, 73, 78–79, 93–94, 98, 101
letters to E. F. Cancrin, 228
letters to Vasily Davydov, 83, 102–3, 244
letters to Anton Delvig, 72, 140, 151, 165–66
letters to N. Goncharova, 187, 190, 193, 206–17, 221–22, 229–30, 246
letters to N. Goncharova's mother, 186
letters to V. Gorchakov, 61, 67, 72
letters to N. Grech, 81
letters to G. Heeckeren, 251
letters to A. Ishimova, 251
letters to A. Kern, 135–36
letters to Elizaveta Khitrovo, 197
letters to N. Krivtsov, 169
letters to P. Mansurov, 49
letters to P. Pletnev, 128, 189–93, 199, 204, 242
letters to M. Pogodin, 155, 157, 194
letters to Alexander Raevsky, 109–10
letters to K. Sobańska, 65, 110
letters to V. Tumansky, 78–79
letters to Alexander Turgenev, 80, 116
letters to Alexei Vulf, 136
letters to P. Vyazemsky, 27, 78, 102, 141–42, 157, 162, 193–94

Index

A
Adrianople, 288
Aesop, 308
Africa, 72
Akatuy, 280
Aksakov, Sergei Timofeevich, 11, 266, 299
Alaska, 308
Alatyr, 299
Alexander I, Emperor, 2–3, 7, 13, *passim*
Alexander II, Emperor, 212, 273, 275, 282, 307–8, 312
Alexander III, Emperor, 312
Alexander Yaroslavich (Nevsky), Prince, 9, 264
Alps, 284
Alupka, 64
Alyabyev, Alexander, 269
Amsterdam, 203
Anna Jagiellon, Queen, 295
Annenkov, Pavel, XV, 276
Apraksina, Ekaterina Vladimirovna, 301
Apuleius, XVIII–XIX
Arakcheev, Alexei, Count, 3, 7, 36, 42, 49, 86, 95, 115, 140, 144, 146, 260–61, 269, 273, 279
Arbeneva, Natalia, 274
Arina Rodionovna (Yakovleva), XVI, XXIII, 12, 118, 131, 209, 266
Ariosto, 29, 139, 276, 307
Arkhangelsk, 276
Arsenyeva, Elizaveta, 266
Arzamas, 18, 26, 28, 31, 38–39, 43, 48, 174, 202, 224, 256, 265, 271–72, 278–79, 291, 308, 311
Arzrum. *See* Erzurum
Asia, 155, 214, 288
Astrakhan, 265, 299–300
Athens, 288
Augustus, Emperor, 72–73, 277–78, 287
Austerlitz, 37, 278, 289, 303, 310
Austria, 201, 259, 286, 294, 297, 308
Avdeeva, Ekaterina Alexeevna, 304

B
Baden, 308
Baevo, 299
Bagration, Prince, 278
Bakhchisarai, 64, 79
Bakhmetev, Alexey, 292
Bakhtin, Mikhail, VII–XI, XI
Bakunin, Alexander, 302
Bakunin, Mikhail, 299
Bakunina, Ekaterina, 302
Balaklava, 293
Balashov, Alexandr Dmitrievich, 3, 259–60
Balzac, Honoré de, 111, 286, 293–94, 304
Baratynsky, Evgeny, 27, 47, 122–23, 130, 230, 245, 269–70, 273–75, 295, 304, 307, 313
Baryatinsky, Alexander Petrovich, 104, 262, 293, 299
Basin, Pyotr, 295
Báthory, István, 133, 295
Batyushkov, Konstantin, XV, 25, 39, 44, 47–48, 66–67, 81, 271–73, 311
Bautzen, 291
Bavaria, 308
Begichev, Stepan Nikitich, 104, 293
Bekes, Gáspár, 295
Bekleshov, Pyotr, 296
Belarus, 268, 293
Belgium, 193, 201
Belinsky, Vissarion, 27, 149, 196, 213, 237, 245–46, 274, 299
Beloselsky-Belozersky, Alexander, 300
Benckendorf, Alexander Khristoforovich, 7, 111, 144–47, 156, 158–60, 163, 170–76, 179, 185–86, 195, 202, 207–8, 212, 216, 219, 222, 225–28, 238, 240, 245, 254, 256, 263, 269, 281, 291, 309
Benucci, Alessandra, 276

Berlin, 210, 293, 297, 308
Bessarabia, 56, 103, 282–83, 286, 290
Bestuzhev (Marlinsky), Alexander, 75–78, 127, 130, 163, 172, 262, 269, 273, 281, 288, 293
Bestuzhev-Ryumin, Alexei, 297
Bestuzhev-Ryumin, Mikhail, 4, 50, 141, 260, 262, 281, 297
Bestuzhev, Mikhail, 27, 50, 273, 281, 288
Bibikova, Ekaterina, 284, 303
Biron (Bühren), Ernst Johann von, 3, 260
Blok, Alexander, 195, 258, 306
Bludov, Dmitry, 202, 224–25, 272, 275, 291, 311
Bobrinskaya, Sofia Alexandrovna, 220, 223, 309
Bobrinsky, Alexey, Count, 309
Bock, Timofei Eberhard von, 3–4, 260
Bodisko, Mikhail, 262
Boileau, Nikolas, 266
Boldino, 120, 126, 154–55, 187–93, 195–98, 239, 285, 305
Bologovsky, Dmitry Nikolaevich, 100, 292
Bolyaev, Murza Aka, 299
Bonivard, François, 74, 287
Boshnyak, Alexander Karlovich, 111, 146, 294
Botkin, Vasily, 299
Bourbon, 1, 192, 305–6
Brandenburg, 290
Branicki, Wladislaw, Count, 113, 294
Briullov, Karl, 206–7, 274, 307
Brussels, 193
Brutus, Marcus Junius, 36, 52–53, 277, 282
Bulgakov, Alexander Yakovlevich, 215–17, 308–9
Bulgaria, 301
Bulgarin, Faddei Venediktovich, 17–18, 76, 78, 156, 170, 172–77, 180–82, 186, 189, 202, 213, 244, 268–69, 285
Bulwer-Lytton, Edward George, Earle Lytton, 250, 315
Burtsev, Ivan Grigoryevich, 20, 270
Buturlin, Mikhail Petrovich, 282, 305
Buturlina, Anna Nikolaeva, 191, 305
Byron, George Gordon, Lord, XXII, 58, 60, 64, 71, 74, 79, 109, 117, 125, 285, 287, 293

C
Cádiz, 292
Calderón de la Barca, Pedro, 302
Camões, Luis Vas de, 265
Campbell, Barbara, 306
Cancrin, Egor Frantsevich, 189, 225, 228, 305
Caspian Sea, 299
Cassius, Gaius, 53, 277, 282
Catherine II, The Great, Empress, 40, 64, 140, 158, 213, 236, 246, 259–60, 271–72, 283–84, 286, 289, 292, 294, 296–97, 309–311, 313
Catiline, Lucius Sergius, 277
Caucasus, 63–66, 70, 79, 81, 117, 155, 162–63, 186, 234, 262–63, 266, 270, 273, 286–88, 302, 315
Cerkovic, Stefan, 110, 286
Chaadaev, Pyotr, 26, 35, 44, 51–53, 55, 70, 92, 202, 206, 238, 249, 271, 291, 295, 304
Champollion, Jean-François, 303
Chateaubriand, François-René de, 169, 243, 293, 298
Chénier, André, 64, 128, 131, 159, 167, 286, 301
Chernigov, 57, 152, 263, 281
Chernyshev, Alexander Ivanovich, 37, 278, 300
Chernyshevsky, Nikolai, 233, 313
China, 155, 162
Chirkov, Nikolai, 278
Chirkova, Sophia, 278
Chișinău (Kishinev), XXIII, 26, 45, 64–66, 69–70, 73–74, 79, 82–84, 86–87, 90–91, 93–96, 98–101, 103–4, 107–8, 110, 112, 261, 280, 282–83, 287, 290–92
Chizhov, Nikolai, 262
Choiseul, Cesar de, Count, 306
Chuguev, 6
Cicero, XVIII–XIX, 36, 277
Circassia, 265
Coleridge, Samuel Taylor, 304
Constantinople, 9, 33, 100, 264, 279, 311
Cortes, 102
Courland, 260, 286, 294
Crimea, 63–66, 286, 302
Cyprus, 286
Cyvilsk, 299
Czartoryska, Isabella, 313
Czartoryski, Adam Jerzy, 284, 312

D

d'Anthès, George, Baron, 223, 231, 247–49, 252–53, 255–56, 309–11, 315
D'Este, Ippolito, Cardinal, 276
Dahl, Vladimir Ivanovich, 251, 315
Danube, 72, 278, 288
Danzas, Konstantin, 251, 316
Danzig, 295
Dargomyzhsky, Alexander, 269
Darmstadt, 193
Dashkov, Mikhail, Prince, 224, 308, 311, 313
Dashkova, Ekaterina, Princess, 236, 294, 313
Davydov, Denis, 39, 58, 70, 83, 90–91, 96, 103, 111, 244, 262, 278, 291
Delarue, Mikhail, 216, 308–309, 313
Delvig, Anton, XVI–XVII, 18–21, 25, 28, 30, 47, 57, 61, 72, 122, 129–30, 138, 140, 151, 165, 173–74, 176, 181, 189, 194, 200, 204, 241, 269–70, 273, 284–85, 295, 302–4, 307–9, 316
Denisevich, major, 51
Denmark, 259
Derpt, 134, 137, 239
Derzhavin, Gavriil, XVII, 25, 29–31, 178, 256, 268, 271, 284
Descartes, René, XXI, 58, 285
Dmitriev, Ivan, XIV–XV, 54, 259, 278, 311
Dmitrievich, Aleksandr, 259
Dmitriev-Mamonov, Alexander, Count, 289
Dmitriev-Mamonov, Matvei Alexandrovich, Count, 85, 88, 102, 162, 289
Dmitrov, 101
Dnipro, 56, 63
Dolgorukov, Alexander Sergeevich, 309, 216
Dolgorukov, Ilya, 279
Dolgorukov, Pavel, 89, 290
Dolgorukov, Sergei, 309
Dolgorukov, Vasily, 279
Dolgorukov, Yuri, 299
Dolgorukova, Olga, 309
Dolgoruky, Ilya Andreevich, 44, 279
Donne, John, 271
Dörnberg, 315
Dostoevsky, Fedor, 107, 198, 268, 287, 300, 306
Dresden, 193, 261, 280, 286
Drusus, 277
Dubelt, Leonty Vasilyevich, 7, 156, 263, 269
Dubrovitsy, 289
Dunai, 72

E

Edinburgh, 303
Egorov, Boris, XI
Elets, 291
Engelhardt, Lev, 23, 273, 309, 313
England, 101, 114, 267, 276, 300, 306
Enlightenment, IX, 45–46, 53, 104, 106, 178, 224, 249, 269, 271, 273, 275, 282–84, 286, 313
Erivan, 288
Ermolov, Alexey Petrovich, 84, 86, 140, 270, 288–89
Erzurum (Arzrum), 155, 191, 245, 251, 254
Estland, 116, 294
Estonia, 263
Ethiopia, 265
Eylau, 289

F

Fichte, Johann Gottlieb, 298
Ficquelmont, Charles–Louis de, Count, 192, 222, 247, 306, 310
Finland, 259, 263
Florian, 298
Fock, Magnus Gottfried von, 171
Fouché, Joseph, 146, 298
France, 24, 114, 146, 200–201, 247, 259, 268, 272–73, 275–76, 278, 280–81, 287, 291, 293, 295, 297, 304–6, 308, 313, 315
Franklin, Benjamin, 313

G

Gagarin, Fedor, 294
Gagarin, Ivan, Prince, 314
Gagarin, Pavel, Prince, 301
Gagarina, Vera, Princess, 265
Gaius Octavius Thurinus. *See* Augustus, Emperor
Galich, Alexander Ivanovich (born A. I. Govorov), 16–17, 268
Gandhi, Mahatma, 266
Gangeblov, Alexander, 163, 302
Gatchina, 267
Ge, Nikolai, 124, 295
Geneva, 74, 272, 287, 302
Genlis, Stéphanie Félicité, Comtesse de, 298
Georgia, 270, 294
Germany, 247, 259, 267, 273, 295, 308
Gershenzon, Mikhail, 87, 120, 295
Gigou, Jean, 293

Glinka, Fedor, 26, 42–43, 46, 48, 55, 269, 303
Glinskaya, Elena, 299
Gnedich, Nikolai, 27, 81, 87, 271, 273
Goethe, Johann Wolfgang von, 60, 155, 271, 300, 302
Gogol, Nikolai, 18, 27, 33, 107, 155, 197, 213, 233, 244–45, 253, 266, 269, 274, 304, 307, 316
Goldman, Emma, 313
Golenishchev-Kutuzov, Pavel Vasilyevich, 143, 284, 298
Golitsyn, Sergei, Prince, 280
Golitsyna, Elizaveta, Princess, 46, 280, 290
Goncharov, Nikolai, 268, 300, 304, 310
Goncharova, Natalya Nikolaevna, 155, 167, 186–87, 199, 231, 265, 301, 303–4, 309–310, 315
Gorbachevsky, Ivan, 50, 281
Gorchakov, Dmitry, 160, 174, 301–2
Gorchakov, Mikhail, 301–2
Gorchakov, Peter, 301
Gorchakov, Vladimir, 61
Gorstkin, Ivan, 44, 262, 279
Göttingen, 35, 40, 48
Govorov, Alexander. *See* Galich, Alexander Ivanovich
Grabbe, Pavel Khristoforovich, 36, 277
Grech, Nikolay Ivanovich, 63, 81, 156, 175, 182, 244, 269, 285
Greece, 82–83, 102, 283, 285, 288, 315
Griboedov, Alexander Sergeevich, XII, 4–5, 18, 34, 62, 104, 156, 163, 172–73, 210, 224, 251, 260, 269, 274, 276, 279, 293
Gribovsky, Mikhail Kirillovich, 95, 146, 291
Grigoryev, Apollon, VIII
Guizot, François, 240, 313–14
Gulianov, Ivan, 168, 303
Guryev, Dmitry, 310
Gurzuf, 63–64, 77
Gusyatnikova, Elizaveta, 272

H
Hamburg, 261
Hannibal, Abram, 264, 266
Hannibal, Pavel, 51
Hannibal, Marya Alekseyevna (née Pushkina), Pushkin's grandmother, XVI
Hańska, Ewelina, 286, 293–94
Hański, Wacław, 109

Hartung, Leonid, 307
Heckern (Heeckeren), Louis (Georges Charles de), Baron, 247–49, 251–52, 310, 315
Heine, Heinrich, 275, 314
Herzen, Alexander Ivanovich, 46, 156, 268, 280, 302
Heytman, Georg, 79
Homer, 273, 287
Horace, 12, 268, 287
Hugo, Victor, 304, 309, 313
Hungary, 288

I
Iakushkin, Ivan Dmitryevich, 276
Iași, 83
Idar (Idarov), 265
Illichevsky, Alexey, XX, 19, 270
Ilovaiskii, Dmitri, 312
India, 88
Inzov, Ivan, 55–57, 63–64, 69, 90, 97, 99–100, 283, 290, 292
Iogel, Pyotr, 186
Irkutsk, 270, 279–81
Ishimova, Alexandra Osipovna, 251, 315
Istanbul, 100, 264
Italy, 44, 112, 193, 259, 268, 276, 283, 289, 292, 294, 302
Ivan the Terrible, Tsar, 150
Ivanov, Nikanor, 241–42
Izmail, 284, 302
Izmailov, Vladimir, 148, 288, 298

J
Jaffe, 194
Jakobson, Roman, 275
Jerusalem, 276
Julius Caesar, Emperor, 52, 277, 282, 287

K
Kachenovsky, Mikhail Trofimovich, 188, 305
Kakhovsky, Pyotr Grigoryevich, 122, 141, 262, 297
Kaluga, 155, 290, 301
Kamchatka, 283
Kamenka, 53, 90, 96, 99
Kant, Immanuel, 267, 298
Kantemir, Antiokh, 35, 221, 276
Kapnist, Vasily, 271

Kapodistrias, Ioiannis (Ivan), 56–57, 283, 294, 308
Karamzin, Nikolai, IX, XIII, XV, XXII, XXIV, 10, 25–26, 28, 31, 39, 47, 54–55, 128, 133, 140, 151, 170, 172, 178, 180–81, 224, 265, 271–73, 275, 278, 294, 305, 307, 310–311, 314
Karazin, Vasily Nazarovich, 54, 283
Kars, 155
Katenin, Pavel, 6, 130, 262
Kaverin, Pyotr Pavlovich, 26, 35, 98, 272, 275
Kazan, 6, 11, 239, 266, 290, 300, 309
Keats, John, XXIV
Kern, Anna, 134–37, 165, 265, 296, 302
Kharkiv, 6, 283
Kheraskov, Mikhail, 278
Khitrovo, Daria, 306
Khitrovo, Ekaterina, 199, 247, 310
Khitrovo, Elizaveta, 168, 192, 197, 222, 306, 310
Khitrovo, Nikolay, 303
Khomyakov, Alexei, 150, 274, 300, 304
Khovanskaya, Ekaterina, Princess, 281
King, Martin Luther, Jr., 266
Kireev, Pyotr Alexandrovich, 190, 305
Kireevsky, Ivan, 27, 149, 202, 274, 298, 300, 304
Kirillov, 150
Kiselyov, Pavel Dmityevich, 37–38, 86, 115, 278, 293
Kishinev. *See* Chişinău
Kliuchevsky, Vasily, 312
Klokachev, Alexey Fedotovich, 33, 276
Kobrino, 267
Kochubey, Viktor P., Count, 267
Kokoshkin, Fedor, 150
Koloshin, Pyotr, 261
Koltsov, Alexey, 27, 245, 257, 274
Kolyvan, 270, 275
Konovnitsyn, Peter, 13, 267
Konshin, Nikolai, 200, 307
Korf, Modest Andreevich, 51, 174, 282
Korsakova, Anna Nikolaevna, 267
Koshelev, Alexander, 275
Kostroma, 265, 282, 302, 307
Kozlov, Nikita Timofeevich, 57, 78, 101, 116, 285, 288, 295
Krasheninnikov, Pyotr, 314
Krasnoyarsk, 291
Krivtsov, Nikolai, 26, 169, 272

Krupensky, Matvey Egorovich, 100, 292
Krylov, Ivan Andreevich, XXIV, 210–211, 244, 269, 288, 304, 307–8, 314
Küchelbecker, Wilhelm, XII, 19, 22, 34, 51, 139, 174, 269–70, 275, 284, 302
Kulm, 272, 289
Kunitsyn, Alexander Petrovich, XX–XXI, 16–17, 267–68
Kurgan, 270
Kursk, 265, 291
Kutuzov, Mikhail, 56, 168, 199, 267, 284, 301–3, 310
Kyiv (Kiev), 57, 62, 90, 99, 156, 182, 264, 299, 304

L
La Fontaine, Jean de, 12, 308
Lacroix, Jules, 286
Laibach, 311
Lamartine, Alphonse Marie Louis de Prat de, 101, 292
Landa, Semen Semenovich, 85–86, 289
Langeron, Theodor de, 295
Lanskaia, Varvara, 3, 259
Lanskoi, Pyotr, 303
Lanskoi, Sergei, 259
Leipzig, 2, 24, 56, 291
Lenin, Vladimir, 313
Lenz, Wilhelm von, 218
Leopoldov, Andrei Filippovich, 159, 301
Lermontov, Mikhail, XIV, 11, 59–60, 66, 74–75, 124–25, 193, 236, 252, 264, 266, 274–75, 307, 310, 316
Liebermann, August von, 256, 316
Lifland, 116
Liprandi, Ivan Petrovich, 103, 112, 157, 292–93
Lithuania, 268, 293, 295
Litt (Litta), Julius Pompeevich, Count, 219, 309
Livonia, 294–95
Lobanov-Rostovsky, Alexei Yakovlevich, Prince, 121, 295
Lomonosov, Mikhail, 227, 256, 279, 282, 312
London, 272, 286, 293–294, 313
Lopukhina, Evdokia Fedorovna, 264
Lotman, Mikhail, VII–XI, XI–XIV, XVI, XIX, XXI–XXIII, XXV, 51, 119, 124, 136, 246, 250

Lubomirska, Julia, 313
Lubomirski, Stanisław, 313
Luga, 57
Luginin, Fedor Nikolaevich, 51, 282
Lunin, Mikhail Sergeevich, 43–44, 260–61, 279–80
Lützen, 291
Luxembourg, 306
Lvov, Nikolai, 271

M

Macarius, Metropolitan of Moscow, 264
Maksimovich, Mikhailo, 181–82, 304
Malinniki, 155, 165, 296
Malinovskaya, Maria, 270
Malinovsky, Vasily Fedorovich, 15, 17, 19, 29, 267
Mamonov. *See* Dmitriev-Mamonov, Matvei Alexandrovich, Count
Mansurov, Pavel Borisovich, 49, 281
Maria Fedorovna, Empress, 3, 14, 66, 77, 111, 143, 146, 152, 210, 223, 233, 259, 263, 265–67, 270, 286, 301, 306–7, 309–310
Marie Thérèse of Savoy, Princess, 305
Markovic, Svetozar, 313
Martynov, Nikolai, 266
Marx, Karl, 313
Masséna, André, 284
Matiushkin, Fedor Fedorovich, 20, 270
Maturin, Charles Robert, 60, 108, 293
Matveev, Fedor, 267
Maximilian II, Emperor, 295
Mayboroda, Arkady Ivanovich, 98, 292
Mazepa, Ivan Stepanovich, 235, 268, 313
Melnikova, Aleksandra Grigoryevna, 312
Mérimée, Prosper, 275
Merzlyakov, Nikolai, 304
Meshchersky, Elim, Prince, 281
Michael (Mikhail Pavlovich), Grand Duke, 13, 143, 267, 270, 279, 282
Mickiewicz, Adam Bernard, 110–111, 275, 286, 293
Mignet, François-Auguste, 240, 314
Mikhailovskoe, VIII, XIV, XVII, XXI, XXIII, 12, 27, 57, 111, 117–21, 123–27, 129–31, 133, 135–39, 141–42, 146, 148, 155, 157, 164, 166, 198, 229, 239, 242, 254, 267, 285, 295–96
Milan, 284

Miller, Pavel Ivanovich, 216, 309
Miloradovich, Mikhail Andreevich, 43, 56, 140, 279, 297–98
Milton, John, 243, 314
Minin (Minich), Kuzma (Kozma), 85, 183, 289
Mirovich, Vasily Yakovlevich, 140, 297
Mniszech, Josephine Amalia, 313
Modzalevsky, Boris, 170–71, 174, 218
Mogilev, 57
Molchanov, Pyotr Stepanovich, 204, 307
Moldova, 70, 82–83, 86, 99, 278
Molière, XV, 266
Molostvov, Pamfamir Khristoforovich, 26, 35, 272
Montesquieu, Charles Louis Secondat de, 287
Mordvinov, Alexander, 156
Mukhanov, Vladimir, 14
Muravyov, Alexander, 20, 261, 270
Muravyov, Mikhail, 20, 260–61, 271
Muravyov, Nikita Mikhailovich, 38, 43–44, 132, 156, 260–62, 278, 300
Muravyova, Alexandra, 152, 300
Muravyov-Apostol, Matvey, 260–61
Muravyov-Apostol, Sergei Ivanovich, 50, 141, 260–62, 281
Murphy, Dennis Jasper, 293

N

Nadezhdin, Nikolai, 177–79, 303–4
Nailantis, Demetrios, 290
Naryshkin, Mikhail, 262
Naryshkina, Ekaterina, 312
Nashchokin, Pavel Voinivich, 27, 254, 274
Naumov, Dmitrii, 303
Naumova, Ekaterina Nikolaevna, 303
Nechkina, Militsa Vasilyevna, 44, 279
Nekrasov, Nikolai, 268
Nepenin, Andrei Grigorievich, 95, 291
Nerchinsk, 139
Nesselrode, Karl, 116, 223, 249, 294, 310–311
Netherlands, 193, 315
Neva, 206, 264
Nevsky Prospekt, 35, 52, 143, 251, 269
Nicolas I, Emperor, 7, 13–14, 16, *passim*
Nicholas II, Emperor, 290, 209
Nietzsche, Friedrich, 287
Nikitenko, Alexander, 228, 312–13

Nizhny Novgorod, 49, 85, 155, 187, 191, 209, 272, 305
Novgorod (Veliky Novgorod), 200, 264, 271, 281, 299–301
Novikov, Nikolai, 56, 134, 172, 278, 283
Novorossiysk, 56, 98, 285, 287, 294

O

Obolensky, Evgeny, 260, 262, 299
Octavianus Augustus, Emperor, 72–73, 277–78, 287
Octavius Gaius, Senator, 36, 278
Odesa (Odessa), XXIII, 26, 64, 66, 73–74, 78, 83, 97–102, 105, 108, 110–113, 116–17, 119, 123, 126, 139, 283, 287, 294
Odoevsky, Vladimir Fedorovich, 149, 247, 259, 262, 274, 298–99, 307
Ogaryov, Nikolai, 280
Oka, 215
Okhotnikov, Konstantin Alexeevich, 87, 96, 290
Olenin, Alexei Nikolaevich, 271, 295
Olenina, Anna Nikolaevna, 121–23, 167, 186, 295
Olonets, 271, 276
Opava, 95
Orenburg, 239, 305
Orlov, Alexei, Prince, 37–38, 272, 278, 290
Orlov, Fedor, Count, 272, 278, 286
Orlov, Mikhail, Count, 26, 37–39, 50, 65, 69–70, 72, 74, 78, 84–91, 94–96, 98, 100, 102–3, 105, 111, 132, 156, 238, 263, 272, 278, 286–87, 290
Orlova, Ekaterina, 87, 287
Oryol (Orel), 155, 265, 296
Osipov, Ivan, 296
Osipova, Praskovya, 134, 239, 265, 295–96
Oudinot, Marshal, 268
Ovid, 70, 72–73, 91, 283, 287, 295, 309
Ozerov, Ivan Petrovich, 308
Ozerova, Rosalia, 308

P

Panin, Valerian Alexandrovich, 286, 299, 301
Paris, 1, 26, 51, 85, 162, 187, 192, 200, 203, 272, 278–79, 281–82, 286, 289, 293, 304, 307, 316
Parkyns, Charlotte, 306

Parma, 306
Paskevich, Ivan Fedorovich, 84, 163, 288, 302
Pasternak, Boris, 164, 302
Paulucci, Filippo, 294
Pavel I, Emperor, 259
Pavlishchev, Nikolay, 276
Pavlishcheva, Olga Sergeevna, 276
Pelym, 260
Penza, 101, 279, 299
Perfilyev, Afanasy, 297
Perovskaya, Sophia, 312
Perovsky, Alexey (pseud. Antony Pogorelsky), 156, 312
Persia, 163, 260
Peter I, The Great, Emperor, 9, 133, 145, 153, 164, 203, 232, 234, 236–37, 240, 245, 256, 264, 276, 296–97, 301, 312
Peter II, Emperor, 297
Peter III, Emperor, 259–60, 286, 297, 311
Peterson, Eleonore, 314
Petrashevsky circle, 156, 306
Phemistoclus, 288
Philemon, Ioannis, 86, 290
Piedmont, 82, 201
Pimen Cherny, 150, 299
Pinas, Emmanuel de, 247, 315
Platonov, Sergei, 312
Pletnev, Pyotr Alexandrovich, 27, 128, 189–92, 199, 201, 204, 242, 265, 269, 273
Plutarch, 36, 277
Pnin, Ivan Petrovich, 56, 271, 284
Pobedonostsev, Konstantin, 300
Poe, Edgar Allan, 304
Poggio, Alexander, 162, 262, 302
Pogodin, Mikhail Petrovich, 27, 149–50, 155, 157, 194, 274, 298, 304
Pogorelsky, Antony (pseud.). See Perovsky, Alexey
Poland, 200, 259, 263, 270, 272, 284, 286, 288, 293, 295, 301, 311
Polevoi, Nikolai, 149, 151–52, 177–79, 182, 195, 225, 298, 304
Polevoi, Ksenofont (Xenofon), 178, 298, 304
Polignac, Jules de, Count, 192–93, 305–6
Poltoratskaya, Ekaterina Ivanovna, 302
Poltoratskaya, Lizaveta, 296
Poltoratsky, Alexander, 161, 302

Poltoratsky, Pyotr, 165, 302
Poludenskaya, Varvara, 282
Poniatowski, Stanislav, 311
Portugal, 259, 308
Posa, Rodrigo de, Marquis, 52
Posse, Euphrosinia Ulrika von, 304
Potemkin, Grigory, Prince, 267, 309
Potocka, Constance, Countess, 313
Potocki, Jan, 234, 313
Potocki, Stanisław Szczesny, 313
Pozdeev, Osip, 311
Pozharsky, Dmitry, Prince, 85, 183, 289
Priiutino, 121
Propertius Sextus, 128, 287, 295
Protasova, Elizaveta, 275, 310
Prussia, 259, 268, 286, 290, 294, 297, 316
Prut, river, 83
Pskov, 106, 116, 130, 132–33, 157, 159, 257, 294–96, 302
Pugachev, Emelyan, 140, 193, 203, 220, 226, 228, 232, 236, 239–40, 271, 297
Pushchin, Ivan, XVI–XVII, 19, 22–24, 28–29, 37–38, 50, 87, 91, 124–25, 138–39, 162, 174, 260, 262, 268, 270, 281, 290, 292, 302, 316
Pushchin, Mikhail, 162
Pushkin, Grisha, 204, 209
Pushkin, Sasha, 204, 209
Pushkin, Vasily Lvovich, XV, XXI, 10–11, 75, 96, 129, 138, 187, 265, 291
Pushkina, Masha, 204, 209
Pushkina, Natasha, 204, 209

R
Radishchev, Alexander Nikolaevich, 56, 134, 172, 284
Raevskaya, Ekaterina, 78, 272, 287
Raevskaya, Maria. *See* Volkonskaya, Maria Nikolaevna
Raevsky, Alexander, XXIII, 53, 85, 107–8, 283
Raevsky, Andrey, 290
Raevsky, Nikolai, 50, 62–64, 66–67, 74, 77, 86, 89–90, 110, 162, 272, 282, 286, 301
Raevsky, Nikolai, Jr., 285
Raevsky, Vasily, 87, 290
Raevsky, Vladimir, 45, 74, 84, 95–97, 103, 105, 159, 280, 291
Raguzinsky, Savva, 264
Rastopchin, Fedor V., Count, 308

Rastrelli, Bartolomeo, 297
Razin, Stepan, 150, 299
Razumovsky, Alexei, Count, XX, 224, 286, 311–12
Renaissance, 288
Repnin, Nicholas, 284
Reval, 263, 273, 275
Richardson, Samuel, 109
Riego y Flórez, Rafael, 102, 292
Riga, 136, 263
Rimskaya-Korsakova, Alexandra, 157, 301
Rimsky-Korsakov, Alexander, 301
Riznich, Amalia, 112–13, 294
Robespierre, Maximilien, 45, 280
Rodzianko, Arkady Gavrilovich, 159–60, 301
Romanovs, 86, 200, 263, 275, 284, 289–90, 296–97
Romanticism, XIV, XXI–XXII, 28, 33, 58–60, 62, 65, 71, 74, 79, 82, 117, 124, 126, 149, 178–79, 241, 266, 286, 293, 303, 307, 314
Rome, 259, 273, 277, 287, 293, 300
Rosen, Olimpiada Vladimirovna von, Baroness, 290
Rousseau, Jean-Jeaques, 25, 67, 87, 89, 267, 271, 284, 287, 298
Runich, Dmitry, 268
Rurik, Prince, 86, 265, 289–90, 300
Ryleev, Kondraty, 45, 50–51, 58, 75–76, 130, 132, 138, 141, 172–73, 262, 269, 273, 288, 293, 297, 312

S
Sabaneev, Ivan Vasilyevich, 97, 103, 159, 291, 293
Saburov, Yakov Ivanovich, 35, 276
Saltykov, Mikhail, 269
Saltykov, Sergei, 218, 309
Saltykova, Ekaterina, Princess, 279
Saltykova, Sofia, 122, 269
Saltykova, Praskovya, Countess, 310
Saltykov-Shchedrin, Mikhail, 264
Samborskaya, Sophia, 267
Samoilov, Alexander, Count, 309
Saransk, 299
Schelling, Friedrich, 268, 298, 314
Schiller, Friedrich, 25, 45, 52, 271, 302
Schlegel, Friedrich, 298
Schlippenbach, Karl, Count, 308

Scott, Walter, 176, 293, 303
Semenovsky regiment, 6, 47, 51, 95, 293, 296
Senkovsky, Osip Ivanovich, 243–44, 314
Serbinovich, Konstantin, 275
Seredkina, Evdokia, 280
Sevastopol, 64
Severin, Dmitry Petrovich, 224, 311
Shakespeare, William, VIII, XXIV, 140, 265, 302
Shakhovsky, Pyotr, Prince, 305
Shalikov, Pyotr, Prince, 78
Shcheglov, Nikolai Prokofyevich, 190, 305
Shcherbatov, Mikhail Mikhailovich, 51, 282
Sheremetev, Dmitry Nikolaevich, 227, 312
Sheremetev, Nikolai, 312
Sheremetev, Peter, Count, 312
Sheremeteva, Anastasia, 277, 312
Sherwood (Shervud), John (Ivan Vasilyevich), 98, 292
Shevyrev, Stepan Petrovich, 149, 298
Shulgin, Dmitry Ivanovich, 301
Shuysky, Vasily Ivanovich, Tsar, 289
Sicily, 290, 306
Simeiz, 64
Simferopol, 64
Sivers, Elizaveta, 275
Skavronskaya, Catherine, 309
Skobelev, Ivan Nikitich, 159, 301
Slavophiles, 149, 274, 280, 299
Smirdin, Alexander Filippovich, 243, 314
Smirnov, Dmitry, 290
Smirnov, Nikolai, 90, 307
Smirnova, Alexandra Osipovna, 210, 212, 307
Sobańska (Sobanskaya), Karolina (Karolina-Rosalia-Tekla), XXIII, 65, 109–112, 286
Sobański, Hieronim, 286
Sobolevsky, Sergei Alexandrovich, 27, 259, 274–75
Sollogub, Vladimir, 253, 255, 316
Solovyev, Sergei, 225
Solovyov, Vladimir, 300, 312
Solovyova, Polyksena, 312
Somov, Orest Mikhailovich, 176, 269, 303
Southey, Robert, 185, 304
Spain, 82, 172, 259, 268, 290, 306
Sparta, 288
Speransky, Mikhail, XVI, 13–15, 42, 263, 266–67

Spinoza, Baruch, 298
Staël-Holstein, Anne Louise Germaine de, 287
Stankevich, Nikolai, 149, 274, 299
Stavropol, 284
Stürler, Nikolas, 297
Sukhomlinov, Mikhail, 175
Sukhorukii, Kozma, 183
Suvorov, Alexandr Vasilyevich, 56, 203, 256, 283–84, 289, 291
Sveaborg, 270
Sviatie Gori, 257
Svinyin, Pavel Petrovich, 304
Svyatogorsk, 279, 285
Sweden, 259, 264, 278, 288
Switzerland, 193, 259, 284, 289, 293, 295, 302, 311

T
Tacitus Publius Cornelius, 36, 277, 287
Taganrog, 7, 292
Tambov, 265, 271, 276, 301–2
Tarkhany, 266
Tasso, Torquato, 29, 276
Tatishcheva, Varvara, 300
Tavrida (Tauride), 63, 302
Tehran, 260
Themistocles, 83, 288
Theresa, Order of, 308
Tibullus, 295
Tiesenhausen, Theodor Ferdinand von, Count, 303, 310
Tiflis, 155, 162, 260, 270
Timkovsky, Ivan Osipovich, 57, 285
Tiraspol, 45, 103, 159, 280, 291
Titus Livius, 277
Tobolsk, 270, 293
Tolstaya, Alexandra, 218, 309
Tolstaya, Sofia Andreevna, 309
Tolstaya, Stepanida, 295
Tolstoy, Alexei, 312
Tolstoy, Fedor, 54, 283, 295
Tolstoy, Leo, 11, 25, 186, 211, 218, 221–22, 248, 260, 266, 287, 303, 309–310
Tolstoy, Yakov, 48, 281
Tomashevsky, Boris Viktorovich, 19, 77, 287
Trigorskoe, 118–19, 134–37, 139, 239, 295–96
Troppau, 311

Trubetskaya, Ekaterina, Princess, 309
Trubetskoy, Sergei, Prince, 48, 56, 104, 260–62, 280, 283
Trubetskoy, Nikolai, Prince, 56, 283
Trubetskoy, Pyotr, Prince, 280
Tsargrad, 100
Tsaritsyn, 299
Tsarskoe Selo, XVII–XIX, 13, 15, 17, 21, 28, 32, 34, 57, 138, 199–200, 263, 267–28, 276, 282, 284, 290, 307
Tumansky, Ivan, 78–79, 288
Turgenev, Alexander, 18, 26, 41–42, 48, 80, 116, 133, 138, 202, 213, 224, 231, 256–57, 268, 275, 278–79, 285, 308
Turgenev, Andrey, 18, 26, 41, 224, 278–79, 308
Turgenev, Ivan, 278, 295, 299
Turgenev, Nikolai, 18, 26, 38–42, 47, 51, 132, 141, 156, 224, 262, 272, 278–79, 308
Turgenev, Sergey, 18, 26, 41, 224, 278–79, 308
Turin, 284
Turkmenchay, Treaty of, 260, 288
Tver, 155, 265, 296, 307
Tynyanov, Yury Nikolaevich, XII, 28–29, 270, 275
Tyutchev, Fedor, 245, 275, 314–15

U
Uglich, 289
Ukraine, 56, 182, 293, 295, 313
Ural, 239
Ushakov, Nikolai, 303
Ushakova, Elena, 167–68, 303
Ust Sysolsk, 304
Uvarov, Sergei, Count, 202, 224–28, 249, 304, 312
Uvarova, Ekaterina Alexeevna, Countess, 312

V
Vadkovskaya, Ekaterina, 272
Vadkovsky, Fedor Fedorovich, 98, 272, 291
Varlamov, 269
Vasilchikov, Illarion, 51, 282
Velikie Luki, 57
Venevitinov, Dmitry, 149, 298, 304
Veresaev, Vikenty, XIV, 68, 286–87
Vidocq, Eugène François, 181, 213, 304

Vielgorskaya, Sofia Mikhailovna, 316
Vienna, 3, 88, 193, 201, 315
Vigel, Philip Philipovich, 93–94, 107, 115, 291
Viljandi, 4
Vilna, 267, 312
Vitebsk, 57
Vladimiresco, Theodore (Vladimirescu, Tudor), 82, 84, 288
Volga, 299
Volkhovsky (Valkhovsky), Vladimir Dmitryevich, 19, 162, 270, 302
Volkonskaya, Maria Nikolaevna (née Raevskaya), 77, 111, 152, 286, 300
Volkonskaya, Zinaida, 152, 300
Volkonsky, Sergei Grigoryevich, 97, 115, 262–63, 286, 291, 294, 300, 308
Volkova, Maria Apollonovna, 3, 259
Vologda, 276, 292, 304
Voltaire, 29, 275
Voronezh, 265, 272
Vorontsov, Mikhail Semenovich, 73, 98–99, 101, 113–16, 119, 198, 287, 291–94, 308, 313
Vorontsova, Elizaveta Ksaveryevna, 112–14, 294, 311, 313
Voyeykov, Alexander, 271
Vrevskaya, Evpraksia Nikolaevna, 296
Vrevsky, Boris, 296
Vsevolod the Big Nest, Prince, 264
Vsevolozhsky, Nikita Vsevolodovich, 48, 127, 280–81
Vulf, Alexei Nikolaevich, 134, 136, 296
Vulf, Anna Nikolaevna, 296
Vulf, Nikolai Ivanovich, 134, 136–37, 295–96
Vulf, Praskovya Alexandrovna, 295–96
Vyazemskaya, Natalya, Princess, 290
Vyazemskaya, Vera Fedorovna, Princess, 113, 117, 290, 294
Vyazemsky, Pyotr, Prince, 10, 27, 39, 41, 51, 78–79, 82, 102, 113, 118, 122, 129–30, 133, 141, 149, 152, 156–57, 161, 167, 176, 181–82, 192–93, 202, 213, 215, 225, 245, 254–55, 259, 265, 271–72, 274–75, 281, 290, 293–95, 298, 301, 304–5, 307–8, 310–311, 315
Vyndomsky, Alexander Maximovich, 134, 296
Vyzhigin, Ivan, 268

W
Wallachia, 86, 278, 301
Witt, Ivan Osipovich de, XXIII, 110–111, 146, 286, 294
Wittgenstein, Ludwig, 266
Wittgenstein, Pyotr Christianovich, Count, 82, 86, 140, 268, 288, 293
Wordsworth, William, 304
Wrangel, Ferdinand von, 270–71, 290, 303, 306, 310

X
Xerxes I, Shah, 288

Y
Yakovlev, Mikhail Lukyanovich, 57, 284, 299
Yakushkin, Ivan, 35–36, 44, 53, 96, 260–61, 276–77
Yakutsk, 273
Yaropolets, 304
Yaroslavl, 85, 260, 307
Yasnaya Polyana, 218, 221
Yazykov, Nikolai, 27, 134, 269, 274, 296, 300, 304

Yekaterinoslav, 56, 63
Ypsilantis, Alexander, 2, 70, 83–84, 86, 259
Yulaev, Salavat, 297
Yushnevsky, Alexey, 262

Z
Zagryazhskaya, Elizaveta, 265, 304, 310
Zagryazhsky, Ivan, 304
Zakrevskaya, Agrafena Fedorovna, 122–23, 295
Zakrevsky, Count, 295, 308
Zamoyski, Jan, 295
Zaporozhye Sich, 284
Zelenskaya, Sofia Borisovna, 298
Zemsky Sobor, 290, 300
Zherebtsova, Olga, 278
Zhukovsky, Vasily, 27–28, 30, 39, 45, 47–48, 58, 63, 66, 74, 129, 135, 139, 147, 172, 202, 204, 213, 224, 230, 245, 256, 259, 269, 271–75, 294, 304–5, 307–8, 311–32, 314–15
Zilber, Leah Abelevna, 275

www.ingramcontent.com/pod-product-compliance
Lightning Source LLC
Chambersburg PA
CBHW071811230426
43670CB00013B/2425